# TOURISM AND PUBLIC RELATIONS

# TOURISM AND PUBLIC RELATIONS

Annamalai Murugan

KALPAZ

ISBN : 978-81-7835-975-5
₹ 1200

First Published 2013

*Published by*

**Kalpaz Publications**
C-30, Satyawati Nagar,
Delhi-110052
Ph.: 9212142040
E-mail: kalpaz@hotmail.com

*Laser Typesetting* : Rudra Computer Graphics, Delhi
*Printed at* : G. Print Process, Delhi

**Cataloging in Publication Data—DK**
Courtesy: D.K. Agencies (P) Ltd. <docinfo@dkagencies.com>

**Murugan, Annamalai, 1969-**
**Tourism and Public Relations** / Annamalai Murugan.
p. cm.
Includes index.
ISBN 9788178359755

1. Tourism. 2. Public ralations. I. Title.

DDC 338.4791 23

# Contents

**PART 4: MARKETING PUBLIC RELATIONS**

# Preface

This book presents tourism and public relations as a practice and a discipline. Public Relations have been the driving force behind the evolution of travelers and tourism. In this changing scenario, Tourism and Public Relations as one of the key communication disciplines need to develop newer strategies and suitable techniques to build enduring relations with all stake holders of tourism industry and closely understand the global environment and design publicity packages and tourism campaigns for domestic and foreign tourists to meet the new challenges.

Public Relations profession is increasingly getting importance and recognition in Indian tourism as a management function and has become an essential part of integrated communication mix. The profession has grown in its stature with public relations consultants specializing on event management, image management of brands and with marketing other tourism products also, etc.

Public Relations are the fifth "P" of marketing after Product, Positioning, Pricing and Promotion. Public Relations bring more credibility and it is more focused because of emerging trends in tourism and travel industry.

India's travel and tourism industry is seeing subdued demand for the ongoing season. India has carved a niche for itself in the world of tourism, attracting domestic and international tourists every year. The Government has set its target to welcome 10 million inbound tourists by 2015. Since tourism is related activities with internationalization more importance to be given to that. In India, tourism is commodification. Brands become invisible. Things become commodities and therefore PR would never end.

The book is aimed at people involved in PR activities with tourism and travel industry. The content of the book would be of immense value of PR consultants, public relations officer, including teachers, students as well as for members of the general public concerned public relation with tourism and travel industry. Finally, I am grateful to the Kalpaz Publications, Delhi, who has taken a lot of interest and full support in bringing out this book. To all of them, my heart-felt thanks.

**Puducherry** **Dr. Annamalai Murugan**

# Introduction

**"Visit your own country and love your own country"**

The objective of this book is to provide access to a broad spectrum of practical knowledge relating to the discipline of public relations and tourism for students and professionals looking for practical principles and perspectives.

***Contemporary issues and the way forward for the Indian Tourism Industry through Public Relations***

**Domestic Tourism** – The average growth rate of the domestic tourism in India in the last 20 years has been 14 per cent. Last year it was 13.8 per cent. This trend is continuing. The main reason for this significant growth is the increasing disposable income. Earlier domestic tourism was ruled by religious tourism and VFR, but now the trend is changing. Our strengths is in the leisure sector is on a high. Domestic tourism laid the foundation of a tourism business in the country. We develop domestic tourism which later becomes a springboard for International tourism. We need to constantly evolve our tourism offerings. Wherever tourism is big, it's both domestic and international. Domestic tourism also needs the active involvement of private sector, to improve the conditions.

Tourism is a way to strengthen the national unity among people. We want people to travel to the other parts of their own country and learn about the diverse cultures. We have designed our plan for tourism keeping in mind not only economic but also for social, political and cultural purposes. Domestic tourism is most vibrant, we established and ever growing and is a huge potential segment of the travel tourism industry that requires no passport, no visas and no foreign exchanges.

India has over 800 million domestic tourists as compared to 6 million inbound and 13 million outbound. This tells the story that domestic tourism has potential much beyond its activity. Domestic tourism flow is ten times that of international arrivals. The accommodation sector has seen a growth in hotels and motels catering to international tourists. The growth of low-cost carriers (LCC) in India is an aid to the domestic market, but road and rail transportation continue to dominate domestic tourism.

The road ahead for improving domestic tourism includes necessity for viable statistics, tourism satellite accounts and household surveys, role of public and private sectors, safety and security, replication of good practices, accommodation, transport, information and promotional public relations.

Several countries in Asia and the Pacific have turned attention to Domestic Tourism. Domestic tourism is dependent on two vital assets : the population and the surface area of the country.

**International tourism :** According to UNWTO, tourism creates one out of every 12 jobs and generates US $ 1.2 trillion in exports in the world. UNWTO works towards turning the one billion tourists into one million opportunities. Moving forward the world will see a major shift in the distribution of shares of the market by 2030. In 2030, 57 per cent of international arrivals will be in merging economy destinations (versus 30 per cent in 1980). By regions, the biggest growth will be seen in Asia and the Pacific, where arrivals are forecast to increase by 331 million to reach 535 million in 2030 (+ 4.9 per cent per year).

By 2015, emerging economies will receive more international tourist arrivals than advanced economies, and by 2030, their share is expected to reach 58 per cent. There will be increases in the global market shares of Asia and the Pacific (to 30 per cent in 2030, up from 22 per cent in 2010), the Middle East (to 8 per cent from 6 per cent) and Africa (to 7 per cent from 5 per cent), and further declines in the shares of Europe (to 41 per cent from 51 per cent) and the Americas (to 14 per cent from 16 per cent), mostly due to the slower growth of North America. A large proportion of the arrivals of the next two decades will originate from the countries of Asia and the Pacific, growing at a rate of +5 per cent a year and generating and average 17 million additional international arrivals every year.

With an additional 39 million international tourists, up from 996 million in 2011, international tourists arrivals surpassed one billion (1.035 billion) for the first time in history in 2012.

Among the top ten tourist destinations, receipts were up significantly in Hong Kong (China) (+16 per cent), the USA (+10 per cent), the UK (+6 per cent) and Germany (+5 per cent). At the same time, a significant number of destinations around the world saw receipts from international tourism increase by 15 per cent or more - Japan (+37 per cent), India and South Africa (both +22 per cent), Sweden and the Republic of Korea (both +19 per cent), Thailand (+18 per cent) and Poland (+16 per cent). Growth is expected to continue in 2013 only slightly below the 2012 level (+3 per cent to +4 per cent) and in line with UNWTO long term forecast.

**PPP-P-PR-model must for tourism growth**

*Public Private Partneship-People - Public relations (5 - P Model)*

Tourism in India are all inter-dependent, the tour operators depend on the service providers such as airlines, railways, tour guides, tourist attractions, accommodation and many other elements. Tourism also dependent on the state tourism boards and NTO's for promoting a particular destination as a tourist attractions. In future, to develop tourism one more P to the public private partnership-People. People play a very important role in any tourism destination. At lasts it is the locals who are employed as guides or staff at the hotel.

13 years ago, Kerala wasn't considered an upmarket leisure destination. The Kerala Travel Mart Society was formed with a vision to encourage the PPP model to develop tourism in the State. The private palyers and the state tourism ministry worked together over the years in the partnership and today Kerala is one of the most famous leisure destination. Tourism as an Industry has multiple stake holders through prominent focus always remains airline, hotel, tour operators and travel agents, whereas the focus should be on building partnership with the people at local levels, who are primary points of contact for travelers.

The government organisations will also play a very important role by enabling a responsible policy that can provide a strategic framework for guiding decision making not only at macro level but also at an individual levels and encouraging greater consistency with sub-regional and regional strategies.

**Targeted public relations a necessity to push inbound**

To achieve the target of 10 million inbound tourists, the Ministry of Tourism, Govt. of India, needs to diversify its public relations and promotional strategy. Experts in the industry believe that the Ministry should open more overseas offices and start imparting to foreign and inbound tour operators so that they can sell India in a more aggressive manner. They believe that investing in training systems is quite necessary.

We can take clue from those National Tourist Offices which have aggressively been promoting their destinations in India with great results. Almost all the foreign countries promoting their tourism products in India have been witnessing a double digit growth in Indian arrivals. So, what they do to woo Indian outbound traffic? Most of these NTO, have their own tourism promotion offices in India, and apart form regular promotional exercises, they have implemented destination-centric specialist training programmers like the Aussie Specialist Programme and Kiwi Specialist Programme, among others.

Experts opine that the Ministry should launch "Incredible India" specialist programme in overseas markets. Their logic is right: if the international travel industry does not know the destination, how can we expect them to sell it to their clients? According to them, "Incredible India" campaign has helped build a presence in the international market through participation in travel marts and by organizing road shows in overseas countries, but nothing beyond that has ever been implemented. Hence, we need to proactively impart training to main tour operators with better and more comprehensive knowledge of Indian tourism products. Moreover, we need it promote standalone products.

It is also important that the Ministry of Tourism works in close synergy with other related ministries to fuel inbound arrivals. It has seen the Ministry of Tourism sign MoUs with Information and Broadcasting, Civil Aviation and Railway Ministries but nothing concrete has taken place on the ground. There seems to be complete disconnect among the concerned ministries. It is believed that all major airports around India want to expand US services but this has not been supported by the tourism bodies. What they are forgetting is that the tourism bodies will benefit the most out of this, as will the other private bodies such as the hotels, tourist attractions etc.

However, we are quite optimistic that the "Incredible India Take-II", if promoted with public relations strategically, will help us in welcoming more overseas tourists.

# PART I

# TOURISM AND TRAVEL

# 1

# Tourism

## Introduction to Tourism

### *Travel and Tourism as an Integrated Discipline*

Tourism embraces nearly all aspects of our society. Apart from its importance to economic changes, human socio-cultural activities and environmental development, tourism is related to other academic subjects such as geography, economics, history, languages, psychology, marketing, business and law, etc. Therefore, it is necessary to integrate a number of subjects to study tourism. For example, subjects such as history and geography help us understand more about the development of the historical and geographical resources of a tourist destination. Besides, subjects like marketing and business help us understand the promotion and marketing of tourism products.

Tourism is a complex field of study because it includes a variety of disciplines which are either directly or indirectly related to the understanding of tourism. The study of information technology enhances our understanding of the importance of the global distribution system and its effect on tourism business. The study of religion and culture provides information on the cultural resources of a destination and opportunities to develop it as a cultural destination. Tourism is so vast, so complex, and so multifaceted that there are a wide range of subjects related to tourism.[1]

## Integrated Model of Tourism and its Major Components

The vast majority of business organizations such as travel agents, meeting planners, and other service providers including accommodation, transportation, attractions and entertainment are classified as travel and tourism related business. In practice, these organizations are closely linked in

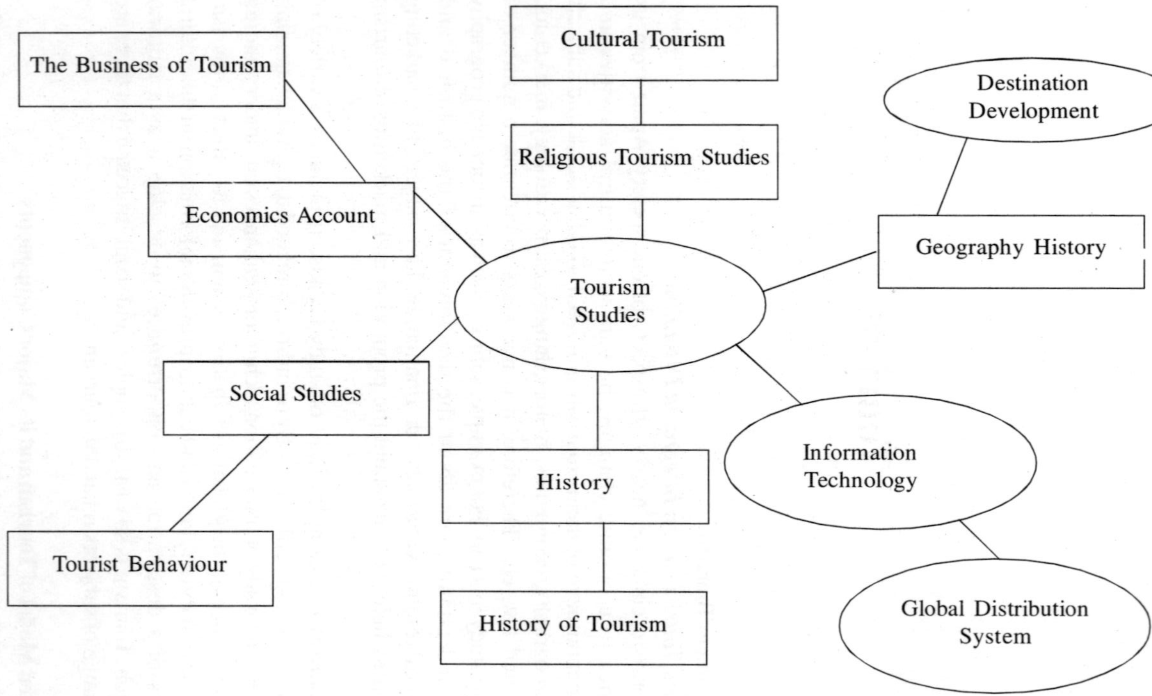


*Source* : Integrated Disciplinary Model
(adopted from Jafari, Jafar, Ritchie, J.R. Brent, Towards a Framework for Tourism Education : Problem and Prospects, Annals of Tourism Research, 1981, VIII (1)

the provision of services to the travellers. Tourism is so vast, so complex, and so multifaceted that the practitioners need to obtain a wide range of knowledge related to tourism.[2]

*Travellers*

Travellers are at the centre of the model where all tourism activities are focused. Radiating from the centre are three large bands containing several interdependent groups of tourism participants and organizations.

*Tourism Promoters*

Tourism promoters are in the first layer, in close contact with the Travellers. Organizations in this layer include tourism boards, direct marketing companies, meeting planners, travel agents and tour operators. The tourism boards and direct marketing companies provide information and marketing services to travellers whereas travel agencies, tour operators and meeting planners provide services such as making travel arrangements and giving professional advice on tourism related matters. All these organizations usually deal directly with individual travellers.

*Tourism Service Suppliers*

Tourism service suppliers, such as airline companies, bus operators, railway corporations, cruise ship operators, hotels and car rental companies, etc. usually provide services to travellers independently. The service suppliers may also collaborate to provide tour packages for travellers by combining the various services such as accommodation, air transportation, theme park entrance ticket, etc.

**External Environment**

All of the participants, either individually or as a group, are constantly responding to a variety of societal/cultural, political, environmental, economic and technological forces. It is the interaction of these forces that determine how closely the individuals and organizations work together.

Societal/Cultural forces such as the local skill and know how, the indigenous cultures of the destination and the attitude of local people towards the tourists would have a significant impact on the tourist experience in a destination. One example of encouraging the local community to take part in tourism is the "Be a Good Host" campaign launched by the Hong Kong Tourism Board. It aims at enhancing the tourist experience which helps to promote Hong Kong through "word-of-mouth".

Political forces such as government support on infrastructure, its policy on tourism planning, the diplomatic relations between tourist generating countries and tourist destination countries, etc, determines the environment of tourism development. For example, because of political instability in the

Middle East, tourism development in the region and the attractiveness of these countries to tourists has been adversely affected.

Environmental forces such as the problems of congestion, pollution, hygienic conditions, loss of green belts caused by excessive urbanization and development of tourism may destroy the pleasant ambiance of the destination which visitors look for. For example, Hong Kong's air pollution problem as a factor discourages tourists to come to Hong Kong.

Technological forces such as the popularity of using the Internet for searching information, reservation or purchasing of tourism products affect the tourists' buying behaviour. The traditional way of distributing tourism products through intermediaries, such as travel agents, tour wholesalers is facing a great challenge. Now that Travellers can deal directly with the suppliers, such as airlines, hotels and operators of attractions to purchase tourism products, they can almost by-pass travel agents.

## History of Tourism

### *Roman Empire Period*

During the Roman Empire period (from about 27 BC to AD 476), travel developed for military, trade and political reasons, as well as for communication of messages from the central government to its distant territories. Travel was also necessary for the artisans and architects "imported" to design and construct the great palaces and tombs. In ancient Greece, people traveled to Olympic Games. Both the participants and spectators required accommodations and food services. Wealthy Romans, in ancient times, traveled to seaside resorts in Greece and Egypt for sightseeing purpose.

### *Middle Age Period*

During the Middle Age (from about AD 500 to 1400), there was a growth of travel for religious reasons. It had become an organized phenomenon for pilgrims to visit their "holy land", such as Muslims to Mecca, and Christians to Jerusalem and Rome.

### *16th Century*

In the 16th century, the growth in England's trade and commerce led to the rise of a new type of tourists - who traveled to broaden their own experience and knowledge.

### *17th Century*

In the 17th century, the sons and daughters of the British aristocracy traveled throughout Europe (such as Italy, Germany and France) for periods of time, usually 2 or 3 years, to improve their knowledge. This was known as the Grand Tour, which became a necessary part of the training of future administrators and political leaders.

*Industrial Revolution Period*

The Industrial Revolution (from about AD 1750 to 1850) in Europe created the base for mass tourism. This period turned most people away from basic agriculture into the town / factory and urban way of life. As a result, there was a rapid growth of the wealth and education level of the middle class, as well as an increase of leisure time and a demand for holiday tourism activities. At that time, travel for health became important when the rich and fashionable Europeans began to visit the spa towns (such as Bath in England and Baden - Baden in Germany) and seaside resorts in England (such as Scarborough, Margate and Brighton).

*19th to 20th Centuries*

In the 19th and 20th centuries, the social and technological changes have had an immense impact on tourism. Great advances in science and technology made possible the invention of rapid, safe and relatively cheap forms of transport: the railways were invented in the 19th century and the passenger aircraft in the 20th century. World War II (AD 1939-1945) was also the impetus for dramatic improvements in communication and air transportation, which made travel much easier today than in earlier times.

*1980s*

The 1980s were called the boom years. Business and leisure travel expanded very rapidly. The baby-boomers were coming of age and had the money to spend. These travellers were looking for a variety of travel products from exciting vacation options such as adventure travel, ecotourism and luxurious travel.

There was not only a significant expansion in the travel market but also in tourist destinations. The fall of the Berlin Wall in Germany in 1989 signified the doom of communism in Europe. Countries such as Russia and the Czech Republic became new tourist destinations both for vacation and business travellers.

*1990s*

The Aviation Industry was facing high operational costs, including wage, oil prices, handling fee of Central Reservation System (CRS), landing charge of the aircrafts and advertising fee, etc. During this decade, CRS also marched towards more sophisticated technology. It became possible for agents to book a huge inventory of travel products, such as hotels, car rentals, cruises, rail passes, and theatre tickets from the CRS.

The introduction of "ticketless traveling" (electronic ticket) brings benefits to the airlines by cutting the amount of paperwork and cost of tickets. At the same time, passengers do not have to worry about carrying or losing tickets. Although, electronic ticketing does not bypass the travel agents as intermediaries, it makes it easier for the airline to deal directly with consumers.

The advance in technology also allows the airlines and other travel suppliers to sell directly to travellers through the Internet and interactive kiosks at airports. The kiosks at the airport usually sell hotel accommodation, transfer tickets such as bus tickets between airport and downtown areas and coach tickets from one city to another.

Travellers can now log on to the Internet easily reach for travel information, book a simple ticket or hotel room through their personal computer at home. There are thousands of new destinations, tour products and discounted airfares for travellers to choose from.

**Trend of Tourism Development**

The important trends of tourism in the world are as follow:

*Increasing Choices of Destinations*

For several decades, Western Europe has been a popular destination for international tourists. However, as tourists have got used to visiting Western Europe, they become curious about the less explored parts of the world such as Eastern Europe, the Asia-Pacific area and the less developed parts of the world including Africa. In general, there appears to be a slow shift of tourist arrivals from the economic advanced countries to the less developed ones.

*Mercurial Responses to Changing Economic Environment*

The potential for tourism growth is enormous throughout the world. As the production of goods and services increases, people have more disposable income and more leisure time. At the same time, a better-educated population would like to travel for different purposes such as recreation, education and health. Although there may be economic setbacks that will discourage tourism development, tourism has always found new ways to flourish. For example, many people would rather change their travel destinations or spending patterns than give up their vacation. Also, there are tour packages to suit every taste and income level.

*Governments Encouraging Tourism Development*

As many countries recognize the potential contribution of tourism to their economy, there will be increasing competition in the development and promotion of tourism among countries in future.

*Sustainable Forms of Tourism*

In future, tourism development will no longer be determined solely by economic consideration. It is suggested that tourism development should not abuse the natural environment. As environmental issues are becoming a worldwide concern, there will be new forms of tourism such as "eco-tourism", "agri-tourism" and "green tourism".

*"Special-Interest Tourism" Changes Forms of Tourism*

Due to cultural and social changes, there have been significant changes in the pattern of international tourism. "Special-interest tourism" (such as weight-losing and mind-broadening) has been developed to cater for the wide range of interests of tourists.

*Increasing Ability to Travel of Young People and the Elderly*

It is suggested that in the next decade, the number of tourists of the senior citizens and young people will increase faster than that of the others. Due to changes in socio-economic conditions such as better retirement benefits, more senior citizens can afford to travel after retirement. Moreover, better education and new travel opportunities enable young people to travel more.

*Information Technology Contributing to Tourism Development*

Information technology will become all-powerful in influencing destination choice and distribution. Travel suppliers and promoters are using information technology to identify and communicate with travellers through promotion and information supply, and to assist the travellers in their choice of destinations. Travellers who are familiar with surfing on the Internet for information and reservations could make their travel arrangements by themselves. As a result, the traditional distribution channels of delivery through intermediaries are being affected.

*Service of Intermediaries Professional and Personalized*

The role of travel agents is now changing from that of intermediaries to that of a provider of personal service and professional expertise.

*Theme Based Tourism Product Diversification*

Theme based tourism product is being developed with a combination of the three E's – Entertainment, Excitement and Education.

*Terrorist Attack Enhanced Concern of Travel Safety*

Air traffic control systems play a major role in overall air travel safety such as collision avoidance, precision landing aids and ground obstacle avoidance. Air security issues such as security screening at airports, permanent reinforcement of cockpit doors, public safety are also being major concerns especially after the September 11 Terrorist Attack in New York and Washington.[3]

## The Meaning of 'Travel', 'Tourism' and 'Tourist'

### *Concepts of 'Travel' and 'Tourism'*

*Travel*

Travel comprises all journeys from one place to another. It includes all journeys made by people who enter a country for leisure, to work, reside, study or who just pass through a country without stopping.

### *Tourism*

A brief summary of the definition is as follows:

Tourism means the temporary short-term movement of people to destinations outside the places where they normally live and work, as well as their activities during their stay at these destinations. (All tourism should have some travel, but not all travel is tourism.)

Tourism comprises the activities of persons travelling to and staying in places outside their usual environment for less than a year and whose main purpose of travel is other than the exercise of an activity remunerated from within the place visited. The term "usual environment" is intended to exclude trips within the area of usual residence and frequent and regular trips between the domicile and the workplace and other community trips of a routine character.

Based on the UNWTO definition on tourism, tourism could be categorized as:

### *Domestic Tourism*

Domestic tourism involves trips made by local residents within their own countries.

Example: An American, who lives in New York, takes a business trip to Los Angeles.

### *International Tourism*

International Tourism involves trips between 2 countries. To a certain country, visits by residents of that country to another country is her outbound tourism; visits to that country by residents of another country is her inbound tourism.

### *Outbound tourism Inbound tourism*

Example: Trips between Hong Kong and Japan. Hong Kong as the point of origin/point of destination:

| *Tourism Generating Country* | *Tourism Receiving Country* |
|---|---|
| Country A | Country B |
| Visits made by Hong Kong residents to Japan are Hong Kong's | Visits made by Japanese to Hong Kong are Hong Kong's |
| **outbound tourism;** | **Inbound tourism** |

International tourists are those who travel to a country other than the one in which they normally live.

The tourist leaves Country A (which is a tourist generating country) to Country B (which is a tourist receiving country). From the point of view of

Country A, this person is an outbound tourist; but from the point of view of Country B, he or she is an inbound tourist.

**Top Tourist Destinations of the World**

According to the figure compiled by UNWTO, international arrivals grew from 25 million in 1950 to 903 million in 2007. In 1950, destinations of the developed countries account for 98 per cent of all the international arrivals. However, this percentage fell to 57 per cent in 2007. In 2007, Europe accounted for 55.6 per cent, Asia and the Pacific for 20.1 per cent, Americas for 16.6 per cent, and the Middle East for 3.1 per cent of the world's total international tourist arrivals. Meanwhile, Middle East region has experienced the highest annual tourist arrival growth rate at 10.6 per cent since 2000. Asia and the Pacific region came second at an annual rate of 6.9 per cent.

***Travellers***

Any person who is taking a trip within or outside his/her own country of residence irrespective of the purpose of travel, means of transport used, even though he/she may be travelling on foot.

***Tourist***

A tourist is a person who travels to destinations outside his/her residence and working place, and stays for at least 24 hours, for the purpose of leisure or business.

***Excursionist***

An excursionist is a person who temporarily visits a destination and stays for less than 24 hours, for the purpose of leisure or business, but not for transit.

Examples:

1. A Canadian resident takes a short trip to the USA without staying overnight.
2. A Hong Kong resident goes to
   - Shenzhen shopping without staying overnight.
   - Macau gambling without staying overnight.

***International visitor***

Any person who travels to a country other than that in which he/she has his/her usual residence but outside his/her usual environment for a period not exceeding twelve months and whose main purpose of visit is other than the exercise of an activity remunerated from within the country visited.

***Domestic visitor***

Any person residing in a country, who travels to a place within the country but outside his/her usual environment for a period of not exceeding twelve months and whose main purpose of visit is other than the exercise of an activity remunerated from within the place visited.

***Tourist (overnight visitor)***
***International tourists***

A visitor who visits another country and stays at least one night in a collective or private accommodation in the country visited.

***Domestic tourists***

A visitor who stays atleast one night in a collective or private accommodation in the place visited within his/her own country.

***Excursionist (same-day visitor or day tripper)***
***International excursionist***

A visitor who does not spend the night in a collective or private accommodation in the country visited.

**Domestic excursionist**

A visitor who does not spend the night in a collective or private accommodation in the place visited within his/her own country.

**World Tourism Organization's (UNWTO) Definitions of "Tourist"**

The International Conference on Travel and Tourism Statistics convened by the World Tourism Organization (UNWTO) in Ottawa, Canada in 1991 reviewed, updated, and expanded on the work of earlier international groups. The Ottawa Conference made some fundamental recommendations on definitions of tourism, travelers, and tourists. The United Nations Statistical Commission adopted UNWTO's recommendations on tourism statistics on March 1993.

(a) *Tourists:* Visitors who spend atleast one night in the country visited
(b) *Crew members:* Foreign air or ship crews docked or in lay over and who used the accommodation establishments of the country visited.
(c) *Excursionists:* Visitors who do not spend atleast one night in the country visited although they might visit the country during one day or more and return to their ship or train to sleep.
(d) *Cruise passengers:* Normally included in excursionists. Separate classification of these visitors is nevertheless preferable.
(e) *Day visitors:* Visitors who come and leave the same day.
(f) *Crews:* Crews who are not residents of the country visited and who stay in the country for the day.
(g) *Members of armed forces:* When they travel from their country of origin to the duty station and vice versa.
(h) *Transit passengers:* Who do not leave the transit area of the airport or the port in certain countries, transit may involve a stay of one day or more. In this case they should be included in the visitor statistics.

(i) ***Purpose of visit:*** Main purposes of visit as defined by the Rome Conference (1963).

**Summary**

According to UNWTO's definition, tourists are classified in 2 categories:

'Tourists', or 'overnight visitors' that would stay overnight in their trips, and 'Same-day visitors', or 'excursionists' that would not stay overnight in their trips.

# 2

# Concerns and Needs of Tourists

## Main Concerns of Tourists

For a number of travelers, safety is their primary concern. Other concerns include health hazards and the crime rate, especially theft at the destination.

### *Personal Safety*

1. Avoid places where crime rates are high, wars are taking place or where there is threat from terrorists.
2. Find out the location of fire exits in the hotel one is staying in.

### *Money and Valuables*

1. Buy traveler's cheques to reduce the possibility of losing the cash.
2. Keep the traveler's cheques, credit cards and cash in separate places.
3. Put valuables in the hotel safe.
4. Take good care of one's travel documents.
5. Make photocopies of one's travel documents in case the original is lost.
6. Keep a list of emergency telephone number

### *Health*

1. Find out whether the country one is traveling to a plague area (whether inoculation is necessary).
2. Find out the sanitation condition in that country (whether it is necessary to bring drinking water).
3. Bring one's personal medication.
4. Be careful with what to eat and drink. Avoid unclean food and water.[5]

***Tourist with Special Needs***

*Very Important Persons (VIPs)*

1. VIPs are usually served by specially trained employees assisting in the departure or arrival procedures.
2. On departure and on arrival, VIPs may benefit from having special immigrations and customs check different from that of normal passengers.

*Senior Travelers*

1. Airlines may provide special care for them, e.g. special meals.
2. Senior travelers may request wheelchair or staff to assist them when boarding and disembarking the aircraft, as well as moving in and out of a hotel.

***Children***

1. Airlines may provide special meals and toys for them.
2. If children fly without adults, airlines must provide staff to take care of them.

***Disabled***

1. Airlines allow the blind to bring along guide dogs on board.
2. Airlines provide the therapeutic air for the needy.
3. Airlines and hotels would provide wheelchairs for those who need.

***Religious Travelers***

1. Airlines prepare special meals for Jews, Muslims, etc.
2. During the flight, they may ask the direction of the aircraft so as to pray to a holy center of their belief.
3. They may ask for a praying room in the concourse area of an airport.

***Pregnant Travelers***

Airlines will accept passengers with pregnancies up to 28 weeks. A medical certificate may be required at check-in.

***Infant Travelers***

Most of the aircrafts are equipped with special baby bassinets, diapers and baby food. Airlines may also offer meet and assist service for passengers traveling with infant when departing from and arriving at the airport.

**Physical Challenge Travelers/ Travelers with Disabilities**

They are slow walkers, wheelchair travelers, dumb and deaf travelers. These travelers have unique needs and they cannot be fulfilled with traditional hospitality facilities. The tourism and hospitality operators must provide a barrier free travel for these travelers.

The typical barriers for these travelers are accessibility, mobility and communication. Airlines, cruises, rails and hotels as well as attractions such as shopping malls, museums, airports, etc should consider providing a barrier-free services to these travelers.

**How to Provide Quality Service to Satisfy Customers' (tourists) Needs?**

***Customer Satisfaction - Quality Service***

Tourism is People Industry. Service is created and performed by people (service providers) for people (customer). What makes service outstanding and memorable is a sequence of events participated by a variety of willingly involved and competent personnel.

Effective Customer Service must be customer-driven and customer-focus so that Total Customer Satisfaction must be achieved. Companies in the tourism industry strive to achieve Total Customer Satisfaction as their corporate culture, their primary objective of corporate success because they realize 'satisfied' customers are the true asset of the companies. Despite the capital investments on aircrafts, hotels and attractions, it is the people that make the difference.

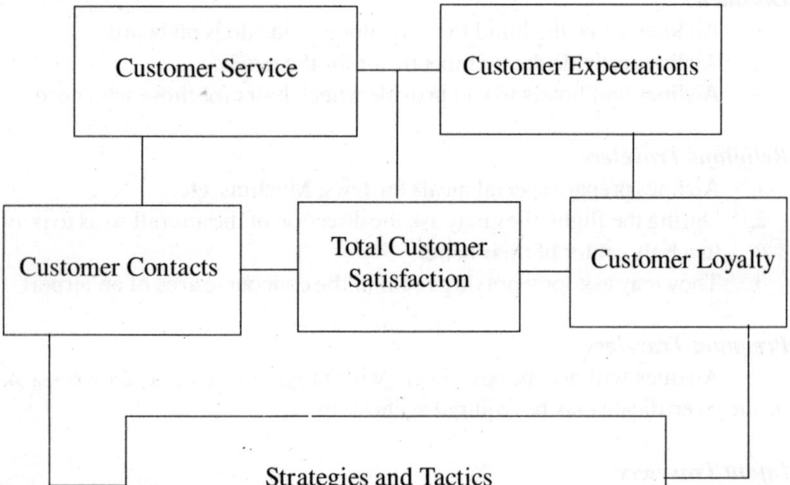


***Total Customer Satisfaction***

Customers can choose what kind of products or services they want to have but service providers have no choice of their customers. Providers are daily meeting all kinds of customers from all walks of life and from all parts of the world. These customers are different in nationalities, genders, ages, life-styles, cultures etc.

Effective customer service must be performed not only with a smile but more important with 'sensitivity'. All service providers must be trained to be observant and alert to respond to different situations and to different customers. The mind-set of positive customer relationship is important and to practice this belief every service provider must develop a positive view towards the customers. In addition, they have to identify their important roles and responsibilities.

***Importance of a Customer***

(a) A customer is the most important person associated with the company, either in person, on the telephone or via correspondence.
(b) A customer is not dependent on us — we are dependent on the customer.
(c) A customer is not an interruption to our work; he/she is the purpose of it. We are not doing the customer a favour by dealing with him/her; the customer is doing us a favour by continuing to do business with us.
(d) A customer is not someone to argue and match wits with. Nobody ever wins an argument with a customer.
(e) A customer is a person without whom we would not continue to prosper. It is our job to ensure the customer continued having pleasure with our products.
(f) The same principle applies to our business partners namely we should not patronize or chastise them. They should be treated as customers.

**Customer Reception**

The front line or customer servicing staff has the responsibility of establishing good relationship with the customers in order to secure business. Greeting is the first reaction of staff to extend his/her hospitality to customer who walks into our workplace. This is an attempt to recognize the existence of

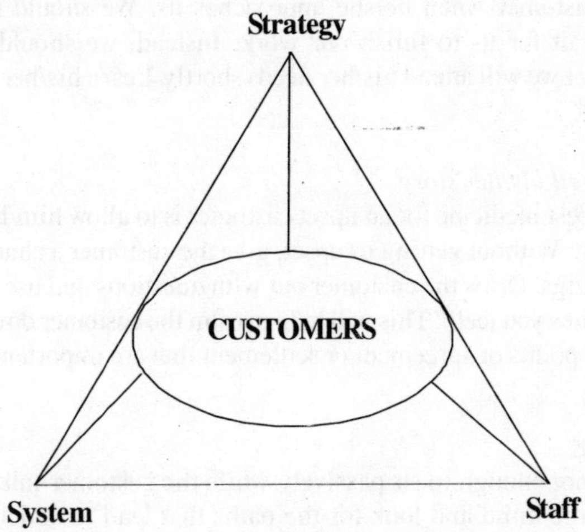

the individual and creates the feeling to the customer he/she is a VIP. Addressing the customer by name such as Mr. .. or Ms. ... will always be welcomed. This will be followed by an offer of service or assistance. Performing effective customer service depends on many factors; the most important being our sensitivity in dealing with the customers.

(a) How well do we understand the feelings, attitudes and beliefs that we bring to our job?
(b) How can these affect our relations with our customers?
(c) How skillful are our communication skills which ultimately have an effect on our relations with others?
(d) How skillful are our evaluation skills in assessing customers' needs and analyzing their behaviours including an understanding of our own feelings and reactions to others?

***Effective Customer Service***

The 9 basic requirements to achieve effective customer service:

1. *Be prepared*

When we know that customers are coming, we have to be prepared. We need to report to work at least 15 minutes earlier so that we can prepare beforehand.

2. *Be presentable*

We need to be properly dressed such as wearing uniform provided by the company. If we cannot look after ourselves, we cannot afford to care for others.

3. *Let customer knows he/she is important*

Everyday we see hundreds of customers but each customer only sees us once. Therefore, it is important that we have to put our work aside and greet the customer when he/she approaches us. We should not make the customer wait for us to finish our work. Instead, we should reassure the customer that we will attend his/her needs shortly. Learn his/her name quickly and use it.

4. *Let him tell his/her story*

The best medicine for an upset customer is to allow him/her to get it off his/her chest. Without getting us upset, give the customer a chance to express his/her feelings. Draw the customer out with questions and use remarks such as "I know how you feel!" This will help to calm the customer down. It will also reveal some points of agreement or settlement that are important in leading to a solution.

5. *Listening*

It is not enough to sit passively while the customer talks. One has to listen with the mind and look for the paths that lead to understanding and problem-solving. Listening requires the ability to turn the speaker's questions reverting back to him/her. In doing so, the speaker will tell his/her story fully before we offer him/her with solutions to the problems. Listening is a very important skill in customer service.

6. *Understanding his/her point of view*

Try to put yourselves in someone's shoes. Doing this, we can appreciate customer's problems, develop emotional maturity and communication skills. Find out what is the customer's interest, talk to the customer in terms of his/her experience, and what are his/her expectations and what brings him/her to us.

7. *Speak their language*

It will never help if we speak the company's language, or industry's jargon when we are dealing with the customers. We should never embarrass our customers or make them defensive and eventually prompting the customer to say, "What Do You Mean?" Use words that the customers can understand when talking about our services. Aim at communicating but not showing off.

Courtesy, respect, consideration are shown in little things; a friendly tone of voice; manner that shows the customer that we consider him/her a person worthy of respect ; a controlled volume to your voice - not too loud yet not whispering and a choice of words that will be meaningful to your customers.

8. *Be honest*

Sometimes when customers approach us for information, we may not have it. In this case we have to be honest. Don't bluff but simply reply that we can find out the information for him/her.

Give accurate directions to the customers and make every attempt to provide good customer service will be appreciated.

9. *Create a lasting impression*

There should always be a courteous opening when meeting customer, and it requires a similar gesture in closing. Customer should be left with a lasting impression, and it is a way to establish a corporate image.

**Travel Products**

There are different type of tourism/travel services which include air passenger transport, rail transport, ferry transport, accommodation services, catering services, meeting and tourist attraction activities, etc. Travel products are a kind of service, and tourism consumers differentiate between travel products provided by different providers on the basis of their own feelings about service quality when making their purchasing decisions. Therefore, tourism providers must pay attention to consumers' views on tourism services and improve clients' level of satisfaction.

### *The Characteristics of Travel Products*

Travel products are intangible, are produced and consumed at the same time, can be differentiated from each other, are non-storable, are mutually complementary, and the ownership rights in them are non-transferable, etc. Each characteristic will influence consumer behaviour.[6]

*Intangible nature*

Tourists can never see, hear, taste or touch travel products before they buy them. This is because what they purchase are the experiences travel gives them, including taking the plane, staying in hotels, visiting museums, enjoying drama performances, taking tourist boat trips, seeing famous mountains and great rivers, having fun, and relaxing in clubs, etc.

After enjoying such services, tourists can only retain these experiences in their memory, and have no way of acquiring physical ownership. Even where travel products require the use of tangible purchases to complete the service process, such as for food and beverages, they do not in any sense represent the ultimate goal of tourists who buy travel products. Tourists hope to achieve intangible goals such as happiness, excitement, relaxation, etc., through their travel experiences.

*The inseparability of production and consumption*

When organizations in the tourism industry provide services to tourists, this is the exact moment that tourists consume such services, and the two cannot be separated in terms of time. For example, when an airplane is in flight, the passengers are consuming flight services at the same time; when a hotel sells a hotel room to a guest for the night, the guest utilizes the hotel's room service at the same time.

*Differentiation*

This means that the elements that make up travel products and their quality standards are difficult to control in a unified manner. This is because the core of travel products is to serve people, even when a tourism enterprise can clearly regulate behavioural standards when service staff are in a certain kind of service situation, the work experiences, personal characteristics and work attitudes of staff will all be different. Because of this, services provided by different service staff in the same environment can never be completely the same.

In addition, the superiority or inferiority of travel products is not only related to the service attitude and ability of service staff, but is also related to tourism consumers. As tourists directly participate in the production and consumption of services, their differences in tourists' knowledge, experience, interests and hobbies all contribute to differences in service quality and satisfaction.

*Perishability*

Travel products cannot be stored like physical products and prepared for sale in the future. Unoccupied hotel rooms or unsold airline tickets have forever lost their chances to be sold. For example, airline companies have no way of storing up spare seats on night time flights to be used to cope with crowded morning or afternoon flights.

*Complementarity*

Tourism is made up of activities such as eating, accommodation, travel, entertainment and touring. Generally speaking, every trip requires the purchase of tourism services provided by various tourism organizations. For example, business travellers, in addition to buying air tickets, also have to pay for taxi transport services, meals and refreshments, and accommodation services provided by hotels. Because of this, one travel product will always be affected by the elements of other travel products. For example, when a famous hot springs tourist attraction becomes less popular, the number of tourists who go to restaurants and shops near the hot springs will also fall, and business on flights to the hot springs tourist attraction will also be affected. Although these products are not from the same organization, they are nevertheless closely linked with each other, and this type of relationship is called complementarity.

*Immobility of Ownership*

This refers to the fact that it is only when services are purchased that activities can be enjoyed or equipment can be used. Tourists will only acquire an experience, but not the ownership of the product. For example, after flying on a plane, a traveller is transported from one place to another, for which he or she acquires nothing other than an air ticket.[7]

## Tourist Destination

People travel for pleasure, looking for tourist resources, facilities and events that provide them with entertainment and interest. Any resources, facilities or events that attract tourists to a particular place are called attractions. Attractions can either be natural or man-made.

### *Tourist Attractions*

An attraction is a destination that pulls or entices a person to it. In general, tourist attractions can be categorized into two types: natural attractions and man-made attractions.

Attractions, no matter physical or cultural, are the main pull factor of tourist flow. Without these attractions, there would be no need for other tourist services. Attraction is a pull factor which entices travelers to a destination. However, the attractiveness of a destination will be different for different people, and it may change with time. Therefore, a combination of attractions may help to create a strong tourist appeal.

*The facilities and services*

Popular attractions will grow into important tourist destinations. Services and facilities such as hotels, restaurants and shops would gather around the attractions for serving the tourists. Most of the world's famous destinations are developed from the major attractions found there.

Example:

(a) Orlando (USA) - Disney World

(b) Luxor (Egypt) – Pyramids

(c) Beijing (China) – Great Wall

*Accessibility*

From a geographical point of view, a tourist destination can be a resort, a city, an area within a country, the whole country or a larger area of the globe. Therefore, the development and maintenance of efficient transport is important in stimulating tourist flows between tourist generating areas and tourist receiving areas.

Referring to the "Overview of Attractions" below, all the attractions are grouped as "Man-made" except those under the heading "Natural Attractions".[8]

*Natural Resources*

There are different types of natural resources:

(a) Climate

(b) Physical features (which could be classified as 'scenery' and 'vegetation and wildlife')

*Climate* : In order to enjoy their holiday, tourists must be physically comfortable with the climatic conditions of the holiday destination. First, they must be comfortable irrespective of their activity, be it passive (e.g. sunbathing) or very active (e.g. surfing, horse riding, snow skiing, etc.). Secondly, climate of the holiday destination must be attractive. People tend to be more relaxed and cheerful when it is sunny and clear than when the sky is overcast and gloomy.

Climate is important to tourism for the following reasons:

1. Climate itself is an attraction

In winter, people from Northern Europe are attracted to the warmer Mediterranean countries for enjoying the sun. At the same time, thousands of people travel to the Alps of France, Switzerland, and to the Rockies in the United States to ski. It is the promise of sunny, clear and cold days that attracts the tourists to spend their holidays on these ski-slopes.

2. Tourists must feel comfortable whether they take part in passive or active activities.

A comfortable warm climate is determined by a combination of humidity and wind. Traveling in hot, dry conditions is more comfortable than in hot, humid conditions. A comfortable cold climate is determined by wind. Wind increases the feeling of winter cold by causing rapid heat loss.

The following climatic elements are associated with human comfort:

- Temperature
- Relative humidity
- Wind

This figure shows the range of temperature and relative humidity within which a person feels comfortable.[9]

*Physical features and scenery*

Natural features and scenery are fascinating attractions for tourists. They can be classified broadly as:

- landforms
- natural vegetation and wildlife

*Landforms*

(a) Mountains and hills attract tourists for:

- Their fascinating natural features;
- The clear and fresh air;
- Activities such as climbing hills, photography, etc.; and
- Winter sports.

(b) Coastlines with beaches, bays, lagoons, islands and reefs attract tourists for:

- Their beautiful scenery of sun, sand and sea; and
- Activities such as surfing, swimming, diving, fishing, etc.

(c) River systems with lakes and waterfalls attract tourists for:

- Their beautiful scenery; and
- Activities such as swimming, canoeing, fishing, etc.

(d) Special natural phenomena such as volcanoes, hot springs, geysers are important attractions. Special geological formations such as karst (limestone) landscape with caves and stalactites and stalagmites are impressive enough to be major attractions on their own. Examples :

Underground river, Philippines
Taal volcano, Philippines
Coral Reef Stystem, Philippines[10]
Mount Titlis, Switzerland
The UNESCO Biosphere Entlebuch, Switzerland[11]

*Natural vegetation and wildlife*

Observation of natural vegetation and animals in their natural environment is increasingly popular. Tourists go into the Amazon for its rich rainforest and wildlife.

Tourist activities related to wildlife can be further divided into *observation and hunting.*

***Hunting***

*Observations :*

There are various wildlife attractions including animals in national parks, forests and game parks/safari parks.In safari parks, tourists remain in their cars and drive through, watching animals in their natural environment. They hunt animals with cameras instead of guns.

*Hunting* :

Hunting of wildlife can be important to the tourism industry. In Kenya and other countries of South Africa, wildlife safaris are becoming more popular. Some rich people are willing to pay high prices for shooting big game. Some countries in Africa and some Eastern European countries such as Poland and Hungary offer expensive hunting trips to western tourists.

*Vegetation and animals as tourist attractions*

*Why do tourists find natural resources attractive?*

Tourists are attracted by natural resources because they want to:

(a) Appreciate the natural wonders of the world - features such as great waterfalls (e.g. the Niagara Falls), volcanic phenomena (e.g. hot springs, sulphur pools, geysers such as Old Faithful in Wyoming, USA), geological phenomena such as caves or rock formations (e.g. Ayers Rock), or spectacular views (e.g. across the Grand Canyon).

(b) Pursue activities that require a natural landscape setting or that depend on rurally located resources, rather than for the scenic quality of the rural backdrop. Activities such as sailing, canoeing, potholing, shooting, climbing, hang-gliding and skiing are examples of the latter where the quality of the resource is more significant than the landscape in which it is set, whereas activities such as cycling, horse riding and walking perhaps depend more closely on high quality landscapes.

(c) Visit the countryside as a destination in order to experience a non-urban way of life for a period, as a relief from the congestion and pressures of the urban environment.

(d) See wildlife in its natural habitat rather than in the zoo or safari park setting.

(e) Visit the countryside purely for the pleasure of looking at, and being in attractive rural landscapes.

## Historic Attractions

People have always been interested in their past, so historic monuments, buildings, and places have become important tourist attractions. Historic attractions include historic relics, sites, history museums and buildings. All of these have special significance in relation to historical events or people.

Each country and the various cultural groups within a country have their own unique history which attracts many interested tourists.

*Examples of Historic Sites*

(i) Stonehenge in England
(ii) Aboriginal rock paintings in Kakadu National Park, Australia
(iii) Archaeological ruins at Mohenjodaro in the Indus valley in Pakistan
(iv) Maya site of Copan in Honduras
(v) Historic center of Florence
(vi) Auschwitz concentration camp run by Nazi Germany in Poland during World War II

*Famous Constructions*

The Great Wall of China
The Parthenon, Athens, Greece.
The pyramids of Egypt
Taj Mahal in India

***History Museums***

British Museum in United Kingdom
The Louvre in Paris

***Historic Relics***

Qin Terra Cotta Warriors, Xian, China.
Crown Jewels of the Queen of England

## Cultural Attractions

Cultural attractions include the cultural traditions and activities originating from the history and customs of a group of people.

***Traditions***

The traditions of societies in Asia or throughout the world provide a focus of interest for many tourists.

**Art**

Most tourists like to visit places where art such as paintings, sculpture, graphics and architecture is being produced or displayed.

### *Handicrafts*

Handicrafts of many cultural groups are of interest to tourists, and demonstration of the craftsman's skills in making the handicrafts also attracts interest. Sale of arts and crafts as souvenir items or gifts is created by:

- the demand of tourists to bring back a souvenir to remind them of their visit; and
- the desire of many tourists to enhance their prestige among friends and relatives by having something to show that they have visited an exotic destination.

### *Food*

Differences in the types of food and the way in which they are prepared provide one of the most interesting ways to learn about another culture. Since people have to eat and usually enjoy doing so, trying new food is a novel experience that is enjoyed by most tourists.

### *Music and dance*

Music and dance are probably the most entertaining and appealing cultural attractions for tourists.

### *Lifestyle*

The lifestyle of a particular culture would be represented by elements of daily life such as:

- work
- food and eating habits
- traditional celebrations
- religion
- language

In Asia, the lifestyle of Buddhist monks in Tibet and Thailand also provide a point of interest for tourists who wish to find out more about the influence of religion upon the host society.

### *Cultural Villages*

With the establishment of "model villages", the lifestyles of particular cultures have been "packaged" for tourists who have a limited amount of time. In order to fit the tight schedules of tourists and to make it convenient for them, the development of such villages enables tourists to experience various aspects of one or a number of cultural groups.

Examples of model cultural villages are the Shenzhen Splendid China Folk Culture and Polynesian Cultural Center in Hawaii. The cultural villages are designed as living museums where the lifestyles of various cultural groups are recreated for visitors to experience. Traditional dances, ceremonies, and music are usually featured. Demonstrations of cooking or craft skills are also provided to educate and entertain visitors.

***Some Famous Traditions/Handicrafts/Food and Dance***

***Traditions***

Dragon dance

***Art***

The Edinburgh Festival in Scotland

***Handicrafts***

Italy is famous for its leather goods
Czech Republic for its crystal

***Food***

Thai food
Chinese "dim-sum"

***Music & dance***

Thai dancing
The Vienna Boys' Choir

***Lifestyle***

Shenzhen Splendid China Folk Culture Village

*Why do tourists find historic/cultural resources attractive?*

- Tourists may be attracted by the age of ancient relics of their own cultural origins. For example, Americans visit Europe in order to see the cities and buildings where their ancestors lived. Likewise, Hong Kong and overseas Chinese travel to the mainland of China to look for their roots and to experience the culture of their own country.
- Tourists of different cultural backgrounds may enjoy visiting historic sites purely for the appreciation of the beauty of the art and architecture, e.g. Greek temple at Sounion, Taj Mahal in India.
- Visitors may be attracted to buildings and places for their historical/ cultural meaning rather than their visual appeal, e.g. the site of 1911 Revolution in Wu Chang, Waterloo Battlefield in Belgium, Mecca in Saudi Arabia and the holy city of Jerusalem in Israel.
- Tourists are interested in how other people live, work and play. They are attracted by the local/native dances, ceremonies and work skills.

**Religious Attractions**

This type of tourism may include pilgrimages, meetings or historical sites. This form of tourism may stem from the curiosity of a tourist.

| | **Types** | **Examples** |
|---|---|---|
| 1. | Places of pilgrimage with illness | Mecca by Islamic believers<br>Lourdes in France by Catholic |
| 2. | Religious Headquarters | Catholic to Rome<br>Jews to Israel |

| | Types | Examples |
|---|---|---|
| 3. | Religious Sites | The birth place of Jesus Christ<br>Westminster Abbey in London |

***Buildings***

Architecture Modern civilizations have created new scenery in cities with their high-rise buildings.

***Theme and amusement parks***

Theme and amusement parks are developed from circuses, carnivals and tournaments of Asia and Europe. Disneyland in Anaheim (California) changed the local amusement park business by integrating shops, shows, and restaurants into a theme embracing adventure, fantasy, history, and science fiction. Another one is in Hong Kong Disneyland.

| | Types | Examples |
|---|---|---|
| 1. | Theme Parks | 1. Disneyland in California<br>2. Splendid China and<br>3. China Folk Culture Village in Shenzhen, China<br>4. Ocean Park in Hong Kong |
| 2. | Parks & Gardens | 1. Palace of Versailles in Paris, France<br>2. Yiheyuan in Beijing , China<br>3. The gardens in Suzhou, China |
| 3. | Convention Centers | 1. Hong Kong Convention and Exhibition Center (In recent years, many resorts have also constructed convention facilities in order to even out the seasonality of their tourist numbers.) |
| 4. | Modern Constructions | 1. Golden Gate Bridge in San Francisco,U.S.A.<br>2. Petrona Towers in Kuala Lumpur, Malaysia<br>3. The Eiffel Tower in Paris, France<br>4. The Tsing Ma Bridge and International<br>5. Airport at Chek Lap Kok of Hong Kong<br>6. Sydney Opera House in Sydney, Australia |
| 5. | Zoos | 1. Singapore Safari Park |
| 6. | Aquariums | 1. Ocean Park in Hong Kong<br>2. Underwater World, Singapore |

| | **Types** | **Examples** |
|---|---|---|
| 7. | Science Museums | 1. Science Museum of Hong Kong |
| | | 2. National Air and Space Museum (Washington, D.C.), U.S.A. |

*Zoos*

Zoos have function similar to that of museums and parks. They entertain and educate visitors and preserve the wildlife in their charge. Zoos serve as centers for scientific research in all areas of zoology and biology, and many zoos are involved in an effort to rescue endangered species through carefully controlled breeding programs.

*Aquariums*

Aquariums are special buildings for fish and aquatic mammals, such as dolphins and seals. Visitors are able to observe aquatic animals, from and below the waterline.

**Special Events and Festivals**

There are many international events that attract a large number of tourists that have no origin in history and are not particularly associated with any one regional culture. These events are of three basic types: sports events, festivals of the arts and commercial events.

| **Type of Events** | **Examples** |
|---|---|
| ***Sports events*** | · Olympic Games<br>· World Championships (various sports)<br>· FIFA World Cup Soccer Games<br>· Asian Games<br>· Hong Kong Rugby Sevens<br>· Formula One Motor Racing |
| ***Arts and culture*** | · Edinburgh Festival<br>· Cannes Film Festival<br>· Mardi Gras (in Rio de Janeiro, New Orleans)<br>· Hong Kong Arts Festival |
| ***Commercial events*** | · World Wine Fair<br>· Munich Beer Festival<br>· Hong Kong Food Festival<br>· World Expo |

**Leisure, Amusement and Sports**

Sometimes, leisure, amusement and sports are the main attractions for a vacation trip.

*Sunbathing*

Sun and surf have always been natural attractions. As people become wealthier, they tend to move farther south where the sun is warmer and more pleasant in winter. They visit beaches not only for the sunshine, but also for sports, such as sailing or surfing.

*Nightlife*

Cinemas, theaters, nightclubs and discos are a part of nightlife. Nightlife is in a special category because certain cities and resorts have such unique and interesting activities that attract large number of people.

*Gambling*

There are 4 types of gambling: pari-mutual wagering, casino gambling, the activities of nonprofit making organizations (mainly bingo and raffles) and lotteries. The travel industry is mainly involved in casino gambling, as well as horse races and dog races. Casino gambling consists of playing slot machines or table games.

*Skiing*

Skiers look for snow and mountains in the wintertime. Skiing has been the fastest growing attraction of all in the past 30 years.

*Hunting and fishing*

In some countries, visitors pay fees for licenses to fish or hunt.

*Shopping*

Shopping has been a by-product of traveling. Recently, shopping has become a reason for traveling. People visit a certain city partly due to the quality of its shops.

# 3

# Forms of Tourism

## Leisure / Holiday Tourism

Leisure/Holiday tourism can be divided into 2 forms:

1. Relaxation
2. Sightseeing

The destinations for relaxation tourism can be attractive scenery or sun, sea and sand. Examples of these tourist destinations are the coasts, beaches, countryside and mountainous regions.

## Sight Seeing

Sightseeing tourism includes the tourists who may travel around sightseeing and staying in different places. The main reasons for sightseeing tourism are a desire for self-education and for self-esteem. These kind of tourists take a lot of photographs. Urban centers are their common destinations, for example, Bangkok, Taipei, Seoul, etc.

## Business Tourism

The business travelers may travel for various purposes, for example, trade, meeting, convention and exhibition. Business people buy similar products as do other tourists. They would also spend money on entertainment and recreation while they are at their destinations.

The characteristics of business tourism are:

(a) Business tourists frequently travel to destinations not usually seen as tourist destinations. Cities such as London, Frankfurt, New York, Tokyo and Hong Kong are important destinations for the business travelers.

(b) Business travel is relatively price-inelastic; business people cannot be encouraged to travel more frequently by the offer of lower prices, nor will an increase in price discourage them from traveling.

(c) Business travel is not greatly affected by seasonal factors such as variation in climate or holidays.
(d) Business tourists take relatively short but frequent trips to major business destinations.
(e) Business tourists may require different services, such as communication facilities or secretarial service.
(f) Business travelers expect, and generally receive, a higher standard of service. Much business travel is first-class or business-class, and thus receives higher levels of service from the suppliers, including the travel agencies.

**Cultural Tourism**

Cultural tourism is related to the transmission of knowledge and ideas of the destination area or host community.

As tourists are curious about different kinds of experiences and cultures in various parts of the world, they travel to learn and experience the culture of a tourist destination. This becomes the prime motivational force for their travel. This kind of tourist likes to visit museums and attend musical, theatrical or folklore performances.

**Eco-tourism**

Tourists of this kind enjoy traveling to natural areas. They will minimize their impact on the environment as well as protect the natural resources during their travel. Therefore, eco-tourism is characterized as a force for conservation and preservation of nature.

For eco-tourism, the managing authority of wildlife areas (e.g. national parks) will spend most of the income from tourists (e.g. entrance fees and donations, etc.) on the conservation work in the area. In some areas, the authority may offer tour guides to educate tourists and modify their behavior so that they will cause less impact on the environment.

**Study Tourism**

Students travel to overseas learning or training centers, such as universities, for short or vacation courses. There is an increasing number of local study tours ranging from half-a-day to a week.

Study tour on board a cruise ship in Hong Kong

**Religious Pilgrimage**

People are motivated by their religious beliefs. The demand for this kind of tourism is quite stable. The destinations of religious pilgrimages usually have a long tradition, such as Muslims to Mecca and Christians to Jerusalem.

**Health Tourism**

Since the development of spas (mineral springs) in the 18th century, there have been visitors to centers of medical treatment. The spas in the mainland of China and Japan are still popular attractions in some tour programs.

**Visiting Friends and Relatives (VFR)**

Some tourists travel abroad because they want to visit their friends and relatives. It is sometimes said that those visiting their friends or relatives (VFR) are not really tourists at all in the conceptual sense. They do not usually buy accommodation or much food or drink or other services at the destination; but they do consume food and beverages from the supermarkets used by their hosts, and household consumption of other services (e.g. electricity, water) is increased during their stay.

Some of the VFR tourists' destinations may not be tourist attractions, but they are the population centers where friends or relatives live. Tourists are therefore visiting "non-tourist" areas. In Hong Kong, the popular VFR destinations are the mainland of China, Canada, U.S.A. and Australia.

**Sports Tourism**

Many tourists travel for sports. They may:

- participate in sports, such as skiing or mountaineering;
- watch sports, such as attending the Olympic Games or World Cup Soccer. For example, the International Rugby-Sevens Competition in Hong Kong attracts both sport players and spectators.
- White water rafting, Philippines,
  Scuba diving, Philippines and
  Rugby Seven, Hong Kong.

**Classification of Tourists (typologies of tourists)**

**Cohen's Classification**

Cohen's classification of tourist is based on the theory that tourism combines the curiosity to seek out new experiences with the need for the security of familiar reminders of home.

Most tourists prefer to explore the destinations from a familiar base. The degree of familiarity of this base underlies Cohen's typology in which he identifies four tourist roles:

| *Role* | *Category* | *Characteristic* |
|---|---|---|
| Organized mass tourists | Institutionalized tourism | - are dealt with in a routine way by the tourist establishments, such as travel agencies, travel companies, hotel chain and other tourism related institutions which cater to the tourist trade |
| Individual mass tourists | | |

| *Role* | *Category* | *Characteristic* |
|---|---|---|
| Explorer | Non-institutionalized tourism | - are loosely attached to the tourist establishment;<br>- act as a "spearhead for mass tourism" as well as<br>- a "demonstration effect" to the lower socio-economic groups of the host community |
| Drifter[12] | | |

*The Organized Mass Tourist*

The organized mass tourists are the least adventurous and spend most of their time in their comfortable "environmental bubble" throughout their trip.

"Environmental bubble" means the tourists surrounded by his/her similar living environment while he/she is abroad.

A guided tour in an air-conditioned bus traveling through the countryside is a typical example of the organized mass tourist. The itinerary is decided in advance, and all the attractions and stopping points are well fixed and guided. Tourists have almost no decisions on their trip.

*Individual Mass Tourist*

This type of tourists is similar to the organized mass tourist, except that the tour is not entirely fixed. The tourist has a certain amount of control over his/her time and itinerary, and is not bound to a group.

However, all the major arrangements are still made through a tour agency. The tour does not bring them much further a field than the organized mass tourists do. They are still confined by their "environmental bubble".

*Explorer*

These type of tourists arranges their trips alone. They try to go somewhere unusual, but still look for comfortable sleeping places and reliable means of transportation. They retain some of the basic routines and comforts of their native way of life. They try to mix with the people they visit and also try to speak their language. The explorers dare to leave their "environmental bubble" more readily than the organized mass tourists and individual mass tourists, but they are still careful about their ventures.

*Drifter*

This type of tourist goes further away from the "environmental bubble" and from the accustomed ways of life in their home countries. They keep away from any kind of connection with the tourism establishment, such as hotels and tour coaches. The drifters have no fixed itinerary or timetable. They tend to make their trips wholly on their own, live with the local people and often take odd-jobs to keep themselves going. They try to live the way the locals live, and to share their houses, food, and habits.

**Plog's Classification[13]**

Stanley Plog proposes a theory that associates the popularity of a destination to the inherent personalities of travelers. Plog suggests that travelers can be classified into the following types based on their different personalities: allocentric, psychocentric and mid-centric.

***Allocentric Type***

An allocentric tourist is a person who seeks new experiences and adventure in a variety of activities. This person is outgoing and self-confident in behavior. An allocentric person prefers to fly and to explore new and unusual areas before others do so. Allocentrics enjoy meeting people from foreign or different cultures.

They prefer good hotels and food, but not necessarily modern or chain-type hotels. For a tour package, an allocentric would like to have the basics such as transportation and hotels, but not be committed to a structured itinerary. They would rather have the freedom to explore an area, make their own arrangements and choose a variety of activities and tourist attractions.

*Psychocentric Type*

Psychocentrics are more conservatively oriented. They tend to be inhibited and non-adventure some. They prefer to return to familiar travel destinations where they can relax and know what types of food and activity to expect.

Psychocentrics prefer to drive to destinations, stay in typical tourist accommodations, and eat at family-type restaurants. When arranging a package tour, psychocentrics would prefer a heavily structured itinerary so that they know what to expect. Safety and security are very important to this group.

*Mid-centric Type*

There is a large number of people falling between the allocentric and the psychocentric types of tourists. This type of tourists is called mid-centrics. Mid-centric tourists are not particularly adventurous, but they are receptive to new experience.

| *Psychocentrics* | *Allocentrics* |
|---|---|
| 1. Prefer familiar travel destinations.<br>2. Like commonplace activities in destinations. | 1. Prefer "non-tourist" destination and few developed tourist attractions. |

*(Contd.)*

*(Contd. Table )*

| *Psychocentrics* | *Allocentrics* |
|---|---|
| 3. Prefer relaxing sun-and-fun spots.<br>4. Prefer low activity level.<br>5. Prefer staying at familiar hotel chain, dining at restaurants offering cuisine of their home country.<br>6. Prefer familiar rather than foreign atmospheres.<br>7. Prefer purchasing complete tour packages featuring a full schedules of activities. | 2. Enjoy discovering new destinations before others have visited them.<br>3. Prefer unusual destinations.<br>4. Prefer high activity level.<br>5. Prefer simple services, such as adequate to good accommodations and food.<br>6. Enjoy interacting with people from different cultures.<br>7. Prefer tour arrangements that include basics (transportation and accommodations and allow for considerable flexibility).[14] |

*Source* : Plog, Stanley. C (1974, February). Why distrinations rise and fall in popularity? The Cornell Hotel and Restaurant Administration Quarterly, 55-58

Other than Cohen and Plog's typologies of tourists, there are a number of typologies which attempt to group tourists on different variables such as vacation experiences, preferences and travel determinants. Below table gives a summarized list of research on the typologies of tourists.

| *Researcher* | *Theory* | *Date* |
|---|---|---|
| Murray | Needs theory of personality | 1938 |
| Masl | Hierarchical Theory of Needs | 1943 |
| Hebb and Thompson | Different levels of optimal stimulation | 1954 |
| Berlyne | Optimal level of stimulation | 1960 |
| Dann | The need to escape | 1977 |
| Schreyer and Roggenbuck | Experience and expectation concept | 1978 |
| Crompton | Different motivations for different markets | 1979 |
| Lopez | Needs motivation and expectations of tourists | 1980 |
| Zuckerman | Sensation seeking concept | 1990 |
| Dann | Push Pull concept | 1981 |
| Cheron and Ritchie | The concept of risk as motivation | 1982 |
| Lounsbury and Hoopes | Needs motivation and expectations of tourists | 1985 |
| Maddox | Needs motivation and expectations in tourism behavior | 1985 |
| Parasuraman, Zeithaml and Berry | Expectations, desires and wants of consumers | 1988 |
| Geva and Goldman | Needs motivation and expectations of tourists | 1991 |
| Hall and McArthur | Motivation of adventure tourists | 1991 |

*(Contd.)*

*(Contd. Table)*

| *Researcher* | *Theory* | *Date* |
|---|---|---|
| Morgan, Moore and Monsell | Motivation in adventure tourists | 1991 |
| Ross and Iso-Ahola | Motivation and satisfaction concept | 1991 |
| Mansfield | Motivation and satisfaction concept | 1992 |
| Oliver | Disconfirmation of expectations theory | 1993 |
| Ivancevich and Matteson | A particular act will result in a particular outcome concept | 1993 |
| Rossi and Cereatti | Objective risk and subjective risk concept | 1993 |
| Anderson, Fornell and Lehmann | Changing and adapting expectation concept | 1994 |
| Gnoth | Push Pull concept | 1997 |
| Fulker and Turner | Needs motivation and expectations of novice adventure tourists | 2000 |
| Stewart | Motivation and desired needs | 2001 |
| Leep and Gibson | Risk avoidance motivation by tourist | 2003 |

*Source* : Cassidy, Francisl, What Motivates Event Tourists ?, P. 11-12.

In the understanding of the typologies of tourists, this topic is highly complex and depends on a range of factors. We cannot hope to encompass the complex patterns of behaviour we see in the real world with one single typology. Some of the above historical research on tourists' needs, motivations and expectations may actually come up with fairly similar dimensions but may label them differently (Plog, 1987). Furthermore, the dynamic nature of the tourism industry may not be able to represent the many changes in consumer behaviour which have taken place over the years. Finally, some typologies are generally used as if they can be applied to people in all countries (example of Plog's psychocentric position of destination). They appear to ignore national and cultural differences, which surely weakens their validity. In view of all these, we may need as many typologies as there are tourism products, tourism markets, countries and cultures.

# 4

# Travel Motivations

## The Motivation Process

Travellers are motivated to satisfy a need, and they have a perception of what will satisfy their need. At the same time, travellers have a perception of the attractions of the destination and whether the attractions satisfy their needs. If both sides are agreed, travellers are motivated to visit that destination.[16]

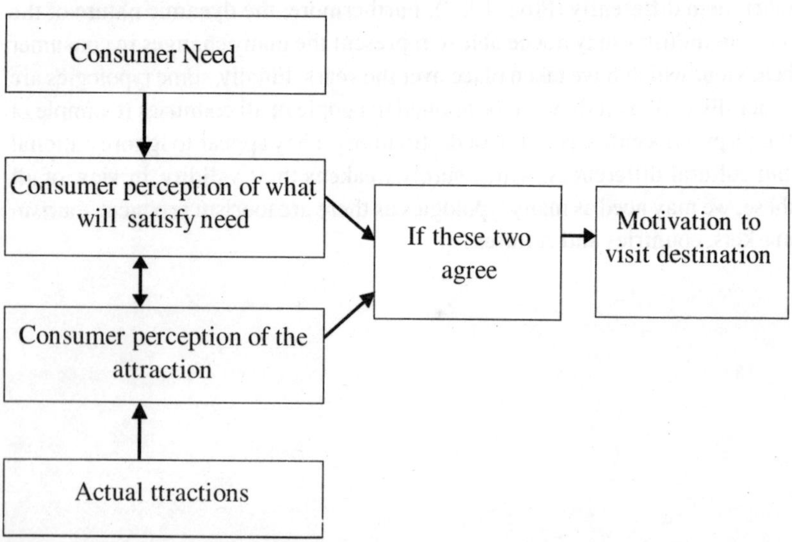


*Source* : Holloway J. Christopher, *The Business of Tourism*, 4th ed., Pitman Publishing, 1994, p. 48.

### *Consumer Behaviour – Travel Motivations*

In this chapter we will use theories on consumer behaviour to explain tourism. Wierenga & Van Raaij (1987) define consumer behaviour as 'all the actions of individuals which are directly involved with the purchase, use and disposal of products and services in order to satisfy one's needs'. The tourism product is a complex mixture of services (e.g. aircraft seats, hotel rooms) and goods (e.g. food, souvenirs) (Holloway, 1989) which are bought by a special kind of consumers, namely tourists.

To provide a high-quality service to tourists effectively, you must understand what psychological factors can stimulate and influence people to make all types of travel decisions. Travel psychology is a science that involves researching tourists' psychological activities and their objective rules, the basic objective of which is to explain why people travel, what factors influence people's travel decisions, and how the motivations for such decisions are formed. Apart from the consumer behaviour approach we also use aspects of personality to describe travelling behaviour.

### *The Definition of "Motivation"*

A motivation is a wish that prompts people to take action, work hard to achieve a goal, and satisfy a certain kind of need. For example, when a person is hungry and there is a need to appease his or her hunger, a motivation to search for food is formed. Therefore, people's activities of all kinds are driven by their motivations, and they govern people's actions.

Why do we go travelling?
Why do we choose to travel to a certain place?
Why do we participate in a certain travel activity?

These are essentially questions about tourists' travel motivations. Travel motivations directly spur people's travel activities.

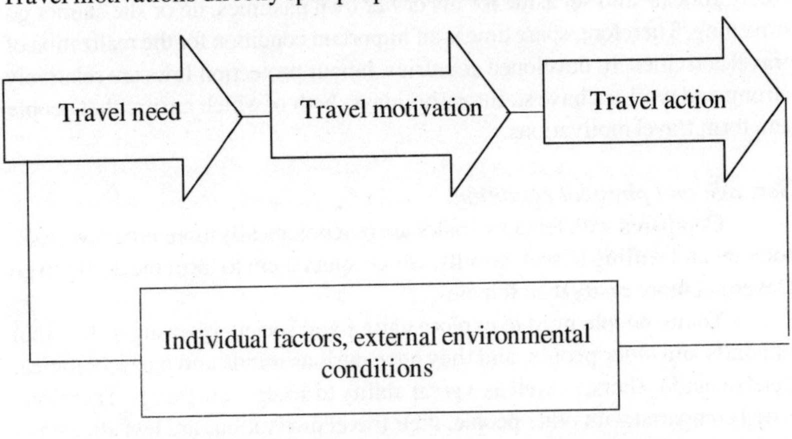


**Fig. The Formation of Travel Motivations and Travel Actions.**

A travel motivation is the psychological need of a person to participate in travel activities, and this kind of need will directly promote the travel motivation; if you have a motivation, a travel action will result. However, in real life, the process from the formation of a travel motivation to the occurrence of an actual travel action is a complex one.

During this process, when people have a need to travel, they must also have corresponding individual factors and external environmental conditions, such as physical fitness, financial status, weather and transport, etc. Otherwise, this kind of need can only remain a wish, and no travel motivation or action will arise.

### *Factors that Influence Individual Travel Motivations*

#### *Economic capacity*

Economic capacity is the basis on which all needs are formed. Because travel is a kind of consumer behaviour, the ability to pay the various types of charges involved is of course necessary. When a person's economic income can only support his or her basic living needs, he or she will not form a motivation to go travelling. As an economy develops, in countries and regions where citizens' income increases, the tourism industry becomes more developed, and the number of people who go travelling climbs, or drops when the opposite applies.

#### *Spare time*

Spare time refers to the time that people can freely allocate to taking part in pastimes and entertainment or anything else they enjoy participating in after their daily work, study, living and other compulsory time commitments. Travel necessarily takes up a certain amount of time, and if a person cannot get away from official business or family matters and has no spare time to freely allocate and set aside for his or her own pastimes, he or she cannot go travelling. Therefore, spare time is an important condition for the realization of travel activities. In developed countries, labour protection laws are relatively strong and workers have statutory holidays, both of which ensure that people can form travel motivations.

#### *Sex, age and physical condition*

Compared with females, males are psychologically more proactive, risk-tolerant and willing to seek novelty, which spurs them to form the desire to go travelling more easily than females.

Young people need to explore nature and society is stronger than that of adults and older people, and they have curious minds and a psychological need to outdo others, as well as a great ability to accept new things. Therefore, when compared with other people, their travel motivations are less affected or limited by reality.

Physical condition is an important factor that influences travel psychology. For example, older people are limited by factors such as health and lack of strength. They will generally have a relatively large number of requirements relating to the travel destination, travel resources and the travel environment.

*Psychological factors*

Travel motivations are a form of individual psychological activity, and are inevitably influenced by various aspects such as individual interests, hobbies, profession, attitude to life, understanding of the surrounding environment, level of education, and family.

***Social Factors that Influence Travel Motivations***

*Overall Development of the Tourism Industry*

It is only when the economy of a country or region is developed that it will have enough resources to improve and construct travel facilities, develop tourist attractions and promote transport development. Road transport facilities, accommodation, catering, and service standards at a destination are important factors in the tourists choice of destination, and also affect their formation of travel motivations to a large degree, especially for tourists with relatively high hospitality expectations.

***Group, family and social atmosphere***

Group or social pressure can also influence people's travel motivations. For example, travel activities organized by enterprises, or travel awards, etc. encourage people to form their own travel motivations involuntarily, and travel activities subsequently take place.

Social surroundings can also influence people's travel motivations. Colleagues, friends and relatives travel behaviour and travel experiences can always influence others, or lead to the formation of a comparative psychology, making people form identical travel motivations, and leading to the formation of a kind of imitative travel behaviour.

**Typologies and Researches on Travel Motivation**

**Erik Cohen**

Sociologist Eric Cohen concludes there are 5 motivations Travelling; See which type applies to you. You may have never realized that you have this kind of travel objective.

(a) My job and family are both in India. Every day I go to work, leave work and go home; I can never get away from this narrow world.
My body and soul are always being pulled between family and work, and I really want to get away to "recharge" my body and soul.

(b) I feel that life has no meaning. My life has basically been "alienated" by work. To earn money I work repeatedly every day, and my biggest fear is losing my job.
I just want to let go of my insignificant and formulaic lifestyle, and allow my taut nerves to relax a little. Relaxation is actually allowing my "alienation" process become more bearable.

(c) I don't know what's missing, but I simply feel that life is shallow. I have no goals, so I've decided to do something and seek a change.
I want to go travelling and put the life I'm used to aside for a time, go elsewhere and get to experience the lives of other people/nationalities, and understand the real meaning of life.

(d) I like trying out alternative lifestyles, different religions, underground music…I'm constantly seeking things that can strike a cord in myself. The purpose of travel is to experience other cultures.

(e) Apart from my day-to-day life, there is a setting or place (e.g. a farm in my hometown or a sacred religious place) calling me.
Going there is just like retreating to the centre of my life and feeling I actually exist.[17]

**Plog's Theory**

Based on Plog's theory, travel motivations are related to a very narrow spectrum of psychographic types.

***Allocentric Motivations***

- Educational and cultural motives to learn and to increase the ability for appreciation, scientific research; trips with expert leaders or lecturers
- Study of genealogy such as visits to their ancestor's homeland to trace their root
- Search for the exotic, such as the North Pole and the South Pole, the Amazon, etc.
- Satisfaction and sense of power and freedom such as anonymity, flying, control, sea travel, fast trains
- Gambling – Las Vegas, Atlantic City, Monte Carlo, Bahamas, Puerto Rico
- Development of new friendships in foreign places
- Sharpening perspectives such as to awaken one's senses, heighten awareness
- Political campaigns, supporting candidates, government hearings
- Vacation or second homes and condominiums

***Near-Allocentric Motivations***

- Religious pilgrimages or inspiration
- Participation in sports events and sports activities
- Travel as a challenge, sometimes a test of endurance such as exploring mountain climbing, hiking, diving

- Business travel, conference, meeting and conventions
- Theatre tours, special entertainment
- A chance to try a new lifestyle

***Midcentric Motivations***

- Relaxation and pleasure travel just for plain fun and enjoyment
- Satisfying personal contacts with friends and relatives
- For health reasons such as to change the climate, sunshine, spas, medical treatment
- The need for a change for a period of time
- An opportunity to escape from life's problems
- The real or imagined glamour of the destination
- Appreciation of beauty such as national and state parks, forests, lakes, wilderness areas, canoe trips, ocean shores
- Sensual indulgence such as food, comforts, luxuries for the body, romance, sexual enjoyment, rest, relaxation
- Shopping such as souvenirs, gifts, expensive possessions like cameras, jewels, furs, cars, antiques, art
- Joys of transportation – cruise ships, gourmet meals, buffets, comfortable trains, buses, airplanes, autos
- Pleasure of pre- and post-travel includes planning the trip, anticipation, learning, dreaming;
- Family or personal matters

***Near-Psychocentric and Psychocentric Motivation***

- Ego enhancement, quest for status
- Travel for acceptance, to be comfortable socially
- Travel as a cultural norm – paid holidays required by law
- Visit to places seen or read about in the news
- Visit to amusement parks[18]

**Maslow – "Hierarchy of Needs"**

Maslow (1971) distinguished five different levels of psychological needs ranging from physiological needs to self-actualization. According to his theory, satisfaction of people's basic needs is a prerequisite for the satisfaction of the higher needs . Maslow argues that all behaviour is motivated by psychological needs, for behaviour serves to fulfill those needs.

***Physiological needs***

These are needs required by humans to sustain their existence and prolong their lives, and are the minimum basic needs, including needs relating to food, water, oxygen, sleep, a place to live and warmth, as well as clothing, food, shelter, mobility, sex and other psychological functions. If these needs cannot be fulfilled, human existence becomes a problem.

***Safety needs***

These are needs that represent human desires to protect their own bodies and minds from injury, and to guarantee safety and stability. For example, needs relating to health, a safe and orderly environment, a stable career and the avoidance of unforeseen accidents. When a person's physiological needs have been fulfilled, he or she will want to fulfill such safety needs.

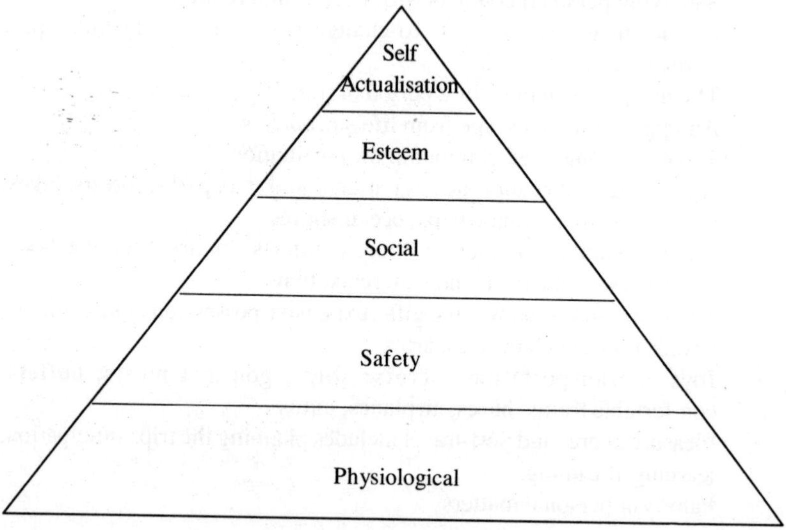


**Maslow's Hierarchy of Needs**

***Personal interaction needs***

Personal interaction needs include the need for love and a sense of belonging. The need for love refers to the fact that people all hope to achieve harmonious relationships with friends and colleagues or to maintain friendships; everyone wants to love others and be loved.

In addition, the need for a sense of belonging refers to the fact that people all want to have a sense of belonging, and want to gain the acceptance of a certain group and to be included and valued by it, as well as for its members to care for and look after each other.

***Esteem needs***

These are human desires to gain other people's respect, a satisfactory status, due human rights, reputation and prestige, and to realize a certain social position.

***Self-actualization needs***

These are human desires for the needs to give full play to one's own potential and to realize one's own ideals and aspirations, including the seeking of knowledge, the appreciation of beauty, creativity, achievements, etc. Maslow considered self-realization to be mankind's highest level of needs, which signify a full, enthusiastic, wholehearted experience of life.

**Interpretation of Maslow's Theory in the context of Tourism Activity**

***Physiological***

To fulfill the physiological needs of travellers, tour operators may designate frequent rest stops in the tour itinerary. The food and beverage outlets are located in easily accessible areas. Motels are designed along highways to provide shelter for travellers using automobile as their means of transport.

***Safety***

To satisfy the safety needs of the travellers, tour organizers provide guided services for exotic or unfamiliar locations. Also travellers tend to prefer making reservations or travel arrangements through government approval agencies or services.

***Belonging or love***

Airlines, hotels, restaurants usually provide frequent-user programs to fulfill the belonging and love needs of travellers. As members of these organizations, travellers develop a sense of belonging towards these organizations. Travellers would join tours or groups with a similar interest and/or background. They may also like to join tours to explore one's ancestral roots.

***Esteem or self respect***

The elite status of the frequent-user programs such as gold, silver, or bronze "membership" are established by the travel industry to fulfill the self esteem needs of the travellers. In recognition of special occasions, travel organizations sometimes offer flowers and champagne to travellers.

***Self-actualization***

Travellers join educational tours to fulfill their self-actualization needs. They may travel to testify their ability, such as climbing the Himalayas or achieve self-fulfillment by taking educational tours, etc.[19]

***Extended activity***

According to the different levels of needs described in Maslow's Theory of Needs, make a list of travel promotion products that can fulfill those needs. Then try to find a kind of travel promotion product that can fulfill multiple levels of needs.

Common travel motivations could be summarized into the following types:

**Common Travel Motivations**

1. ***Relaxation, health***

- People who have stressful or monotonous daily lives or work participate in travel activities such as relaxing, travel and recuperation holidays in order to relax and loosen up, as well as keeping healthy and finding entertainment. For example, natural scenery, historical monuments, parks, the seaside, hot springs recuperation areas, etc., are all tourist choices for this type of travel motivation.
- Travellers who are curious, knowledgeable and adventurous, such as Himalayas climbing parties and North Pole explorers.

2. ***Exploration, risk-taking***

- For travellers with this kind of motivation, their travel activities are mainly directed at distinctive, beautiful things and phenomena in the natural world, as well as to visiting museums, exhibition halls and famous tourist attractions, and participating in various types of theme-based travel activities, etc.

3. ***Spirit and the appreciation of beauty***

- People all go travelling to meet friends and relatives, to find their roots and search for their ancestors, and to get to know new friends, etc. Travellers in this category require that the personal relationships they maintain in the course of their travels be friendly, cordial and warm-hearted, and want to be cared for.

4. ***Social Interaction***

- People who have a religious faith go travelling to participate in religious activities and take part in religious studies, and those who travel driven by religious faith motivations do so mainly to satisfy their own spiritual needs. Religious travel is divided into two categories: pilgrimages, and missionary work.

5. ***Religious Faith***

- People go travelling for various types of business and official activities, such as special trips to buy goods or diversions to a certain place to go travelling; business trips to a certain place to take part in academic observation, communicate, etc.; and travel activities participated in by groups, government delegations and business associations, etc., that go to a certain place for discussions, etc.

6. ***Business affairs and official matters***

- Because they are busy at work, people will normally neglect to take care of and look after their family members and friends. For these people, they go travelling to satisfy a responsibility or obligation to their parents, wife or children, or to relax and have fun with friends. Therefore, every summer, the number of family-based tour groups will increase greatly.

**7. *Family Responsibilities***

Apart from the above common travel motivations, there are other typologies and research as well:

**Hudman's Motivators of Travel**

***Health***

People travel for improving their health. They would go for leisure and medical treatment to relax and entertain themselves. Natural landscapes, historical sites, coastline, spa and resort are the destinations of these travellers.

***Curiosity***

People travel because of curiosity, inquisitiveness and adventure. Politics, culture, public figures, physical features and disaster would attract these travellers.

***Sports***

People travel for sports to release their pressure and fantasize about being an athlete. Being a spectator could experience the atmosphere of the competition, and have social contributions such as connecting with other audience and meet new friends.

***Pleasure***

Vocation relates to pleasure because it could give routine life a break. People would try new things and participate in activities that would make them feel happy, such as visiting art museums, watching operas and gambling etc.

***Religious and spiritual appreciation***

People travel for spiritual needs. They visit religious headquarters usually because of religious reasons. In this way they could have stronger believe in their religion. On the other hand, many travellers gain satisfaction by appreciation of natural landscapes, art performances, and visiting museums and historical sites.

***Professional and business***

People travel for business such as scientific expeditions, business meetings, conventions and education.

***Friends and relatives***

People travel because they want to visit their friends and relatives; it shows their care of family and friends.

***Roots syndrome***

People travel to trace the root of their family or the culture of their homeland. Pedigree research and hometown exploration are the common activities of these travellers.

***Esteem***

Many people travel for gaining respect from others and a satisfying social status because one with plenty of travel experience and knowledge of different countries is usually admired by others.

**Krippendorf: 8 Reasons for Travel**

Research on reasons for travel uncovers an endless list of travel motivation. Apparently, people want to 'switch off, relax'. They want to 'get away from everyday life', 'recover strength' and 'experience nature' (Krippendorf, 1997).

Krippendorf (1997) distinguishes eight reasons for travel:

1. ***Recuperation and regeneration.*** People get tired during working weeks, and use vacations to replenish their 'bodily and mental strength'.
2. ***Compensation and social integration.*** Tourism compensates for everyday social failure by presenting another world next to everyday dreariness.
3. ***Escape.*** Everyday life contains more and more aspects of stress; people want to escape from this.
4. ***Communication.*** Travelling abroad gives people a chance to gain human warmth, to establish contact with other people.
5. ***Broadening of the mind.*** People want to satisfy their interests in other cultures and nature.
6. ***Freedom and self-determination.*** Tourists are in a position to largely make up their own rules; they are free from any obligations.
7. ***Self-realization.*** An unfamiliar and strange environment offers a great chance for investigating and enhancing the self.
8. ***Happiness.*** Vacations are highly associated with joy and pleasure, so happiness becomes a reason for embarking on a holiday trip.

This list is not conclusive, yet one can conclude that reasons for travel encompass more aspects of 'going away' than aspects of 'going to' (Krippendorf, 1997).

Along with the diversification and complexity of people's living needs in modern society, travel motivations are becoming more varied and diversified. Different tourists go travelling based on their own differing motivations, and each travel activity allows them to acquire different experiences and knowledge. Travel is a complex social action, and tourists use travel to satisfy their own various needs.

At the same time, under the influence of external environmental conditions, motivations always change as the environment changes. Therefore, the same tourist's motivations for going on different trips will differ from each other. At the same time, a lot of travel motivations do not just involve one motivation, but may include various kinds of motivations.

**Nickerson's Travel Motivations**

Furthermore, following the above reasons for travel, tourism seems to serve psychological needs. Nickerson (1996) too argues that deep psychological needs are the basic motivators for tourism. She uses Maslow's "Hierarchy of Needs", a theory about psychological needs and motivation to describe people's motivation to travel.

Within the five levels of needs, physiological needs are the most easily fulfilled, and the higher the level, the more difficult it is to achieve fulfillment. However, for any type of need, it doesn't disappear just because a higher level of needs appears; it's just that once a higher level of needs has arisen, the influence of lower levels of needs on one's actions will be reduced.

Applied to tourism, social and ego factors influence people to travel in order to gain social acceptance and admiration in their social environments (Nickerson, 1996). For example, in the Western world people who are not able to go on a holiday trip are often pitied. So, a reason for travel could be the avoidance of pity (Nickerson, 1996).

Another example is provided by the process of conformity. If all people in a person's social environment are apt to travel, the social pressure on that person to travel is high (Holloway, 1989).

Fashion plays a role too, partly in being part of the conformity process, partly in being a determinant in choosing a travel destination (Holloway, 1989).

Nickerson applied the Maslow's Hierarchy of Needs to describe travel motivations as below:

***Physiological needs***

This can explain why people go to the seaside or a mountain retreat to avoid the heat; these are all actions required to be performed by certain physiological conditions inside the human body.

***Safety needs***

To travellers, safety needs are expressed in terms of the safety of people's life, property and psychology. They hope that in the course of a journey, no vehicle or boat accidents occur, they don't get sick, they're not robbed, they don't have things stolen, and that they safely complete the entire journey, etc. They also hope to achieve a psychological feeling of security. For example, they hope there is no political upheaval or war in the country they go to and that social order is sound there, etc.

Although the natural scenery and human cultural landscape of some countries are extremely rich, tourists would lose the motivation to travel there if the country has been involved in a long period of upheaval or war. Therefore, the need for safety is one of the most important factors that influences people's travel behaviour.

***Personal interaction needs***

Tourists' personal interaction needs have diverse characteristics. People who go travelling all want to be able to travel together with close friends, get to make new friends in the course of their journey, understand different cultures and customs through interaction with local people, or enhance their friendships by visiting friends and family.

Therefore, travel is one of the most effective activities for people to make new friends, meet up with old friends around the world, and promote contact between people.

***Esteem needs***

A person who has experience of frequent travel and knows a lot about different countries and regions are often admired and respected by others, which helps to fulfill the need to be respected as an individual.

***Self-actualization needs***

Travel can involve a search for stimulation, challenging oneself and acquiring knowledge about new things, and this kind of travel involves expressing one's own self-value to fulfill self-actualization needs. For example: climbing Mount Everest.

**The Push-and Pull Theory**

In 1977, Dann, a U.S. academic, put forward the push-pull theory of travel motivations. He considered that travel behaviour was influenced by both push factors and pull factors.

People travel because they are "pushed" into making travel decisions by internal, psychological forces, and "pulled" by the external forces of the destination attributes.

***Push factors***

These are internal or intangible factors that lead to the formation of travel desires among potential tourists. Anything that can relieve and fulfill tourists' desires can thus become a focus or target. In short, these are socio-psychological factors that motivate or create a desire to satisfy a need to travel. Therefore, under the influence of push factors, tourists who go travelling do not necessarily have specific, clear choices.

For example, tourists who hope to improve their relationships with family members don't really care where they go, the key is to spend quality time together with family.

**Pull factors**

These are factors that influence where tourists go travelling. Pull factors are the attractiveness or "drawing power" of the destination as perceived by the traveler, and they are likely to help traveler to make an actual destination choice. Tourists form pull-type travel motivations on the basis of their perception, expectation and knowledge of destinations. Because of this, tourists who go travelling under the influence of pull factors always have a clear destination.

For example, a newly married couple may go to the sunshine and beaches of the Maldives to testify to their love, and will not choose other travel destinations.

Other than the above factors there are the factors below which motivate a person to travel

| **(A) Push Factors**<br>**Psychological Factors** | **(A) Pull Factors**<br>**Destinations Attributes and Type of Facilities (knowledge)** |
|---|---|
| Motivations (psychological)<br>Escape<br>Rest and relaxation<br>Prestige<br>Health and fitness<br>Adventure<br>Social interaction<br>Benefits<br>Interests | Climate<br>History sights<br>Scenic beauty<br>Sunshine<br>Beaches<br>Snow<br>Cultural events<br>Recreational opportunities<br>Benefit expectations |
| **(B) Socioeconomic and Demographic Factors** | **(B) Accessibility and Marketed Image (perceptions and expectations)** |
| Age, gender, income, education, family life-cycle and size, race/ethnic group, occupation, second home ownership<br>**Market knowledge**[20] | Formed negative or positive destination image<br>Quality of services<br>Quality of facilities |

*Source* : Mahmood Khan, Michael Oslen and Turgnt Var (1993) *VNR's Encyclopaedia of Hospitality and Tourism*, New York, pp. 798-810.

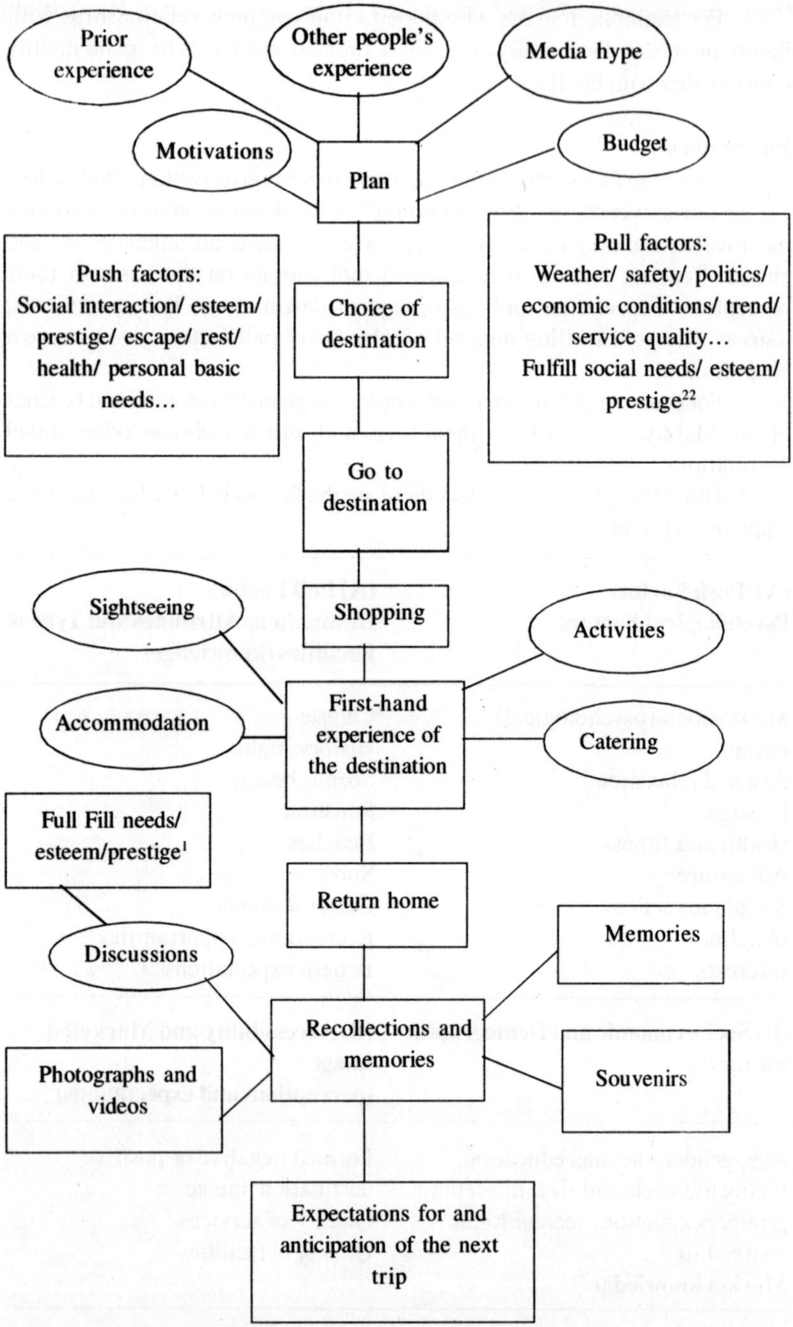


*Source* : Adapted from Du Jing Chuan and Zen Ping's translations of "Travel Relaxation" Yunnan University of Publishing, p. 14.

**Interpretation of Push and Pull Factors Often Used in Travel Motivation Research**

| *Push factors* | *Pull factors* |
|---|---|
| 1. To see culture and history, admire beautiful scenery, or enjoy the weather. | 1. Tourism products, tourism charges |
| 2. Increase knowledge | 2. Distinctive lifestyles at one's destination |
| 3. Experience different lifestyles | 3. Interesting nightlife |
| 4. Fulfill one's travel dreams | 4. All kinds of good food |
| 5. Visit family and friends | 5. Convenient transport |
| 6. Be together with family members or friends | 6. Accommodation, sports facilities, and information |
| 7. Establish friendships, develop relationships | 7. Quality of service |
| 8. Escape day-to-day life | 8. Abundant historical and cultural resources, beautiful scenery, sunshine and comfortable weather |
| 9. Rest and relax body and mind | 9. Safety |
| 10. Relieve work pressure | 10. International metropolises |
| 11. Seek stimulation and excitement | 11. Peace, hygiene, comfort |
| 12. Physical challenges | 12. Familiarity |
| 13. Get close to and understand nature | 13. It's a good place to understand nature |

*Source* : Extract from Wu Qing Jin, "A Study of Tourists Consumer Behaviour", Tourism Education Publishing.

**Exercise:**

Michael decides to spend US$15,000 to travel to Singapore in the summer holidays. But after discussing with his family and friends, he decides to give up on his Singapore travel plans. What reasons spurred Michael to change his original decision?

**The Motivation-Opportunity-Ability Approach to Tourism**

Jager et al (1997), in their Motivation-Opportunity-Ability (MOA) approach to consumer behaviour, do not use Maslow's hierarchy of needs to describe motivation. Instead, they propose Max-Neef's (1992) description and classification of human needs. However, both Maslow's and Max-Neef's theories aim to describe the same phenomenon, and therefore both offer a starting point in modelling human needs (Jager et al, 1997).

Although Jager et al (1997) state that Max-Neef's theory is more sophisticated than Maslow's hierarchy of needs, we propose Maslow's theory, for it does serve our purposes, it fits the MOA approach, and is also used in Nickerson's theory about tourist motivation.

MOA approach uses 4 personality dimensions to describe tourists in order to indicate motivations for different types of travel.

Jager et al (1997) have developed a conceptual model for consumer behaviour. Applied to tourism this model can be used to assess reasons for travel. Jager et al (1997) argue that consumer behaviour is the result of 3 factors:

1. **Motivation:** Motivation is created by psychological needs.
2. **Opportunity:** The availability of factors that create the possibility for gratification of psychological needs.
3. **Ability:** Personal skills and resources needed to use the opportunities.

**Motivation**

Applied to tourism, motivation is represented by social, ego and self-actualization needs (Nickerson, 1996). Tourism is an opportunity to fulfill these needs.

For example, one might climb Mount Everest in order to gain esteem, which is a part of ego needs. The tourist must also have the ability to use the opportunity. For example, one needs a lot of money to climb Mount Everest, which means that few people have the ability to use the opportunity of climbing Mount Everest.

**Opportunities**

Opportunities are products and services one can use to fulfill one's needs (Jager et al, 1997). In this case tourism is the need-satisfier. According to the theory one's need can be satisfied by many different opportunities. This is in line with the existence of the many different tourism types and needs.

We presented a typology of 5 different types of tourism (coastal tourism and water recreation, mountain tourism, city-tourism, rainforest-tourism and other nature tourism). These can be regarded as five different opportunities to satisfy one's psychological needs.

Of course, those 5 types of tourism can each be divided into smaller types of tourism. In repeating this, one would end up having single destinations as tourism types. This implies that each destination is an opportunity for satisfying one's psychological needs, yet specific needs and a specific personality lead to a specific ranking of destination.

In exploring the relation between needs and opportunities, 5 types of satisfiers can be discerned (Max-Neef, 1992 as cited in Jager et al, 1997).

An interesting one for tourism is the inhibiting satisfier, which satisfies one need, but inhibits the satisfaction of other needs in the process.

Especially interesting is the interpersonal need inhibition. People who seek to satisfy their esteem needs by visiting a certain destination are dissatisfied by other people seeking the same satisfaction or the satisfaction of social needs. On the other hand, people seeking to satisfy social needs are more satisfied when other people come visit the same destination.

So, people seeking satisfaction for some need, may in the process inhibit, and simultaneously stimulate, another's need-gratification.

The phenomenon of the need inhibiting satisfier can explain the pleasure periphery (Prosser, 1994), which describes the spatial spreading of tourism, initiated in Western Europe and North America, across the globe.

After the elites or first-movers have reached a new destination, they are often soon followed by growing numbers of emulators. In turn, this crowding leads the first-movers to recognize that the destination is not a good opportunity anymore to satisfy their esteem needs. So they move on to even more remote areas. The tidal wave of tourism has recently reached Antartica.

**Abilities**

Each opportunity demands a certain set of resources. Individuals (or households) not having these resources at their disposal are not able to make use of certain opportunities.

To return to our Mount Everest example, one needs a lot of money to even travel to Mount Everest. Second, one needs great climbing skills to climb Mount Everest. A lot of people do not have those resources (money and climbing skills) at their disposal.

Jager et al (1997) distinguish 4 different kinds of resources:

**(i)** ***Physical resources***

These resources refer to people's physical state (e.g. health, strength), and to physical tools and circumstances (e.g. a car, space for storage) people have at their disposal. This is closely related to the macro-level factors for example, technological developments, accompanied by economic wealth and public health measures.

**(ii)** ***Permitted and licensed resources***

Many opportunities demand having certain permits and licenses available. Examples are driver licenses and educational grades. Limits to these resources are set by the political and institutional factors.

**(iii)** ***Financial resources***

These resources refer to income. The higher the income, the more opportunities a consumer can use. On a macro-level this ability is provided by a certain level of economic development.

***(iv) Social and cognitive resources***

This category of resources comprises knowledge resources, cognitive capacities and skills, attitudes, values and norms. These resources determine whether someone can foresee outcomes of opportunity-use. Demographic and cultural factors exert a certain influence on these kind of resources.

# 5

# Travel Personality and General Personality Theories

## (a) Travel Personality

As stated before, motivation, opportunity and ability are not the only determinants of tourist behaviour. Personality influences travelling behaviour too (Nickerson, 1996). For example, people who want to climb Mount Everest in general have certain personality traits in common. Most of those people will have a tendency to sensation seeking, for climbing mountains is performing risky behaviour (Carver, 1995).

## (b) General Personality

The personality dimensions used by Nickerson and Ellis (1991) are commonly used in personality psychology. Therefore it seems relevant to explore a few basic aspects of these theories. Nickerson and Ellis (1991) use 4 personality dimensions to describe tourists in order to indicate motivations for different types of travel:

1. *Activation:* A guest's level of excitement, alertness or energy.
2. *Variety:* The need for change or novelty.
3. *Extraversion or introversion*: The extent to which a person is outgoing and uninhibited in interpersonal situations.
4. *External or internal locus of control:* The way people perceive whether or not they themselves are in charge of the happenings in their lives.

In this model, activation and variety are covariant.

As noted above, different types of travel can be regarded as specific types of opportunities. In other words, Nickerson and Ellis (1991) link personality dimensions to preferred opportunities.

Using the 4 dimensions mentioned above, Nickerson and Ellis (1991) describe eight different tourist types

| *Tourist personality* | *Locus of control* | *Extrovert / Introvert* | *Activation and Variety* |
|---|---|---|---|
| **Voracious tour-taker** | External | Extrovert | High |
| **Private cultural traveller** | External | Introvert | High |
| **Repeat tour-takers** | External | Extrovert | Low |
| **Non-traveller** | External | Introvert | Low |
| **Outgoing experimental traveller** | Internal | Extrovert | High |
| **Private explorer** | Internal | Introvert | High |
| **Repeat visitor** | Internal | Extrovert | Low |
| **Private low-key traveller** | Internal | Introvert | Low |

*Source* : Tourist types as described by Nickerson and Ellis (1991).

The concept of locus of control was worked out by Rotter (1982). It is a personality trait describing the perceived determinants of rewards and punishments (Pervin 1997).

At the one extreme are people who believe to be in control of their lives (internal locus of control), at the other extreme are people who believe in factors like chance, luck or fate are determining the events in their lives. Interestingly, Maslow (1971) argues that self-actualizating people have an internal locus of control, whereas people lower on Maslow's pyramid (e.g. social and ego needs) have a more external locus of control.

The introvert-extrovert dimension is very popular among trait personality psychologists. It is described in the Big Five personality theory (Goldberg, 1981), Eysencks personality theory (1970) and Cattell's sixteen factor-theory of personality ( Cattell, 1947).

Nickerson and Ellis (1991) regard sociability as being an important aspect of extroversion. A lot of psychologists hold this believe, although there is no agreement on this subject.

As the activation and the variety dimension are covariant, it seems legitimate to regard them as one. The advantage of this approach is the fact that the combination of these dimensions closely resemble what Zuckerman (1971) understood to be sensation seeking.

Nickerson and Ellis emphasize a traveller's level of excitement, alertness or energy, and his need for novelty and change, whereas sensation seeking is defined as the tendency to seek out varied, unusual and exciting stimuli (Carver, 1995).

They ascribe different destination preferences to the different tourist types (Nickerson and Ellis 1991).

| *Tourist type* | *Destination preference* |
|---|---|
| Voracious tour-taker | Cities and popular campgrounds |
| Private cultural traveller | Museums, art, culture, for richness and variety |
| Repeat tour-takers | Package tours (likes other people performing the same behaviour) |
| Non-traveller | Home |
| Outgoing experimental traveller | Cities, resorts, places with lots of action |
| Private explorer | New, different places, away from people (e.g. wilderness sites) |
| Repeat visitor | Keeps visiting the same favourite resort or destination. |

*Source* : Destinations Preferences by Tourist Type (Nickerson and Ellis 1991).

The Mount Everest climber might best be described by the private explorer tourist type. Beside destination preference, Nickerson and Ellis (1991) also argue that travel personality is a determinant of interaction with local cultures, degree of activity, and preference in type and number of travel companions, which in turn are determinants of opportunity preference.

**Linking it All Together**

We propose motivation opportunity-ability approach to tourist behaviour, combined with a tourist personality based on three personality dimensions to model opportunity preferences. According to our approach, motivation and travel personality infer as to which opportunities suit a certain person, whereas ability limits the number of opportunities that person can use. The final result, tourist behaviour, consists of the chosen opportunity.

***Case Study***

In China, the domestic golf tourism market is still a middle and upper class consumer market in which the sport functions as a way to improve one's quality of life and as a symbol used to show off one's status and position. To a certain degree, price is no longer a major factor that influences the travel motivations of these high-level consumer tourists. What they demand is to experience a feeling of relaxation in which they are at one with nature.

Gibson (1998) defined sports tourism as "travel activities away from home that focus on relaxation as the main objective, including both participation in and watching sports activities." (Quote from Liu Xiang Xing, 2007)

Sports tourism can be divided into (1) participants, whose main intention is to participate in sports, such as canoeing, skiing, golf, etc.; (2) spectators, including those who travel to watch sports events, such as the Olympic Games

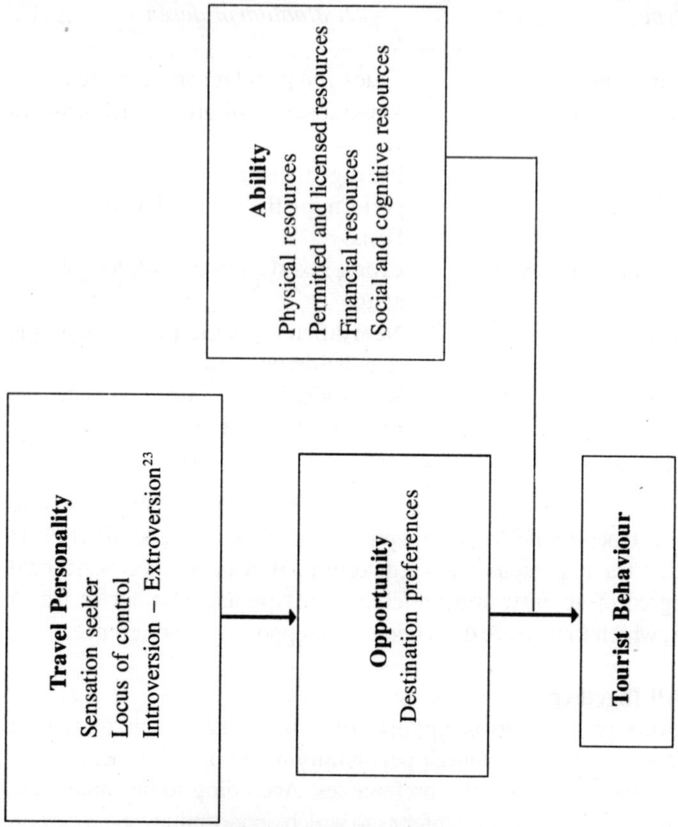


**Pressures on tourist behaviour**

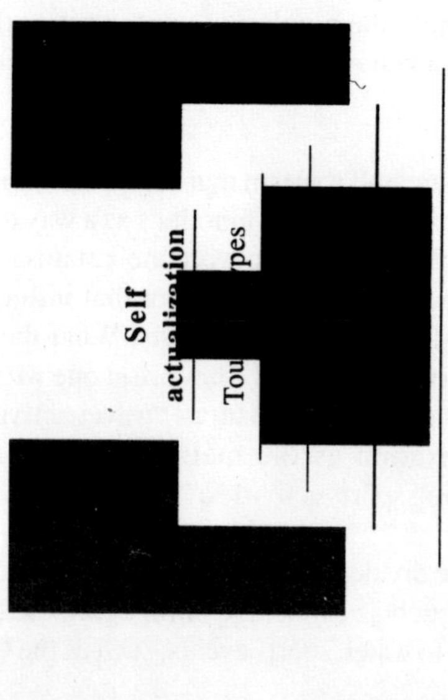


*References* : Swarbrooke, John (1990), Consumer Behaviour in Tourism, 2nd Edition, Butterworth-Heinemaun.

and the World Cup Football Tournament, etc., or travellers who visit sports museums or are involved in sports-related industries, such as the Sports Hall of Fame and sports fields and stadiums, etc. (Quote from Liu Xiang Xing, 2007)

**Question for discussion:**

1. Analyze the travel motivations of golf tourists in the Indian region.
2. Discuss how sporting events and sports can stimulate people's travel motivations.

**Case Study:**

In recent years, the sport of golf has been developing rapidly in the Indian region, motivating golf enthusiasts to travel overseas to play. Because of its geographical proximity and convenient transport links, the number of Japanese and American golf enthusiasts who choose to play in India has been increasing rapidly in recent years.

**Questions for discussion**

Recall your most recent travel experience, and write down in the table below the factors you took into account when you went travelling and when you decided on your travel destination.

Factors that influenced my decision to go travelling

Factors in my choice of travel destination

# 6

# Tourists Flows

### The Concept of Tourist Flows

'Tourist flows' refers to the statistical measure of the volume and direction of movement of tourists into or out of a destination for a given period of time or as a trend. The push and pull theory can be used in explaining travel patterns.

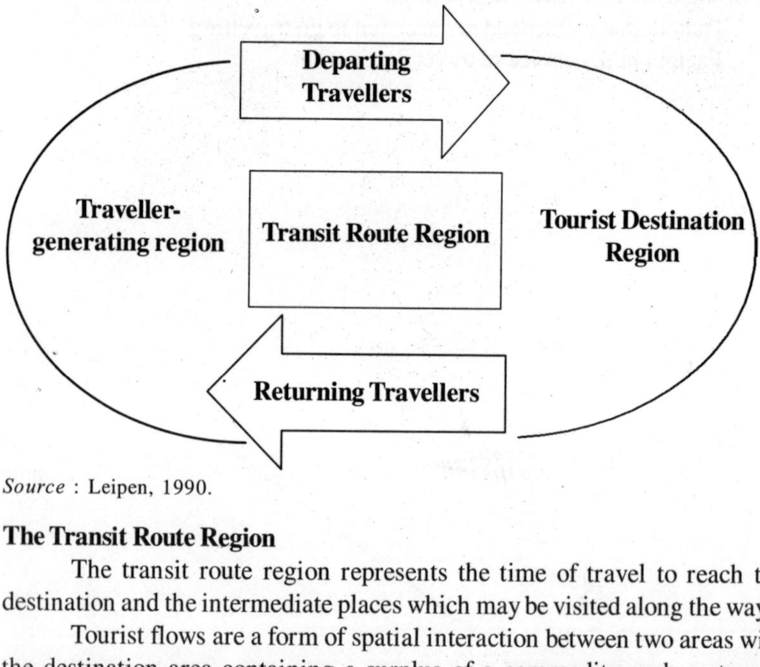


*Source* : Leipen, 1990.

### The Transit Route Region

The transit route region represents the time of travel to reach the destination and the intermediate places which may be visited along the way.[24]

Tourist flows are a form of spatial interaction between two areas with the destination area containing a surplus of a commodity such as tourist attractions (pull factors) and the generating area having a deficit, or demand for that commodity (push factors).

## Micro Factors influencing Patterns of Tourist Flows

### Push factors

Traveller-generating region represents the generating market for tourism and in a sense provides the "push" to stimulate and motivate travel. Push factors are considered to be those sociopsychological constructs of the tourists and their environments that predispose the individual to travel and help explain the desire to travel. Most of the push factors are intangible desires of the individual travellers. Some of the psychological motivations are:

- escape
- adventure
- rest and relaxation
- social interaction
- prestige
- satisfying needs (based on Maslow's Hierarchy of Needs)
- health and fitness

## Macro Factors Influencing Patterns of Tourist Flows

### Pull factors

A destination faces with many different types of tourism push factors. They are the attractiveness or "drawing power" of the destination as perceived and valued by the travellers. The attractiveness is called "pull factors".

Destination attributes can either by tangible resources or the perceptions and expectations of the travellers. Factors influencing patterns of tourist flows are:

- General attractiveness of the destination for the tourists:
- Natural and man-made attractions

Tourist flow will be strong if one place can provide the attractions (e.g. beaches, landscapes or historic resources) that the other place lacks.[25]

### *Climate*

There is a general trend of travel towards places of better (i.e. warmer, sunnier or drier) climatic conditions.

### *Political, cultural and business ties*

Other things being equal, travel is more likely to occur between places with stronger political (e.g. friendly relationships between countries, shared political system), cultural (e.g. common language and religion) or business ties.

### *Relative costs (cost of living and exchange rates)*

If two places have significantly different costs of living, tourist flow will be encouraged from the more expensive place to the place with lower living cost.

***New cultural experience***

Many tourists are interested in experiencing a culture which differs from their own. Therefore, the culture of a host population is an important factor of attracting tourists to a particular destination.

***Attitude of the host community***

Positive attitude of the host community towards tourism may increase tourist flow (attitude of the host community depends on how they perceive the impacts brought about by tourism).

***Political factors***

Government policies can affect both inbound and outbound tourism in two ways:

- currency control (more common in Communist countries); and
- the necessity of obtaining visas.

The long-term political stability of a place will make it relatively more attractive both for investors in tourism and for the tourists themselves. Wars with other nations, civil war within the country/region or terrorism will quickly reduce the demand for travel to that country or region.

***Economic development of a country***

Everyone buys goods and services out of his/her income. The size of that income is then a very important factor of tourism demand. Therefore, for a country/region which is developing fast and increasing its income, tourism generation is likely to be greater. China is a good example in Asia. More developed countries generate more tourists while less developed countries have less tourist generation.

As cities grow and attract more international tourists, more jobs will be provided in the tourism and tourism-related sectors. This produces more potential clients for both domestic and international travel. In addition, the money generated from other sectors of the economy also stimulates tourism.

***Trend in tourism***

Tourism demand is easily affected by the changing trend. Some tourist destinations become more popular while others decline in popularity. For example, taking a trip to Maldives has been very popular to Hong Kong people in the 1980s.

But nowadays, independent travel is getting more popular such as fly and drive package, accommodation and transportation (hotel and airline) package and cruise and air package.

**Personal Factors**

***Income***

People with better jobs and higher income have greater demand for travelling. The frequency of travelling and the amount of travel expenditures increase rapidly as income increases.

Nowadays, total income of an urban family increases due to:

- Double income household (income from spouse)
- Smaller size of a family.

As a result, there is more money for travelling.

***Employment***

Those secured in their jobs are more likely to travel than those unemployed. People with employment uncertainty will have more domestic holidays, but less overseas holidays, shorter length of stay and lower spending levels.

***Holiday entitlement***

The longer the paid leave people get, the greater distance they are likely to travel. In general, excursionists spend on average about 1.5-2 hours travelling to a destination, 1- week tourists spend about 4-6 hours, and 2-week tourists spend about 8-12 hours.

***Time availability***

People with more free time travel more. People in the following cases travel less:

- Many people cannot leave their business or jobs for vacation purposes; and
- Couples with young children also have less time and money to travel.

***Education level***

Differences in education level affect the types of new experiences a person is willing to accept (university graduates are more willing to go somewhere unfamiliar). People with a high level of education generally earn more money and are of higher social status. They usually travel a lot more.

***Personal attitudes and perceptions***

Differences in people's attitudes and perceptions have strong influence on travel decisions such as:

- Whether to travel or not;
- Tourist destinations; and
- Travelling styles, etc.

**Other Factors**

***Time distance and cost of travel between origin and the destination***

The greater the time distance, the greater the travelling expenses, the smaller the volume of flow.

***Transport routes***

Tourism between places will be encouraged where good transport infrastructure exists. Tourism will flourish particularly when travel between places can take place without a change of mode of transport.

***Location of destination***

Tourist flow towards destinations on major transport routes will be stronger, e.g. Hong Kong lies in the major transport routes between China, Europe and America.

**Ways of Measuring Tourist Flows**

**How Can We Collect Information About Tourist Flow?**

To get information about international tourist flows, the frontier survey is one of the methods commonly used. Tourists can be counted as they enter or leave India

There are 3 Types of Statistics:

1. Statistics of Volume
2. Statistics of Tourist Characteristics
3. Statistics of Expenditure

**Statistics of Volume**

These provide the number of tourists leaving an area or visiting a destination in a given period of time, and provide a basic count of the volume of tourist traffic.

**Statistics of Tourist Characteristics**

These measure the quality of the tourist flow and include information on types of tourist (sex, age, socio-economic group, etc.). They also measure the tourists' behavior, e.g. structure of trip, attitudes to the destination, etc.

**Statistics of Expenditure**

Measurement of tourist expenditure can be obtained by asking tourists directly how much they have spent on their holidays, or indirectly through suppliers of tourist services :

- In-Town Visitor Per Capita Spending by Major Market Area
- Overnight Visitor Spending Patterns
- Main Items bought

**Why Is It Important to Measure Tourist Flow?**

It is important to understand tourism statistics because we can prepare an accurate visitor profile:

(i) Know how many visitors visited a destination (such as Hong Kong) in the past;

(ii) Find out whether the number of visitors has increased or decreased;
(iii) Predict future numbers of tourists and identify where they come from (market trends);
(iv) Plan and develop sufficient infrastructure (e.g. hotel and transport) for the future development of tourism; and
(v) Promote a destination (such as Hong Kong) to the potential visitors (those who are likely to come here).

# 7

# Different Sectors of the Travel and Tourism Industry

## Accommodation

To an ordinary person, the essence of a good holiday away from home composes of three main elements - satisfactory accommodation, safe transportation, and suitable entertainment. However, to the members of the tourism industry, a good holiday or a good trip would also include the services of responsible intermediaries and the availability and provision of travel related services.

Accommodation is the temporary home for travellers. It ranges from simple sleeping places to deluxe suites for eating, entertainment, and sleeping. Travellers can stay overnight in any kind of lodging from an African tree house to a castle in Europe.

The accommodation industry is made up of hotels, motels (motor hotels), resort hotels, campgrounds, hostels and guesthouses. Hotels are classified in various ways. One of the most common ways is by location, such as resort, city center, airport, suburban, or highway.

## Types of Hotels

### *Resort hotel*

Resort hotel can be considered as a destination itself. It offers a full range of services and amenities for the guests to enjoy their vacations within the property. Typical features of a resort hotel include restaurants, shops, sporting facilities, pools, spas, casinos, and even the private beaches.

Examples : Hong Kong Gold Coast Hotel, Mission Hills Resort Shenzhen in China.

### *Airport hotel*

Airport hotels are located in or near airports. This type of accommodation is selected by travellers for necessity. A major feature of airport properties is convenient for early morning departures or late evening arrivals. It is mainly for airline crew members and passengers with overnight layovers or cancelled flight.

***Bed & Breakfast (B&B)***

B&B is a guest house or private house providing a clean, attractive accommodation and breakfast. The B&Bs offer a home-like atmosphere. The owner of the B&B usually lives on the premises and provides all the necessary labor. Community breakfasts with other lodgers and hosts enhance this atmosphere.

Example:

B&Bs operate in Paddington district in London, U.K.[26,27]

The other way of classification is rating (grading), for example, five-star, four-star, three-star, two-star hotels. This grading system is commonly used in China.

As for India, hotels are categorized depending on published room tariff and staff / room ratio.

**Transportation**

How can a traveller get to his/her destination?

The actual movement of travellers is usually categorized as air, water, road, rail. Transport is acknowledged as one of the most significant factors to have contributed to the international development of tourism. It provides the essential link between tourism origin and destination areas. It also helps to facilitate the movement of travellers either for leisure or business.

The various types of transport modes with their subdivisions are as follows :

*Air*

- Domestic (Guangzhou to Beijing)
- Regional (Hong Kong to cities in China)
- International (Hong Kong to London)

*Water*

- Ferry
- Cruise

*Road*

- Coach/bus
- Private car

*Rail*

- Domestic (Guangzhou to Beijing)
- Regional (Hong Kong to Guangzhou)
- International (Beijing to Moscow)

### *Air Transport*

*First-class travellers* enjoy the privacy of their own private cabin area with seats that can be converted into 6′6″ flat beds. Plenty of good food, in-flight entertainment and personal video screen are provided. They are also welcome to use arrivals lounge.

*Business-class travellers* have wide comfortable seats with plenty of legroom. They can also enjoy good food, free drinks, and complimentary newspapers.

*Economy-class travellers* though have narrower seats, still are provided with suitable services and meals.

In general, most of the airlines provide different classes on board; they are first, business and economy class. Some airlines nowadays introduced 'premium economy class'. This class of service offers better individual service (e.g. more comfortable seat) to passengers at a lower price comparing with business class service.

### *Types of flight*

*Scheduled flights*

- refer to those flights operated regularly according to a published timetables and fares.
- irrespective to the number of passengers to be carried on any one flight, they serve on a routine basis.

*Non-scheduled flights*

- also known as chartered flights
- do not operate on any set schedule or have predetermined fare structure
- chartered flights could go anywhere and at anytime when scheduled service do not cover, and very often they supplement the service on regular routes during peak seasons.

### *Sea / Water Transport*

*Cruise ships*

What is a cruise? A cruise is a vacation trip by ship. This definition excludes travelling by water for primarily transportation purposes.

It offers the passengers a chance to relax in comfortable surroundings, with attentive service, good food, and a liner that changes the scenery from time to time.[28]

It is projected that cruise ships make an important contribution to Hong Kong tourism. In 2008, there were more than 7,80,000 overseas travellers visiting Hong Kong. However, there has until now been a lack of detailed information about the market, and in particular, the type of experiences cruise visitors have in Hong Kong.

Despite the potential positive impact of cruise tourism to the local economy, there is also danger the local tourism industry faces is that cruise tourism can displace other forms of tourism as hotels and tours fill with cruise passengers, reducing capacity for other tourists.

Cruise ships are basically self-contained destinations where guests live, eat, are entertained, and travel. Cruises are voyages taken for pleasure and not only for the purpose of transport. Most cruises start and end at the same port.

A cruise with all-inclusive fare nowadays may combine:

- Transportation costs such as airfare between cruise passengers' point of origin and the destination port. Sometimes the cost of accommodation at the destination port is included in the all-inclusive fare.
- On-board activities; and
- Shore excursions

*Ferry services*

Ferry service is a short distance sea-journey between ports. Both the local commuters as well as tourists use this mode of transport. The demand for ferry services between Hong Kong and Macau is very high and three operators offer year-round scheduled services.

**Road Transport**

Travelling by road is the most flexible and economical form of mass transportation. Modern motorway networks have made major cities easily accessible.

***Coach Services***

- Local – services operated in Hong Kong
- Regional – between Hong Kong and Shenzhen
- International express services – services between Canada and United States in North America
- Tour and sightseeing operations
- Shuttle buses for airport transfers

***Car Services***

Car travellers have greater freedom in choosing their route, destination, and timing of their journey.

(a) Private cars for rental;
(b) Taxis; and
(c) Private cars.

***Car Rental***

Business and vacation travellers book car rentals for different reasons: Business travellers are looking for a convenient and reliable form of ground transportation to get them from point A to point B with minimum amount of fuss and bother.

Vacation travellers are looking for a comfortable form of transportation to places where they plan to visit but these places are not easily accessible by public transportation.

**Rail Transport**

The importance of rail travel has given way to private cars and air travel, but is picking up now since a number of services have been designed specifically for the tourist trade on a local and international level. Examples include "Orient Express" in Europe and "Indian-Pacific" across Australia. Others include the "Trans-Siberian Railway" and the "Bullet Train" of Japan.

Examples of Other Rail Transport:

Underground train services in most urban city;

Airport express train service; and Scenic rails

One of the world's eminent travelling experiences is to travel on luxury train. Traversing the world's varied landscapes along alternative train routes, the train combines all the comfort and luxury of a five-star hotel with a globally unparalleled journey.

The Blue Train

Reference: http://www.bluetrain.co.za

Orient Express Trains

Reference: http://www.orient-express.com

**Table summarizes the major characteristics of various transport modes:**

| | | Air |
|---|---|---|
| 1. | Carrying unit and Capacity | • Aircraft<br>• Medium to High passenger capacity<br>• Suited to long distance journeys |
| 2. | Advantages | • Speed and range |
| 3. | Disadvantage | • High fuel consumption<br>• Stringent safety regulations make air transport an expensive mode |
| 4 | Significance for Justice | • Speed: shortened the travel distance and reduced the time of travel<br>• Range: Increased accessibility to places, opened up most parts of the world for tourism.<br>• Stimulate the growth of international mass tourism |

*(Contd.)*

*(Contd. Table)*

| | | **Water** |
|---|---|---|
| 1. | Carrying unit and Capacity | • Ship/cruise<br>• Can have a high degree of comfort<br>• Medium to High passenger capacity |
| 2. | Advantages | • Suited to either long or short distance ferry operations<br>• Relaxation |
| 3. | Disadvantage | • Comparatively slow<br>• Seasickness<br>• High labour costs<br>• Feeling of Confined while most of the activities limited in the cruise |
| 4 | Significance for Justice | • Cruising became a popular form of leisure travel since 1980. |
| | | **Road** |
| 1. | Carrying unit and capacity | • Car, bus, or coach.<br>• Low capacity for passengers |
| 2. | Advantages | • Door-to-door flexibility.<br>• Suited to short distance journeys |
| 3. | Disadvantages | • Way shared by other users leading to possible congestion<br>• Door-to-door flexibility allows tourist to plan routes. |
| 4. | Significance for Tourism | • Allows carriage of holiday equipment.<br>• Acts as a link between terminal and destination.<br>• Acts as mass transport network for excursions in holiday areas. |
| | | **Rail** |
| 1. | Carrying unit and Capacity | • Passenger carriages<br>• High passenger capacity |
| 2. | Advantages | • Convenience: it usually arrives at and depart from the central business district of a city, thus saving transit time between city and airport. |

*(Contd.)*

*(Contd. Table )*

| | | |
|---|---|---|
| 1. | Carrying unit and Capacity | • Suited to medium or long distance journeys, and to densely populated urban areas,<br>• Environmental friendly |
| 2. | Advantages | • High fixed costs |
| 3. | Significance for Tourism | • In the mid-nineteenth century, it opened up areas previously inaccessible for tourism.<br>• Special carriages can be added for scenic viewing,<br>• Trans-continental routes and scenic lines carry significant volume of tourist traffic.[29] |

**Intermediaries**

Intermediaries are "Middle-Men", acting as a link between the customer and the supplier. In the travel business, the suppliers consist of airlines, cruise and ferry companies, coach/bus companies, railways, hotels and motels, and car rental agencies. The customers include holiday makers, business travellers, and those visiting friends and relatives.

**Definition of Travel Agency**

The United Nations World Tourism Organization (UNWTO) defines a travel agency as "a retail service organization that provides information about the cost and conditions of possible travel, accommodation and associated services. Before travel demands are made, travel organizations, suppliers or wholesalers prepare for travel and tourist accommodation by organizing transport, booking different kinds of accommodation and advancing all other services."

**Tourism and the Structure of the Tourism Industry**

Travel agencies, in their role as "middlemen," combine tourism activities originally carried out on an unconnected, individual basis, linking customers with tourism service suppliers and thereby promoting the development of the tourism industry. Tourism service suppliers include airlines, hotels, restaurants, car hire companies and companies that operate reception services at destinations.

Types of tourists

Overseas tourists

Local residents

**Intermediaries**

- Travel agencies
- Tour operators (wholesalers / retailers)
- Service industries associated with tourism

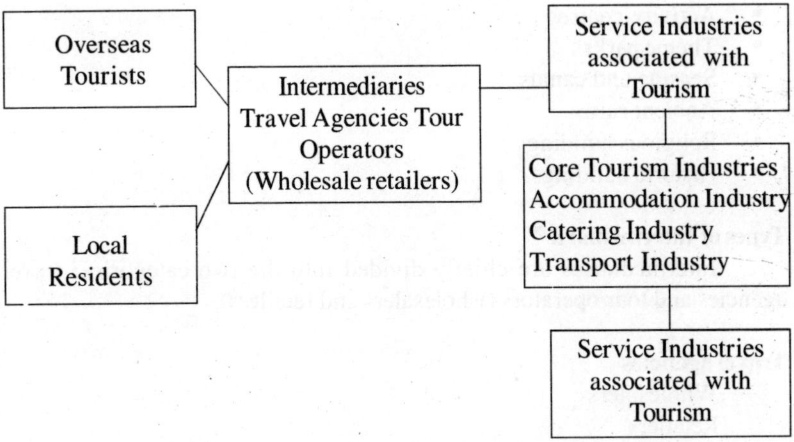


**Tourism and the Structure of the Tourism Industry**

***Connections Between Tourists and Product Suppliers of Different Categories in the Tourism Industry***

**Government institutions**

- Travel guide services
- Travel insurance and financial services
- Travel publications
- Travel training and education
- Retail shops and restaurants
- World Tourism Organization
- Local tourism institutions and statutory groups
- Government departments
- Travel visa institutions
- Travel course and training institutes

**Transport Industry**

- Air routes
- Water routes (ferries and cruise liners)
- Rail route
- Land routes (tourist coaches/car hire)

**Accommodation**

- Hotels/guesthouses
- Villas/holiday villages
- Holiday apartments
- Camping grounds/campervan parks
- Motor inns
- Youth hostels

**Man-made Tourist Attractions**

- Historic memorials

- Activity centres
- Theme parks
- Seaside and canals
- Ancient ruins
- Religious buildings
- Historic buildings

**Types of Intermediaries[30]**

Intermediaries are chiefly divided into the two categories: travel agencies and tour operators (wholesalers and retailers).

**Travel agencies**

Wholesalers
Retailers
Inbound travel agencies / outbound travel agencies

**Tour operators (wholesalers/retailers)**

- Inbound tour group operators / outbound tour group operators
- Corporate client travel services
- Sightseeing tour companies
- Tourism service retail channels commonly found.

**Types of Intermediaries**
**Travel agencies**

- Appointed representatives such as tourism service suppliers or wholesalers are authorized to sell customers a series of tourism-related products and services such as airline tickets, cruise liner berths, hotel rooms, car rentals and train tickets etc. Their role is to provide guests with relevant tourism consultant services, book travel products on

**Three Types of Retail Channels**

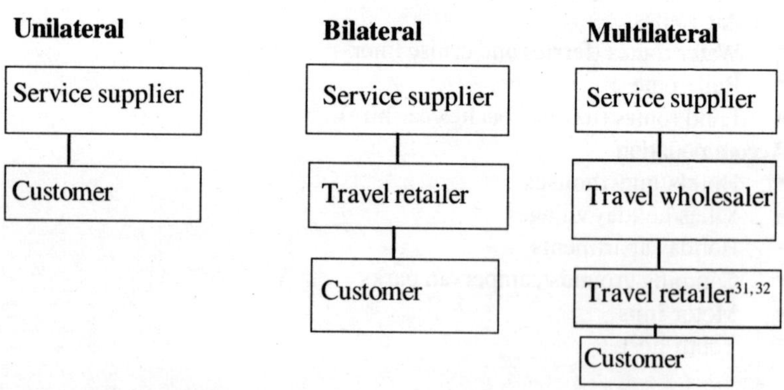


*Source* : Wu Xiao Huai : "An Introduction to Tourism Studies", Electronics Industry Publishing House, 2008, pp. 85-86.

behalf of customers and provide special services for customers in accordance with their needs etc. Their income is mainly derived from agency commissions.

- Travel agencies can be divided into *inbound travel agencies* and *outbound travel agencies*.

**Wholesalers**

- Wholesalers buy large volumes of products at a relatively low price from tourism service suppliers such as transport companies, hotels and tourist attractions, and then sell them to tourism retailers that then sell to the retail market. They won't normally sell travel products directly to the general public. However, some powerful travel agencies will also establish retail departments to sell these products directly to customers. There are also some wholesalers that are operated by a number of airlines and chain hotels, and promote package tours put together from their own products.

**Retailers**

- Retailers order large volumes of various different types of travel products from tourism service suppliers or wholesalers such as transport company, hotel and tourist attraction products and services, then design and combine these individual products and add in their own services such as tour guide services etc., turning them into packaged travel products, which are then sold to customers.
- They differ from wholesalers in that they will open branches in each district as their sales channels and arrange for attractive travel brochures to be printed and produced, then given to customers.

**Inbound tour group operators**

- Inbound tour groups are normally domestically (locally) operated tour groups that specialize in looking after individual tourists or tour groups when they arrive at a local destination. They provide services to all sorts of tour groups (including sightseeing groups) on an individualized or group basis, or provide tour guides.

- In addition, various types of promotional pamphlets for local tour groups will be displayed at the service desk in the lobby of hotels. Examples in Hong Kong include the "Two Day/One Night Trip to Macau," "Ocean Park/The Middle Kingdom One Day Trip," "Hong Kong Disneyland One Day Trip" etc.

**Outbound tour group operators**

- Outbound tour groups will take locals to another city or country and provide travel products such as transport, accommodation and tickets to tourist attractions. Generally speaking, this type of intermediary will regularly organize groups to take people from Hong Kong all over the world, wherein they will be accompanied by a group leader or tour guide from the very start.

Wing On Travel, Hong Thai Travel Services

**Corporate client travel agencies**

- This type of travel agency mainly caters to business or corporate clients rather than the general public. This kind of client often travels for meetings or exchanges, or to discuss business etc. This type of client's travel mode involves a lot of flying, usually requiring late bookings and short stays.
- Most companies appoint one travel agency to arrange all air tickets for business trips undertaken by their staff. Some companies that have staff with extensive travel requirements have independent travel departments that handle travel arrangements and provide other special services, such as applying for travel documentation and visas etc.

  Sightseeing tour companies
- These companies provide travel products such as tourist attraction visits and entertainment for customers, and will also provide services such as tour guides, transport and catering.
- The relevant services will either be sold directly to customers or provided to customers via different tourism retail channels such as inbound tour group operators, travel agencies or hotels, etc.

**The Role and Function of Travel Agencies**

The function of travel agencies includes the following 3 aspects:

**Providing one-stop travel products**

In the course of travel, customers have a wide variety of needs from the moment they leave home until they return to their home base, which includes food, accommodation, transport, touring and sightseeing, shopping, entertainment etc. To satisfy tourist needs in all respects, tourists have to be provided with relevant travel products and services from different types of enterprises. This is where travel agencies come in, by linking tourists with tourism service providers. Playing the role of middlemen between the two parties, travel agencies transform a number of purchases made by the original customer from travel product suppliers into a one-off purchase. They combine all tour operators' products and provide them to the customer. Therefore, the involvement of travel agencies breaks local boundaries.

**It is the most important retail channel for travel products**

Although core areas of the tourism industry, such as transport, accommodation and catering organizations will also sell their own products/ services directly to travellers, in light of developments in modern-day mass tourism, different parts of their travel products are sold to customers in the retail market via travel services. Therefore, the main function of travel services is to sell travel products in the retail market.

**Facilitating customers' tourism activities and promoting the development of the tourism industry**

Travel agencies bring together many types of services needed by customers, thereby facilitating customer purchases; in addition, travel agencies can book the relevant travel services before the customer departs, guaranteeing that the trip will go smoothly; furthermore, tourism agents also provide customers with information, assistance and professional opinions that can help customers to plan their journeys.

**Merits of using Intermediaries (Travel Agency)**

There is usually an intermediary between the supplier and the customer in all channels of distribution. Although tourism industry suppliers such as airlines, hotels, restaurants and car rental companies may reach their customers directly, they can also use the distribution services provided by one or more intermediaries. The advantages are:

- offer suppliers' services available to large numbers of potential customers;
- serve as a one-stop shop for a wide variety of travel related services; and
- provide clients with information, assistance and personalized advise for making the travel arrangement.

**Travel-related Services**

**Travel Insurance**

One important aspect of maintaining "peace-of-mind" while people travel is to purchase travel insurance, especially when travellers are using "special" tickets which are mostly non-refundable. This is because the insured travellers may get a partial compensation in case they are unable to get on the plane due to various reasons. By travel insurance, we usually refer to personal insurance, but in other cases, it is best to include vehicle insurance as well.

***Why is it important to buy travel insurance?***

It is because travel insurance covers the following:

(a) Medical and hospitalization expenses;

(b) Personal accident involving loss of life or limb;

(c) Loss of baggage (including a small amount of cash);

(d) Baggage delay over 12 hours after scheduled time of arrival (reimbursement for the urgent purchase of basic personal hygiene items such as toothbrush, underwear, basic medication, etc.);
(e) Cancellation charges in the event of illness, injury or death. This includes non-refundable deposits and tour costs;
(f) Some cash;
(g) Personal liability; and
(h) Losses involved in the event of a curtailment of the journey due to death, injury and illness (nowadays, some insurance companies include strikes, poor weather, hijacking, etc. as well).

Travel insurance is valid for specific periods of time, e.g. "within 7 days", "under 2 weeks", "1 month and over", etc. It is important that the traveller must make sure he is covered for the entire travel period, or else if anything happens only in the period that is not insured, his cover can be disqualified.

It is essential that the dates of travel are accurate. Please note that different insurance firms have different limits to age (some firms will not cover anyone over 75 years old), and their special conditions of coverage.

**Foreign Exchange**

Nowadays, a lot of travelling expenses can be paid by credit cards, it seems that foreign currency exchange is no longer important. However, when it comes to shopping, hiring a taxi, or making a phone call, travellers would need cash in local currency and petty change. These can be obtained from banks (in some countries), post offices, large international hotels, some foreign exchange booths in busy business centers, airports, railway stations and quays.

**Credit Cards**

Credit card is important to the automated payment system of travel nowadays. It represents simplicity, instead of paying in cash or traveller cheques, purchase is charged to a credit account. Credit card offers speed, safety, security and convenience to travellers.

**Retail Shops and Restaurants**

Retail shops and restaurants are important areas of the tourism industry anywhere over the world. Shopping is one of Hong Kong's favorite tourist attractions. Tourists can also enjoy food of many countries, with a great price range that can fit with different tastes and budgets of the visitors.

**Travel Publications**

Travel publications is one of the booming travel-related industries nowadays. Tourists can obtain a wide range of travel information from various forms of publications.

To help readers get better prepared for traveling to an overseas country or destination, such guide books often contain basic information about the country or destination such as climate, geography, history, culture, religion and economy. Readers are also briefed on the formalities and operational aspects of travelling such as visas, customs, accommodation, transportation, tourist offices, postal services, and even laundry service.

Travel magazines show a similar variety of information and they can bring major up-dated information to readers. Many large operators and companies in the tourism industry and the consumer goods industry make use of these magazines to advertise their products and services. The advantage goes both to tourists, who can get in touch with the latest products and services and plan their trips accordingly, and to the operators, who can promote their seasonal products and services to the prospective consumers.

Hotels and airlines are among the major contributors of advertisement out of which the magazine publishers can make profit. Travel magazines also have their unique function of providing articles catering for specific travel needs and interests, as well as giving seasonal updates on different aspects of travel.

Electronic publication is a rapidly growing industry. It provides a real-time visual and audio base of information to computer users. Airlines, National Tourist Offices (NTOs), major hotel groups and some well-established travel intermediaries have already established their Internet websites to promote their products and services. They have also built up a two-way communication with their prospective customers. Tourists can obtain updated travel information from the Internet at a click of the mouse.

Moreover, all NTOs publish reading materials for tourists, including leaflets, brochures, magazines and CDs. Airline companies would also provide informative and interesting magazines for the passengers. Large hotel groups publishes magazines, leaflets and brochures of nearby restaurants and attractions.

**Internet Solution Provider**

Electronic commerce on the Net provides customers with an opportunity to have direct access to the principal service providers such as airlines, hotels and car rental companies or to its distribution channels like travel agencies.

In addition to displaying the basic product features, potential customers can enjoy a variety of services such as information display, reservation, ticketing, accommodations, and entertainment.

A sample of travel related companies offering information on the Internet:

- Hong Kong Trade Development Council
- ANTOR
- Tourism Board

- Cathay Pacific Holidays Ltd
- Egl Tours
- Farrington American Express Travel Service Ltd
- Travelex Hong Kong Ltd

**The Role of Technology in the Travel and Tourism Industry**

Technology has greatly influenced the way travel is carried out, sold and distributed from producers to consumers. It will continue to change and all participants in tourism will have to constantly adjust to new and often very different forms of technology.

**Transportation**

All tourists have to get to and from their holiday destinations by one form of transport or the other. In the 21st century means of transport have become faster, more reliable and more comfortable. Examples include:

Airbus A380 and Boeing 787 Dream liner aircrafts
Mega Ships
Fast Trains
Private cars
Tourist Attractions

From the management of natural attractions to sophisticated, computer run theme park rides and IMAX cinemas technology has greatly impacted the tourist industry.

**Communications Technology**

Traditional:

Messengers
Mail
Telex
Telegram
Fixed line telephone
Fax

21st century:

E-mail
Skype
Internet
SMS
Mobile Phone
Satellite phone (Iridium)
Blackberry etc.

**Distribution of Travel Products**

The vast majority of travel products are services and as such they are different from physical products in several ways.

- Consumers must travel to consume the product
- Intangibility (can't be touched from the distance) of product means that pre-testing of tourism products is not possible
- Perishable – hotel rooms, airline seats or events tickets can't be stored
- Simultaneous production and consumption

*Traditional Travel Product Distribution*

- Airlines, hotels, cruise companies, restaurants, attraction etc. 'manufacture" the product or service.
- Tour Wholesaler or consolidators package the various products and offer them as packages to the market.
- Travel agents acting as agents of the producers of the services or agents of the tour wholesalers sell the products and services for a commission.
- The consumer buys the travel product from the travel agent.

*21st Century Travel Product Distribution*

- Supplier/Manufacturer direct to consumer via the Internet no need for middlemen like travel agents
- Advantages for both parties – cost effective and quick
- This works out to be fast, efficient and reliable communications are at the fore-front of modern tourism. The days when most bookings were made through travel agents are well and truly over and the internet now plays a major role in the provision of travel information and in the booking of trips.
  Example ZUJI http://www.zuji.com

**Benefits of Technological Advances for the Services Providers and Tourists**

***Improve on cost effectiveness***

(i) staff scheduling, catering production and fuel costs.

(ii) a seamless GDS (Global Distribution System) or web-based system helps to reduce the bureaucracy and paper-work free employee time for better customer services and relations.

(iii) consolidate a better integration of departments and functions of organizations towards better services and reduction of operation costs.

***Enhance forecasting techniques***

- reservation (yield management), routes planning and marketing programs.
- develop a better understanding of consumer needs thus reducing the gap between consumer expectations and perceived experience.
- obtain accurate and much richer marketing research data from all

transactions and enquire made by consumers through the Internet or GDS.

***Consolidate fragmented tourism products (distribution channel)***

- offer one stop shopping for tourists via CRS or GDS,
- destination promotions with airlines via CRS,
- consolidate a better integration of departments and functions of organisations towards better services and reduction of operation costs.

**Benefits of Technological advances to the consumers**

***Ease of purchase***

(i) Eliminate complicated distribution intermediaries, direct dealing with suppliers, reduce incurred costs such as commissions, shop at home.
(ii) Automation of routine passenger check-in procedure by the passengers through the Internet is considered by the passengers as a personalized service.
(iii) Transform the traditional multilateral tourism distribution channel to a unilateral channel via the Internet platform. Thus, enabling consumers to deal directly with Internet-based travel intermediaries, and name the price they are willing to pay for their products.
(iv) Express check-in services for airline passengers at airports - Kiosks and touch-screen terminals.

***Speed up purchasing decision***

(i) direct dealing with service providers' reservation department, one stop shopping.
(ii) ease of access of information on the Internet empower consumers to get information on products and services of interest.

***Provide more product information***

(i) enhance travel experiences through consolidation of tourism products such as destination attractions, accommodation, and transportation.
(ii) massive availability of travel websites offer consumers more information and enjoy greater choice.
(iii) GDS provides a reliable yield management solution to service providers, therefore, consumers can enjoy great discounts for last-minute, targeted offers and special promotions.
(iv) Mobile-based reservation systems.

**CRS**

CRS is the key link between the airline computer (which controls all the selling of seats on the airline flights) and the travel agents. The CRS can act as a provider of information (price, seat availability, schedules) and can also help the travel agent administer the flight with computerized itinerary printing and ticketing. This computer holds a great deal of information and needs to be kept permanently up-to-date since new bookings, cancellations and travel arrangements are constantly changing.

**The main roles of the key players in the CRS**

**Travel agents**

The travel agents benefit from having CRS installed in their offices since they can get access to all the information about several airlines flights at the touch of a button, or through just one phone call. The airlines benefit since they have their flights advertized in a wider marketplace, in a competitive screen situation with other airlines.

Travel agents are the customer's representatives in the booking process. They act as a provider of information on prices, destinations and availability, and offer their own experience to the customer. Once the customer decides on the destination and flight, the travel agents act as a travel administrator for the customer by booking, confirming and ticketing the travel plans. Being the customer's representatives, the travel agents should be unbiased in the reporting of flight availability and prices to customers.

**Airlines**

Airlines send their updated reservation availability and prices to the CRS, either on-line (immediately when they are changed) or on a periodic basis, e.g. once per day.

# 8

# Role of Government, Private and International Tourism Organizations in the Development of Tourism

## Role of Government

### *Planning and facilitating tourism*

Governments devise policies and plans for development. These include the generation of guidelines and objectives for the growth and management of tourism, both in short and long term, and devising of strategies to achieve their objectives.

The planning of tourism requires research. This is to access the level of demand or potential demand to the region, as well as to estimate the resources required to cater for that demand, and how these are best distributed. Planning implies the provision of training. Through hotel, catering and tourism schools, for the skills that the industry requires.

The planning and facilitating function of the government may be delegated to the National Tourism Office of that country.

## Control and Supervision of Tourism

The government plays an important part in controlling and supervising tourism. This is necessary to prevent undesirable growth, to maintain quality standards, to help match supply and demand and to protect tourists against industrial malpractice of failure.

### *Refusal or granting of permission in planning*

Refusal or granting of planning permission is an obvious example of the exercise of control over tourism development.

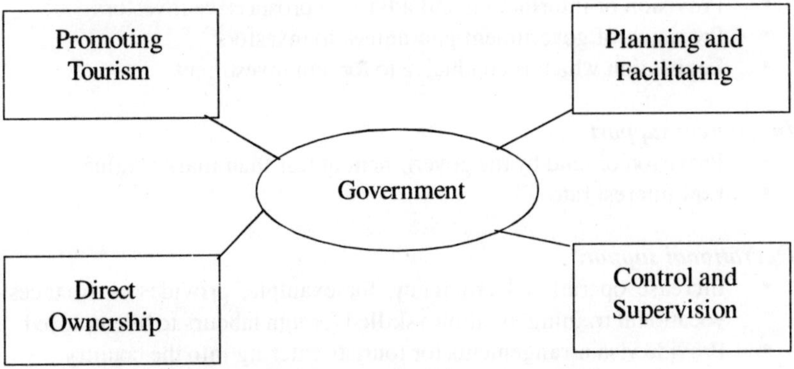


***Control of the export currency***

Government sometimes exercise control over tourism flows for economic reasons. Government may protect their balance of payments by imposing currency restrictions or banning the export of local currency in an attempt to reduce the number of local tourists traveling abroad.

***Supervision of tourism industry***

Supervision and control is also exercised over the various sectors of the tourism industry. The need to ensure passenger safety has led not only to the licensing of airlines and other forms of public transport, but also of tour operators and travel agencies.

Perhaps the most common form of government supervision of the tourism industry in all countries is in the hotel industry, where compulsory registration and grading is imposed in many countries.

***Direct ownership of components of the tourism industry***

Some governments own parks, airlines and airports, galleries, museums, historic sites, streets and highways railways, buses, harbors and ferries, subways, hotels, resorts, swimming pools, golf course, and even liquor stores, so as to facilitate the development of the tourism industry.

***Promoting tourism to home and overseas markets***

Government produces and distributes maps, charts, and tourism literature; operate information centers; advertise, organize sales promotion and public relations activities directed at home and overseas markets.

Government attempts to increase tourism growth by effective marketing, concentrating their publicity on less popular attraction or geographical regions and doing more promotional work during off-season.

***Active involvement***

Government action covers the following areas:

- Provision of information and advice to prospective investors
- Provision of government guarantees to investors
- Legislation which is conducive to foreign investment

***Investment support***

- Provision of land by the government at less than market value
- Low interest rate

***Operational support***

- Increase operational efficiency, for example, provides or finances vocational training, or allows skilled foreign labours to be employed
- Provide visa arrangements for tourists entering into the country
- Negotiate with tourist generating countries on air traffic rights and airlines routes

***Research and planning***

- Carry out research to find out the most suitable places and ways to develop tourism
- Plan for a well-built infrastructure to meet the needs of developing tourism
- Evaluate the resources (attractions, facilities, labour) available in the country for further tourism development[33, 34]

**Exercise**

Tourist Confidence and the Role of Government

Tourist attractions are important elements in the travel industry for attracting tourists to a certain destination. However, the occurrence of serious incidents weakens the attraction of a destination, and causes tourists to lose confidence in travelling there. A recent string of terrorist attack at Taj Hotel, Mumbai and incidents in which mainland tourists have been cheated etc., have seriously damaged the image of the Indian tourism industry.

When such problems occur, how should relevant government authorities restore tourist confidence in India?

**Quiz: How much do you know about Indian tourist attractions?**

. List four Indian tourist attractions you like to visit and guess which category of tourist attractions they belong to:
Please use a ✓ (Tick) for each separate category of tourist attraction
Indian tourist attractions I like to visit
Different categories of tourist attraction

(i) Natural landscapes
(ii) Historical remains
(iii) Culture and customs
(iv) Religious and sacred objects and sites

(v) Architectural sites
(vi) Special items and programmes
(vii) Entertainment and leisure, sports activities

**Public Sector**

Government departments and public organizations are involved in tourism policy, planning control and education. For example, travel formalities are administered by consulates and departments in charge of immigration, border security and customs. There are departments responsible for monitoring, licensing and regulating major tourist businesses like hotels and travel intermediaries. Besides, the design and provision of career training in different schools also depend upon the support from the government. In all, the planning and co-ordination of future tourism development require the collaborative efforts of many departments. The following are the possible tourism related departments:

Ministry of Tourism, Government of India (e.g. Indian Tourism)
Department of Commerce
Education Department
Marine Department
Immigration Department
Customs and Excise Department
Transport Department
Planning Department
Environmental Protection Department
Civil Aviation Department
Agricultural and Fishery Department
Health Department etc.

**Travel Formalities**

Since the world is divided into many territories and travelers have different citizenship, some travel formalities are needed for international traveling.

**Passport**

The most important travel document is passport. It is the official document with which the citizenship of a tourist can be clearly identified. Passports are issued by their respective sovereign governments, stating the status of citizenship of the holder and some basic personal information such as date of birth, gender, correspondence and emergency contact. The holder's photo is stuck on the main page with an official stamp/chop certifying the validity of the document. The issue date and valid period of the passport are also stated. The holder needs to renew his/her passport for usually every 10 or longer years.

Each passport contains blank pages, allowing embassies of other sovereign government to stick or stamp their visas, also allowing border officials of the host countries to stamp the dates of entry and exit. For national security reason, all passports are carefully designed and made to prevent forgery. Modern sophisticated printing technologies such as laser markings help this in a great deal.

A passport is an official document issued by a government to identify an individual, and it is usually issued for five to ten years. In general, the following items can be found in a passport:

Name of passport holder

Photo of passport holder

Personal details (e.g. nationality, date of birth) of passport holder

Date of issue

Issuing authority

Expiry date

Passport's holder often ignores the expiry date on the passport. Some countries require passports to be valid for a certain period, normally it requires no less than 6 months of validity for travelling abroad.

***Types of passport:***

*Joint passport*

Some countries allow persons travelling together on a joint passport which may include a spouse, children or both. Any member of the family included in a joint passport cannot travel without the principal passport holder.

The joint passport holder can travel alone without the dependents, provided those included in the passport are staying in their country of residence. For example, a mother and her child enter Australia together on one passport. The mother cannot proceed to, say, United Kingdom, leaving the child in Australia as the child would have no evidence of legal entry into Australia and would be unable to leave Australia without the mother.

*Aliens passport*

Some countries issue this type of passport to alien residents. An alien is classified as a person living in a country of which he is not a citizen.

*Diplomatic or consular passport*

Issued to diplomats, consular and other government officials on missions entitling the bearer to diplomatic or consular status under international law and custom.

*Other passports*

Nansen passport is a temporary document issued by internationally recognized organizations such as the UN and International Red Cross. This temporary identity card is mainly issued for refugees or displayed person who were unable to obtain an ordinary passport.

*Official, special or service passports*

Issued to government officials or other persons on government missions. The passport's issuing authority has to specify the travelling purpose on the passport.

**Visa**

Along with passports, visas play the most significant role among other formalities. Tourists from an overseas country that has no strong political tie with the host country are often required to apply for a visa from the host country's embassy or representative office in their home country before departure.

Documents such as passport, an employer's letter, return air tickets, and receipt(s) of hotel booking or proof of arranged accommodation in the host country are often required. Embassy officials may also ask for other papers such as bank statements (proving the applicant's financial capacity to travel) and travel insurance receipt. Applicant must submit photo(s) along with the application.

Every visa has a valid period. If a tourist wants to stay in the host country beyond that period, he/she must apply for an extension that can be arranged during the stay. Tourists who want to study abroad may be required to apply instead for a student visa. In this case, documents from the concerned educational institution would be necessary.

A visa specifies the authorized length of stay, the period of validity and the number of entries into the country allowed during the period. To apply for a visa, applicant may need to provide the following supporting documents:

- Proof of sufficient funds to cover the period of stay
- An employer's certificate (optional)
- A return ticket
- Proof of continuation of the trip
- Vaccination certificates (optional)

**Health Requirements**

To prevent the spread of epidemics diseases, tourists departing from a port which has been declared to have an epidemics problem are usually required to present a proof of health or vaccination issued by an officially recognized medical officer or institution. Aged travelers usually need a travel medical insurance receipt or even a medical certificate stating good health in order to get a visa.

Travellers arriving from an 'infected area' are normally required to prove that they have duly been vaccinated against specific diseases. The World Health Organisation produces an international certificate of vaccination for this purpose.

If a passenger arrives in a country without evidence that he has had the necessary vaccinations, he could be:

(a) denied entry to the country
(b) put under medical surveillance
(c) put into quarantine
(d) vaccinated 'on the spot'

**Customs and Taxes/Duties**

For trade, hygiene and security reasons, different host countries have their list of items of forbidden goods that overseas tourists and their citizens are not allowed to bring into their territory. Dangerous drugs are mostly strictly prohibited. Tourists bringing in firearms or other lethal weapons could face severe penalty or punishment. For example, tourists convicted of the offence of drug trafficking in some countries such as Thailand could face capital punishment.

Taxed items such as tobacco and alcoholic products are usually restricted to a limited amount (in weight or volume). Items other than travelers' accessories including electrical household appliances may also be taxed. Tourists who wish to travel with their pet(s) often need prior permission, and a proof of vaccination may be required. Some countries such as the United States have strict policies on bringing in agricultural produce or even herbs and plants. Tourists bringing in non-duty-free items need to fill in a custom declaration form and submit it at the point of entry.

Some host countries that adopt sales tax system offer tax refund benefit to tourists who are big spenders, so as to attract them to buy more during the stay. The customs office usually operates refunding procedure before the visitors return home. Most countries also have a policy on the value of both the foreign currency and their national currency that a tourist can bring into and out of their territory. Usually before arrival, transport operators help the host country distribute customs declaration forms and arrival cards to visitors to fill in and submit at the point of entry.

**Public Security**

Public security is one of the major issues to governments around the world, in particular public security at the airports. Many airports have adopted a tight security measure in ensuring the safety of air passengers.

**The Role of the Major International Organizations**

**United Nations World Tourism Organization (UNWTO)**

The United Nations World Tourism Organization (UNWTO) is concerned with tourism on a global level. Its headquarters are in Madrid, Spain, and it maintains regional offices around the world.

The organization was established in its present form in 1975. The WTO acts as a clearing house for information on international and domestic travel.

It encourages nations to regard tourism as a way to promote economic development and international understanding. It also advocates tourism as a way to ensure peace and protect human rights. The organization gathers and distributes statistics data on a host of tourism-related topics, including new technology, employment, and training.

In addition, it makes available information concerning travel facilities, special events, and legal protection available to those who travel. Its technical department studies the economic and trading factors that influence the flow of tourists.

Basically, the UNWTO has 5 principal responsibilities. These are to promote the following:

(i) The free and unhindered movement of tourists within individual countries and between all countries of the world;
(ii) The role of tourism in world trade;
(iii) The economic development of all countries and revival of declining areas of the globe through tourism;
(iv) The social and cultural functions tourism fulfills within nations; and
(v) The interests of tourists and tourism in general.

In addition to promoting the positive aspects of tourism, the WTO lobbies against measures that it believes would be harmful to tourism.

**Pacific Asia Travel Association (PATA)**

Pacific Asia Travel Association (PATA) was founded in Hawaii in 1951 to develop, promote, and facilitate travel to and among the destination areas in the Pacific Ocean.

PATA brings together governments, airlines and steamship companies, hotel owners tour operators, travel agents, and a wide range of other tourism-related organizations.

PATA headquarters are in San Francisco, California, Branch offices are located in Singapore to serve the East Asia region and in Sydney to serve the South Pacific. Marketing representatives are located in London, Frankfurt, and Paris.

*Roles and responsibilities:*

PATA represents countries in the Pacific and Asia that have united to achieve a common goal – excellence in travel and tourism growth in the vast region. Its work has been to promote tourism through programs of research, development, education, and training.

The Association has become an important source of accurate and up-to-date information for its members in the fields of marketing, development, research, education, and other travel-related activities. PATA's marketing efforts are directed to influencing more individuals to travel and within the Pacific area.

Development activities are geared to improving and advancing facilities and services in new destinations, increasing the handing capacity of existing destination, and preserving their heritage and quality. In research, PATA concentrates on the operation of an annual travel research conference, the publication of an annual pacific area statistical report, and the conduct of cooperative research studies.

**International Air Transport Association (IATA)**

The International Air Transport Association (IATA) was established in 1945 in order to promote safe, regular, and economical air transport. The members of IATA are individual international airlines.

Functions of IATA include:

(i) To act as a ticket clearing house ; and
(ii) To ensure the standardization of prices, tickets, and baggage checks.

The main role of IATA is coordinating international commercial airline industry activities and compromising on international airfares.

**Universal Federation of Travel Agents Association (UFTAA)**

The objectives of the Universal Federation of Travel Agents Association (UFTAA) are:

(i) To act as a negotiating body for various branches of the tourism and travel industries on behalf of travel agents;
(ii) To give professional and technical advice and assistance to travel agencies on the world economy and tourism;
(iii) To improve the prestige and public recognition of travel agents; and
(iv) To provide training courses to travel agency personnel.

**World Travel and Tourism Council (WTTC)**

The World Travel & Tourism Council (WTTC) was founded in April 1990. It provides a global forum for members who are chief executives from all industry sectors, including accommodation, catering, entertainment, recreation, transportation and other travel-related services.

The WTTC is led by the executive committee and the day-to-day operations are carried out by the President and a small staff based in London, Brussels, and Washington D.C. The goals of the council are:

- to work with governments to make tourism strategic economic development and employment as priority
- to move toward open and competitive markets
- to pursue sustainable development
- to eliminate barriers for growth and to realize the full economic potential of tourism and its job generating ability.

The WTTC also conducts extensive research to determine the sheer market size of travel and tourism, and its contribution to world, regional, and national economies.[35]

**International Civil Aviation Organization (ICAO)**

ICAO established in 1994, is an organization of governments joined to promote civil aviation on a worldwide scale. It serves as a means to secure international cooperation in the highest possible degree of uniformity in regulations and standards, procedures and organization regarding civil aviation matters.

The organization has adopted the "Guiding Civil Aviation Into the 21st Century" to deal more effectively with the constantly evolving challenges facing civil aviation, particularly in the area of flight safety. The strategic action plan focuses on eight major objectives to further the safety, security, and efficiency of international civil aviation. The eight objectives are as follows:

- Foster the implementation of ICAO Safety Standards and Recommended Practices to the greatest extent possible worldwide.
- Develop and adopt new or amended standards, recommended practices, and associated documents in a timely manner to meet changes.
- Strengthen the legal framework by developing new international air law that is required to govern the international civil aviation, and to encourage the ratification of existing infrastructure.
- ·Ensure the currency, coordination, and implementation of Regional Air Navigation Plans and provide the framework for the efficient implementation of new air navigation systems.
- Respond on a timely basis to major challenges to the safe and efficient development and operation of civil aviation.
- Ensure that guidance and information on the economic regulation of international air transport is current and effective.
- Assist in the mobilization of human, technical, and financial resources for civil aviation facilities and services.
- Ensure the greatest possible efficiency and effectiveness in the operations of the organization. Reference: URL: http://www.icao.org

**The International Eco-tourism Society (TIES)**

The International Eco-tourism Society was founded in 1990 to foster a true sense of synergy between outdoor travel entrepreneurs, researchers and conservationists. The organization assists those committed professionals around the world who are working to make eco-tourism a genuine tool for conservation and sustainable development.

The Society provides internship, training and education programmes on a wide spectrum of topics, ranging from marine eco-tourism management to eco-tourism business operations. The Society also has a exhaustive list of publications on ecotourism.

# 9

# The Impacts of Tourism

### Tourists' Code of Behaviour

1. Travel in a spirit of humility and with a genuine desire to learn more about the people of the host country.
2. Be sensitively aware of the feelings of other people, thus preventing what might be offensive behavior on your part. This applies very much to photography.
3. Cultivate the habit of listening and observing, rather than merely hearing and seeing.
4. Realise that often the people in the country you visit have time concepts and thought patterns different from your own; this does not make them inferior, only different.
5. Instead of looking for that "beach paradise", discover the enrichment of seeing a different way of life, through other eyes.
6. Acquaint yourself with local customs - people will be happy to help you.
7. Remember that you are only one of the thousands of tourists visiting this country and do not expect special privileges.[36]

### Behaviour of a Responsible Tourist

Tourism involves the movement of large numbers of people from their normal places of residence to new locations. Tourism results in certain impacts on the environment, social, cultural and economy of the host destinations. In order to minimize the negative impact of tourism on the host destination and so as to enable tourists to enjoy the originality of the destination, tourists should be aware of the effect of their behaviour on the host destination.

### Understanding human differences

Do not impose your thinking on the others. The local community may have a different concept of time, thought pattern, customs, values and the way they behave may be different from your home country.

- It is necessary to understand the taboos and protocols of a destination and to avoid any acts that may offend the host community.
- Appreciate all aspects of the host destination
- By understanding the indifferences, tourists should appreciate all aspects of the destination including their customs, heritage and environment.
- Protect the environment, heritage and be concerned with the feelings of the host community
- Tourists should assist in protecting the physical environment so that the attractiveness of the destination would not be depreciated.
- It is necessary to respect the culture of the host community.
- The tourists' own culture is not superior than the others and they should not expect any privileges from them.

**Understand** → **Appreciate** → **Protect**

***Voluntary Code of Conduct***

When cultural tourism and ecotourism are the major forms of tourism of a destination, the code of behaviour of the travellers on culture and environment of the community is very important. For example, the Himalayas in Nepal is a popular trekking destination and a culturally distinct area. The British-based organization, Tourism Concern has set up a voluntary code of conduct for tourists as a guideline when they visit the country. This guideline was launched in 1991 which aims to:

- promote greater understanding of the impact of tourism on host communities and environments;
- raise awareness of the forms of tourism that respect the rights and interests of people living in tourist receiving areas, promoting tourism that is just, sustainable and participatory;
- work for change in current tourism practice such as vast tract of forest depleted in order to fulfil fuel-wood needs and accommodation for tourists. This has resulted in soil erosion and flooding;
- to enable tourists and travellers to travel with critical insight and understanding.

The guidelines were distributed to all British tour operators carrying visitors to the Himalayas. They also encourage tour operators to include the Code in their brochures. Copies were also sent to major ticket outlets, such as Campus, Trail-finders to ensure they reach independent travellers.

The set of tourist code is as follows:

(i) Limited deforestation– do not set open fires and discourage others from doing so on your behalf. Where water is heated by scarce firewood, use as little as possible. When possible choose accommodation that uses kerosene or fuel effective wood stoves

(ii) Remove litter, burn or bury paper and taking away out all non-degradable litter, graffiti are permanent examples of environment pollution.

(iii) Keep local water clean and avoid using pollutants such as detergents in streams or springs. If no toilet facilities are available, make sure you are at least 30 metres away from water sources, and bury or cover wastes.

(iv) Plants should be left to flourish in their natural environment –taking cuttings, seeds and roots is illegal in many parts of the Himalayas.

(v) Help your guides and porters to follow conservation measures. 184

(vi) When taking photographs, respect privacy – ask permission and use restraint.

(vii) Respect Holy places –preserve what you have come to see, never touch or remove religious objects. Shoes should be removed when visiting temples.

(viii) Do not give to children as it may encourage begging. A donation to a project, health centre or school is a more constructive way to help.

(ix) You will be accepted and welcomed if you follow local customs. Use only your right hand for eating and greeting. Do not share cutlery or cups, etc. It is polite to use both hands while giving or receiving gifts.

(x) Respect for local etiquette earns you respect – loose, light-weight clothes are preferable to revealing shorts, skimpy tops and tight fitting action wear. Hand holding or kissing in public are disliked by local people.

(xi) Observe standard food and bed charges but do not condone overcharging. Remember that when you're shopping the bargains you buy may only be possible because of low income to others.

(xii) Visitors who value local traditions encourage local pride and maintain local cultures, please help local people gain a realistic view of life in Western Countries.[37]

**Types of Tourists and their Social and Cultural Effects on Local Communities**

Tourism is an activity that involves the movement of people from one place to another. In the process, tourists bring along customs and cultures of their own countries to the host countries on the one hand, and learn and bring those of the host countries back home, on the other. Along the process, tremendous socio-cultural impacts, positive and negative, are made upon both the tourist and host communities. In this unit, social impact refers mainly to the results of interaction between tourists and host communities reflected in the social dimension such as moral behaviour and religion, while cultural impact includes issues in such areas as heritage conservation, respect and tolerance for each other's culture, imitation of visitors' culture, commercialization of host's culture, revival of national identity and cultural degradation, etc., brought about, directly or indirectly by tourist activities.

| Factors that affect cross-cultural contact |
|---|
| • Opportunities for contact<br>• Attitudes to each other<br>• Social motivators / purpose of travel<br>• Cultural background |

*Positive Effects*

*Social*

- Developing positive attitudes towards each other (host-guest)
- Developing friendships
- Increasing self-esteem of hosts and tourists
- Reducing negative perceptions and stereotypes
- Positive changes in the way of life

*Cultural*

- Learning about each other's culture and custom
- Developing pride in, appreciation and understanding of, as well as respect and tolerance for each other's culture
- Heritage conservation

*Negative Effects*

*Social*

- Developing negative attitudes towards each other
- Generating feelings of inferiority (host) and superiority (visitors)
- Difficulties in forming friendship
- Ethnocentrism
- Negative changes in the way of life
- Congestion
- Increased crime
- Segregation, tension, hostility and misunderstanding

*Culural*

- Cultural shock
- Imitation of host's/visitors' culture
- Commercialisation of culture
- Disrespectful behaviour of tourists such as noise and impoliteness[38]

**Travis – Benefits and Costs of Tourism Development**

Tourism development can bring about the benefits to a destination, but at the same time the host society may be adversely affected by it. Travis came up with a detailed and comprehensive table showing the benefits and costs of tourism development for the socio-cultural aspect of the host society. (1982)

***Benefits and Costs of Tourism Development***

***Benefits***

Increased knowledge of host culture by visitors. Awareness of its music, cuisine and arts, and possibly language.

*Host culture*

Develops because of demand for traditional entertainment, demand for traditional art, crafts and music.

Education and learning aided. Boost for heritage protection, interpretation and management. Increased social range and experience. Cultural interchange, peace and understanding. New experiences, new ideas, new cultures.

*Costs*

Host culture debasement.

Unacceptable rate and scale of cultural conflict and change.

Damage to cultural systems and to cultural resources.

Minority languages at risk.

Improved reputation and visibility of host community to outsiders.

Rich visitors come to poor communities, creating tension.

Cultural commercialization and commodification of society.

Increased social contacts, new ideas, new values, new ways of life.

Pressures to change social values, dress, mores, habits and behavioral norms.

Folk art becomes airport junk-art. Deeper values and ideals at risk.

- Loss of original state and stability. Loss of cultural pride. Status relationship between host and guest cultures changes.
- Consumption changes. Introduction or expansion of gambling, prostitution, drunkenness and other excesses; vice and drugs, theft and petty crime.

By provision of services, amenities and facilities not otherwise available to hosts – there is increase in commercial activity.

Short-term and transient social relationships with visitors are not real and meaningful links. They often result in the following :

Misunderstanding, Hostility, Debasement and Diseases .

- Increasingly mass-entry of visitors makes contact diminish and relationship meaningless.
- Visitors have little understanding or knowledge of the hosts, their culture and language.[39]

**Cohen – Tourists and their Impact on Host Country**

While the impact of tourism on a host country is unavoidable, the nature of such impact depends on the type of tourist concerned., Cohen has classified tourists into 4 main categories: explorers, drifters, organized mass tourists and individual mass tourists. These four types of tourists could further be categorized according to their travel motives:

*Tourists who are seriously interested in the local host* (explorers and drifters)

Primarily, these two types of tourists are very interested in the culture of the local host. While their open and friendly attitude helps break down part of the communication barriers between local residents and tourists, their eagerness to know more helps to create more opportunities for host-tourist interaction and even in-depth contact, resulting in an ultimate better understanding of each other.

*Tourists who are looking for superficial pleasure* : (organized mass tourists and individual mass tourists)

Mass tourism is characterized by superficial pleasure. When the tourist-resident relations are maintained at a superficial level, communication barriers between tourists and residents, caused mainly by cultural shock, cannot be broken down easily.

Three signs that *cultural shock* is at work :

- If you find yourself repeatedly puzzled by other peoples' behaviour
- If you find yourself stereotyping or making generalizations about a culture
- If you find yourself getting angry at other cultures

Tourists who seek for local culture vs tourists who look for superficial pleasure.[40]

**Number and type of tourist and their adaptation to local norms**

| **Type of tourist** | **Number of tourists** | **Adaptation to local norms** |
|---|---|---|
| Drifter | Very limited | Adapts fully |
| Explorer | Uncommon | Adapts well |
| Individual mass tourist | Steady flow | Seeks western amenities |
| Organized mass tourist | Massive arrivals | Demands western amenities[40] |

*Source* : Tourism the State of the Art.

**Smith – Tourists and their Adaption to Local Norms**

Based on Cohen's classification on tourists, a typology of tourists is developed which focuses on the types of tourist, number of tourists, and adaptation to local norms.

The four types of tourists vary in their number and their way of

**Frequency of types of tourists and their adaptations to local norms**

| *Types of tourist* | *Numbers of tourists* | *Adaptations to local norms* |
|---|---|---|
| Explorer | Very limited | Accepts fully |
| Elite | Rarely seen | Adapts fully |
| Off-beat | Uncommon but seen | Adapts well |
| Unusual | Occasional | Adapts somewhat |
| Incipient mass | Steady flow | Seeks Western amenities |
| Mass | Continuous influx | Expects Western amenities |
| Charter[41] | Massive arrivals | Demands Western amenities |

*Source* : Smith, 1977 quoted from Pearee, 1989 : 217.

adaptation to local norms. A more detailed version, which was developed by Smith, is shown below:

***Summary***

To simplify, tourists may be identified and grouped under two categories, namely independent tourist and package tourist. The categorization of these two types of tourists has implications on the development of the tourism product and for the influence they exert on the host society.

*Independent Tourists*

(i) They are usually fit in better with the environment and social structure of local society.

(ii) They are associated with relatively slow growth rates and often lead to local ownership of tourism products.

(ii) According to Cohen's classification, drifters and explorers are the types of visitors that could be categorized under this heading.

*Package Tourists*

(i) They usually demand Western amenities, e.g. hotel accommodation with good facilities.

(ii) They are associated with rapid growth rates and often lead to the restructuring of the local economy, e.g. influx of foreign investors because of the upward development of tourism industry.

(iii) According to Cohen's classification, individual mass tourists and organized mass tourists are the types of visitors that could be categorized under this heading.[42]

**Tourism Effects on Community – Social Effects**

In spite of certain social impact of tourism upon the host culture, it should be recognized that tourism is usually not the main cause of degradation or loss of the host's culture. Very often, the latter are inevitable and will occur whether tourism development exists or not. Tourism may speed up the process of change, but it is not necessary the cause of it.

**Community problems associated with the development of tourism**

*Culture with a price tag:* Cultural costs altering locally promoted ceremonial or traditional values to suit tourists' preferences. The pursuit of economic gain is conducted at the expense of cultural breakdown.

*Conflict of land use:* Lack of regard for the quality of life of local residents.

Possible friction between visitors and local residents over shared usage of local recreational facilities.

***Problems associated with the development of tourism***

(i) Increase in crime rates: robbery, prostitution, etc.
(ii) Additional demands on social services and supporting infrastructures
(iii) Segregation: Tourists stay in luxurious areas isolated from the residents.
(iv) Antagonism: Employees relate this to the difference between their own lifestyles and that enjoyed by the tourists

*Community problems associated with the development of tourism*

Community problems associated with the socio-cultural impact of tourism are usually concerned with the following aspects :

- Lifestyles: Living condition, personal mobility (shopping, entertainment and dining away from home), changes in labour structure
- Culture and value: Preservation and/or degradation of culture; changes in moral standard
- Social facilities: Infrastructures, social services and transportation

***Assessment Frameworks***

Many possible and actual social impacts can be summed up, but unfortunately not many frameworks are available to assess them in a coherent way. Mathieson and Wall (1982) mention two such frameworks. In a sense these frameworks offer a possibility to assess perceptions by locals of tourism development.

The first one is the ***irritation index of Doxey (1976),*** which describes a transitory development of host attitudes through 5 stages:

level of euphoria: locals err enthusiastic and thrilled by tourist development '
level of apathy: tourists become targets for profit'-taking
level of irritation: locals cannot handle the large number of tourists
level of antagonism: tourism is a scapegoat for all that is bad
final level: locals must learn to live in an altered environment

In this framework, change can only be in one direction, from euphoria

| | | Behaviour | |
|---|---|---|---|
| | | *Active* | *Passive* |
| Attitude | Positive | FAVOURABLE: Aggressive promotion | FAVOURABLE: Slight acceptance and support |
| | Negative | UNFAVOURABLE: Aggressive opposition | UNFAVOURABLE:: Silent acceptance but opposition |

*Source* : Bjorklund and Philbrick (1972).

to the final level. No movement in the other direction is possible. Another underlying assumption of this framework is that the host population can be viewed as a homogeneous group.

A probably more realistic approach is taken by Bjorklund and Philbrick (1972). Here, the host population is not seen as a homogeneous group, but as made up of individuals with varying interests and other characteristics.[43]

In the Bjorklund-Philbrick framework, four responses to tourism development are identified, ranging from aggressive promotion to silent opposition. People's responses are dependent on the distribution of advantages and disadvantages from tourism development. Entrepreneurs making a profit out of tourism and not bearing a significant part of the costs associated with it, can be expected to be aggressive promoters. On the other hand, fishermen seeing their fishing grounds become polluted and less accessible will be aggressive opponents.

People's place in the matrix may change, however, in any direction. Fishermen, for example, may find a job as a tourist guide. Then, costs and benefits to them are more equilibrated, possibly leading to a response shift towards slight support of tourism development.

**Social Impacts of Tourism**

Many possible social impacts of tourism have been put forward in the literature, most of which are negative. Not every form of socio-cultural change is necessarily bad, however. In order to reach a higher standard of living, some socio-cultural changes are often needed. But this does not need to damage social or cultural identity. Unfortunately, no generally accepted classification of social impacts seems to exist in the literature. The existing classifications lack a logical structure and their impact categories are overlapping.

In here, we construct our own classification based on Pearce (1989) and France (1997), consisting of the following 8 categories:

1. Local resentment resulting from the "demonstration effect"
2. Impact on population structure
3. Transformation of forms and types of occupation
4. Congestion
5. Transformation of values
6. Modification of consumption patterns
7. Health problems
8. Neo-colonialism

***Local resentment resulting from the "demonstration effect"***

Especially young people tend to imitate the tourists' behaviour. They are attracted by the tourists' clothing and eating habits and their spending patterns. This is called the demonstration effect. The problem is that the local population often cannot afford the tourists' behaviour, which may lead to feelings of frustration. Older people can also become frustrated with tourism development. On the one hand they see the advantages of tourism in terms of employment and income, but on the other hand they see the disadvantages, for example in terms of loss of culture. This ambiguous attitude may produce feelings of resentment.

***Impact on population structure***

Population structure can be affected by tourism. First of all, by strengthening the economic basis of the local community, tourism may foster population growth. This population growth often comes about by immigration. People from other areas are lured to the tourist destination by the possibility of finding a better paid job. Movements of people appear to be both age- and sex-selective. For example, according to Pearce (1989), people aged twenty to thirty and females are overrepresented in the tourist destination of Queenstown, New Zealand.

One of the main characteristics of tourism is its seasonal nature. During the high season, employment opportunities are far greater than during the low season. This is often reflected in population structures. Workers flow in and out of the destination together with the tourists. This makes it hard for the local population to develop a sense of community. Moreover, the seasonal workers do sometimes not belong to the same culture as the autochthonous population. In the case of English-spoken Belize, for example, people working in the tourism industry often have a Hispanic background (Pearce, 1989).

***Transformation of forms and types of occupation***

Tourism offers new employment opportunities, which may draw workers from other sectors of the economy - for example, agriculture - with consequent effects on class or social structure. Also, activities may become financially rewarded, which were not paid for in earlier times. Here one can think of cleaning and washing.

Tourism can place people, especially women and young people, in a financially less dependent position. This can drastically alter hierarchical structures in society.

### *Congestion*

By using facilities and resources in the destination, tourists can have a serious impact on daily life. Tourism may for example lead to water shortages as aggregate demand for water is greater than supply. This phenomenon may be worsened by the earlier discussed demographic processes. The described forms of congestion usually occur when a rapid pace of development or marked seasonality is combined with a large number of tourists compared with local population.

### *Transformation of values*

According to Figuerola (1976) values in society can be grouped into four categories:

- political
- social
- religious
- moral

The transformation of values is related to the demonstration effect, which occurs when different groups of people are brought together. Lambiri-Dimaki (1976) notes the democratization and modernization of attitudes amongst the young, arising out of contact with youthful Western tourists.

Often negative developments of moral behaviour are attributed to tourism. Such developments include prostitution, gambling and crime. It is hard to determine the exact role of tourism in these developments. All of them are present in almost every society, with or without tourism. However, tourism may have created locations and environments which prostitution, gambling and crime need to flourish. In the case of prostitution, Mathieson and Wall (1982) mention, among others, the following hypothetical processes:

- Tourism means that people are away from the puritanical bonds of normal living and money is available to spend hedonistically.
- Tourism affords employment for women, so it may upgrade their economic status. This, in turn, may lead to their liberalization and, eventually, to their involvement in prostitution to maintain or acquire new economic levels.

The latter hypothesis is of course closely related to earlier comments on the transformation of forms and types of employment.

***Modification of consumption patterns***

Contact between hosts and tourists may give rise to changed consumption patterns. This may be due to the demonstration effect or to increased income levels. If a tourist is rich and successful in the eyes of the host, the latter may try to emulate the formers behaviour and consumption pattern. In the process the host may forget that the tourist often seems better off than he really is. After all, tourism is a hedonistic experience which most tourists cannot afford on a sustained basis. The significance of the demonstration effect for changing consumption patterns probably increases with increasing cultural and economic distances.

Tourism may indirectly change consumption patterns by increasing abilities. A higher income level means more consumption possibilities.

***Health problems***

Tourism may give rise to health problems in at least two ways. First of all, by moving around the world tourists may spread diseases such as AIDS, cholera or malaria. Second, the movement of tourists or of people employed in the tourism industry may lead to excessive use of facilities such as sewage treatment which may present health risks.

***Neo-colonialism***

Tourism is sometimes accused of being a neo-colonialist industry. It is directed from the large metropolitan areas in the Western world, leaving the rest of the world without much control and in a dependent situation. Neo-colonialism can give local people a feeling of frustration and inferiority. In the case of tourism, neo-colonialism is closely related to the magnitude of the profit and wage repatriation flows discussed in earlier chapter. Once large multinational corporations gain control in a destination, a large part of tourist expenditure ends up in the Western home countries of those corporations.

Another expression of neo-colonialism may be the intensification of racial or ethnic differences. Tourism is highly related to the service sector. Therefore one could argue that the local population is serving the (Western) tourist, just like in the colonial times. It is feared that this undermines the local population's self respect. However, service is not the same as servility. People can work in the service industry without losing their self esteem.

## Insight into the Social Impacts

***Demonstration Effects***

It is a term given to the notion of local people seeking to imitate the consumption patterns of visitors and their standard of living. In other words, foreigners bring along their values while vacationing in a destination and have them transferred to and adopted by the host population.

One should notice that demonstration effect is not to be traced solely to tourism. Advanced information technology namely the internet is bridging people together from different parts of the world. In addition, the popularity of televisions provides a very convenient way for viewers to get adequate exposure to the world of developed countries at a very affordable price. Therefore, the phenomena of host residents seeking to imitate the ways of their visitors are not necessarily contributed by tourism activities. Nevertheless, social demonstration effect gets further enhanced by tourists who introduce and spread their social and cultural values to the host community in person.

Demonstration effect can easily be detected in the following two areas:

- Value system: the ideology and attitudes of the host population
- Lifestyle: dressing style, accommodation demands, eating habits and demand for consumer goods

**Lifestyle: Traditional retail shops in Macau.**

*Impact on lifestyles*

When under demonstration effect host residents try to work hard to strive for the things they lack, the effect can be regarded as a positive one, "good". As a matter of fact, tourist developments do offer increased job opportunities to young adults, resulting in their becoming less dependent on their parents and traditional jobs. The same holds for women who used to work at home but may now be more independent from their husbands and families. Besides, demonstration effect can help widen the horizon of the host population and let them gain a better understanding of the outside world.

**Lifestyle : Impact on values**

The influence of visitors' value, namely dress code, ways of life and moral standard on the host community is especially noticeable among young people. Tourism could aggravate social problems by encouraging social and cultural deviations which usually take the form of alcoholism, prostitution, gambling, fraud and robbery and in the extreme situations, racism and even sexual exploitation. And where deviation from the host tradition occurs, social disagreement among the host community may arise.

**Positive demonstration effects**

1. Positive attitude towards work: Hard working and willingness to work in the pursuit of the things they lack.
2 Employment shifted from traditional jobs to tourism related jobs, which in turn further enhances cross-cultural interactions.
3 More women participate in the workforce especially in the tourism related industry.
4 The exposure to different cultures helps cultivate a better understanding of and relationship with tourists. This will minimize or remove stereotyping between the host and the tourists.

5 Tourists become aware of local culture through participating in and viewing local cultural performances as well as purchasing handicrafts as souvenirs.

**Negative demonstration effects**

1. *Vanishing hope:* Locals work very hard but find themselves unable to afford the tourists' lifestyles. When the hope is gone, locals will become frustrated and antagonized.
2. *Employment shifted.* Young people, in particular, abandon their traditional livelihood (fishing or farming) and seek jobs in the tourist industry. Traditional skills may thus lack inheritors. In addition, family togetherness may be jeopardized by the shift duty system common in the tourist industry.
3. The exposure to different cultures affects especially the young people who are easily susceptible to the forces of westernization. It means a more relaxed western moral standard in terms of sexual morality, dress code and

Traditional cultural performances and handicrafts may be modified to suit the tourists' preference. Eventually, the authenticity is gone. Furthermore, cultural heritage has been attached with a price tag. Patriotically speaking, it could be humiliating to the host community.

***Changing Stereotyping Image***

Another social problem that needs to be addressed is stereotyping. It is a good indication of the existence of obvious social and cultural barriers between the host and the tourists. It is difficult to remove stereotyping from people but close interaction between tourists and their hosts could minimize the negative impact. When interacting with groups of tourists, it is advisable for host residents not to stereotype or classify them according to their expectations about tourists' behaviours or characteristics. By the same token, tourists should not stereotype the host. An open attitude towards tourists from different countries may help change one's stereotypical impressions about them. As a result, knowledge of different cultures and people would be improved and the ability to understand tourists with different cultural backgrounds would be enhanced. Eventually, this will remove the stereotyped views of one another.

**Tourists**

- When western tourists visit destinations in the developing countries, they usually have a superior feeling towards local communities. This attitude could at some point be transformed into prejudiced or discriminating perception towards the local residents, which might result in stereotyping.

- Tourism in some developing countries is associated with sex tours by certain western tourists. Examples are the Philippines, Thailand and Vietnam. As a result, the tourists sometimes stereotype girls from these countries as prostitutes.

***Residents***

- Residents of the host countries are primarily concerned about the economic effects of tourism. Therefore, they often categorize tourists according to their spending power. This categorization by the host is considered as stereotyping.
- In Hong Kong, Japanese tourists are stereotyped as the wealthy tourists because they have tremendous spending power. But there is a general belief that tourists from developing countries are not as willing to spend as tourists from other places. Therefore, tourists from developing countries are stereotyped as penny-pinching tourists.

***Impacts on the Host Society***

*Doxey's Irritation Index*

With the development of the tourist industry and the influx of tourists, the contact of tourist-host becomes more frequent and intensified. Demonstrating effects and stereotyping are two of the issues that go along with tourism development in the host society. Unlike environmental and economic impacts, it is always difficult to measure how far tourism development influences the population of the host society. To get a clear picture on the local population responses towards tourists, Doxey (1976) has developed an index to measure the level of irritation generated by the contact between tourists and the host society.

According to Doxey's irritation index (as discussed earlier) tourist destinations will pass successively through stages, namely euphoria, apathy, irritation and antagonism, then eventually to the final stage. The number of tourists could be a determining factor in leading the sentiment of the local society to the final level. It is because an ever-increasing number of tourists will finally outweigh the capacity that local people can accommodate and consequently brings pressure to the host society. For example, local people may tolerate a few tourists who behave as if they are in their home country, e.g. dress code, but if the number of tourists exceeds certain level, it may be considered as an annoyance by the host society.

Doxey's index of tourist irritation

1. ***The level of euphoria.*** People are enthusiastic and thrilled by tourist development. They welcome the stranger and there is a mutual feeling of satisfaction. There are opportunities for locals and tourists bring in money.

2. ***The level of apathy.*** As the industry expands people begin to take the tourist for granted. He rapidly becomes a target for profit-taking and contact on the personal level begins to become more formal.
3. ***The level of irritation.*** This will begin when the industry is nearing the saturation point or is allowed to pass a level at which the locals cannot handle the numbers without expansion of facilities.
   Parking is a problem in Mumbai Zuhu Beach.
4. ***The level of antagonism.*** The irritations have become more overt. People now see the tourist as the harbinger of all that is bad. 'Taxes have gone up because of the tourists.' 'They have no respect for property.' 'They have corrupted our youth.' 'They are bent on destroying all that is fine in our town.' Mutual politeness has now given way to antagonism and the tourist is 'ripped off'.
5. ***The final level.*** All this while people have forgotten that what they cherished in the first place was what drew the tourist, but in the wild scramble to develop they overlooked this and allowed the environment to change. What they now must learn to live with is the fact that their ecosystem will never be the same again. They might still be able to draw tourists but of a very different type from those they so happily welcomed in early years. If the destination is large enough to cope with mass tourism it will continue to thrive.[44]

Cultural conflicts may give rise to antagonism towards foreigners but the unequal status between local people and foreigners is another catalyst for bringing about similar conflicts. For instance, foreigners from developed countries see themselves as superior to the local population. Such perception paved the way for certain forms of exploitation or abuse. There are more examples of socio-cultural conflict between host society and tourists. In many cases, tourists see things from their perspective and fail to consider the feeling of the host population. This explains why host people are sometimes hostile towards tourists .

*Illustration 1 : Irritation due to tourist behavior*

In many Muslim countries, strict standards exist regarding the appearance and behaviour of Muslim women, who must carefully cover themselves in public. Tourists in these countries often disregard or are unaware of these standards, ignoring the prevalent dress code, appearing half-dressed (by local standards) in revealing shorts, skirts or even bikinis, sunbathing topless at the beach or consuming large quantities of alcohol openly. Besides creating ill-will, this kind of behavior can be an incentive for locals not to respect their own traditions and religion anymore, leading to tensions within the local community. The same types of culture clashes happen in conservative Christian communities in Polynesia, the Caribbean and the Mediterranean.[45]

Tourist development in certain countries, especially developing countries, often means the deprivation of host in using local facilities or consuming local resources. In order to develop tourism business so as to earn more revenue, local resources, e.g. usage of means of transport, will be reserved for tourists or the priority of using such facilities will be given to tourists. Such deprivation will undoubtedly leads to social discontent which eventually will lead to antagonism towards tourists

*Illustration 2: Depriving local people of access*

There are numerous examples where local residents have lost access to local natural resources because of tourism development. On Boracay Island in the Philippines, one quarter of the island has been bought by outside corporations, generating a crisis in water supply and only limited infrastructure benefits for residents. Similarly, in Bali, Indonesia, prime agricultural land and water supplies have been diverted for large hotels and golf courses, while at Pangandaran (Java, Indonesia), village beach land, traditionally used for grazing, repairing boats and nets, and festivals, was sold to entrepreneurs for construction of a five-star hotel (Shah, 2000).[46]

Tourism development is always regarded as beneficial to local population; however in reality, local people may not be the ones who enjoy the benefits. On the contrary, they are the ones who are exploited. Such phenomenon brings about the discontent of local people towards tourist activities and tourists.

*Illustration 3: Income Inequality in Taman Negara National Park, Malaysia*

In Western Malaysia, the Taman Negara National Park, is a privately owned park and resort which can house 260 visitors at a time. The park employs 270 people and 60% of the staff in the administrative headquarters are locals. In 1999 these local staff earned about US$120 a month; for comparison, Malaysians living off the land at that time were earning on average about US$40 a month.

Despite the positive effects of increased park employment, the difference in income between the two local groups has led to social tension and driven up boat fares and the cost of everyday goods. Little of the tourism money generated by the park stays in Malaysia, and park employees spend almost 90% of their income outside the region or on imported goods. Thus, local inhabitants, whose culture has been marketed to attract tourists, benefit only to a very limited extent. Indeed, many have been taken to illegal hunting and fishing in the park, contrary to its protective regulations.[47]

## Impacts on Habits and Customs

Two theories are available to describe tourism's impacts on habits and customs: acculturation theory and cultural shift theory.

According to the acculturation theory cultural changes brought about by tourism are permanent. This theory states that when a strong and a weak culture meet, the weak culture adopts the habits and customs of the stronger culture.

A competing view is that hosts indeed change their behaviour when interacting with guests, but that these changes are only temporary and context-dependent. This is called cultural shift. Here, the changes are merely cosmetic instead of fundamental as in the case of acculturation. However, when cultural shift occurs over long periods of time, it may become more and more instituitionalized, beginning to form part of local culture. In this way, cosmetic change may give rise to fundamental cultural change.

**Host Attitudinal/behavioural Responses to Tourist Activity[48]**

Since there may be different attitudes towards tourism within the host society, the framework developed by Bjorklund and Philbrick (1972) includes four types of responses from local people towards tourist activities. According to the matrix, the attitudes and the behaviour of local people toward tourism may be either positive or negative, and active or passive. Social impacts of tourism are not static and will change from time to time. A new tourism development scheme or project may lead to attitudinal and behavioural change of groups or individual towards tourism.

For example, some people from the host society originally may show slight acceptance and support for tourist activity. But attitude may change when they are deprived of enjoying the activity or facilities.

**(Arrow indicate Possibility of Change)**

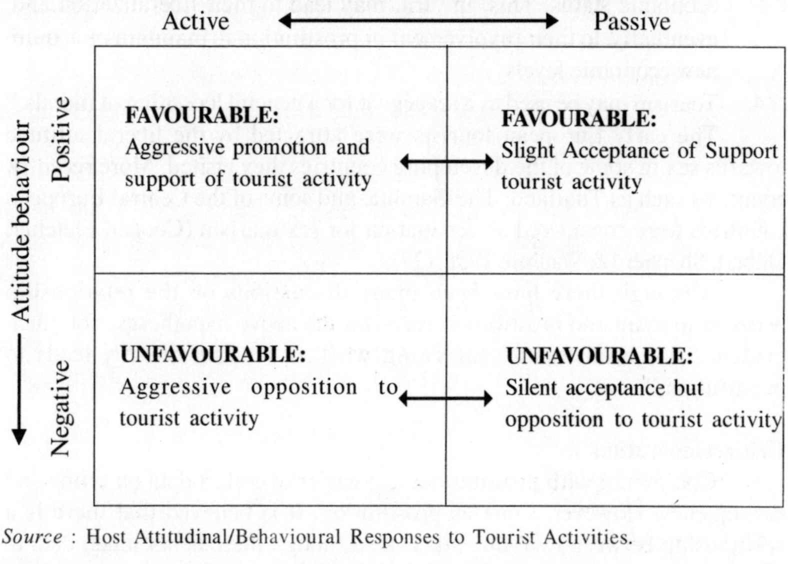


*Source* : Host Attitudinal/Behavioural Responses to Tourist Activities.

Tourists gathered late in the evening could deprive local residents from enjoying their quality time with family members or friends while taking a stroll or break at this major tourist attraction – the Ruins of St Paul's, Macau.

Also, the local business sectors who are actively involved in promoting tourism business activities may not like the idea of having to share the market with overseas/foreign investors as they feel threatened. The arrows in the matrix reflect the potentiality of such changes in attitude and behaviour in reality.

**Tourism versus Moral Conduct and Other Community Problems**

While the host society might enjoy the benefits brought by the growth of the tourism industry, many believed that lot of social problems such as: prostitution, sex tourism, child abuse, crime, and gambling are the consequences of/by-products of the tourism development.

***Prostitution and Sex Tourism***

The following hypotheses are usually used in explaining the increase in prostitution in tourist resorts:

1. The processes of tourism have created locations and environments which attract prostitutes and their clients;
2. By its very nature, tourism means that people are away from the puritanical bonds of normal living, anonymity is assured away from home, and money is available to spend hedonistically. These circumstances are conducive to the survival and expansion of prostitution;
3. As tourism affords employment for women, it may upgrade their economic status. This, in turn, may lead to their liberalization and, eventually, to their involvement in prostitution to maintain or acquire new economic levels;
4. Tourism may be used as a scapegoat for a general loosening of morals.[49]

The early European tourists were attracted by the liberal attitude towards sex in some of the developing countries they visited. More recently, countries such as Thailand, The Gambia, and some of the Central European countries were considered as destination for sex tourism (Cooper, Fletcher, Gilbert, Shepherd & Wanhill, 1998:177).

Although there have been many discussions on the relationship between tourism and prostitution based on the above hypotheses, not much evidence has been found concerning whether tourism directly leads to prostitution.[50]

**Crime Generation**

Comparing with prostitution, it is easier to collect data on crime and delinquency. However, same as prostitution, it is believed that there is a relationship between tourism and crime although there is not much data to prove it. 3 factors that can influence relationship between tourism and crime rate are:

1. The density of the population during the tourist season;
2 The location of the resort in relation to an international border;
3 The per capita incomes of hosts and tourists, large differences between them tending to encourage robbery[51]

Crime rates are usually higher in urbanized areas than remote areas. The development of mass tourism provides rooms for the growth of crime rates. Such situation is more obvious when it is during the peak season. Mass tourists who are preparing to spend large amount of money on shopping, may be carrying video recorders or cameras and wearing expensive ornament, these attract criminals such as pickpockets and robbers.

**Gambling**

There are numerous examples that both legalization of gambling and establishment of casinos are considered as remedies for the downturn of a destination's tourism business.

Many tourist destinations build up their fame and notoriety through their gambling industry, e.g. Macau, Monte Carlo and Las Vegas. Gambling is always perceived as business associated with loan shark and prostitution. In addition, violent crime is often associated with gaming because of the monetary interest involved. Gambling is always perceived as business associated with negative social impacts. Example : A casino hotel (center) in Macau, Crown Casino in Melbourne, Australia.

**Tourism Effects on Community – Cultural Effects**

*Introduction of Culture*

According to Hudman, curiosity is one of the key motivators of travel. Curiosity means desire to learn about things foreign. For tourists, the cultures of foreign countries are naturally what they are most curious about. Speaking of culture, there are basically three things to bear in mind. Culture is something that:

- is learned; we are not born with culture.
- is shared, it is something collective.
- includes much more than the performing arts or high culture.

As a broad term, culture comprises a variety of material and non-material elements, ranging from language, traditions, food, history, religion, and architecture etc. Non-material culture can be divided into habits and customs and non-material art forms.

***Elements of culture***

The elements of culture have been identified as attractions for tourists:

*Language*

The learning of and the ability to use a foreign language by a tourist provides a means for developing an interest in another culture.

*Traditions*

Traditions that characterize a destination or a country provide a focal point of interest for tourists who seek to learn about the way of life in the host community.

- ***Handicrafts*** : Handicrafts provide a source of interest for tourists who wish to see the craftsmanship of a traditional or popular item. Handicraft items can also be purchased by tourists as souvenirs.
- ***Art*** : Art, being country or culture-specific, often reflects the past and present cultural heritage of the host community.
- ***Dress*** : The styles of dress of the local residents are usually a feature of popular interest to tourists. The styles of dress also highlight distinctive characteristics of an area. Items of dress and clothing unique to an area make good souvenirs too. For the wearer, his or her status and self-esteem is enhanced as the dress and clothing become an object of discussion or admiration.

*Food*

Trying and enjoying the cuisine or food at a destination is one of the main activities tourists engage in when travelling.

*History*

The oral, written, and landscape history of an area reflects its past and serves as a reminder for both locals and tourists of the way of life of the host society in earlier times. Important events which shaped the existing nature of an area and its people also provide insights for tourists about the community.

*Works and technology*

The works or technology particular to a destination area, either in the past or at present, are a source of interest for tourists. They provide knowledge about the nature of the host's economy and lifestyle.

*Religion*

Religion of particular significance to an area influences the lifestyle and festivities of the host community. It is a source of interest amongst tourists as it provides further insights about the spiritual aspects of the culture of the host community.

*Architecture*

Architectural features provide physical evidence of the cultural attributes of an area. Often a distinctive architectural style is associated with a particular community or country. Architecture also reflects the availability of local building materials, the way the community adapts to climatic conditions, or a particular design style.

**Culture: bridge or barrier?**

People from different countries have different cultures. Cultural difference is one of the many reasons that attract tourists to a particular destination.

However, language and religion are often the major barriers between the hosts and the visitors. Tourists are usually less interested in communicating with local residents when there is a language barrier which nevertheless hinders effective mutual understanding. Apart from language barrier, visitors may not be aware of their ignorance of and arrogance towards the local tradition and religion. Disrespectful behaviours can be considered offensive or even unacceptable to the host community. In fact, it is culture that usually enables and disables communication between residents and tourists.

When hosts and tourists are not willing to learn, share or accept each other's cultures, a series of socio-cultural barriers would result. Demonstration effect, stereotyping, segregation, tension, misunderstanding and ethnocentrism are typical socio-cultural barriers. It is an irony that while a local culture in its own right might attract tourists, the very same culture can dispel tourists.

**Impacts on Material Culture**

The forms of material culture which are most important for tourism are handicrafts and architecture (Shaw and Williams, 1997). Tourism often leads to the commercialization of art forms and especially handicrafts. Artefacts with cultural or religious meaning are sought by tourists as souvenirs. As more and more tourists visit a destination, souvenir production is increased, often leading to mass production. In the process, the cultural artefacts may loose their cultural meaning.

On the other hand, tourism may also stimulate a renewed attention for old cultural traditions and art forms, often combined with insights from other parts of the world. According to Mathieson and Wall (1982) this has been the case in the United States where Pueblo Indians combined Indian and Western techniques to create new forms of art. This development could not have taken place without the financial stimulus of tourism.

Possibly, both observations belong to the same process (Mathieson and Wall, 1982):

(a) The disappearance of traditional artistic designs and art and crave forms, particularly those with deep religious and mythical affiliations. This is followed by;

(b) The growth of a degenerate, unsophisticated replacement which develops in association with mass production techniques. This is often followed by;

(c) The resurgence of skillful craftsmanship and distinctive styles incorporating the deeper cultural beliefs of the host society. This phase is a response to the deleterious impacts evident in phase 2.

*Impacts on architecture,* which is another form of material culture, are of another nature. These arise mostly because tourist buildings are not built according to local architectural standards. To give an example, whereas in many less developed countries high-rise buildings are rare, hotels are often many stories high. This, coupled with high level of international building standardization, may lead to complete alterations of the local scenery.

**Impacts on Non-material Culture**

Impacts on non-material culture, such as dance or religious manifestations, are similar to impacts on material art forms. Here too, cultural expressions may lose their deeper significance when confronted with commercialization. But tourism may also give rise to a revival of old art forms, perhaps mixed with influences from other cultures.

Maybe these two impacts are not as mutually exclusive as they may seem at first sight. Commercially produced art forms without significance, also called fake art or airport art, may be used to distract tourist attention from the real cultural expressions by the local population. A good example is to understand the concept of staged authenticity.

***Authenticity and Commoditization in Tourism***

To experience the host culture is one of the motives among the visitors from the tourist-generating countries. The increasing exposure of the aboriginal or native peoples to the outside world, which is usually referred to as contacts with people from the developed countries, makes local cultures become 'pseudo-native'.

***Re-structured Authenticity***

In order to satisfy the expectation of tourists who may have a pre-conception on the host culture learnt from travel guidebooks, the host society may modify their rituals, for example, in a form which will match the tourists' desire and expectations. This creates a phenomenon in which what tourists see is not authentic. This will result in what has been called "re-structured ethnicity" according to United Nations Environmental Programme. There are countless examples of "re-structured authenticity" ranging from the Polynesian dance of the Western Samoa in the South Pacific, to wedding ceremony of the minorities held at China Folk Culture Village in Shenzhen, China. Once the culture, for example religious ritual, traditional ethnic rites and festivals, is commercialized and commoditized for tourism purposes, the true meaning and value of these cultural performances and events will be destroyed.

**Staged Authenticity**

As tourists would like to have a glimpse of the local culture, they always look for opportunities to experience the authentic culture in the host society. This incurs the emergence of different levels of cultural penetration. Normally, local culture could be expressed and manifested in the forms of rituals and ceremonies. To adapt such cultural events to the tastes of the tourists and at the same time to retain its true identity, the local people provide an alternative of a more realistic but de facto modified performance of cultural heritage, i.e. staged authenticity.

According to the level of cultural penetration jumps to B from A. In doing so, a cultural curtain is set up between the staged authenticity and true cultural heritage. This cultural curtain serves as a firewall curtain which is set to prevent the tourists from penetrating behind the curtain. However, due to the influx of tourists and levels of penetration, the firewall curtain will keep on retreating so as to satisfy the desire of the tourists as well as to get more share in the competitive tourism market. In this case, tourists may reach the true cultural heritage and eventually, host culture will be exposed to impacts from tourists and finally loses its true identity, i.e. level C.

**Levels of cultural penetration**

Further interpretation the arena is divided into three distinct areas:

| Previous Level of Cultural Penetration | Staged Authenticity |
|---|---|

| A<br>**Tourists** | B<br>**Cultural Curtain** | C<br>**True Cultural Heritage** |
|---|---|---|
| The previous level of tourist penetration into the host culture; | The new level of cultural penetration that is considered to be authentic by the tourist but is, in fact, staged authenticity; and | The true cultural heritage of the host society that maintains its integrity by keeping tourists on the other side of the firewall curtain. |

In general, tourists are looking for "typical" forms of local culture. These can be offered to them in the form of typical souvenirs or exhibitions of the local way of life in specially designed imitation villages. In such settings, visual or audible art forms, such as local dances or songs can be performed. At the same time, locals can enjoy their own cultural manifestations, which may be less typical in they eyes of the tourist but more authentic and contemporary.

**Tourism Effects and Preservation of Cultural Heritage**

**Ruining of the Local Heritage Culture**

The popularity of an attraction could lead to the overloading of visitors. When this happens, the attraction may be damaged or destroyed through:

1. Erosion of resources which usually takes place in the form of wearing of floors and steps of a building or the pathways around it.
2. Effects of visitors' perspiration. Acidity of perspiration has the same effect of acid rain. Thus, it erodes the interior walls, carvings, sculptures and paint works.
3. Air pollution due to increased car and bus traffic. Emissions from automobiles lead to the deterioration of the condition in an attraction.
4. Littering and hawking are an eye sore to the attraction.

   Due to the ruining of local heritage caused by tourism, there is an increasing concern in preservation.

**UNESCO (1972)**

According to the definition adopted by UNESCO (1972) in the World Heritage Convention, heritage is divided into (1) Cultural heritage and (2) Natural heritage. Since heritage is very broad in its meaning, different countries might have different concepts of heritage. In Hong Kong, the Antiquities and Monuments Office (AMO) has its own definition of heritage.

*Cultural heritage*

- A monument, group of buildings or site of historical, aesthetic, archeological, scientific, ethnological or anthropological value

*Natural Heritage*

- Designating outstanding physical, biological and geological features; habitats of threatened plants or animal species and areas of value on sor aesthetic grounds or from the point of view of conservation

**AMO**

*Archaeological heritage*

*Historical heritage*

Focuses on early municipal government buildings, Western style residences and churches

*Cultural heritage*

Focuses on village life and ancestor worship

Emphasises 6,000 years of prehistory

***Definition of Cultural Heritage***

It is a broad concept that "includes the natural as well as the cultural environment.

- It encompasses landscapes, historic places, sites and built environments, as well as biodiversity, collections, past and continuing cultural practices, knowledge and living experiences.
- It records and expresses the long processes of historic development, forming the essence of diverse national, regional, indigenous and local identities and is an integral part of modern life.
- It is a dynamic reference point and positive instrument for growth and change.
- The particular, the heritage and collective memory of each locality or community is irreplaceable and an important foundation for development, both now and into the future.[53]

*Tangible Cultural Heritage*

Tangible cultural heritage includes all forms of physical construction such as architectures like temples and imperial tombs, heritage sites etc. Examples are ranging from The Great Wall in China, Taj Mahal in India and Borobudur Temple Compounds in Indonesia to Peking Man Site at Zhouko The Ruins of St. Paul's, Macau Great Wall, China[54]

*Intangible Cultural Heritage*

Intangible cultural heritage "might be defined as embracing all forms of traditional and popular activities, i.e. collective works originating in a given community and based on tradition. These creations are transmitted orally or by gesture, and are modified over a period of time through a process of collective recreation. They include folklore, customs, languages, music, dance, rituals, festivities, traditional medicine and pharmacopoeia, the culinary arts and all kinds of special skills related with the material aspects of culture, such as tools and the habitat." - United Nations Educational, Scientific and Cultural Organization (UNESCO).

**What is cultural and heritage tourism?**

*Cultural tourism*

It covers all types of cultural attractions, ranging from concrete attractions such as museums and monuments, cultural performances to other cultural manifestations, such as the consumption of the way of life of certain cultures.

*Heritage tourism*

It is anything from historical buildings to art works and beautiful scenery.

According to Murphy, cultural heritage tourism serves to cultivate a form of awareness from a domestic and international perspective:

- Domestic perspective refers to the renewal of interest and pride in their own cultural heritage among the locals
- International perspective refers to the widening of horizons

Paradoxically, cultural tourism is increasingly being recognized as an influential tourism activity which exerts considerably positive impacts on the cultural awareness of the locals. The genuine admiration of local culture by tourists helps trigger in the host country an increased appreciation of its own cultural heritage and adds another dimension to the search for national identity. Tourism may in a sense serve as a mechanism through which to prevent the disappearance of certain artistic and cultural features. Tourists' appreciation of local art, crafts, folklore, history, religion or language may create a desire among the local residents to renew their cultural pride. Along the process, tourists can help the residents appreciate their own cultural heritage and look for their national identity.

According to Morin, international tourism acts as a powerful force in the universal standardization of culture and society. Many people have argued that the development of cultural villages such as China Folk Cultural Villages in Shenzhen and Hawaii Cultural Village in Hawaii are too commercialized and the shows are over-modified to suit the tourists. Some people consider this kind of staged culture a poor representation of the local heritage culture. The stage shows lack cultural authenticity, and are at the verge of treating culture and heritage as a commodity. Nevertheless, some people believe that cultural village is an ideal solution to preserve the local heritage. According to de Kadt, some of the cultural heritage, without tourist development, would become completely extinct.

Therefore, it is difficult to determine whether cultural tourism is effective in preserving the local heritage.

**Preservation of the Local Heritage Culture**

The effects of cultural tourism extend beyond national identity and cultural preservation. Cultural tourism provides the necessary improvement and enhancement to the attractions and their peripheral supporting developments.

1. ***Restoration:*** Income arising from tourism provides funding for restoration of the attractions, especially historic buildings, sites and monuments.
2 ***Infrastructure:*** Better access namely pathways, roads, car parking lots, bus and train stops and lighting is provided to the attractions.
3 ***Amenities:*** Amenities namely toilets, food kiosks, landscaping, shelter, transport facilities, hotels, and restaurants are provided for visitors.

These improvements would make an attraction more attractive to both the tourists and local residents. In Hong Kong, many historical buildings have been restored and have become important cultural attractions for locals and tourists. Examples are Sam Tung UK Village in Tsuen Wan, Western Market in Sheung Wan, Hong Kong Museum of Medical Sciences, and Flagstaff House in Central.

The example found in Bali shows the benefit of tour development in preserving local heritage culture . Preservation of Balinese culture.

"Tourism has forced the Balinese to reflect on their artistic output as just one cultural identifier. The presence of visitors who continually praise Balinese art and culture has given people a kind of confidence and pride in their art, and made them truly believe that their culture is glorious and thus worthy of this praise and therefore justly admired. This realization removed any possibility in the people's mind that their art was in any way inferior to the art of advanced nations, and plays an important role in conserving and developing the art in general."[56]

***The Renaissance and Deterioration of Traditional Art Forms***

Tourism development has both advantages and disadvantages onto host culture. The income generated from selling traditional artifacts and staging cultural heritage may provide budget for preserving indigenous culture. The fact that employment opportunities created by tourism in the fabrication of handicrafts implies a renaissance in the production of art forms. Culture itself is not static but is under a process of being invented and reinvented. A change of traditional art forms may not necessarily mean a disaster for local culture.

Nevertheless, in reality, tourism does encourage the production of 'pseudo-traditional' art forms. The most typical example is the last-minute purchase of souvenirs by tourists at the airport before taking flight back to their home countries. Such 'airport art' is normally under mass production and does not reflect the creativity of the art makers or the true meaning of the arts and crafts.

***Framework for Preservation***

An ideal heritage preservation programme requires the cooperation of the public and private sectors. The two sectors should work within a planned framework to make sure that the local culture and heritage is properly preserved for the enjoyment and appreciation of both the local residents and foreign visitors.

*Criteria for the framework:* Government sets standards on the quality of its cultural resources.

A Arts and handicrafts: The sale of arts and handicrafts either at government centres or shops that meet the standards established by the government.

B Performing arts: Performances must be authentic in nature. There should be no compromise between authenticity and tourists' preference. In other words, they must adhere to the cultural authenticity as well as the unique character. The performers must meet the minimum performance standard. Thus, traditional training may be required for stage performance.

2. Develop cultural heritage tourism that can strike a balance between economic and social goals.
3. Develop educational heritage tours that teach local residents and foreign visitors about the culture and history of a destination.
4. Establish a benchmark on social carrying capacity. It is either the capability or tolerance of a community towards tourism activities. The aspects to be considered are moral standards, cultural authenticity, misunderstandings and conflicts between hosts and visitors, conflicts between different generations in a community, shifted employment from traditional jobs, and the development of infrastructure.
5. Maintain an equilibrium of restoration of heritage and the national identity. In other words, the restoration, conservation and preservation of heritage culture are to attract tourists as well as develop a sense of cultural pride. This equilibrium will not be balanced when the community depends heavily on cultural resources to generate income through tourism. For this reason, culture is modified to suit the tourists' preferences and packaged as a commodity with a price tag.

**Conclusions**

Tourism may seriously alter the social and cultural setting in a destination, especially when tourism development is rapid and economic and cultural distances between hosts and guests are large.

The actual assessment of social and cultural impacts is very difficult, because tourism is only one of the factors of societal change. Ascribing social and cultural developments to tourism is therefore a very difficult task. Moreover, a great handicap of the assessment of impacts appears to be the lack of a logically structured impact classification. The construction of such a classification seems to be an important research goal.

# 10

# Economic Impacts of Tourism

## POSITIVE IMPACTS

### Creating Jobs

Tourism is a highly labour intensive industry. It depends very much on a large number of people with various levels of skills and abilities (e.g. waiters, tour guides, hotel managers, etc.). In general, tourism industry has a greater capacity to provide more job opportunities than any other industries. There are 2 main types of employment generated by tourism: direct and indirect.

1. *Direct employment* is employment generated from business that directly provides services to tourists.
   Examples:
   - accommodation and catering (hotels)
   - tourist attractions and business facilities (e.g. exhibition and convention centres)
   - tourism promotion and information (e.g. travel agencies or tourist boards)
2. *Indirect employment* refers to jobs of those people who either
   - serve both local people and tourists, or
   - manufacture goods and provide services which are bought or used by business and organisations which serve tourists directly.
     Examples: taxi drivers, shopkeepers.
   - factory workers manufacturing bedroom furniture for sale to hotels
     Sectors which employ the most employees in the tourism industry are:
   - ·food services
   - accommodation
   - transportation

- entertainment
- travel agencies and tour operators

**Providing Tax Revenue**

Tourists may pay tax like most other people. As they come from other regions or countries, their expenses result in an increased tax base for the host country. Government receives these taxes from:

***Direct taxes***

- Salary tax (on personal income)
- Profit tax (on business)

An increase in tourist expenses would result in an increase in

- Income of people working in the tourism industry
- Profit of business owners which therefore increases the tax revenue of the government

***Indirect tax***

- Turnover tax
- Expenditure tax
- Departure tax and hotel room tax

*Turnover tax* is paid on consumption. Two major types are sales tax and value added tax. Sales tax is levied by the government on goods and services that are passed directly to consumers. Value added tax (VAT) is an indirect tax on goods and services. Tourists pay the tax without knowing the exact amount since it is included in the price of the goods and charge for the services.

*Expenditure tax* is luxury tax paid on specific forms of consumption. They are often known as excise duties paid on goods like alcohol, tobacco and petrol. However, in order to promote international tourism, some countries provide exceptions, usually in the form of duty-free sales for tourists at major shipping and airline terminals.

*Departure tax* is common in many countries for tourists to pay to the destination countries and hotel room tax is paid for staying overnight in a hotel room.

**Improving the Balance of Payments**

The balance of payments is an accounting of the flow of goods, services and capital in and out of a country during a given period (usually a year). If a country pays, or agrees to pay out more money than it receives, it has a deficit balance of payments. If it receives more money than it pays, it has a surplus balance of payments.

Every country wants a surplus balance of payments rather than a deficit one. A thriving tourism industry (especially an inbound tourism industry) can improve the balance of payments by bringing in a large amount of foreign exchange.

A country's inbound tourism is its invisible export as it brings in foreign exchange through providing services to overseas visitors. A country's outbound tourism is its invisible import as local residents spend money overseas. (But not all of their expenses would be earned by other countries as a portion of the expenses may be paid to local tour operators.) If inbound tourists spend more than outbound tourists do, a country will have a net surplus that will help improve the balance of payments.

According to the UNWTO Tourism Barometer, international tourist arrivals reached 924 million, up 16 million from 2007, representing a growth of 2%.[57]

**Generating Income and the Linkage Effect**

Income is generated from wages and salaries, interest, rent and profits. In a labour-intensive industry such as tourism, a large part of income comes from wages and salaries earned by people who are directly or indirectly involved in the industry. Moreover, the benefits of tourism can spread throughout the whole economy by creating more jobs in other sectors of the economy. For example, a hotel receptionist may save up and buy a car or a TV set, thus creating business for manufacturing industries and shops; a tour bus driver may go out for dinner with his family and this creates more business for restaurants.

On the whole, income is greater in areas where a large number of tourists of high spending power are attracted to stay for a longer time. Furthermore, contribution of tourism to the income of a tourist destination is greatly increased by a process of tourism income multiplier. This occurs when money spent by tourists in an area is spent again by those who have received the initial amount of money.

**Economic Growth and Living Standard**

Most developing countries face a foreign exchange shortage problem and have difficulties financing their economic development. Tourism industry plays an important role as a foreign exchange earner. This is very important to those developing countries with limited potentials for exporting agricultural products and manufactured goods.

Tourism contributes greatly to the diversification of the economy. Through the linkages with other economic sectors such as construction, transport, food production industries, etc., the industry may spread its effect throughout the economy and bring about economic growth.

Tourism may also raise the living standard of local residents. They may have more jobs that are better paid than the traditional ones such as farming and fishing. Local people may enjoy better facilities and a wider choice of goods and services.

**The Phenomenon of Tourism Multiplier**

**Approach 1: Three-tiers Approach looking at Tourism Multipler**

The concept of the multiplier is based upon the recognition that the various sectors which make up the economy are interdependent, that is, in addition to purchasing primary inputs such as labour, imports, etc., each sector will purchase intermediate goods and services produced by other establishments within the local economy. Therefore, any autonomous change in the level of final demand will not only affect the industry which produces that final good or service, but also that industry's suppliers' suppliers, etc. (Fletcher and Archer, 1991:28)

***Flow of money***

In order to gain insight into the net economic benefits, we will trace the flow of money from tourists through the economy of a destination area. Three steps are distinguished in this flow scheme; each of them will be discussed below.

*First order effects*

The initial spending of tourists is at the start of the economic chain. Tourists can buy tourism products or services either directly or indirectly. In turn, these products and services can be provided either inside or outside the destination country. From these observations, the following table emerges:

**A classification of tourist expenditure with some examples**

| | **Final recipient** | |
|---|---|---|
| | ***Inside destination*** | ***Outside destination*** |
| **Direct purchase** | (a) accommodation, food | (b) tax free shopping |
| **Indirect purchase** | (c) accommodation via tour operator | (d) air-fare via tour operator |

The inflow of money from tourism into the destination country (the gross effect on the balance of payments) depends on (a) and on the percentage of (b) the tour operator spends in the destination country. Clearly, if (b) is important compared to (a), the destination country is sensitive to changes in tour operators' spending patterns. Moreover, if (b) is large, tour operators can often negotiate a significant price discount, resulting in a smaller inflow of money.

*Second order effects*

Having received the initial spending by tourists and tour operators, the tourism industry in its turn spends this extra income on inputs (consumption) and on the payment of the production factors, labour (wages), capital (interest) and entrepreneurship (profits).

*Third order effects*

Returning to the flow of money, we see that buying inputs means extra consumption and sometimes also taxation in the form of value added taxes (Holloway, 1989). The owners of the production factors spend their income on consumption, savings or taxation. Savings and taxation can be seen as leakages from the spending cycle. However, these leakages are usually only temporary. Savings are simply postponed consumption, while part of tax revenues flow back into the economy in the form of government expenditure.

The extra consumption expenditures from buying inputs and from spending production factor income can be directed towards imported products or locally produced products. A large percentage spent on imports means a large import leakage, influencing the balance of payments.

It is good to remember that the net contribution of tourism on the balance of payments depends not only on initial spending, but also on the magnitudes of the import leakage and the repatriation of money.

***Closing the cycle***

Now, the amount of money spent on locally produced goods enters the spending cycle again. This amount is, of course, smaller than the initial expenditure due to the various leakages. After having gone through the spending cycle for the second time, less money remains still and so on, until the effects of the initial expenditure have vanished. The cumulative effect of the initial tourist expenditure going through various spending cycles is called the tourism income multiplier (TIM).

**Approach 2: Two-tiers Approach looking at Tourism Multiplier**

How tourism multiplier works in local economy. The concept of multiplier has been widely used for studying the impact of tourism on a destination's economy. Nevertheless, there is much controversy on the usefulness of multiplier effect in analyzing the economic impact of tourism. For instance, it is not easy to measure how much amount of revenue could be generated from every dollar spent by tourists in the first circulation, the second circulation and so on. Nowadays, some other concepts have been used for studying this issue, e.g. linkage effect.

***The multiplier process*[58]**

Very often, only tourism-related sectors such as accommodation like hotels, transport like airlines, or tour operators and travel agents, are considered as the ones who are benefited from tourism development. However, tourism is virtually a multi-faceted industry, the revenue generated benefits various sectors of the economy. For example, manufacturers of electrical appliances and suppliers of foodstuff who provide their products and services to hotels are also benefited. In this sense, there is always a linkage amongst different sectors and industries that jointly support the running of the tourism business and in return, they are all benefited from tourism.

The initial spending of tourists triggers the economy boom of the host society. There are a number of multipliers working in the economic system including transactions multiplier, output multiplier, income multiplier, employment multiplier and government multiplier.

*Transactions (or sales) Multiplier*

It measures the amount of additional business revenue created in an economy as a result of an increase in tourist expenditure.

*Output Multiplier*

It measures the amount of additional output generated in an economy as a result of an increase in tourist expenditure. The principal distinction between transactions and output multipliers is that output multipliers are concerned with changes in the actual levels of production and not the volume and value of sales. Not all sales will be related to current production (some sales may have been made from inventories and some productive output may not be sold within the time frame of the model and, therefore, result in an increase in inventories). Therefore, the value of an output multiplier may well be larger or smaller than the value of the corresponding transactions multiplier.

*Income Multiplier*

It measures the additional income (wages and salaries, rent, interest and profits) created in the economy as a result of an increase in tourist expenditure.

*Employment Multiplier*

It is a measurement of either the total amount of employment generated by an additional unit of tourist expenditure or the ratio of the total employment generated by this same expenditure to the direct employment alone.

*Government Revenue Multiplier*

It measures the impact on government revenue, from all sources, associated with an increase of tourist expenditure. This multiplier may be expressed in gross terms, that is the gross increase in government revenue as a result of an increase in tourist spending, or in net terms when the increase in government revenue is reduced by the increase in government expenditures associated with the increase in tourist activity.

This multiplier effect is explained as follows:

Tourists visit India and spend money on their meals in restaurants. This provides income for the restaurant owners. They then pay tax, save some money and spend the rest. Some of what they spend goes to the purchase of goods and services from other suppliers and producers in India. Some is spent as wages and salaries of staff and some is used to pay interest to banks and rents to landlords.

The people who receive money from the restaurant owners will pay tax, save some money and spend the rest for goods and services. Thus, the money spent by tourists is used again and again by other people. It is spread throughout the whole economy. As a result, the additional income created is far greater than the initial spending of the tourists.

Not all money circulates in the economy. Some has gone to pay tax; some has been saved or used for imported goods and services. Money which stays out of the circulation system will reduce the multiplier effect. The multiplier effect is great when there are strong linkages among various economic sectors. Linkages are strong and the income multiplier effect are high if all the goods and services are locally supplied.

## NEGATIVE IMPACTS

Tourism profits motivate many countries encourage tourism development, however, there are costs for tourism.

### High Consumer and Land Prices

A flourishing tourism industry will place great pressure on the limited resources such as food, land, transport, electricity and water supply, etc. of the host economy.

An increasing demand on these resources and facilities may result in inflation, thus causing negative effects on local residents. Higher consumer and land prices may result.

### Over-dependency on Tourism

Tourism depends very much on external demand factors. A large proportion of expenditure of international tourism is generated from a small number of developed countries. A change in the economic condition of these countries will greatly affect the number of tourists going to tourist destinations. Also, tourists' taste is somewhat "fickle"; the once popular destination may become out of fashion quickly. High dependence on tourism should be avoided.

High dependence occurs when a region becomes too dependent on tourism. Subsequent decline in the tourist flow to that region may greatly affect the economy of the area.

**Leakage**

Additional income generated from tourism may not be as much as it should be if there is leakage. Leakage is anything that causes the profits from tourism to drain out of the economic system.

Leakage can be:

- expenditure on imported goods and services required by tourists
- expenditure on imported goods and services required by tourist business
- money earned and sent home in overseas countries by foreign workers in tourism industry
- profits of foreign-company-owned tourist facilities diverted overseas

The host countries enjoyed substantial economic benefits through the multiplier process. However, part of the revenues earned by tourism industry may leak out from local economy.

As claimed by UNEP, for most tourists who have purchased all-inclusive package tours, about 80% of their expenditures will go to companies in the private sector such as airlines, hotels and other international companies (who have their headquarters in the tourists' home countries), and not to local companies and workers. Such leakage is particularly serious in developing countries. For each US$100 spent by a tourist from a developed country on a vacation tour in a developing country, only about US$5 will actually be put back into the economy of the destination country

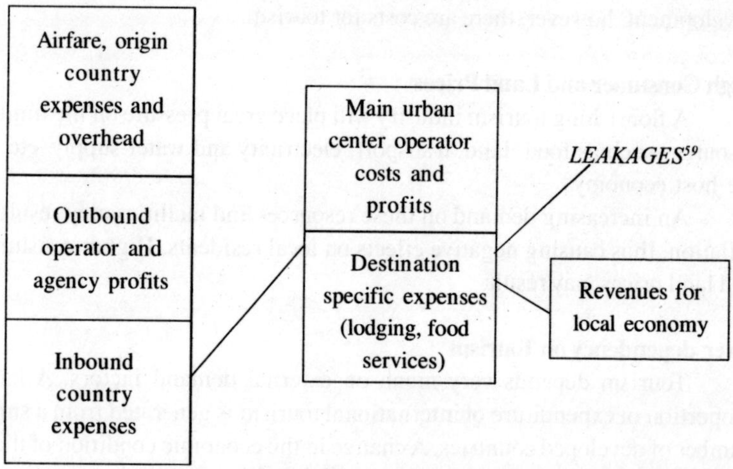


**Fig. How Leakages Happen.**

There are two types of leakages:

***Import Leakage***

When the host country cannot supply the products required, it is common that destination countries will import goods and products from abroad to satisfy tourists' demands, e.g. equipment, foods and drinks. On the other hand, it is due to the inferior quality of the products provided by the host country that cannot meet the standards of the international hotel chain.

***Export Leakage***

As proclaimed by UNEP, 'multinational corporations and large foreign businesses have a substantial share in the import leakage. Often, especially in poor developing destinations, they are the only ones that possess the necessary capital to invest in the construction of tourism infrastructure and facilities. As a consequence of this, an export leakage arises when overseas investors who finance the resorts and hotels take their profits back to their country of origin.'

In other word, the host society 'exports' their products, which are the tourist facilities and services in the destination where visitors enjoy. But since most of these facilities and services suppliers are financed and controlled by foreign investors, the profits earned will be taken back to the investors' home country.

**Conclusions**

As we saw in this unit, spending on tourism is huge on a global scale. However, this does not mean that tourism is the universal remedy for economic problems. The net contribution of tourism to a destination's economy depends largely on the spending leakages. If much of initial tourist spending leak away through imports, taxes and repatriation of profits and wages, net receipts may very well be small.

# 11

# Environmental Impacts of Tourism

## POSITIVE IMPACTS

### Preservation and Conservation of Environment

One of the arguments in favour of tourism is that uncontrolled urbanization, modernization and industrialization cause great damages to the natural environment.

Tourism can be seen as an alternative economic development which provides the necessary motive and money for preserving the archaeological treasures and ancient monuments, and conserving the natural resources for the continued enjoyment of both tourists and local residents.

Wildlife and forest reserves have been set up and scenic lands have been preserved partly due to their ability to attract tourists. For example, some east African countries such as Kenya and Tanzania have established large natural parks and game reserves for wildlife as they know that wildlife is the most important tourist attraction in East Africa. Without the economic return provided by tourism, these areas might well be converted to agriculture, mining or other forms of industrial development which cause great harm to the natural habitats.

### Enhancement of Environment

It is often the environment itself that attracts tourists to a destination. An example is the beautiful mountain scenery of Switzerland. Any tourist destination hoping to attract tourists will try to improve its image by planting flowers, developing well-designed tourist facilities such as attractive landscaped hotels.

Tourism also provides incentive for "cleaning up" the overall environment. This can be done through control of air, water, and noise pollution, littering and other environmental problems.

**Increasing Environmental Awareness**

Economic success of tourism will encourage local awareness (both the government and residents) of the importance of conservation of natural environment. This leads to the adoption of administrative controls and planning (e.g. stricter anti-pollution control, better land use zoning, etc.) by government to maintain the quality of the environment.

## NEGATIVE IMPACTS

Tourism development is not without cost. When the carrying capacity of a destination is exceeded, there will be a number of negative effects on the environment.

**Carrying Capacity Problems**

- ***What is carrying capacity?*** Carrying capacity can be defined as "the maximum number of people who can use a destination without unacceptable changes in the environment and without unacceptable changes in the enjoyment gained by visitors."

  ***Types of carrying capacity :*** There are three types of carrying capacity: physical, environmental, and psychological.

*Physical carrying capacity*

The physical carrying capacity of a destination is related to:

- the amount of suitable land available for accommodation, tourist facilities, and services like roads and water supply;
- the finite capacity of facilities such as car parking spaces, seats in theatres or restaurants; and
- the capacity of local transport systems e.g. maximum 3,000 cars per hour for Tate's Cairn Tunnel.

*Environmental carrying capacity*

Most tourist destinations suffer some forms of environmental wear and tear whether it is:

- the trampling of grassland at picnic sites;
- disturbance of wildlife; or
- physical erosion of important historic monuments by visitors' feet.

*Psychological or perceptual capacity*

The psychological or perceptual capacity of a destination is exceeded when the visitors' experience or enjoyment is significantly impaired. This depends on:

- visitors' attitudes to both the number and behaviour of other users, e.g. crowded and noisy environment; and

- visitors' tolerance of the physical wear and tear or pollution at a destination.

  Whenever or wherever these capacities are exceeded, environmental problems occur. For example, if too many people try to use a barbecue site at Goa Beaches, Ooty all at the same time, problems will occur. They may make too much smoke from their fire, occupy all the seats, and drop a lot of litter. Some people need to sit on the ground and wait a long time for a barbecue. The place gets very crowded. The picnic site becomes unpleasant rather than enjoyable. In other words, the barbecue site has exceeded its carrying capacity.

***How (Where) do carrying capacity problems happen?***

The problems may arise:

- in tourist-generating areas, like Hong Kong, where public holidays and school holidays are fixed. This leads to a concentration of outbound demand at those particular times;
- on transit routes, e.g. Shenzhen and Guangzhou. Delays may occur at these bottlenecks if the transport system cannot cope with the demand; and
- in tourist-receiving areas, e.g. Beijing. Tourist resources such as the Great Wall and the Forbidden City may come under great usage pressure.

**Other Ways in which Tourism do Harm to the Environment**

The natural environment rarely escapes damage when a large number of tourists are found. The quality of water and air, the amount and species of vegetation and wildlife are inevitably changed in one way or another.

**Environmental Pollution**

***Water Pollution***

Water pollution in rivers, lakes, and the sea may result from recreational and tourist transportation. For example, oil spills from cruise boats in resort harbours, untreated sewage from kitchens and bathrooms of island resorts may cause adverse effect on the aquatic ecosystem and reduce the enjoyment of the tourists swimming there.

***Air Pollution***

Air pollution from tourism development may result from excessive use of vehicles (cars, buses, and motorcycles) by and for tourists at major tourist attraction areas that are accessible only or mainly by road.

Shops and restaurants in Stanley's tourist areas installed their air-conditioners' exhaust outlets close to the local residents' homes.

***Noise Pollution***

Noise may be generated by a concentration of tourists, vehicles, aircraft and motor boats. Sometimes certain types of tourist attractions such as amusement parks, car or motorcycle races may generate noise that is unacceptable and irritating.

***Visual Pollution***

Visual pollution may result from several sources:

- Poorly designed buildings, e.g. hotels that are not compatible with local architectural style or environment
- Use of large and ugly advertising signs
- Overhead utility (electricity and telephone) lines and poles
  Illegal parking
- Buildings obstructing scenic views
- Poor maintenance of buildings

***Waste disposal problems***

Littering is a common problem in tourist areas. It is due to a large number of people using one area and the kind of activity they engage, like picnicking.

***Impact of Vegetation***

Overuse of fragile natural environment by tourists may lead to ecological damage in the following ways :

- Collection of flowers, plants and fungi may change the species composition
- Tourists trample the vegetation in parks and conservation areas
- Hikers and campers cut trees to make campfires and soil erosion results from overuse of hiking

***Impact on wildlife***

- Wildlife loses their natural habitats wherever tourist facilities and roads are constructed
- Feeding and breeding patterns of animals may change as they are prevented from hunting or breeding in usual places

***Impacts on geology***

- Tourists like to collect or buy minerals, rocks and fossils as souvenirs of their trips
- Inscriptions, carving or painting of initials and names leave unpleasant scars on rock

***Damage to archaeological and historic sites***

Overuse or misuse of environmentally fragile archaeological and historic sites may cause damage to these features through excessive wear, increased humidity, vibration, vandalism, graffiti writing, etc.

**A framework for the study of tourism and environment stress**

| *Stressor activities* | *Stress* | *Primary response environment* | *Secondary response (reaction) human* |
|---|---|---|---|
| ***Permanent environmental restructuring***<br>**(a)** ***Major construction activity***<br>- urban expansion<br>- transport network<br>- tourist facilities<br>- marinas, ski-lifts, sea walls<br>**(b)** ***Change in land use***<br>- expansion of recreational lands | Restructuring of local environments<br>- expansion of built environments<br>- lands being taken out of primary production | Change in habitat<br>Change in population of biological species<br>Change in health and welfare of man<br>Change in visual quality | *Individual* – impact on aesthetic values<br>Collective measures<br>- expenditures on environmental improvements<br>- expenditures on management of conservation<br>- designation of wildlife conservation and national parks<br>- controls on access to recreational lands |
| ***Generation of waste residuals***<br>- urbanisation<br>- transportation | Pollution loadings<br>- emissions<br>- effluent discharges<br>- solid waste disposal<br>- noise (traffic, aircraft) | ***Change in quality of environmental media***<br>- air<br>- water<br>- soil<br>Health of biological organisms<br>Health of humans | ***Individual defensive measures***<br>Locals<br>- air conditioning<br>- recycling of waste materials<br>- protests and attitude change<br>Tourists<br>- change of attitude towards the environment<br>- decline in tourist revenues |

*(Contd.)*

*(Contd. Table )*

| *Stressor activities* | *Stress* | *Primary response environment* | *Secondary response (reaction) human* |
|---|---|---|---|
| | | | ***Collective defensive measures***<br>- expenditure of pollution abatement by tourist-related industries<br>- clean-up of rivers, beaches |
| ***Tourist activities***<br>- skiing<br>- walking<br>- hunting<br>- trial bike riding<br>- collecting | Trampling of vegetation and soils<br>Destruction of species | Change in habitat<br>Change in population of biological species | ***Collective defensive measures***<br>- expenditure on management of conservation<br>- designation of wildlife conservation and national parks<br>- controls on access to recreational lands |
| *Effects on population dynamics*<br>- Population growth | Population density (seasonal) | Congestion<br>Demand for natural resources<br>- land and water<br>- energy | *Individual* – Attitudes to overcrowding and the environment<br>*Collective* – Growth in support services, e.g. water supply, electricity[60] |

*Source* : Organisation for Economic Co-operation and Developement quoted from Pearce, 1991, 230-231.

### *The Environmental Impact Assessment Process*

It has been agreed that limited environmental resources are being consumed by tourists and the tourism industry and in reality, the environmental impacts of tourism on the host country could be extensive. According to Romeril (1989), environmental impacts are generally categorized under three main headings: physical, biological and socio-economic (which includes cultural). Nowadays, both public and private sectors are becoming more and more concerned about the tourism impacts on the physical environment.

Environmental impact assessment (EIA) is often conducted for evaluating how serious the environment could be affected by new tourism development projects. It is believed that preventing the environment from being spoiled is easier and less costly than taking remedial action afterwards.

Although EIA is widely used for evaluating tourism impacts, there are no generally accepted models. However, it is important to note the followings before conducting EIA:

- To understand the motivation that underlies a particular EIA before an appropriate methodology is selected. It is because certain types of EIA may concern about the cost of environmental correction. If so, the EIA is mainly for evaluating the net economic returns of tourism activity and there may be attempt to retrieve some of these costs from the industry.
- One of the functions for conducting EIA is to compare alternative developments so as to allocate resources more effectively. That is, to maximize the economic benefits of a development and to minimize the negative environmental impacts.
- Another function of EIA is to raise the profile of environmental issues.

**Green's Checklist of the Environmental Impacts Caused by Tourism**

**The Natural Environment**

*(a) Changes in floral and faunal species composition*

(i) Disruption of breeding habits

(ii) Killing of animals through hunting

(iii) Killing of animals in order to supply goods for the souvenir trade

(iv) Inward or outward migration of animals

(v) Destruction of vegetation through the gathering of wood or plants

(vi) Change in extent and/or nature of vegetation cover through clearance or planting to accommodate tourism facilities

(vii) Creation of a wildlife reserve/sanctuary

*(b) Pollution*

(i) Water pollution through discharges of sewage, spillage of oil/petrol

(ii) Air pollution from vehicle emissions

(iii) Noise pollution from tourist transportation and activities

*(c) Erosion*

(i) Compaction of soils causing increased surface run-off and erosion
(ii) Change in risk of occurrence of land slips/slides
(iii) Change in risk of avalanche occurrence
(iv) Damage to geological features (e.g. tors, caves)
(v) Damage to river banks

*(d) Natural resources*

(i) Depletion of ground and surface water supplies
(ii) Depletion of fossil fuels to generate energy for tourist activity
(iii) Change in risk of occurrence of fire

(e) *Visual impact*

(i) Facilities (e.g. buildings, chairlifts, car parks)
(ii) Litter

**The Built Environment**

*(a) Urban environment*

(i) Land taken out of primary production
(ii) Change of hydrological patterns

*(b) Visual impact*

(i) Growth of the built-up area
(ii) New architectural styles
(iii) People and belongings

*(c) Infrastructure*

(i) Overload of infrastructure (roads, railways, car-parking, electricity grid, communications systems, waste disposal, and water supply)
(ii) Provision of new infrastructure
(iii) Environmental management to adapt areas for tourist use (e.g. sea walls, land reclamation, man-made mudflat in Hong Kong Wetland Park

*(d) Urban form*

(i) Changes in residential, retail or industrial land uses (move from houses to hotels/boarding houses)
(ii) Changes to the urban fabrics (e.g. roads, pavements)
Emergence of contrasts between urban areas developed for the tourist population and those for the host population (e.g. Mission Hills Resort of the Mission Hills Golf in Shenzhen, China)

*(e) Restoration*

(i) Re-use of disused buildings

(ii) Restoration and preservation of historic buildings and sites
(iii) Restoration of derelict buildings as second homes

*(f) Competition*

(i) Possible decline of tourist attractions or regions because of the opening of other attractions or a change in tourist habits and preferences

***Exercise:***

Ways in which tourism do harm to the environment in India?

**Environmental Impacts – Impact Typology**

The environment plays a vital role in the tourism industry. Among other things, it serves as an attraction and as a sink for waste residuals.

In order to assess tourism's impacts on the environment one can take various viewpoints. One can use a tourism typology and see what impacts are related to the different types of activities. Or one can use an impact typology and see how tourism influences the different types of impact. We will use the latter approach, because an impact typology is easier to construct.

We will distinguish between two types of environmental impacts of tourism: emissions to air, water and soil and changes in biodiversity.

The first category deals with changes in the abiotic environment, while the second one deals with biotic changes. Obviously, these two are related. For example, emissions can change ecosystem conditions, resulting in changes in biodiversity.

***Emissions to Air, Water and Soil***

Tourism activities emit waste to all environmental compartments, being air, water and soil.

*Emissions to the atmosphere*

The most apparent tourism-based emission to the atmosphere is caused by transport. In the case of international tourism, this transport first of all involves the movement of the tourist from the country of origin to the destination country. Because tourists cover ever larger distances, emissions grow. Moreover, a change in travel distances influences the choice of transport mode (modal split), favouring the aeroplane.

Apart from this long haul transport, tourism triggers other types of transport as well, such as the movement of tourists inside the destination country and the transport of goods needed to support the tourists.

Clearly, transport is not the only source of emissions. The heating of accommodations and swimming pools and the use of snow machines are other examples of the consumption of significant amounts of energy.

From a global point of view, the most important consequence of these emissions may be their contribution to global warming. Regionally, the emissions can be a cause of smog and acidification.

*Emissions to the aquatic environment*

The greatest tourism impact on water resources is sewage. First of all, sewage disposal causes water pollution through the usage of chlorine-based cleaning agents, which threaten marine life. Second, in many tourism destinations sewage systems are malfunctioning, resulting in emissions of untreated sewage water to the environment. Often, sewage problems occur when tourism flows grow faster than the underlying supportive infrastructure, including sewage systems.

Emissions of sewage induce eutrophication, which poses a threat to coral reefs, and can induce excessive growth of algae. Nowadays, water quality is constantly monitored in beaches and coastal tourism areas largely because of its importance for tourism.

Some other direct emissions to the aquatic environment are related to special types of tourism, such as boating. Oil leakage can have severe impacts on water quality and its aptness for human use.

***Emissions to the soil***

Litter is probably the most important emission of tourism to the soil and certainly the most visible. The problem of tourism-/recreation- induced littering is very old, as is illustrated by the ancient Dutch imperative: *"Laat niet als dank voor het aangenaam verpozen, de eigenaar van dit bos de schillen en de dozen."* (Do not leave, in gratefulness for your pleasant stay, your boxes and litter to the owner of this forest.)

**Changes in Biodiversity**

Biodiversity can be defined at three level:

the variety of genes per species;

the variety of species per ecosystem

the global variety of ecosystems.

Tourism affects each of these levels. At the positive side, it may contribute to more protection of species or ecosystems. The entrance fees tourists pay to visit natural areas can be used for better maintenance and protection. Often, maintenance of natural areas is paid for by the government in the form of subsidies. In many (developing) countries these subsidies are under constant pressure, which makes good maintenance difficult. Furthermore, tourism can trigger a change of attitude inside the host country, which may increase the value that people attach to the protection of natural systems.

Although tourism can contribute to better environmental protection, it can also have negative consequences, as discussed below.

***Impacts on the variety of genes per species***

The most direct way in which tourism affects the abundance of a species is through hunting and fishing. Each animal contributes to the gene-pool of a species, maybe even representing unique types of a gene. Extensive hunting has already led to the extinction of species. A lot of species are currently endangered as an effect of hunting.

Other direct impacting tourism activities are plant-picking and -uprooting, which cause loss of vegetation.

Somewhat more indirectly, tourists can influence the number of individuals of a species by buying biotic souvenirs, thereby triggering hunting activities by the local population. Exemplary are the trade in ivory products and products made of crocodile skin.

Perhaps the cutting up of natural areas by the construction of infrastructure also falls into this category. It makes the exchange of genes more difficult, thus hampering the formation of new genetic combinations. Breeding and mating can also be hindered by the noise and the mere presence of tourists.

***Impacts on the variety of species per ecosystem***

Tourism changes ecological processes and will thereby modify the species variety of an ecosystem.

Well known are the effects of tourism on soil compaction and erosion. Soil compaction involves the process in which soil particles are pushed together by pressure. Compacted soils have a less abundant bacterial life, and bigger soil creatures are expelled from the compacted soil. Moreover, compacted soils can hold smaller amounts of air and water, which means that they are less favourable for certain plants (decrease in soil vegetation), and that their surroundings are more prone to water erosion.

Tourism can also have an impact through habitat and ecosystem destruction. For example, turtles, which have sand beaches as a breeding place, are expelled when those beaches are used for tourism purposes. This is happening in the Costa Rican natural reserve of Tortuguero, where more and more hotels are built at the beaches used by turtles. Turtles are very susceptible to light, so their breeding at the Tortuguero beaches is threatened by these developments (Morera and Garcias, 1995).

The affected species can even be homo sapiens. Tourism affects drinking-water resources. Tourists use drinking water to take showers and baths, etcetera. In some cases tourists use much more water than the destination area can offer. For example, golf course in a resort affects the habitat of many birds, insects as well as a possible water shortage for the local population.

An example of more indirect tourism interference with ecological processes is the earlier mentioned eutrophication of water resources. The abundance of nutrients favours the development of some species (algae), while being detrimental to most other species. Oligotrophic ecosystems are very vulnerable to eutrophication. Eutrophication often hinders organisms living in oligotrophic environments, such as coral reefs. Of course, nature can handle an amount of organic waste before eutrophication causes composition shifts. For example, mangroves and marshes often remove a lot of organic matter from the water, thus leaving coral reefs downstream water relatively poor in nutrients. However, nature's cleaning capacity is limited.

Another example are the effects of littering. Bears in national parks have been observed moving to places frequented by tourists. Litter left by tourists also presents a great rat habitat (Ceballos-Lascurain, 1996).

***Impacts on the global variety of ecosystems***

Sometimes entire ecosystems are wiped away by tourism. Building new hotels near the seacoast is an example of an activity that can destroy transitional ecosystems between land and sea (for example, dune ecosystems could be destroyed in such ways). Coral reefs are often used as building material, for it is easy to get and cheap. Sometimes reef flats next to coral reef are transformed into airports.

Introduction of tourist infrastructure often involves the relocation of soils, sometimes destroying whole ecosystems. Evidence for such large relocations of soil can be found in Costa Rica. In the Tambor-project, comprising the construction of 1500 new hotel rooms by a Spanish hotel chain, large amounts of white beach sand from another beach were used to cover the black sand of the beach in front of the new tourist resort. The sand used for other parts of the project was obtained by digging off large parts of a river-bed (Hagenaars, 1995).

A graphic representation of the different forms of environmental impacts is given below :

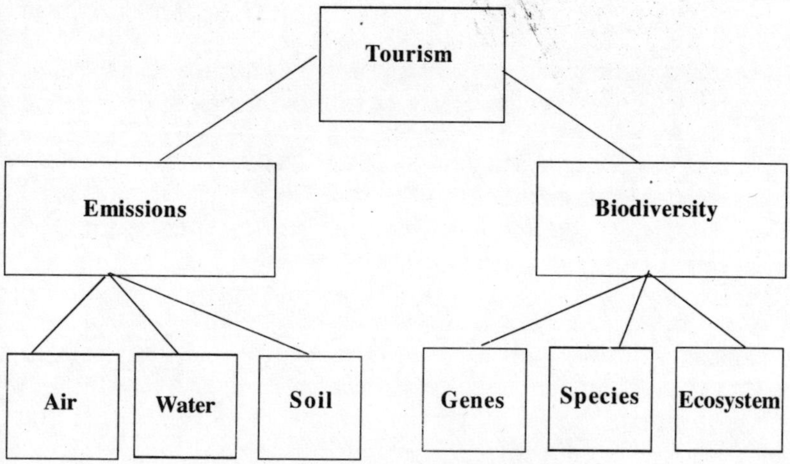


**Environmental Impacts of Tourism**

## Tourist Type, Tourism Type and their Environmental Implications

The actual environmental impact of a given tourist depends on many factors. The tourism type a tourist participates in seems to be of great importance. Possibly each tourism type has it's own specific detrimental effects on the environment. Furthermore, it is possible, given someone's personality, motivation and ability, to assess the tourism type someone will get involved in. Thus, the MOA-personality approach should, when linked to specific tourism types, be able to infer a tourist's contribution to environmental problems.

*A Simple Example for Illustrative Purposes*

Let us assume that tourist 'X' is a private explorer who is going fishing in Alaska. The affected ecosystem is aquatic, for fishing requires a river or a lake. The main impacts are loss of species numbers, due to the death of the caught fish, and change of species composition, due to the abundance of that fish' food, and the possible starvation of the species who feed on that fish.

## Conclusions

Tourism can have important impacts on both the biotic and the abiotic environment. Abiotic impacts arise from emissions to air, water and soil, while biotic impacts are caused by tourist activities such as hunting and processes such as changed land use.

Operationalization of the described method of linking tourism type, tourist type and environmental impacts is difficult, but it offers interesting possibilities for integration.

# 12

# Towards a Synthesis of Impacts

In the previous chapters we have separately described the economic, environmental and socio-cultural impacts of tourism. In this chapter an attempt is made to combine the major findings from these chapters. For this purpose two concepts will be used. The first one is the destination life cycle concept (Butler, 1980), the second one is the concept of carrying capacity. These concepts are useful when explaining the changes a destination goes through.

## The Destination Life Cycle

According to Butler (1980) every destination goes through a life cycle. This life cycle encompasses six major stages: exploration, involvement, development, consolidation, stagnation and decline. Each stage can be associated with specific economic, ecological and socio-cultural impacts.

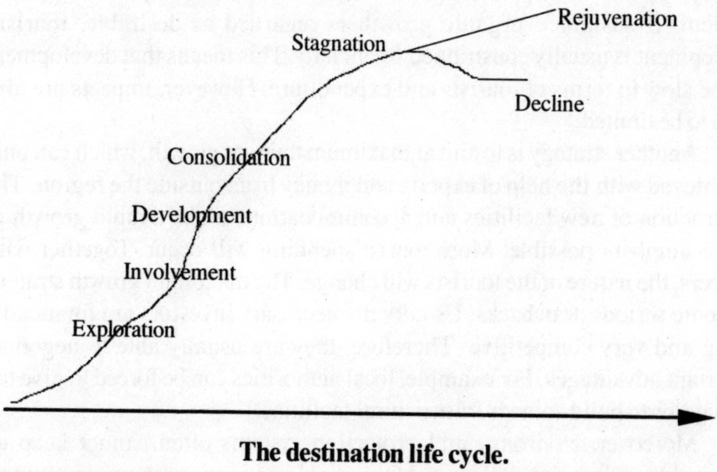


**The destination life cycle.**

*Source* : Butler (1980).

*Exploration*

During the exploration phase, drifters discover a destination. They come in very small numbers and accept local conditions. Contact between hosts and tourists is mutually satisfactory, so the euphoria level on the Doxey scale applies. In this phase no disruption of local society occurs. No tourism facilities or accommodation are available. Although relationships between hosts and guests may be intense, overall impacts are small because numbers are small. Usually leakages from the local economic system are small, since most food and building materials, to name a few examples, are produced locally.

*Involvement*

Once the local population notices that tourism can be (financially) beneficial to them, local initiatives may be employed to build facilities and accommodation. This is the start of the involvement phase. Developments in this phase are usually quite slow, because of social or financial constraints. The destination's destiny is still firmly in local hands.

The phase of involvement involves a marked increase in the number of tourists. Tourists of the drifter type are replaced by explorers. These explorers revel in local conditions. Relationships between hosts and guests, although a little more formalized, are still personal and the scale of tourism and its growth rate are still manageable. Economic benefits per tourist can be quite large, since leakages are small.

*Development*

Take-off for the destination occurs in the development phase. Local people see opportunities for further growth of the tourism industry. However, not enough knowledge and investment capital are available within the region to fully capture the opportunities. Several solutions are possible to this problem. If sustained organic growth is regarded as desirable, tourism development is usually constrained financially. This means that development will be slow in terms of tourists and expenditure. However, impacts are also likely to be limited.

Another strategy is to aim at maximum tourism growth, which can only be achieved with the help of experts and money from outside the region. The construction of new facilities and accommodations make a rapid growth of tourist numbers possible. More tourist spending will occur. Together with numbers, the nature of the tourists will change. The maximum growth strategy has some serious drawbacks. Usually the necessary investors are financially strong and very competitive. Therefore, they are usually able to negotiate important advantages. For example, local authorities can be forced to give tax holidays or to build some infrastructural facilities.

Moreover, environmental protection systems often cannot keep up with rapid tourism development. Many problems occur with waste disposal systems, such as sewage systems. It also tends to be difficult to control tourism development physically. Often, the main tourist attractions are natural resources. It is very attractive for investors to build facilities close to the attractions. Often this wish is not consistent with environmental protection policy.

Many things change in a socio-cultural way as well. Local control over development greatly diminishes because ownership and management is in foreign hands. Very quick development leads to a large demand for labour, which may induce immigration or disruption of other sectors. As the industry expands, people begin to take the tourist for granted. He gradually becomes a target for profit-taking and contact on the personal level formalises. This is Doxey's apathy phase. Cultural shift becomes apparent.

*Consolidation*

When arriving at the consolidation phase enough facilities and accommodations are available to receive early mass tourists. These tourists come in a steady flow and look for Western amenities. In the consolidation phase tourism has become institutionalized. The destination has become a product which is marketed by international tour operators. Local control has diminished even further.

In economic terms, both initial tourist expenditure and leakages may be considerable. Because of the sheer number of tourists, much money enters the economy. However, much of the Western amenities these tourists look for are likely to be imports. And much of the profits and wages earned by foreign employees and companies leaks back to the metropolitan areas of the developed world.

Local support for tourism development may diminish because serious social and environmental impacts become apparent, while the economic benefits may be disappointing. In the Bjorkland diagram, this means a shift away from the "active promotion" response to tourism development.

Unlike in the development phase, in the consolidation phase it is not so much the growth rates that cause problems, but sheer numbers of tourists. These may cause large problems of congestion and may overwhelm any local cultural event, indicating the irritation phase on Doxey's index of tourist irritation.

Because of the large number of tourists, substantial damage can be done to the natural environment as well. Transport emissions and emissions from tourist facilities and accommodations can be quite high, although the initial capacity problems may have been partly resolved.

However, tourist interests can also aid conservation of natural and cultural resources. This can occur by pressure from the tourism industry or by gifts or entrance fees from the tourists themselves.

*Stagnation*

Tourist numbers are highest in the stagnation stage, although growth rates are low. In this stage massive numbers of tourists come on fully standardized packages and they expect Western amenities. To be able to offer these, a destination often separates tourist resorts from the local population. For the tourists, a so-called "environmental bubble" is created in which the tourists can feel at home and safe. However, this separation may have serious consequences for the host population. Often, for example, use of beaches is restricted to tourists.

Contact between hosts and tourists is highly institutionalized. Hosts and tourists only meet at scheduled moments along the itinerary which the tour operator has planned. The increasing distance between tourists and the host population may give rise to the formation of caricaturistic images of each other. The characteristics of Doxey's stage of antagonism may apply, in which irritations become more overt and the tourist is seen as the harbinger of all that is bad (Prosser, 1994).

The economic benefits may significantly decrease. On the one hand, initial expenditure – at least per tourist – can be expected to decrease due to bargaining by the tour operators. On the other hand, leakages are expected to increase. Control is now firm in the hands of foreigners, who tend to repatriate important shares of their profits and wages.

*Decline/ rejuvenation*

After the stagnation stage the succession of tourist types, from drifter to organized mass tourist, has come to an end. Often, this means that tourists and the tourism industry lose interest in the destination. As growth comes to a standstill, so does investment.

Now several scenarios can be imagined, such as decline and rejuvenation. In the decline scenario, the destination does not succeed in changing its image. Tourist numbers will decrease and investors move on, using the destination as a cash-cow. They try to squeeze as much money out of it without investing in improvement.

So, in economic terms, benefits from tourism are gradually declining. People realize that their culture and the environment have changed irreversibly and that it is too late to do something about it. Doxey's so-called final level of tourist irritation may apply in such a case.

Another possible scenario is rejuvenation in which the destination tries to reposition itself in the tourism market. A destination may for example decide to offer more possibilities for an active vacation, whereas the focus used to be on quite passive vacations by the elderly.

**From the Destination Life Cycle to Carrying Capacity**

The destination life cycle is a useful concept for the description of possible forms and consequences of tourism development. It focuses attention on some important mechanisms of tourism development. However, the destination life cycle should not be looked upon as an inevitable process. At any moment adaptations are possible, for example by government policies.

An important contribution of the life cycle concept is its focus on both temporal and physical concentration. The first is related to growth rates, the second to absolute numbers in relation to the destination's resources. Both types of concentration can be analyzed in terms of carrying capacity.

**Carrying Capacity**

In the context of tourism, the concept of carrying capacity can be defined as the maximum number of people who can use a site without an unacceptable alteration in the human and natural environment and without an unacceptable decline in the quality of the experience gained by visitors (Mathieson and Wall, 1982).

The concept of carrying capacity is used mostly when assessing the environmental impacts of tourism. However, the concept is also applicable to other impacts such as socio-cultural and economic ones.

According to Muller (1994) five important dimensions of tourism development exist, together forming the "magic pentagon".

*Tourism development's magic pentagon. Source: Muller, 1994 251*

For at least four of these dimensions one can imagine the existence of a carrying capacity.

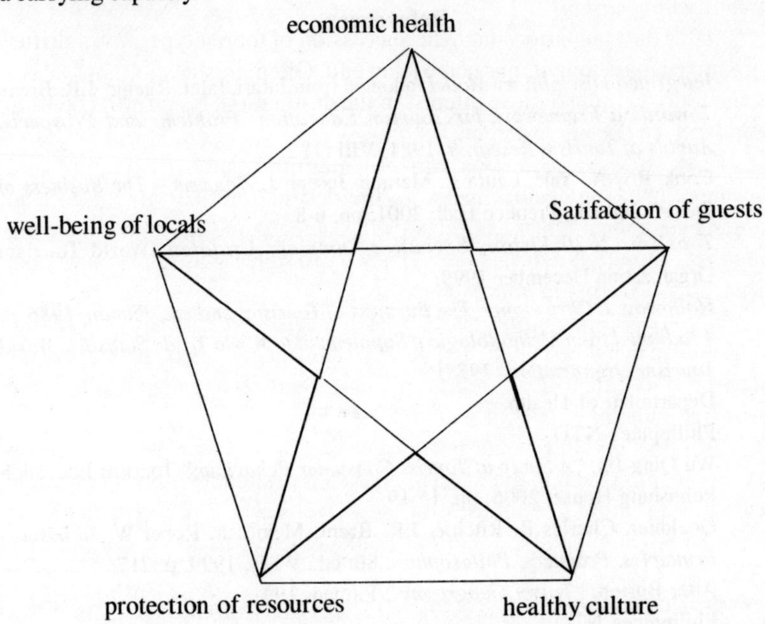


*Source* : Tourism developments Magic Pentagon Muller, 1994.

Assume respect for the economic, social, environmental and cultural carrying capacities respectively. Maybe satisfaction of guests can also be described in such terms: a "satisfactional" carrying capacity.

According to Muller sustainable tourism can only exist if none of the mentioned carrying capacities are violated. In practice, however, there appears to be a trade-off between the short term need for economic development and the long term sustainability interests.

## Conclusions

Economic, environmental and socio-cultural impacts usually do not occur independently. Often, they can all be linked to a destination's stage in tourism development. Crucial factors appear to be scale and rate of change, because these are intimately connected with foreign involvement and environmental and social carrying capacities.

In order to expose the inter-linkages between the different kinds of impact, the concepts of carrying capacity and destination life cycle offer interesting perspectives. However, empirical validation of the processes described in this chapter is crucial and will be an important element of future work.

*Acknowledgement: Reproduced With permission from Drs. Bas Amelung, Global tourism towards an integrated approach, ICIS, 1995*

## References

1. *Integrated Disciplinary Model* (adopted from Jafari, Jafar, Ritchie, J.R. Brent, *Towards a Framework for Tourism Education: Problems and Prospects, Annals of Tourism Research,* 1981, VIII (1) 2.
2. Cook, Roy A., Yale, Laura J., Marqua, Joseph J., *Tourism – The Business of Travel,* 2nd ed., Prentice Hall, 2001, pp. 6-8.
3. *Tourism: 2020 Vision, Executive Summary Updated*, World Tourism Organization December 1999.
4. *Holloway, J. Christopher, The Business of Tourism, 2nd ed., Pitman, 1986, p. 4 (adapted from Methodological Supplement to World Trade Statistics, World Tourism Organization, 1978).*
5. Department of Health.
6. Philippines NTO.
7. Wu Qing Jin, "*A Study of Tourist Consumer Behaviour,*" Tourism Education Publishing House, 2006, pp. 15-19.
8. Goeldner, Charles R, Ritchie, J.R. Brent, Mcintosh, Rober W, *Tourism – Principles, Practices, Philosophies,* 8th ed., Wiley, 1999, p. 217.
9. After Burton, "*Travel Geography*", Pitman, 1991.
10. Philippines NTO.
11. Switzerland NTO.

12. Cohen Erik, Toward a Sociology of International Tourism, *Social Research*, Vol. 39, No. 1, 1972.
13. Plog Research, Inc., *Leisure Travel – Making It a Growth Market Again*, John Wiley & Sons, 1974.
14. Plog, Stanley C. (1974, February). Why destinations rise and fall in popularity. *The Cornell Hotel and Restaurant Administration Quarterly*, 55-58.
15. Plog, S. (1987). *Understanding psychographics in tourism research. In Travel, Tourism, and Hospitality Research: A Handbook for Managers and Researchers* (J.R.B. Ritchie and C.R. Goeldner, eds) John Wiley and Sons.
16. Holloway, J. Christopher, *The Business of Tourism*, 4th ed., Pitman Publishing, 1994, p. 48.
17. "Travel is a Trojan Horse," *Oxfam 'Infinite'*, June 2004, pp. 8-9.
18. Goeldner, Charles R, Ritchie., J.R. Brent., McIntosh, Robert W. (1999). *Tourism – Principles, Practices, Philisophies*. 8th ed., John Wiley & Sons. Inc. pp. 637-644.
19. Maslow, A., *Motivation and Personality*, Harper and Row, 1954.
20. Mahmood Khan, Michael Olsen and Turgut Var (1993) "*VNR's Encyclopedia of Hospitality and Tourism – Push and Pull model of tourism motivations*" Motivation of Pleasure Travel and Tourism, Van Nostrand Reinhold, New York, pp. 798-810.
21. Extract from Wu Qing Jin, "*A Study of Tourist Consumer Behaviour*," Tourism Education Publishing.
22. Adapted from Du Jing Chuan and Zeng Ping's translation of "*Travel Relaxation*", Yunnan University Publishing House, p. 14, Figure 1.4.
23. Swarbrooke, John., (1990). *Consumer Beaviour in Tourism*. 2nd edition. Butterworth-Heinemann.
24. Leiper, 1990 (adopted from Cooper Chris, Fletcher John, Gilbert David, Wanhill Stephen, *Tourism Principles and Practice*, 2nd ed., Longman, 1998, p. 5).
25. Philipine NTO.
26. Walker J.R. (2001). "*Introduction to Hospitality*", 3rd ed., Prentice Hall, Upper Saddle River, NJ, USA.
27. Semer-Purzychki Jeanne (2000), "*Travel Vision: A practical guide for the travel tourism, and hospitality industry*", Prentice Hall, Upper Saddle River, NJ, USA.
28. Ward D (2000), "*Berlitz complete guide to cruising & cruise ships 2001*", Princeton, N.J. Berlitz Pub., c 2000.
29. Extracted & Modified from the Boniface Brian G., Cooper Chris (2001), "*Worldwide Destinations, The geography of travel and tourism*" 3rd ed. Butterworth Heinemann, ch 5. p. 57.
30. Holloway, J.C., *The Business of Tourism*, 7th ed., Prentice Hall, 2006.
31. Wu Xiao Huai, "*An Introduction to Tourism Studies*," Electronics Industry Publishing House, 2008, pp. 85-86.

32. Xie Chan Qun, Chen Cai, Xie Zhong Tian, "*An Introduction to Tourism Studies,*" Dongbei University of Finance and Economics Publishing House, 1999, pp. 165-166.
33. Bodlender J.A. & Gerty M.W. (1992) "*Guidelines on Tourism Investment*" 2nd ed., Horwath consulting, World Tourism Organization (UNWTO).
34. Holloway J.C. (1998), "*The Business of Tourism*", 5th ed., Longman.
35. URL: http://www.wttc.org
36. O'Grady, R. "Third World Stopover:The Tourism Debate ".
37. Davidson, Rob, *Tourism,* 2nd ed., Longman, 1995, pp. 170-171p
Additional information on tourist code:
Useful website for tourist conduct: www.tourismconcern.org.uk
The Nepal Tourism Board also inform tourists on some do's and don'ts through their website aiming to enable tourists to be aware of the local cultures and to minimize the conflicts between tourists and host communities. (www.welcomenepal.com)
GlobalCodeofEthicsinTourism(UNWTO): http://www.unwto.org/code_ethics/eng/principles.htm
38. Tourism the State of the Art.
39. Travis, 1982:260.
40. Tourism the State of the Art.
41. Smith, 1977 quoted from Pearce, 1989:217.
42. Cooper, Fletcher, Gilbert, Shepherd & Wanhill, 1998:170-190.
43. *Host attitudinal/behavioural responses to tourist activity*. Bjorklund and Philbrick (1972).
44. Doxey, 1976:26-7 quoted from Mathieson & Wall, 1992:138.
45. UNWTO website - http://www.unwto.org/code_ethics/eng/1.htm and UNEP website - http://www.unep.fr/scp/tourism/
46. Overseas Development Institute Suggested links: UNWTO website - http://www.unwto.org/code_ethics/eng/5.htm and UNEP website - http://www.unep.fr/scp/tourism/
47. ILO report on human resources development, employment and globalization in the hotel, catering and tourism sector, 2001.
48. http://www.unwto.org/code_ethics/eng/2.htm and http://www.unep.fr/scp/tourism/
49. After Bjorklund & Philbrick, 1972:8. Found in Butler, 1974:12. Quoted from Mathieson & Wall, 1992:139 202
50. Mathieson & Wall, 1992:149.
51. UNWTO website: http://www.unwto.org/code_ethics/eng/9.htm and http://www.unwto.org/code_ethics/eng/2.htm UNEP website - http://www.unep.fr/scp/tourism/
52. Mathieson & Wall, 1992:150.
53. Cooper, Fletcher, Gilbert, Shepherd & Wanhill, 1998:179.

54. International Council on Monuments and Sites (ICOMOS) International Cultural Tourism Charter website, http://www. international. icomos.org/ risk/ 2001/tourism.htm
55. For World Heritage List, please visit the website of United Nations Educational, Scientific and Cultural Organisation, http://whc.nuescoorg/en/35/
    56. Philippines NTO.
57. Bali Vision and UNEP website, http://www.unep.fr/scp/tourism/
58. UNWTOhttp://unwto.org/facts/eng/pdf/barometer/UNWTO_Barom09_1_en_excerpt.pdf
59. Cooper, Fletcher, Gilbert, Shepherd & Wanhill, 1998:133 22.3
60 UNEP website, http://www.unep.fr/scp/tourism/sustain/impacts/economic/negative.htm
61. Organisation for Economic Cooperation and Development quoted from Pearce, 1991:230-231

For more information on Hong Kong's heritage conservation and the revitalization of historic buildings, visit Development Bureau's heritage website "Conserve and Revitalize Hong Kong Heritage" - http://www.heritage.gov.hk/en/buildings/monuments.htm

*Acknowledgement: With permission from Drs. Bas Amelung, Global tourism towards an integrated approach, ICIS, 1995.*

*Acknowledgement: Reproduced With permission from Drs. Bas Amelung, Global tourism towards an integrated approach, ICIS, 1995.*

# PART 2

# PRACTICE OF PUBLIC RELATIONS AND CODE OF ETHICS IN PUBLIC RELATIONS

# 13

# Public Relations: Principles and Model

## 13.1 Objective

The motive of this chapter is to understand the meaning, definition, nature and scope of PublicRelations. Further, in the present chapters, some essential steps are discussed, which play a vital role for PR planning.

After reading this chapter you will be able to understand:

- the meaning of PRs
- the evolution and growth of PR.
- the Principles of PRs

The steps to be followed or not for better PR

## 13.2 Introduction

Public Relation is a management function that involves monitoring and evaluating public attitudes and maintaining mutual relations and understanding between an organization and its public. Public could include shareholders, government, consumers, employees and the media. It is the act of getting along with people we constantly come in touch with. PROs ensure internal cohesion in the company by maintaining a clear communications network between the management and employees. Its first objective is to improve channels of communication and to establish new ways of setting up a two-way flow of information and understanding. Subject of Public relations is a management function that helps organization to compete effectively in the competitive and global era. The job scope of public relations goes far beyond the skills of communicating. To be competent and efficient practitioners urgently need holistic skills and knowledge.

## 13.3 Meaning and Defintion of Public Relations

Public Relations means exactly what the words suggest relations with the public. Human beings can never live in 'isolation, we need someone to talk, and share our views. In this way we practice public relations from the time we take birth. Public Relations, simply defined, are the practice of doing the right thing of performing and communicating the substance of that very performance.The distinctive thing about public relations is that it is deliberate.

Technically defined, public relations are the management function that evaluates public attitudes, identifies the policies and procedures of the organization, and executes a program of action to earn public understanding and acceptance. It includes the followings:

- *Public Attitudes:* What does your community think of your organisation? Is the public's perception the same as the image that you think you are trying to project? Stay in touch with the view of your community, informally, by talking to a neighbour and formally, by doing a small survey.

- *Policies and Procedures:* Ensure that your PR objectives are in line with organisational goals. Should your organisation appoint one person to look after PR? Is your PR plan developed in conjunction with other planning? Has your organisation budgeted any money for its materials? Make sure that PR is a priority for your organisation and is treated equally to other projects and committees.

- *Execute a Plan of Action:* Don't just talk about it. Identify newsworthy projects, list the tasks required to get the publics attention, delegate these tasks, follow through, and thank the media and your volunteers. Do it and do it right. Other statements to help you gain an understanding of public relations:
  (a) It is not paid advertising,,
  (b) It is a communications tool,
  (c) PR seeks to influence attitudes,
  (d) PR is what others say about your organization.

## 13.4 Model of Public Relations

The steps to be followed in the process of public relations are as follows:

1. **Establish a public relations role in the chapter/division**: Needless to say, this is the easiest step in the process. At all times, however, the chapter/division leadership must be committed to the public relations function. Public relations must be treated with the same respect given to professional development, bulletins or newsletters, government relations or membership development. The Committee chair and members must have communications skills and enthusiasm.
2. **Define the objectives of the public relations programme**: A good tool to define objectives is a abrainstorming session. Consider including members of your board. A brainstorming session will lead to the development of public relations objectives on which everyone agrees.

3. **Define the target audience(s):** Whom do you wish to reach with your message? The response will vary, but generally includes members of the Association, potential members, the library/information science community, academe, related professional associations and the media.
4. **Define the message(s):** What is your message? What do you want to get across to any one of the audiences? Again, the message will vary.
5 **Develop the strategy (ies):** The strategies are a key element of your plan. The strategies are used to reach your target audiences and convey your messages, as well as forming the basis of your public relations plan. An abbreviated list of strategies might include:
   (a) Continually develop public relations materials.
   (b) Use a broad spectrum of media to convey the message.
   (c) Promote public relations resource to members.
   (d) Build and develop media contacts.
   (e) Work as the best source of information (credibility building) for the media.
   (f) Work to position the President and Executive Director as spokespersons for the profession and Association.
   (g) Coordinate with other staff members.
6. **Set goals:** What do you want to accomplish? Ideas may include:
   (a) Increase visibility for the profession.
   (b) Effectively promote Association programs and services.
   (c) Enhance the image of the special librarian.
   (d) Meet the public relations needs of Association units.

   The choice is yours, you can make your goals as high as you wish. The key to continuing your work within a committee is to maintain enthusiasm. Overstated goals can drain a committee of valuable energy from trying to reach the stars.
7. **Coordinate with other timetables or appropriate people**: To be effective in your role as a public relations committee chair, you must know what is happening within your unit. In speaking with chapter/division public relations chairs, a frequent complaint is, "I didn't know the event was planned."

   Two major mistakes in public relations programming is not knowing what the other committee chairs have planned and not allowing adequate time to execute your plan. The chief responsibility of the public relations chair, in order to be successful, is to communicate. Ask questions. You must know what is happening or planned. Beyond getting the information you must build your credibility for obtaining the information you need to operate. Build your respect and with any luck at all, the professional development chair will call you and say, "We need your help in promoting the workshop." Part of this access should be established when the board creates the committee.

8. **Prepare a written plan and timetable**: Have a written plan complete with deadline dates. The best plans are yearly, but implement what is most effective given your constraints.

   Edward Bernays, the public relations pioneer, lamented how loosely the term public relations is used. To illustrate his concern, Bernays told about a young woman who approached him for a career advice. He asked her what she did for living. "I'm in public relations," she said. He pressed her for details, and she explained that she handed out flyers (brochures). It's unfortunate, but the term, public relations sometimes is used loosely. Some people think that it is just about good communication skills, talking, and smiling prettily to make people feel good. The fact, however, is that public relations goes far beyond good interpersonal skills. For some individual public relations practitioners, public relation revolves around the following:

   - Public Relations = Advertising
   - Public Relations = Press Agency
   - Public Relations = Sales Promotion
   - Public Relations = Communication

   This all is just a part of what public relations constitutes, industry is growing all over the world, one should be aware of all aspects related to it. A recent trend is to look at public relations in terms of an organization's reputation. A personal favourite is that a public relations is 'the management of reputation'. A public relations personnel is responsible for the communication between an organization and its key stakeholders. In the case of technical marketing, this includes communications relating to products and technologies as well as the corporate values of the organization. Public relations are thus a strategic function, which concerns management at the highest level, employing tactical tools in order to implement defined strategies. For some public relations help an organization and its public to adapt mutually to each other. Public relations helps organizations to effectively interact and communicate with their publics.

   Four steps are necessary for public relations to accomplish goals:

- *Identify Existing Relationships*

  In modern society, institutions have many relationships. A college, for example, has relationships with the students, its faculty, its staff, its alumni, its benefactors, the neighbourhood, the community, the legislature, other colleges, and perhaps unions. The list could go on and on. Each of the constituencies is called public relations.

- *Evaluate the Relationships*

  Through research, the public relations practitioner studies these relationships to determine how well they are working. This evaluation is an ongoing progress. An organization may have excellent relations with the government one year and win major appropriations, after a scandal related to the organizations tax frauds the next year, government may be downright unfriendly. So situation can change at any time, professionals need to work hard and save image of the organization, even before something happens.

- *Design Policies to Improve Relationships*
  The job of public relations people is to recommend policies to the top management to make these relationships work better, not only for the organization but also for the partners in each relationship.

- *Implement the Policies*
  Public relations are not a mass medium itself, but PR uses the media as tools to accomplish its goals. The number of people in most of the publics with each public relations practitioners need to communicate is so large that it can be reached only through mass media. The influence of public relations on the mass media is extensive. Half of the news in many newspapers originates with the formal statements or news releases from organizations that want something in the paper. It is the same with radio, television, and even with the Internet.
  Misconceptions about public relations include the idea that it is a one-way object for institutions and individuals to communicate to the public. But the good practice of public relations seeks two-way communication between and among all the people and institutions concerned with an issue. Public relation affects almost everyone who has contact with other human beings. All of us in one way or another practice public relations daily. For an organization, every phone call, every letter, every e-mail and every face-to-face encounter is a public relations event.
  Unfortunately, public relations is not yet a profession like law, accounting or medicine, in which all practitioners are trained, licensed and supervised. Nothing prevents someone with little or no formal training from hanging out a shingle as a public relations specialist. Such quacks humiliate professionals in the field and bring bad name to the profession. Public relations in North America are totally different than that in India. Canadian Public Relations Society, works on set parameters. For becoming public relations professional, one is required to have specialized education and training in public relations. After finishing education, one is required to practice public relations for five years, after that only the individual can appear for the accreditation test and if he or she qualifies the test then only accreditation certificate is issued. Public Relations Society of India should also change the parameters of enrolling professionals as its members, and it should

also conduct events at least quarterly to keep practitioners aware of the changes in the industry, and this will even give them an opportunity to develop their network.

## 13.5 Basic Elements of Public Relations

1. Objective: What do you want to accomplish?
2. Target: Who do you want to reach?
3. Position: How do you wish to be perceived?
4. Strategy: How do you want to inform your target audience?
5. Action Plan: How do you accomplish your strategy?
6. Results: Have you succeeded?
7. Evaluate: What happened? How can you improve in the future?

## 13.6 Evolution of Public Relations

The increasing incidence of change, conflict, and confrontation in society is yet another reason for the evolution of public relations: Women's rights; senior citizen's rights; consumerism; environmental awareness; layoffs and resultant unhappiness in society. With the growth of Internet, activities have become increasingly more daring and effective. Although modern public relations are a 20th century phenomenon, its roots are ancient. Leaders in every society throughout the civilization understood the importance of influencing public opinion through persuasion. For example, archaeologists found a farm bulletin in Iraq that told farmers of 1800 B.C. the latest techniques of harvesting, sowing and irrigating. It was a good example of planned persuasion to, reach a specific public for a particular purpose; in other words, public relations. Later on, the Greeks put a high premium on communication skills. The best speakers, in fact, were generally elected to leadership positions. When modem day public relations experts agree to represent repressive governments in Serbia or Nazi sympathizers in Switzerland or when Republican communications experts like Dick Morris switch sides to join Democrats like Bill Clinton and then reveal confidential campaign secrets, these ethical questions remain very much a focus of modern public relations.

Even the Catholic Church had a hand in the creation of public relations. In the 1600s under the leadership of Pope George XV, the church established a college of propaganda to "help propagate the faith." In those days the term propaganda did not have a negative connotation; the church simply wanted to inform the public about the advantages of Catholicism. Indeed, the roots of public relations lie in the -development of propaganda, defined neutrally.

- *Into the 1800s*

The practice of public relations continued to percolate in the 19th century. Among the most prominent, yet negative, antecedents of modem public relations that took hold in the 1800s was Press agency. Phineas, T.

Barnum was one of the notorious practitioners of this art. Most public relations professionals would rather not talk about P.T. Barnum as an industry pioneer. To some Barnum was a huckster, whose motto might well have been, 'The Public Be Fooled.' Some defenders suggest that while Barnum may have had some faults, he nonetheless was respected in his time as a user of written and verbal public relations techniques. Like him or not, Barnum was a master publicist. He purposely gave his star performers short names-for instance, Tom Thumb; and Jenny Lind, the singer-so that they could easily fit into the headlines of narrow newspaper columns. In this modern era, some practitioners do practice his techniques.

Barnum's methods to achieve publicity for his museum attractions and circus act pales in comparison with the efforts of today's entertainment publicist. Public relations are also required to generate results, because it is also perceived as part of marketing mix. Today's entertainment publicists play hardball. Indeed modern-day press agents have become so powerful that some publications derisively label public relations practitioners as press agents.

- *Emergence of the Robber Barons*

The American Industrial Revolution ushered in many things at the turn of the century, not the least of which was the growth of public relations. The 20th century began with small mills, and localized business, which served as the hub of the economy, giving way to massive factories. Limited transportation and communications facilities became nation-wide railroad lines and communications wires. Big business took over, and the businessman was the king. Consumer rights were not there to protect the interest of consumers. At that time industry was interested in earning more profit rather than improving the standards of living for the citizens. Railroad owners such as William Vanderbilt, the bankers such as J.P. Morgan, oil magnates such as John D. Rockefeller, ruled the fortunes of thousands and others. The famous and perhaps sarcastic response of Vanderbilt when questioned about the public's reaction to his closing of the New York Central Railroad: "The public be dammed".

Americans cursed Vanderbilt and his type as robber tycoons that cared little for the society. Most of the dependents on these industrialists for their livelihood felt powerless to rebel, the seeds of discontent were being sown liberally throughout the culture. It was just a matter of time before the robber barons got their deserved penalty.

- *Enter the Muckrakers*

When the axe fell on the robber barons, it came in the form of criticism from a feisty group of journalists dubbed "muckrakers." The "much" that these reporters and editors "raked" was related to the scandalous operations of America's business enterprises. Journalistic shock stories soon led to a wave of sentiment for legislative reform. As journalists and the public became more anxious, the government got more involved. Government began passing laws telling business leaders what they could and couldn't do. Trust busting then became the order of the day. Conflicts between employees and employers began to break out, and newly organized labour unions came to the force.

For a while, these men of inordinate wealth and power found themselves limited in their ability to defend themselves and their activities against the tidal wave of public condemnation. To tell their side of the story, the business tycoons first tried using the lure of advertising to silence journalistic critics; they tried to buy-off critics by paying for ads in their papers. It didn't work. Next, they paid the press agents, to present their companies position. Often, these hired guns painted over the real problems and presented their clients view in the best possible light. The public saw through this approach. Business leaders were discovering that a corporation might have capital, labour, and natural resources, yet be doomed to fail if lacked intelligent management, particularly in the area of influencing public opinion. The best way to influence public opinion, as it turned out, was through honesty and frankness.

## 13.7 Growth of Modern Public Relations

With change of era, field of public relations started changing the way of carrying out the business. It was clearly understood by the high-powered companies that individuals have responsibility to inform their publics. So the practice began to grow in every sector, as detailed below.

1. *Government*

During the World War I, American President Woodrow Wilson established a committee under journalist George Creel. The group composed of the nation's leading journalists, scholars, press agents and other celebrities, worked hard to mobilize public opinion in support of the war effort and to stimulate the sale of war bonds through Liberty Loan publicity drives. With this public relations profession got a boost. The nation was highly impressed with the potential power of publicity.

During World War II, the public relations received an even bigger boost. The proliferation of public relations experts in World War II to a growth in the number of practitioners during the peace that followed. Public relations were recognized as a tool to send across the message to the public efficiently. With growth of the new economies and overall development in the world, public relations got recognition, and are being used in most of the world.

2. *Counseling*

In the 1990s, the counseling business saw the emergence of international super agencies. Most of the agencies have a worldwide recognition these days. Latest to join the ranks of successful public relations agencies are those who specialize in online public relations. It has been quite remarkable to see the dramatic growth of public relations in recent firms. This will continue. Specialist firms in technology, investor relations, health, and government relations will continue to play important role, and of course there will be a strong need for local and regional firms.

3. *Education*

One public relations pioneer who began as a publicist in 1913 was Edward L. Bernays, nephew of Sigmund Freud, a great psychologist and a master of human psychology. Bernays was a giant in the public relations field for nearly the entire century. Bernays was a true public relations scholar. He taught the first course in public relations in 1923. He was the first to disassociate public relations from press agency or publicity work. Bernays wrote later: "At first we called our activity 'publicity direction'. We intended to give advice to clients on how to direct their actions to get public visibility for them. But within a year we changed the service and its name to 'counsel on public relations.' We recognized that all actions of a client that impinged on the public needed counsel. Public visibility of a client for one action might be vitiated by another action not in the public interest. Bernays was also at least indirectly responsible for encouraging the development." of another public relations phenomenon that would take an added impetus in the 1990s-the emergence of women in the field. Boost in Public Relations is due to:

- The growth of large institutions and their sense of responsibility.
- The increased changes, conflicts among interest groups in society.
- The heightened awareness of people brought about by increasingly sophisticated communications technology everywhere.

4. *Growth of Large Institutions*

The public relations profession received perhaps its most important thrust when business suffered its most severe setback. The economic and social upheaval caused by the Great Depression of the 1930s provided the impetus for corporations to seek public support by telling their stories. The conflict between the government and business is unique in America. In other nations-Japan and Germany most prominently government and business work more in concert to achieve common goals. In India, public relations is being practiced by the government organizations but it is restricted to the extent of public affairs, and this very function is not being served properly by the government organizations. Whereas public relations in the private sector is now picking pace and with the change in time public relations would also be considered as one of the best professions. In United States, many businesses, both large and small, complain that government over regulation frustrates their ability to prosper.

5. *Changes and Conflict*

The conflicts during the early part of the decade between private economic institutions-especially large corporations and various disenfranchised elements of society arose from long standing grievances. Women, long denied equal rights in the work place and. elsewhere, began to mobilize into activist groups, to seek justice and equal rights. Environmentalists, worried about threats to land and water by business expansion, began to support groups. Minorities, particularly Blacks and Hispanics, began to protest for rights. Homosexuals, AIDS activists, senior citizens, birth control advocates, social activists of every kind began to challenge the legitimacy of large institutions.

6. *Heightened Public Awareness*

Government played active role in implementation of rules and regulations in the form of action guidelines, senior citizen programs, consumer and environmental protection acts and agencies, aids to education and other laws. Business began to contribute to charities. Managers began to consider community relations a first line responsibility. The general policy of corporations confronting their adversaries was abandoned. By the new century, the vast majority of American homes had television, with millions wired for cable and another 100 million online. As a result of all this communication, publics have become much more segmented, specialized, and sophisticated. Public relations professionals have had to discard many of the traditional methods used to reach and influence these publics.

7. *Global Democracy in the 21st Century*

In the 21st century, with few glaring repressive exceptions, democracy is virtually everywhere in the world. If something happens in a civilized democratic country, the information about that incident spreads all over the world in just matter of seconds. The Berlin Wall's destruction was transmitted live around the world. So was the dissolution of the Union of Soviet Socialist Republics. In 1993, two longtime arch enemies, Nelson Mandela and Nicholas Deklerck, stood together to share the Noble Peace Prize as free elections were held in South Africa and a black former prisoner of the state became the President. Some years later two equally passionate enemies got together to hammer out a peace proposal for their perceptually warring lands. Even in societies slower to pick up the cudgel of democracy, there is change. The Communist China celebrates its anniversary by inviting Western business leaders to tour its new economy.

8. *Growth of Internet and World Wide Web*

In the 21st century, true two-way communication has arrived. Not only have satellite, mobile phones, faxes, scanners, voice mail system, videodisk technologies and all the rest revolutionized the information transmission and receiving process, but the emergence of the Internet and World Wide Web have radically intensified the spread of communication even further.

Internet is a powerful push media, because no one has any control on the pop up windows. The impact of web on public relations practice has been phenomenal. E-mail dominates not only internal communication but external communication too; with just a click of mouse user is able to send the message across the state and even across the country. Journalists now regard the Internet as their number two choice of organizational contact-just behind a human source. Knowledge of and facility with the Internet is no longer an "option" for public relations professional. It is a necessity, which is cheap, impressive, effective and now massively available.

9 *Public Relations Education*

Though in India, universities, colleges and other institutions provide courses in mass media and public relations, but the level of enthusiasm is not up to the required standard. More work is to be done in India and nearby countries to enhance the scope of public relations. Nowadays the western world is looking towards India, as it has a large market place, readily available for multinational organizations. If skilled professionals in the field of public relations were available then it wouldn't be difficult to place public relations into top slot. In business, the practice of public relations has become an integral part of the way companies operate. Therefore, business students should be exposed to the discipline's practical aspects before they enter the corporate world.

The practice of public relations in the 21st century stands as a potent, persuasive force in society. Clearly, the public relations field today whatever it is called and by whoever it is practiced-is in the spotlight. It is a highly paid profession, but to reach on the top slot professionals as well as aspiring professionals need to work hard. This field is highly demanding, and to fulfill the demand of the job, professional needs to keep on updating his or her knowledge to survive in the business, so it should be mandatory for every professional to undergo training.

The *advantages of PR* are : credibility of sources, lower the cost of advertisement, clutter of advertisement avoidance, lead generation, ability to reach specific groups and image building. On the other hand, the major *disadvantage of PR* is the potential for not completing the communication process. And also they may misfire through mismanagement and lack of coordination with the marketing department.

## 13.8 Public Relations Principles

Principles of Public Relations by Mitchell Friedman are as follows:

1. Public relations should support marketing efforts. But public relations lose its value as a truly objective force if it slavishly adopts marketing's orientation and language.

2. Public relations succeeds when it fills three key roles: (1) organizational conscience; (2) overseer of the corporate brand/reputation; and (3) manager of relationships with internal and external audiences. As such, public relations can serve as the ultimate bulwark against the inevitable excesses and miscalculations of maıketing, sales, and other organizational functions.
3. Education and training in public relations must be based on an understanding of the function filling the three aforementioned roles - not simply as publicity or marketing tool.
4. The opportunity to define one's work, as "public relations" should be reserved for those whose responsibilities cover some portion of the three roles identified above.
5. Publicity - the sum total of efforts whose purpose is to generate media coverage - is not public relations. Publicity is part of media relations, which is one of several major public relations functions.
6. The expression "get good PR" is consistent with a view of public relations merely as publicity.
7. "Creating buzz" as a public relations effort is also consistent with a publicity orientation. A focus on "creating buzz" risks diverting attention from the indispensable role public relations practitioners can and should fill.
8. Success in public relations demands strict intellectual honesty and integrity in all aspects of one's professional demeanor.
9. A public relations professional must have access to every aspect of an organization's operations if he or she is to be effective. A skilled practitioner professional possesses an insatiable appetite for information about the organization or cause being represented and,in general, the environment in which it operates.

## 13.9 Do's of Public Relations

1. Do respect reporters and editors.
2. Do invite media people to events and on tours of interesting facilities.
3. Do answer telephone calls from media promptly.
4. Do provide facts and figures when asked.
5. Do have your facts and figures clear.
6. Do get to know your media contacts.
7. Plan, plan, PLAN.
8. Do respect deadlines.
9. Do keep an up-to-date media mailing list.
10. Do create a stylebook.

## 13.10 Don'ts of Public Relations

1. Don't ignore radio and weekly newspapers as important sources of media placement.

2. Don't talk off the record—it doesn't exist.
3. Don't talk to a reporter unprepared. If you do not have an answer, don't make one up. Offer, instead, to gather the information and call the reporter back.
4. Don't become angry with members of the media. Angry letters or calls close doors.
5. Don't attack a newspaper for a negative story or for not using your story. Do investigate other reporters who might be interested in your story.
6. Don't badger or harass busy reporters. If it is clear that a reporter is busy, cut the call short. If it is clear that a reporter isn't interested in a story, end the conversation.
7. Don't say "no comment." This phrase indicates that you're hiding something.
8. Don't give up. Developing an effective public relations campaign is not easy or quick.
9. Don't forget to thank reporters.

## 13.11 Summary

Public relations as a field has grown immeasurably in numbers and respect over the last three decades and today is clearly a growth industry. In the 21st century, while industries such as banking, tourism,utilities, and retailing are vulnerable to recession movements; the public relations profession is expected to thrive, with more and more organizations interested in communicating their story. It is unfortunate that still in India, people have very less knowledge about public relations; it is hard for professionals to define to their peer groups, and relatives as to what they do for living. Indian business organizations think of hiring a charming lady in her 20's to handle public relations for the organization. Now is the time to change in this era of globalization, organizations need to come out of this sick mentality, and should foresee public relations seriously. There are no universally accepted definitions of public relations. Any book on the subject will list a number and add to them. For the purpose of this chapter, it is enough to say that the movement is way from definitions involving persuasion and towards the idea of two-way communication.

## 13.12 Self-Test Questions

1. What do you mean by Public Relations? Why do you think they are important in the society?
2. Detail the evolution and growth of Public Relations in India.
3. What can happen if Public Relations are not available? Comment.
4. What is scope of Public Relations in the Marketing and Advertising Age?

**13.13 Suggested Readings**

1. Belch George E. and Michael E. Belch, *Advertising and Sales Promotion* (5th ed.), Tata McGraw Hill, New Delhi, 2001.
2. Osborn, Michael and Suzanne Osborn, Public Speaking, *Biztantra*, New Delhi, 2004.
4. Sharma, Diwakar, *Public Relations,* Deep and Deep Publications, New Delhi, 2004.
5. Shelburne, Merry, *Effective Public Relations: A Practical Approach, Biztantra*, New Delhi, 2003.

# 14

# Public Relations: Tools, Credibility and Truth

## 14.1 Objective

The motive of this chapter is to understand the tools of Public Relations. Further, in the present chapters, some essential aspects related to credibility of source and truths in PR campaign are also discussed.

## 14.2 Introduction

All public relations professionals as well as all those working in marketing and sales should go ahead meet people, try to talk to them, shout jingles, have fun be cool, calm and patient. Carve out as much as you can do introspection after every such meeting and talk to your inner self about your achievements and try to find out what you missed and work on it. Move ahead, move fast with the spirit of winning hearts of all, use your charm glory, and always be presentable as people judge you most of the time on the basis of our looks. Your moderate style of presenting yourself as a product for sale may develop relations that could last very long and benefit you as a professional in understanding the human anticipations. Therefore go ahead and start working on your public relations.

We live in an age of dependence in which all of us are increasingly reliant upon one another for the satisfaction of our needs. The growing complexities of our society and the inevitable problems created thereby have tended to nullify this formerly concept of independence. Today few people are able to accomplish their aims without the help of others. My "guru" used to tell me, it's whom you know, not what you know that counts. As with most generalizations, this has an element of truth sufficient only to constitute a serious hazard for those who attempt to live by it. A good public relations person must know who, what, when, where, why and how. Otherwise the professional is working in dark, and this can have very horrifying consequences.

Nevertheless knowing people is a great asset and being known is almost equally important. It is true that you have to know others but it is not essential that they should be aware of what you really are, that is you have to portray different pictures of your inner and outer self if you want to be successful in this profession of performance recognition.

This should not be constructed as giving a blanche for a hefty expense account while wining and dining, and getting to know all and sundry. On the contrary, the important contacts are those made day-today in the normal course of business. Most valuable are rarely the most expensive, among these can be counted the local government officers, counselors, neighbours, friends, staff members and customers. Every public relations professional must remember that customers are the actual kingmakers.

From the point of view of Mr. Fixit for any PR person to be, the range of contacts should always be growing and the move of making resourceful contacts should never stop. 'One can never know too many people. Apart from the gentlemen of the press the complete public relations professional must know photographers, printers, contractors, caterers, designers, artists, travel agents, advertising professionals, display and-exhibition specialists.

When public relations job is so difficult even then people say "Wining, dining and mutual appreciation is perhaps, the most appropriate description of the profession." This isn't very hard. Most of these people come to your door or at least they write to you, looking for business. The secret is to establish and maintain personal contacts. It is amazing how many friends you can make in this way and how many more contacts the initial ones lead to. The contacts on the other side of the fence are generally more troublesome to define, and more problematic to define. However, the difficulty in definition is mainly mine not yours. Certainly you should know the opposition-not too well but well enough for mutual recognition and to pass the time of day. But since every business has it's own peculiar range of publics, which changes constantly, it is not possible to know all.

When you have defined your publics, as a basic PR exercise, you should then be able to start a list if contacts are to be made, beginning with your opposite trade associations, and through to typical customers or users of the product or service you are promoting. If you have mutual interest then make the contact worthwhile, the other fellow will want to meet you as much as you want to meet him.

## 14.3 Tools of Public Relations

Once the research has been conducted and the target audiences identified, the public relations program must be developed and delivered to the receivers. A number of PR tools are available for this purpose including press releases, press conferences, exclusives, interviews, and community involvement.

*1. Press Release*

One of the most important PR tools is the press release. To be used by the press, information must be factual, true, and of interest to the medium as well as to its audience. The information in a press release won't be used unless it's of interest to the readers of the medium it's sent to. For example, financial institutions may issue press releases to business trade media and to the editor of the business section of a general-interest newspaper. Information on the release of a new rock album is of more interest to radio disk jockeys than to TV newscasters; sports news also has its interested audiences. While a press release is an essential tool in public relations, it is one of many. It is usually the primary way you communicate your "News" and information to the outside world. A press release should relate some genuine news. It should be brief, clear, factual, accurate, thoroughly proofread and neat. It should answer who, what, where, when and why in the first paragraph and include information in descending order of importance. Name of contacts, phone numbers and the release date should be clearly indicated. Releases should be limited to two pages. If there is more to the story, other information can be added as attachments (Fact Sheets, Biographies or Brochures). Quotes are important in a release. Usually it's best to quote the head of your organization or the person responsible for the program being announced. Quotes flash out the factual presentation, lend meaning and color to the story. They should not sound "stiff." It is best to use quotes that express an opinion or a position. The release itself should be factual. Press releases can be written on election of officers, special events and programs, awards and publications, to name a few. Good press releases tie into local angles. For example, if your division releases a salary survey or local directory of special libraries that's news that might be of interest to an editor. Your news releases will be used if you gain a reputation for submitting timely, newsworthy information that doesn't need massive editorial overhaul. Be brief. If an editor or reporter wants more information, he or she will call you. Write in inverted pyramid style, because editors cut from the bottom of a story. The most important information belongs in the first paragraph, and additional information follows in order of importance. Always tell who, what, where, why, when, and how. Use facts, not hype. The typical editor sees hundreds of "Dramatic, new, State-of-the-Art Improvement" stories each day. Present the facts clearly and simply, and let the editor decide what is important, editors are hired to exercise sound news judgement. Use active voice, subject-verb construction and conversational language. Write in simple sentences (17 words is a good average for readability), with two or three sentences per paragraph.

Address news releases to the editor personally. Information that looks like junk mail usually ends up in the newsroom trash. One page is good; two pages is more than enough. Additional background information can be attached, but don't bury the editor. List a contact name and phone number clearly in the release. Generally, the contact and telephone is listed at the top of the release with the notation, "For Immediate Release." Make the editor's job as easy as possible—double-space your release for easy, clear editing. Use a wide margin for the same reason. Have someone unfamiliar with the subject or contents read your news release. If it doesn't make sense to your test-reader, it probably won't make sense to an editor. Include a photograph whenever possible. Even if the photograph is never printed, a good photograph may get your release a little closer to the top of an editor's crowded desk. When a photograph or other artwork is included with the release, label the top of the release "with photo" or "with art."

Place a typed label on the back of every photograph. Record the subject, news release title, and your company name. This makes sure your photo finds a home in case it gets separated from your release. Photographs can be expensive to reproduce in sufficient quantities to accompany a release and might not be used anyway. Some newspapers will never use a photograph that has not been taken by a staff photographer; others welcome an interesting, creative shot. It is worthwhile, however, to send most types of photographs to smaller, weekly papers. Always indicate on the press release that photos are available. Develop a standard news release distribution list. Include appropriate local newspapers (daily and weekly), radio and television stations, cable news stations, trade publications, and business publications.

Some professionals suggest sending out hundreds of releases; others suggest sending it to only a handpicked list of key media. Usually it's best to do a bit of both. Use judgement. Develop two mailing lists—a large, general list, and one carefully targeted to key media whom you will contact individually. If you want to send news releases to reporters electronically, first send an e-mail asking whether they want to receive them in that format. Some reporters are still paper-based. News releases should be faxed only when they must be distributed in a hurry because of their timely news value — not because you didn't get them done on time.

2. *Press Conferences*

We are all familiar with press conferences held by political figures. While used less often by organizations and corporations, this form of delivery can be very effective. The topic must be of major interest to a specific group before it is likely to gain coverage. Usually major accomplishments (such as the awarding of the next Super Bowl or Olympics location), major breakthroughs (such as medical cures), emergencies, or catastrophes warrant a national press conference. On a local level, community events, local developments, and the like may receive coverage. Companies often call press conferences when they have significant news to announce, such as the introduction of a new product or advertising campaign. Sports teams use this tool to attract fan attention and interest when a new star is signed. TV3, a Malaysian broadcast system, held an international press conference to announce its introduction of an interactive TV service. Hertz held two press conferences regarding O. J. Simpson when he was accused of murdering his wife-the first to announce that it would continue to support him as its spokesman, the second to announce that it would discontinue the relationship.

3. *Exclusives*

Although, most public relations efforts seek a variety of channels for distribution, an alternative strategy is to offer one particular medium exclusive rights to the story if that medium reaches a substantial number of people in the target audience. Offering an exclusive may enhance the likelihood of acceptance. As you watch television over the next few weeks, look for the various networks' and local stations' exclusives. Notice how the media actually use these exclusives to promote themselves.

4. *Interviews*

When you watch TV or read magazines, pay close attention to the personal interviews. Usually someone will raise specific questions, and a spokesperson provided by the firm will answer them. For example, when four people died from eating tainted hamburgers at Jack in the Box restaurants, the company's president gave personal interviews with the press to detail the corrective actions the company would take. Microsoft's president, Steve Ballmer, appeared in a number of personal interviews to present the company's position in a legal case brought against it by the U.S. government. Monica Lewinsky's first TV interview with Barbara Walters of ABC was a major coup for the network, as the ratings were among the highest ever recorded. (The interview just happened to take place during "sweeps") Peter Bijur, the chair of Texaco, met with the press to discuss his plans to eliminate discriminatory practices within his corporation.

5. *Community Involvement*

Many corporations enhance their public images through involvement in the local community. This involvement may take many forms, including membership in local organizations like the Kiwanis or Jaycees and contributions to or participation in community events. For example, after Hurricane Floyd created so much damage in the South, a number of companies came to the assistance of those experiencing losses. Retail Alliance provided Rs. 1 million in interest-free loans to small' businesses. Lowe's stores contributed Rs. 5,000 and the Franciscus Company, a Virginia Beach condo developer, donated furnishings from professionally decorated model homes. In addition, a local trade association raised Rs.53,000 for victims in less than one week. A flood in Venezuela, which killed hundreds, brought aid from governments and businesses from around the world. The media also devoted free airtime to aid victims by coordinating activities, announcing programs and food drop-off points, and so on.

6. *The Internet*

Internet has become a means by which companies and organizations can disseminate public relations information. Just as in the print media, companies have used the Web to establish media relations and government, investor, and community relationships; deal with crises; and even conduct cause marketing. Companies have used their websites to address issues, as well as to provide information about products and services, archive press releases, link to other articles and sites, and provide lists of activities and events. Other Internet tools, including e-mails and e-mail newsletters, have also been used effectively. It is observed that while public relations activities are increasing on the Internet, and will continue to do so, PR people have been some of the slowest to adopt the new technology. However, as more and more media people and PR people gain confidence, the Internet will become a major source of public relations activities. Other methods of distributing information include photo kits, by lined articles (signed by the firm), speeches, and trade shows. Of course, the specific mode of distribution is determined by the nature of the story and the interest of the media and its publics.

## 14.4 Source Credibility

Credibility is the extent to which the receipient sees the source as having relevant knowledge, skill, or experience and trusts the source to give unbiased, objective information. There are two important dimensions to credibility, expertise and trustworthiness. A message is more believable to an audience if the source has credibility, which is why writers try to attribute information and quotes to people who are perceived as experts. If a layman comments that in the coming two months the present ruling party of India will make reshuffle in its party organisation, then no one is going to believe. But if the Prime Minister Manmohan Singh makes this statement, audience will hear and believe it, all due to the credibility of the source. Prime Minister is more credible than a layman, that's why he is being heard.

A communicator -seen as knowledgeable, someone with expertise is more persuasive than one with less expertise. But the source also has to be trustworthy honest, ethical, and believable. The influence of a knowledgeable source will be lessened if audience members think he or she is biased or has underlying personal motives for advocating a position (such as being paid to endorse a product). One of the most reliable effects found in communications research is that expert and/or trustworthy sources are more persuasive than sources who are less expert or trustworthy? Information from a credible source influences beliefs, opinions, attitudes, and/or behaviour through a process known as internalization, which occurs when the receiver adopts the opinion of the credible communicator since he or she believes information from this source is accurate. Once the receiver internalizes an opinion or attitude, it becomes integrated into his or her belief system and may be maintained even after the source of the message is forgotten. A highly credible communicator is particularly important when message recipients have a negative position toward the product, service, company, or issue being promoted, because the credible source is likely to inhibit counterarguments. Reduced counter arguing should result in greater message acceptance and persuasion.

- *Applying Expertise*: Because attitudes and opinions developed through an internalization process become part of the individual's belief system, marketers want to use communicators with high credibility. Companies use a variety of techniques to convey source expertise. Sales personnel are trained in the product line, which increases customers' perceptions of their expertise. Marketers of highly technical products recruit sales representatives with specialized technical backgrounds in engineering, computer science, and other areas to ensure their expertise. Spokespeople are often chosen because of their knowledge, experience, and expertise in a particular product or service area. Endorsements from individuals or groups recognized as experts, such as doctors or dentists, are also common in advertising.
- *Applying Trustworthiness*: While expertise is important, the target audience must also find the source believable. Finding celebrities or other figures with a trustworthy image is often difficult. Many trustworthy public figures hesitate to endorse products because of the potential impact on their reputation and image. Advertisers use various techniques to increase the perception that their sources are trustworthy. Hidden cameras are used to show that the consumer is not a paid spokesperson and is making an objective evaluation of the product. Disguised brands are compared (of course, the sponsor's brand always performs better than the consumer's regular brand, and he or she is always surprised.) Most consumers are skeptical of these techniques, so they may have limited value in enhancing perceptions of credibility.

## 14.5 Limitations of Credible Sources

Several studies have shown that a high credibility source is not always an asset, nor is a low-credibility source always a liability. High-and low-credibility sources are equally effective when they are arguing for a position opposing their own best interest. A very credible source is more effective when message recipients are not in favor of the position advocated in the message. However, a very credible source is less important when the audience has a neutral position, and such a source may even be less effective than a moderately credible source when the receiver's initial attitude is favorable. Another reason a low-credibility source may be as effective as a high- credibility source is the sleeper effect, whereby the persuasiveness of a message increases with the passage of time. The immediate impact of a persuasive message may be inhibited because of its association with a low-credibility source. But with time, the association of the message with the source diminishes and the receiver's attention focuses more on favorable information in the message, resulting in more support arguing. However, many studies have failed to demonstrate the presence of a sleeper effect. Many advertisers hesitate to count on the sleeper effect, since expose to a credible source is a more reliable strategy.

## 14.6 Truths and Public Relation Campaign

It's a phrase I hear over and over again from many entrepreneurs, small businesses owners and inventors: "I'd love to hire someone to launch our publicity campaign professionally, but we can't afford it, so I'm just going to have to do it on my own." Over the past several months, I have been conducting an informal survey among entrepreneurs and business owners who have contacted me about my services. I have found that due to their lack of information or knowledge on the topic, many businesses typically over-estimate or over-budget the cost of a prospective public relations/publicity campaign. During my PR consultation with them, I asked: "How much do you think it will cost to launch a solid, effective PR/publicity campaign for your product/business?" Of the 102 people I've queried:

11% - Thought a professional PR campaign would cost Rs. 10,000+ per month

32% - Thought a professional PR campaign would cost Rs. 5,000-Rs. 10,000 per month

39% - Thought a professional PR campaign would cost Rs. 3, 000-Rs. 5, 000 per month

12% - Thought a professional PR campaign would cost Rs. 1,000-Rs. 3, 000 per month

6% - Thought a professional PR campaign would cost less than Rs. 1,000 per month

The truth is you can get a publicity/PR campaign in all of those prices ranges. What you get for your money and how effective the campaign will be is the real question? It is true that the more you pay the more you get. But getting the most publicity/PR exposure doesn't mean you have to get most expensive PR agency or specialist. A good rule of thumb is to align you with a PR business that best reflects your business size. Most times their rates will be in line with your prospective PR budget. If you are a small business owner with two employees, you need not hire a high-dollar PR agency with dozens of employees. Find a PR business whose office size and capabilities closely resemble your business.

Case in point: there is a large PR agency in a fancy building downtown a few miles from my office. Frankly, we are not even competition to each other end ash; in fact we have even referred clients to each other. Why? They typically work with large corporations and implement campaigns of around Rs. 10, 000 per month. My business works with smaller businesses/individuals a PR/publicity campaign with my company would be about Rs. 10, 000 for an entire year and end; not just a month. Mechanically, the downtown firm and my business do the same thing when it comes to PR campaigns: professional media release composition; extensive media market research; articulate personalized distribution to the media;

months of media relations (article placements/interview scheduling/media request fulfillment, clipping/tracking of media placements, etc.).

Signing up with the big firm doesn't mean you'll necessarily get an experienced associate working on your campaign. So are you getting what you are paying for? A friend of mine who works at a major PR firm gave me the following breakdown of billing fees in his office:

*Interns/Junior Executives and end ash*; bill at Rs. 75 / hour (Very little, if any professional experience)

*Account Executives and end ash*; bill at Rs. 100 - Rs. 125/hour (1-3 years of professional experience)

*Senior Account Executives and end ash*; bill at Rs. 125 - Rs. 200/hour (Multiple years of professional experience. Agency decision makers.)

Compare those prices to many small PR shops or individual PR specialists. Many have started their own PR businesses after years of experience in the industry and typically charge Rs. 50 - Rs. 100 per hour to professionally launch and maintain your campaign. Many times, you can get a seasoned PR veteran who will work directly with you and your staff for cheaper than the "Intern/ Junior" executive rate at a downtown firm. However, one word of advice- when choosing a smaller firm or individual to do your PR, make sure they have the same tools that the bigger agencies do: updated media lists/contacts; personalized media distribution capabilities; professional clipping/tracking services to get copies of each of your media placements (articles, tapes from TV/ radio shows) as well as the intangibles of expert communication/media relations skills and professional pitching prowess. If they are cheaper, but don't have all the tools to help you in the best manner possible, you are probably better off spending a little extra money to make sure your campaign is launched and maintained correctly.

The major *benefits of hiring a professional* to launch your campaign are:

- *Proper Campaign Implementation and end ash*: Improperly composed or poorly pitched campaigns are the major downfall of many PR efforts. Poorly written, over-commercialized media releases; uncalculated, misdirected mass e-mailing of the release pitch; no follow-up media relations/media request fulfillment; etc. Your first impression to the media is a lasting one and end ash; make sure it's a good one.
- *Media Contacts and end ash*: Most PR agencies have established multiple media contacts over several years that can lead to much better and more numerous media placements for your campaign. Let there foot in the door benefits you.
- *Efficiency and Effectiveness and end ash:* PR specialists/agencies generate publicity full time, 8-12 hours per day and know the ins and outs, shortcuts and secrets to getting the job done better and quicker. Sure you could hang your own drywall or do your own plumbing, but do you have the tools, the time and the expertise to make it cost effective. I always tell my

clients, "You do what you do well, I'll do what I do well and we'll collectively move this business further up the ladder." One caveat when it comes to choosing a professional PR agency or individual to work with and end ash; signing up for a higher priced campaign doesn't necessarily mean you will get better results than a cheaper campaign. And the inverse is true as well. Over the past year or so, many "low-cost PR/publicity services" have begun to pop up all over the Internet. Ones that promise to write and launch a press release for as low as Rs. 99. They are low in cost and end ash because frankly many are low in quality. Bigger is not necessarily better, and cheap does not always mean a good bargain. If you have the time, tools and talent to launch and maintain your own campaign, you should definitely do so. If not and end ash; there are a number of public relations/publicity firms, specialists and services out there. Research to find the one whose services and fees match your business plan. Once business owners, entrepreneurs, and inventors learn more about their options when it comes to launching a PR campaign - many find that they can't afford not to have one. The truth is, you can attract the support of those external audiences whose behaviours have the most effect on your enterprise. But you must do it by first achieving the positive changes you need in their perceptions and, thus, behaviours. You'll get both using this strategic approach to public relations, which means your chances of achieving your organizational objectives are enhanced. It all starts with the *fundamental premise of public relations* shown just below.

"People act on their own perception of the facts before them, which leads to predictable behaviours about which something can be done. When we create, change or reinforce that opinion by reaching, persuading and moving-to-desired-action those people whose behaviours affect the organization, the public relations mission is accomplished."

The core strength of those comments lies in the behavior changes that can take place among your key, outside audiences. When those changes occur-and the combined perceptions of members of that important external "public" begin to move in your direction-it can spell public relations success.

For instance, with a strong factual basis, you convince area activists gathering at your plant gate that (1) you don't dump chemicals into the river, and (2) both State and Federal investigations found that to be true. When they finally clear out, you've limited the damage an expensive and long-lasting disruption could have caused. That saved the organization cold, hard cash.

What happened? You managed to change the perception of those activists, which, predictably, led to the change in their behavior that you desired. While public relations can bring real power to bear, and while there's a well-worn path leading to each success, truth is, you can't change perceptions, and thus behaviors of your important outside audiences if you are not in touch with them on a regular and meaningful basis.

That's why it's so important to interact with members of each target audience, and ask questions. What do you think of our services, our programs, or our products? Are you satisfied? Listen carefully for signs of a misconception or a factual inaccuracy. Is there a belief alive out there that simply isn't true? Do you detect a hurtful rumour that must be squashed? The answers you receive let you establish your public relations goal. For example, correct that inaccuracy, clear up that misconception, or get out the facts in order to neutralize that rumour. But how will you actually reach that goal? Fortunately, in dealing with perception/opinion, we have just three options available to us. Create perception/opinion where there is none, change existing perception, or reinforce it. The goal you established would quickly tell you which strategy choice you must make. But, of course, what you say to that target audience, in pursuit of your public relations goal, is crucial. Your message must be persuasive, compelling and clear as a mountain stream. It also must be credible and believable, which means truthful in all detail. It should also address the particular inaccuracy, misconception or rumour head-on and not allow room for any further misunderstandings.

Now, how do you get that carefully chiseled message to the attention of members of that key, target audience? I still call them "beasts of burden" because they carry messages from Point A to Point B. Communications tactics is the answer, and you have a huge selection from which to choose. Everything from open houses, contests, news releases and speeches to brochures, community briefings, letters-to-the- editor, emails, radio/TV and newspaper interviews, and lots more. Sooner rather than later, you will wonder whether you're making any progress. And the only realistic way to nail that down is to go back to members of that target audience again and ask them the same questions all over again.

The big difference this time around is, you're looking for signs that opinion/perceptions have begun to change in your direction. By that I mean clear indications that the misconception is clearing up, or the inaccuracy has been corrected, or that a negative impression is slowly turning around. Truth is, that's when this strategic, and powerful approach to public relations-supported by appropriate tactical firepower-delivers the altered perceptions and modified behaviors promised in the fundamental premise of public relations.

By August 1998, Clinton's goose was cooked. It seemed apparent that he had not only lied to a grand jury about the Lewinsky matter but also to the American public. He would soon be the subject to impeachment hearings in the Congress, and even his closest aides were crestfallen.

So on August 17, six months after the name Monica Lewinsky had burst into the scene, the president made a televised address before the American public. This performance may have been the least ethical of all. Instead of apologizing for lying to the people who had voted for and trusted him, Clinton chose calculated lawyerly language and a flat delivery. "I misled people. I deeply regret that." While admitting that he "did have a relationship with Ms. Lewinsky that was not appropriate," the president spent much of his address attacking Stars and asserting his own right or privacy-both popular themes, according to opinion polls. Understandably, after the speech, polls indicated that although 60 percent of Americans still approved Clinton's performance as president, a whopping 73 didn't believe he was honest or trustworthy.

Three days later, the president ordered assaults on suspected terrorist operations in Afghanistan and Sudan. In light of the half-truths and outright lies that had characterized the Lewinsky saga, some questioned whether Clinton had ordered the attacks simply to divert attention from his domestic ethical miseries.

## 14.7 Measuring the Effectiveness of PR

As with the other promotional program elements, it is important to evaluate the effectiveness of the public relations efforts. In addition to determining the contribution of this program element to attaining communications objectives, the evaluation offers advantages:

1. It tells management what has been achieved through public relations activities.
2. It provides management with a way to measure public relations aehievements quantitatively.
3. It gives management a way to judge the quality of public relations achievements and activities.

A number of criteria may be used to measure the effects of PR programmes. Raymond Simon suggests *additional means for accomplishing this evaluation* process, including the following:

- *Personal observation and reaction*: Personal observation and evaluation by one's superiors should occur at all levels of the organization.
- *Matching objectives and results*: Specific objectives designed to attain the overall communications objectives should be related to actions, activities, or media coverage. For example, placing a feature story in a specific number of media is an objective, quantitative, and measurable goal.
- *The team approach:* Harold Mendelsohn suggests that one way to achieve attitude and behavior modification through public information campaigns is the team approach, whereby evaluators are actually involved in the campaign. By using research principles and working together, the team develops-and accomplishes-goals.
- *Management by objectives:* Executives and their managers act together to identify goals to be attained and the responsibilities of the managers. These goals are then used as a standard to measure accomplishments.
- *Public opinion and surveys:* Research in the form of public opinion surveys may be used to gather data to evaluate program goal attainment.

- *Audits*: Both internal and external audits may be used. Internal audits involve evaluations by superiors or peers within the firm to determine the performance of the employee (or his or her programs). External audits are conducted by consultants, the client (in the case of a PR agency), or other parties outside the organization.

A number of other bases for evaluation can be used. Walter Lindenmann says three levels of measures are involved: (1) the basic, which measures the actual PR activities undertaken; (2) the intermediate, which measures audience reception and understanding of the message; and (3) the advanced, which measures the perceptual and behavioral changes that result.

In summary, the role of public relations in the promotional mix is changing. As PR has become more marketing oriented, the criteria by which the programs are evaluated have also changed. At the same time, nonmarketing activities will continue to be part of the public relations department and part of the basis for evaluation.

## 14.8 Publicity

Publicity refers to the generation of news about a person, product, or service that appears in broadcast or print media. To many marketers, publicity and public relations are synonymous. In fact, publicity is really a subset of public relations effort. But there are several major differences. First, publicity is typically a short-term strategy, while public relations is a concerted program extending over a period of time. Second, public relations are designed to provide positive information about the firm and are usually controlled by the firm or its agent. Publicity, on the other hand, is not always positive and is not always under the control of, or paid for by, the organization. Both positive and negative publicity often originates from sources other than the firm. In most organizations, publicity is controlled and disseminated by the public relations department.

## 14.9 Summary

We noted that public relation and publicity are significant to the marketing and communications effort and are usually considered differently from the other promotional elements. The reasons for this special treatment stem from the facts that (1) they are typically not designed to promote a specific product or service and (2) in many instances it is harder for the consumer to make the connection between the communication and its intent. Public relations were shown to be useful in its traditional responsibilities as well as in a more marketing oriented role. In many firms, PR is a separate department operating independently of marketing; in others, it is considered a support system. Many large firms have an external public relations agency, just as they have an outside ad agency. In the case of publicity, another factor enters in the equation: lack. of control over the communication the public will receive. In public relations and corporate advertising, the organization remains the source and retains much more control. Publicity often takes more of a reactive than a proactive approach, yet it may be more instrumental (or detrimental) to the success of a product organization than all other forms of promotion combined. While not all publicity can be managed, the marketer must nevertheless recognize its potential impact. Press releases and the management of information are just two of the factors under the company's control. Proper reaction and a strategy to 'deal, with uncontrollable events, are also responsibilities. Corporate advertising was described as controversial, largely because the source of the message is top management, so the rules for other advertising and promoting forms are often not applied. This element of communication definitely has its place in the promotional mix. But to be effective, it must be used with each of the other elements with specific communications objective in mind. Finally, we noted that measures of evaluation and control are required for each of these programme elements, just as they are for all others in the promotional mix.

**Self-test Questions**

1. What do you mean by Public Relations? Why do you think they are important in advertising?
2. Detail the tools of Public Relations and what is their role in the digital age?
3. Explain the credibility of source and importance of truth in PR campaign. What are the limitations of a credible source?
4. What is scope of Public Relation tools in the Marketing and Advertising Age?

**Suggested Readings**

1. Belch George E. and Michael E. Belch, *Advertising and Sales Promotion* (5th ed.), Tata McGraw Hill, New Delhi, 2001.
2. Osborn, Michael and Suzanne Osborn, Public Speaking , *Biztantra*, New Delhi, 2004.
3. Sharma, Diwakar, *Public Relations*, Deep and Deep Publications, New Delhi, 2004.
4. Shelburne, Merry, Effective Public Relations: A Practical Approach,*Biztantra,* New Delhi, 2003.

# 15

# Structure and Functions of In-house PR and PR Consultancies

## 15.1 Objective

This lesson would explain the structure and functions of In- house PR and PR Consultancies. Pros and cons of both PR Consultancies and In-house PR department have also been discussed.

## 15.2 Introduction

In a world of increasing complexities chaos and cut-throat competition, it becomes imperative for organization, companies and institutions to stay ahead in the race for success. One good way of doing this is to perform well and better than the competitors. Performing well is not enough so organizations and companies try to maintain good and mutually beneficial relationships with all their publics through the practice of public relations. PR is effective communication to achieve desired results. PR has been defined by many in different ways.

- Public relations help an organization and its public to adapt mutually to each other.
- Public relations is an organization's efforts to win the cooperation of its publics.
- Public relations include the deliberate planned and sustained efforts to win the goodwill of the publics through mutually beneficial, two-way communication.

## 15.3 Functions of Public Relations

John Marston, a professor of communication has identified four functions of PR. These include Research, Action, Communication and Evaluation (RACE)

- *Research* involves finding out what the various publics want from the organization. This involves finding out the attitudes of the public on a particular issue.
- *Action* means planning and finalizing programmes to address this particulars issue.
- *Communication* involves reaching the public with messages designed to gain understanding, acceptance and goodwill.
- *Evaluation* means finding out the effects of the Communication efforts on the public.

Public Relations play the role of a harmonizer of long term relationships amor g individuals and organizations. PR tends to harmonize internal and eternal relationships. Internal relations include employee relations. External relations includes client or customer relations, share holder relations, investors or financer relations, trade relations, Government relations, media relations and community relations etc.

In another sense, the functions of PR fall under three categories-man management, issue management and crisis management.

## 15.4 Organizational Structure of PR Department and PR Consultancies

Strictly speaking, there is no international formula which can guide the basic structure of a public relations department. The nature of the PR set up varies enormously if the organization is different in size, objective, geographical dispersion, nature of ownership, technology and competitive environment.

Business today has reached the open level of information age and announces point blank that "the management of change" is what company officials get paid for. The emerging trends in business and societal demands have thus opened up a new vista for PR to review its own status and position in the organizational structure.

In a model situation, the public relations chief should report directly to the Chief Executive, and the department under him should enjoy an independent status like the other components of management organization. This is applicable to any multi-unit or single unit industrial, commercial or even large trading organization. In the government or statutory department, there are age-old public relations and information bureaucracies who have to work within a strict line of control and guidelines.

## 15.5 In House PR

The ideal set up for an in house PR department envisages coverage of all aspects of public relations and communication activities. The department is expected to possess adequate infrastructure, resources and capacity to fulfill its assigned tasks independently.

Public relations departments employ specialists who do a better and effective job by identifying and anticipating attitudes and trends formulating plans and programmes, implementing them and finally co-coordinating all public relations activities of an organization.

Public Relations departments are organized on the basis of the functions to the carried out , on the basis of staff, or on the basis of the 'media' of ' communication', 'publics' , geographic areas etc.

When organized on the basis of media of communication a PR department has different divisions for print media, radio, T.V., films, Exhibitions, advertising etc.

For example - In India the government PR departments are organized as follows : The Ministry of Information and Broadcasting has several wings like Press Information Bureau, All India Radio, Doordarshan, Films Division, Directorate of Film Publicity, Directorate of Advertising and Visual Publicity etc. The second type divides the PR department on the basis of public so PR departments of many organizations, particularly private sector organizations-have such divisions as Employee Relations, Share holder Relations, Investor Relations, Media Relations, Government Relations, Community Relations etc. Some very big organizations which have branches in many parts of the country or the globe have PR divisions in various geographic locations as part of the PR department.

Also the organizational structure of PR departments differ on the basis of the size of the parent organizations,, the management philosophy, the policies and also the areas of operations, the size and structure of the PR department depend on the degree of importance given to PR by the organization.

*Functions of PR Personnels* - These include public speaking or addressing the various public, writing and editing publicity material, news letters, house journals, speeches (for others ) reports, articles etc. PR personnel deal with the internal and external relationship and various publics.

They also answer and deal with complaints, act upon suggestions and of course, they plan and organize special events ranging from annual day functions, anniversaries, foundation day celebration etc.

## 15.6 PR Consultancy

PR consultancy has changed dramatically in recent years but it is also getting more difficult. The reason is that the client needs are becoming more complex. The unprecedented growth of business, the globalization of operations, the shortage of highly competent professionals, the need for continuous innovations and specialist advice have resulted in the increased demand for PR. Consultants for the management and the in house PR chief realize that the consultant can be helpful but they must know how to use them.

The emergence of PR consultancies is a stimulating factor in the overall PR scene. It has given a healthy push to PR as a profession and provided a much needed boost to its outlook and performance.

*Services of PR Consultants*

The PRSA (Public Relations Society of America) has listed following services for public relations consultants -

- Establishing and defining of short term and long term goals counseling and funding the management on actions and policies that affect public relations goals.
- Support the marketing communications programmers including product publicity by way of news release features, case studies, audio - visual aid and media coverage.
- Stock holder and financial relations including interim, quarterly and annual report, assistance in conducting the annual meeting, liaison with financial organization.
- Employee Relations including any publication, newsletter, house journal etc. and information programmers for the employee.
- Community Relations- liaison with local media for increased and improved coverage, staging events such as pujas, opens house sessions etc.
- Government Relations, Helping build relations with local, state or central government by liaisoning with concerned govt. departments.
- Evaluation - measuring effectiveness of PR programmes.

## 15.7 In House PR

*Advantages*

1. Organizations having people oriented structures will require in-house PR more to promote and maintain good relationship with emphasis on people aspects at all levels of working.
2. In-house PR provides full time service with continuity of functions. They have direct access to decision makers within the organisation.
3. Management can easily ensure value for time and money spent on PR activity in diverse fields.
4. Relations with the media will be more direct which will ensure immediate feedback and prompt action.
5. PR personnel become identified with the aims and objectives of the organisation.

*Disadvantages*

1. As a seal of loyalty to the organisation many PR persons use unbiased behaviours, an essential requirement in the profession.
2. In-house PR people normally do not have, nor are they interested in knowing the good aspects of PR activity in other org.
3. Chief Executives of many organisations are easily bored by the slick talk and appearance of consultant while ignoring the in-house PR capabilities.

4. Employment condition prohibits doing away with inefficient PR persons and in effect they become redundant.
5. In-house PR persons normally fail to elicit information of value from various sources involved and are at a disadvantage pertaining to national or global communication matters.

## 15.8 PR – Consultancy

*Advantages*

1. Consultancy firms are like advertising agencies that can be dispensed with if found inadequate or inefficient.
2. They normally possess wider range of experience and exposure by working with many organizations.
3. Consultants can provide unbiased impartial service facilitating correct assessment of situations by the management during emergencies like strikes, natural calamities etc.
4. They will have location advantage enabling companies situated at distant places for maintaining line of contact with the government, media and other agencies.
5. Consultants are better equipped to collect a host of information from multiple sources which will be of value to the management. They are also able to reach across the world for global communication matters.

*Disadvantages*

1. Lack of continuous functionary is a hindrance to effective build up of reputation and attachment for the consultant.
2. Lack of sufficient knowledge about the organisation for which the consultant is working.
3. While dealing with the Press and the government a consultant will be needed to make frequent reference to the management for seeking approval.
4. Partial service and divided loyalties of consultants create barriers of communication for an organization.
5. Most consultants employ inexperienced personnel with low salaries resulting in half hearted performance by them.

## 15.9 Summary

The structure of a PR department depends on the size, nature of work and organizational structure of the organization. Services of PR consultancy are used when specialized services are required by the organization. Both In – house PR Department and PR consultancies have their pros and cons. Public relations is all about image building and maintaining cordial relations with the public. PR is effective communication to achieve desired results.

**Self Assessment Exercise**

Q.1. Discuss the functions of IN-HOUSE department.
Q.2. Explain the services provided by PR Consultancies.
Q.3. Elaborate the structure of in-house PR department.
Q.4. What are the various pros and cons of PR Consultancies?

**Suggested Readings**

1. Seema Sharma, "*Public- Relation*" Anmol Publications Pvt Ltd. 2005.
2. Caroline Block, "*The PR practioner's : A Handbook*", Viva Books Pvt Ltd., 2003.
3. David. W. Wragg, *An Introduction to Public – Relations*, Blackwell Publishers, 1992.
4. Paul Burton, *Corporate PR*, Reinhold Publishing House, New York.

# 16

# Institutional Public Relations

## 16.1 Objective

The chapter would allow an insight into:

- Corporate Promotion through P.R.
- Scope and contribution of P.R. in growth and progress of Corporate sector
- Relations with corporate public
- Public Sector P.R.

## 16.2 Introduction-Institutional Public Relations

The success in business sector and industry is an assurance to surge in capital flow, export growth and investments. The Indian market is gradually receiving recognition world over for its growth potential. With aspirations and vision for growth, the Indian corporate world is adapting fast to the new age market culture transforming rowdy and rugged "*lalajis*" into urban and astute CEO's, managers and directors. They have reshaped not only their business operations but also their attitudes and business philosophies. Apart from commercial interests, companies have started worrying about their public image to be earned in a cost effective manner. It has finally transpired that the "Performance", however good, shall not be "Recognized" unless projected continually with deliberate efforts. Increasing influence and interference of the marketing community at all levels of functioning in business has further demanded the Company-Public interface for healthy relationship. Strength of this bond of relationship however depends on the means of communication employed, other PR initiatives and *integrity* of the communicator.

*Corporate Promotion through PR*

Like an individual, corporate bodies can not be persuaded to adhere to any ideology. Philanthropy is one of those ideological concepts, which became

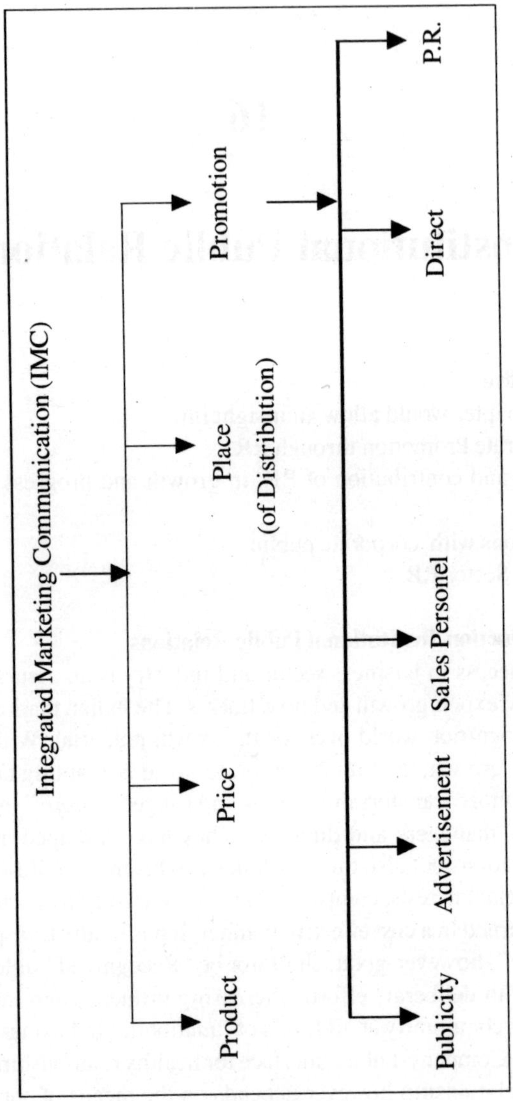
Integrated Marketing Communication (IMC)
Product
Price
Place
(of Distribution)
Promotion
Publicity
Advertisement
Sales Personel
Direct
P.R.

precursor for public oriented activities in the Indian corporate world, still struggling to adjust to the total shift in attention from mere profitability to near- "positive image". With widening variety of business, and stiff competition it has became imminent to appreciate one's public and serving their societal and psychological needs through the product or services in pursuance to the business ideology. Public Relations thrives on this philosophy.

Integrated Marketing Communication (IMC)

Noticed → Judged → Accepted

While committing itself to the organizational goals. The business bodies, companies, institutions and corporations, driven by commercial interests; and the non-commercial organizations also, are well aware that recognition in the market and favorable public attitude ultimately pay dividends and help perpetuate the business activities.

Hence, there is ongoing struggle for achieving business goals and public confidence, envisioned by the management. The yardstick set by the management remains the prime focus of marketing activities including promotional imperatives. PR also remains subject to review and evaluation in terms of identifying human needs, implementing PR programmes, promoting the organization, communicating the target public and maintaining the flow of feedback. It is a misnomer that PR is a magic wand and counting on the fruits of PR efforts is closer to groping in the dark. As a management tool, PR is seen more as a business breather, which is creating space for the organizations for sustenance through various measurable tactics.

## 16.3 Scope and Functions of PR

The corporate sector deals with varied public routinely for business purpose. This public in the form of shareholders, distributors, dealers, employees, consumers, financial institutions, fellow business groups, competitors, media, state administration and others are at some stage or the other, concerned with the activities and operations of the institution. Their cooperation ultimately paves the way for steadfast, successful existence in the market. The scope of institutional PR widens with the expanse of business. The nature of organization – commercial or non-commercial also decides the prospects of PR in an institution. Commercial organisations with profit motto are demanding and result-oriented. Non-commercial institutions on the other hand are willing to bear with sparse budget even while seeking maximum returns. Management philosophy and attitude remains crucial for drawing the bottom lines for PR functions. Public Relations executives receive guidelines from the management and also act as counselors to construct corporate image.

The corporate image is cumulative perceptions about the institution. This image management remains the primary function of the companies PR team. This perception is carefully cultivated through deliberate actions.

*The Image Management is achieved through:*

1. Identifying the current image among various public.
2. Determining the elements of desired image in consultancy with management.
3. Achieving consistency with management philosophy.
4. Building and projecting human face of the institution.
5. Conducting planned activities catering to different public.
6. Measuring returns and feedbacks in terms of institution's market performance and people's perception.
7. Increasing communication activities within and outside, to build healthy work environment. While all PR efforts are directed towards image management the PR department is entrusted with all kinds of communication activities.

*The tasks PR department undertakes* as primary or allied responsibilities include:

1. Building and maintaining relations with corporate public.
2. Projecting image (Image Management).
3. Enhancing communication flow.
4. Becoming responsive and dispelling myths.
5. Counseling management (to improve overall performance).
6. Conducting research (public opinion, product/services, etc.).
7. Planning and producing publications (house journals, brochures etc.).
8. Organizing institutional activities (exhibition, cultural events, seminars etc.).
9. Maintaining media relations (press conference, press notes etc.).
10. Providing promotional assistance (for advertising, direct marketing, sales Promotion etc.).

*Relations with Shareholders*

Economic reforms and liberalization have offered better opportunities of capital investments and returns; hence, there is growing interest in buying shares. To earn confidence of the shareholders the companies strive to perform and project themselves. To attract prospective investors, the company needs to work on its image and establish itself as a progressive institution. PR activities play crucial role in all these endeavors. The annual reports, information booklets, brochures, leaflets, correspondence with the investors etc. contribute to project the institution in a positive light and PR is responsible for coordinating, drafting or planning at various stages.

*Relations with Dealer – Distributor*

For the promotion or sale of the goods or services, the dealer- distributor is the link between manufacturer and the customer. The customer carries a lasting impression of the company taking cue from the services offered by the dealers-distributors. A dealer, say a cell phone Co's authorized dealer's reckless behavior, apathy for complaint about product/service or lack of interest in answering customer's queries would dissuade them to buy and recommend the product further. Here, Public Relations' role in facilitating selection of an honest dealer and training him into the policies, decisions, plans etc., gives an opportunity to build a bond of confidence.

The PR tries to maintain personal contacts, organizes dealer meets, workshops, exhibitions, training programmes, publishes booklets, magazines, floats best dealer award etc. These activities serve the purpose of affecting dealer's attitude, building his confidence into the company and its product/ services, apprising of the facilities/offers given them and to the customers through them, finding ways to understand and settle problems, highlighting the importance of the counter and after sale services and maintaining thereby cordial relations.

*Relations with Financial Institutions*

Capital is the backbone of any business and the company's demand for capital is fulfilled by the investors and the creditors. The creditors constitute a bigger group who affect the decisions of investors and other public in a big way. The creditors can be categorized into:

1. Development Banks e.g. IDBI, ICICI, HDFC, BIFR, SFC, FFCI etc.
2. Insurance companies (various plans)
3. Mutual funds e.g. Commercial Banks, UTI, LIC etc.

Another category could include:

(a) Financial Experts and Advisors,
(b) Share Brokers,
(c) Credit Rating organizations like CARE, CRISIL, ICRA etc.

These groups or service providers evaluate the status and standing of the company objectively. Publicity doesn't impress them while PR makes the relevant information available to them. Keeping these creditors in dark or providing wrong information could bounce back in the form of lost credibility or bad impression.

PR also contributes in publicity campaigns before and after the public issues released, preparation or draft of the annual reports, publicizing Co's plans, advertising, lobbying, liasioning, publication etc. All these efforts are simultaneously targeted to win the financial opinion leaders including experts, insurance companies, banks, and brokers among others.

*Relations with other Business Groups*

Maintaining cordial relations with the business persons and groups in the market is something hard to achieve, but professional ethics demand that in the larger interest of business, competitors and business groups must learn to co-exist without strain.

*Community Relations*

The corporate world is a social phenomenon. For this reason the corporate community can not afford to be indifferent towards the society. Here the ethics and moral duties come into play. The practice of the corporate social responsibility is regarded as the PR task where the company undertakes the activities outside its scope of business existence. The primary purpose of these activities remains earning goodwill, and support by establishing itself as a responsible company sensitive to the society.

The area of community PR can not be limited. It encompasses charity, endowments, scholarship, philanthropic activities, social campaigns (AIDS awareness, hygiene. etc.), support to state administration to solve local problems, adoption of villages, slums etc. for development works, special events (e.g. health, medical camps, hobby classes), awareness rallies (e.g. national integration) and other communication activities to convey the companies sense of belongingness towards the community.

*Consumer Relations*

The consumer culture has spread awareness about the consumer rights and the companies have intensified efforts to satisfy customers. Consumer organizations also work on their toes to redress consumer grievances while the companies are legally bound to serve in the interest of customers. The PR executives, therefore, gear themselves to achieve consumer satisfaction. Among other imperatives for success and image, quality of goods/ services comes first. Assured of the quality, the comparative status and standing isevaluated with the assistance of professional research and survey agencies if required. A deeper understanding of the factors affecting the attitude of consumers, conveying the outcomes to the personnel, production, marketing and related departments while simultaneously persuading the management to adapt to the consumer demands in terms of image, quality, price, availability etc., remains prime areas of PR functioning.

**16.4 Public Sector PR**

Public sector poses challenges before PR. Central and state information and PR departments carry loads of responsibilities. The activities undertaken by the PR departments in PSUs are aimed at publicizing plans, policies, and decisions. The PSUs are controlled by the government and are accountable to the Parliament and the government. These are not the commercial organizations but their performance has direct bearing on the public for this reason their activities and functioning are constantly watched by the government, the public and the media. It is also expected of the PSUs, that they maintain a balance between social concerns and commercial viability.

Keeping the sensitive nature of PSU's existence, the PR has to be extra careful and watchful. PR has to be vigilant about the following duties:

(1) Government interference and accountability to the Parliament keeps the activities, appointments, quality, and prices under constant scrutiny in public eyes. Irregularities or inefficiencies at any level invite criticism from all quarters. PR has to be alert to deal with such situations and keep the channels of communication open.

(2) Keeping the parliamentarians and policy makers abreast of the progress and problems to help them use the relevant information for future plans and policy decisions. PR facilitates this information flow.

(3) With a large workforce in public sector and being big service provider it is imperative to maintain good relations with masses, keeping them informed and ensuring their participation for institutional growth.

(4) Maintaining media relations, keeping an eye on the image projected through media and informing the media about all developments.

(5) Attending all meetings and deliberations to remain updated.

**Summary**

The Indian market is gradually receiving recognition world over for its growth potential. Increasing influence and interference of the marketing community at all the levels of functioning in business has demanded the company-public interface for healthy relationship. Strength of this bond of relationship however depends on the means of communication employed and other PR initiatives. The corporate sector deals with varied public routinely for business purpose. Public relations aim at building a positive image, while committing itself to the organizational goals. Integrated marketing communication is being done i.e. getting noticed, judged and accepted. The purpose is to have fruitful relations with the shareholders, dealer-distributor, financial institutions and other business groups. Community relations are important where ethics and moral duties come into play. The consumer culture has spread awareness about there consumer rights and the companies have intensified efforts to satisfy customers. Public sector poses challenges before PR. Central and state information and PR departments carry loads of responsibilities.

The activities undertaken by the PR departments in PSUs are aimed at publicizing plans, policies and decisions.

**Self Assessment Exercise**

Q. 1. What are various dimensions of the Institutional PR?

Q .2. How PR facilitates business promotion in the competitive market?

Q.3. Illustrate various facets of "Image Management."

Q.4. Describe the measures taken by the institutional PR to maintain good relations with various corporate public?

Q.5. What are the challenges before public sector Public Relations?

**Suggested Reading**

1. Seema Sharma, "*Public- Relation*" Anmol Publications Pvt Ltd., 2005.
2. Caroline Block, "*The PR Practioner's : A Handbook*", Viva Books Pvt Ltd., 2003.
3. David, W. Wragg, *An Introduction to Public – Relations*, Blackwell Publishers, 1992.
4. Paul Burton, *Corporate PR*, Reinhold Publishing House, New York.

# 17

# International PR, Image Building and Pressure Groups

## 17.1 Objectives

This chapter would give an insight into :

1. Facets of International PR.
2. PR tools for managing international face of business.

## 17.2 Introduction

Brodeur Worldwide, a global communication consultancy has taken lead in PR for technology companies. They don't advertise, they don't do direct marketing, but focus on exclusive PR work for the clients.

World over, marketing functions have realized the PR potential and world market for the need for communication strategies. PR in the blooming stage in India has already made strides in developed nations of the world, where corporations have wider networks and extensive business activities. With expanding markets and global nature of businesses, PR has range of cross-border functions and hence growing need for experts in finance, international business, marketing communication or a journalist to become PR professionals.

## 17.3 Approaching International Public and Appreciating Local Realities

The Indian markets are seen as one of those with greater possibilities of investments, but the market realities here could be shocking for those unaware of the Indian psychology .The markets here are complex and the business and customers both are considered calculative.

Although standardization of Indian markets is difficult to achieve, because of the variation in language, customer and attitudes from region to region, yet it is one of the fastest expanding and biggest markets. The consumer behaviour is therefore very crucial for the transnational companies to understand. The success of international PR would depend mainly on how quickly the companies adapt to the local traditions, customs, mindsets and systems.

**PR Works Abroad**

Understanding the local cultures help to plan for actual PR works of reaching and communicating public. China is a big manufacturing market and technologically advanced. They chose Indian market for dumping their products, were able to get returns since their products were reasonably priced and gradually Chinese stores were raised once the quality was assured. The Colgate Company devised a strategy to launch its product only after analyzing the market specifications in various countries. The packaging of toothpaste tube was green for the Pakistani market as the colour has religious overtones for Muslim community while it was kept red for the Indians.

The company PR for its international business across the globe shall have to realize the need for PR and its scope in respective nations keeping certain things under consideration:

*Factors to be Considered*

1. The starting point for PR work is exploring the possibilities of company's business and analyzing markets.
2. Market research for analyzing strengths and weaknesses of the competitors.
3. Demarcating the key areas of functioning and planning accordingly.
4. Conveying company's core culture and adapting it according to indigenous realities.
5. Understanding the behavioral patterns of the target societies before launching PR programmes.
6. Delineating PR plan for all kinds of public – media, employees, shareholders, distributors, etc.
7. Engage local PR firms or consultancies to coordinate.

When the companies are working for culturally and geographically diverse customers, drawing an international communication strategy to support the marketing plans remain the major task. PR consultancies offer their specialized services to plan and carry out communication functions and often act as nodal agencies for coordinating these programmes. These agencies help analyze markets, plan activities, design strategically tailored and positioned messages for each country and generate interest from the press.

Amongst other things, there are several *responsibilities the PR agency or consultancy or firms undertakes for international PR:*

1. Provide marketing support to the customer company.
2. Operate a worldwide network with regional subgroups in the native country.

3. Develop resources and systems for strategic planning and delegating.
4. Work on agreed upon strategies and adapt them to local needs.
5. Involve lead partners and work on each other's advice.
6. Conduct research and survey to measure potential and scope for communication works.

Whether it is the company's self generated PR system or the hired PR consultancy firms working as intermediaries overseas, the PR have to be *vigilant and conversant with the prevalent systems in the native countries.*

(1) An understanding of technological and developmental status of the societies would allow designing the PR programmes according to the need. Hygiene campaign could be successful in South Asian nations not in Europe.

(2) Media operations are both complex and crucial. All PR functions are carried out with the objective of clinching mass media attention to receive favours from media. PR has to understand closely the practices in the professional circles, media's news sense, attitude towards PR activities and the overall operations. While Indian media enjoys freedom of expression in countries like Pakistan and Bangladesh, media works under constant pressure and threats from various quarters.

(3) Knowledge of business regulations, legislations, legal impositions and ethical norms relevant to the corporate functioning, dealing and educating the company to comply with them remains the PR concern.

(4) An awareness about the social make-up, stratifications and dichotomies in the society help at every stage in business. The countries have group and subgroups whose demands and wants vary. Greater the diversity, greater the urgency for the PR to be well versed with group specifications.

(5) The pressure groups and the local communities' perception about the overseas companies remains a big challenge. The areas with dominant communities or religions or ideological fanaticism would make it harder for the MNCs. The Companies activities will be under constant watch and hence, the PR.

(6) The customs, mores, habits and attitudes are specific to cultures. While the communities differ in all these respects, the communication patterns also vary. Exaggerated facial expressions are part of normal behviour in western countries while its just opposite in the oriental nations. Standing closer to each other in a formal gathering is a prevalent non-verbal communication in the Western world while in South Asian nations standing too close is abnormal .

(7) Every language has denotations and connotations, proverbs, idioms, slang etc. Grammatical sense of language is insufficient to comprehend the complete meaning

### 17.4 Image Building and Pressure Groups

It is said that PR is 90 per cent doing good and 10 per cent talking about it. PR as a management philosophy has been hyped as a publicity activity. Though, publicity is one of the many functions PR undertakes to project one's organisation, it is not the only one. The PR does support the marketing plans (and this marketing PR is directly supporting corporate promotion and image building). PR is basically concerned with influencing the public, seeking their attention, building a favourable opinion about the organisation.

PR is often accused of projecting the organisations in a manner contrary to the act of conduct. This is propaganda-oriented communication not the PR. Since, PR is the spokesperson of the organisation, he/she good on all the communication activities on behalf of the company whether it is publications, event management, press relations, speeches, public oriented activities, advertising etc. All these functions are conducted with the objective of managing the image. The image is a perceptional entity affected by many activities. Affecting or influencing the public opinion, therefore, remains the core of PR activity.

Opinions are public expressions of active attitudes or opinions are activated by attitudes. Its a psychological phenomena where the interplay of persons beliefs, values, ideology together form the attitude. The outer stimuli (if communication on part of organisations) further guided by the attitude, half formulate opinions.

Though new PR activities have gone beyond image building and PR practitioners have long way to go. In the result orientation campaigns. The terms "image-builders" or "image-managers" still seen as negative connotations and after associated with propaganda. The constant criticism is that the image concept of the PR is generally contrary to the actual work done by an organisation which is against the very basis of PR work and of honest communication in PR. While it needs to be understood even the seasoned PR practitioners can not earn good image for their organisation if there are confusion, counter views of information and lack of knowledge, among the customers and non-performance and negligence of human sentiments law of the land and good standards on part of the organizations.

The people's opinion rests primarily on the goodwill, the organisation earns over a period of existence. Not one but a chain of factors ultimately keep the organisations in good stead. PR activities supported by performance and supported activity forwards the society have an impact on these factors, finally to be immerse in the people's subconscious mind, when it comes to action, subconscious mind of the public recollects and connects all those impressions gathered through self-experience, word-of-mouth, press coverage, grapevine, publicity advertising etc. and decide about the course of action – to accept, reject or ignore an organisation.

## 17.5 Steps for Public Opinion for Image

1. Identifying the Public Opinion among various public through public opinion surveys, researches, feedbacks and one-to-one interactions.
2. Locating the factors influencing public attitudes, individuals and group opinions.
3. Analyzing the complexity of the meanings of attitudes, the reasons and influences.
4. Devising a communication plan for each group of public in order to shape and reshape the image.
5. Impressing upon the opinion builders and receiving the criticism to adopt correctional measures.
6. Managing and facilitating the two-way communication flow.

In the 70's the leading public sector company, the Indian Airlines earned bad reputation because of the frequent mishaps, delays and accidents. There was a public outcry to improve the services which pushed the Government to take measures like termination of chairperson and MD of the airlines, and induction of retired Air Force chief P.C. Lal to let the house in order.

Mr. Lal did all that a PR person ought to do in the times of crisis to restore public confidence and goodwill. He organised meetings with senior executives, sought three months time to study the situation before suggesting rem....., net union leaders, public representatives and finally drew.

## 17.6 PR Concerns and Pressure Groups

In the case of airlines tangle, there were pressure groups in the form of remains, and groups of parliamentarians, to press their demands or view points, Crisis PR took special care of them. There are other lobbies and groups with common interest and objectives.

The public relations practitioners have to be aware of those lobbies, which leave an impact on their organisations while seeking favours from and associating with the groups which influence the legislators, decision makers and opinion builders. In every society there is one diverse interest group which differs not only in terms of goals but also in methods, means, motivation, etc to achieve these goals. In India, besides religious, political and caste based groups, there are women organisations, human rights activists, environment protection groups, consumer rights bodies, civil rights movement etc. There are examples like Medha Patakar and group agitating against the construction of bridge on Narmada river under the banner of Narmada Bachao Andolan, Chipko Movement as a campaign for environment conservation receiving wider support, women group in South successfully stopping the sale of liquor in their villages.

In this context, the PR's job is to tackle the situations arising because of the unrest among pressure groups and also to carry out lobbying work by associating with the pressure groups with similar interests as that of the organisation represented by the PR executives. PR keeps track of the moves and sentiments of the pressure groups as they affect the public opinion. Recklessness on part of PR towards the pressure group might impair the image.

## 17.7 Summary

The Indian market is seen as one of those with greater possibilities of investments, but the market realities here could be shocking for those unaware of the Indian psychology. The success of international PR would depend mainly on how quickly the companies adapt to the local traditions, customs, mindsets and systems.

Understanding the local cultures help to plan for actual PR works of reaching and communicating public. PR consultancies offer their specialized services to plan and carry out communication functions and often act as nodal agencies for coordinating these programmes.

PR as a management philosophy has been hyped as a publicity activity. PR is primarily concerned with influencing the public, seeking attention, and building a favorable opinion about the organization. Opinions are public expressions of active attitudes or opinions that are activated by attitudes. The people's opinion rests on the goodwill the organization earned over a period of existence. The public relations practitioners have to be aware of those lobbies which impact their organizations while seeking favors from and associating with the groups which influence the legislators, decision makers and opinion builders.

**Self Assessment Exercise**

1. What is the importance of 'image building' in an organization?
2. What are the factors affecting the image of an organization?
3. How PR department of an organization deals with the pressure groups?
4. Write a note on the functions of International PR.
5. What communication strategies should be adopted for International PR?
6. Is it required for PR to understand the local realities to function in the global market?

**Suggested Readings**

1. Seema Sharma, "*Public- Relation*" Anmol Publications Pvt Ltd., 2005.
2. Caroline Block, "*The PR Practioner's : A Handbook*", Viva Books Pvt Ltd, 2003.
3. David, W. Wragg, *An Introduction to Public – Relations*, Blackwell Publishers, 1992.
4. Paul Burton, *Corporate PR,* Reinhold Publishing House, New York.

# 18

# Code of Professional World

## 18.1 Objectives

This chapter would allow an insight into:

1. Ethical code for professionals
2. Internal – External codes
3. Personal codes for accountability

## 18.2 Introduction

The PR department is the company's conscience and the ethical heart. Many corporations in the Western and European nations have adopted clearly spelt and general rules of corporate behaviour on social, environmental and other relevant issues. These codes, though generalized for the whole corporate fraternity are well adopted by the companies, or independent associations to suit their needs.

The nature of the codes also vary depending on whether company itself designs or any outside agency like professional society, association, government or academic institution or any other group drafts them.

The Corporate world's concern over ethical issues can be traced to the rising instances of insider trading and also growing social expectations and stakeholders' demand to be responsive. It has been realized by the corporate world that ethical codes are essential not only for the corporate but also for the PR field as well and that these ethical principles result in all positive output, hence, good for the overall health of an organization. Many PR case studies also suggest that PR's role in designing communication strategies, counseling, decision making, trouble shooting, crisis management, media dealing, organizing events and upholding social commitments etc., have resulted in better work environment and improved communication, performance and satisfaction levels.

The empirical studies in PR suggest that:

1. The corporate management must set ethical guidelines.

2. The practioners can not ignore ethical issues.
3. The practioners are continuously evaluated on the basis of the professional conduct.
4. The ethical behaviour benefits the practioners individually, the organization as a whole and the social community at large. The prime duty of any corporation is to "keep faith" of all the concerned community and the codes provide directions to all the practioners to serve the following purpose :

1. Offer guidelines for professional activities.
2. Enumerate the expectations from PR practioners by the client, the company, the stakeholders, the investors.
3. Define the Do's and Dont's of conduct.
4. Prescribe rules to deal with press.
5. Help handle the internal communication.
6. Inculcate a sense of duty towards the company and the community.
7. Becomes a yardstick for drafting company's mission statements, strategies, vision etc.

It must be discussed in this context that the concept of voluntary codes has largely failed to instill a sense of solidarity among the practitioners.

The PR practioners and the corporate world still don't subscribe to the concept and believe the conduct be governed by their own understanding of the personal morality. Another aspect is the absence of enforcement mechanism for the ethical codes. In the 45 years of existence of PRSI hardly any case of misconduct of PR person or corporate world was ever focused or discussed leave alone the action or indictment. PRSA's codes of standard were drafted in 1959 and between 1952 and 1985, some 168 cases were investigated, with 10 cases resulting in sanctions.

### 18.3 Internal – External Code

Every institution seeks to attain minimum standard of practice. Levi Strauss and Company adopted "Global Sourcing and Operating guidelines" in 1991. These codes aimed at managing labour practices of its global chains of apparel suppliers. The code commits Levi Strauss to work only with suppliers who do not use child or prison labour, who maintain reasonable work hours and benefits, who permit union organizing and who maintain adequate health and safety standard. Levi Strauss consulted the NGOs and based its codes on principles elaborated by the International Labour Organization (ILO) and United States Labour Law.

The Bennet and Coleman Company has designed code of conduct for the staff journalists and had appointed an ombudsman to look into the complaints and grievances against the company.

Internal codes have become intrinsic part of any system as a measure of check and balance. The internal codes are meant for the employees and staff to make them clear, aware and conscious about their rights, duties, responsibilities, constraints and liberties.

There are two mechanisms in operation-one the company generated codes developed primarily by the corporate management. These are broad statements of business practice and professional commitments. The responsibility to follow these standards is fixed on individual staff members. The extent to which these standards act as a disciplinary-pressure rests on the fact of how serious the management is about its implementation and whether the management keeps track of the trends in the company and the conduct of the staff. Another mechanism is for the trade association or a flagship body who develops a code, which is then adopted by a group of firms. The idea here is to committ a whole business sector to a certain minimum standard of practice, with peer pressure helping to enforce compliance. Members of the Advertising Standard Council of India (ASCI), a representative body of the advertisers have to abide by the guidelines regarding advertising. The Kenya Flower Council, representing a group of Kenyan growers and exporters of cut flowers, crafted a "Code of Practice" that commits members to minimize pesticide use, dispose of chemical safely, and be audited on their commitments twice a year. Some codes are crafted through negotiations among diverse stakeholders, including non-governmental organizations and these tend to be more exacting and insistent on accountability measures. One example is the Forest Stewardship Council's (FSC) code for forestry operations – a set of standards for sustainable management of timber producing lands that harvesters must prove they meet in order to market their wood as "certified" and to use the FSC trademark logo (FSC 2003). Some NGO's also propose model codes of conduct that they would like to see industries follow. Amnesty International for instance, offers a set of human rights principles that companies can use in building their own code of conduct (Amnesty International 1998).

There have been instances when the transnational corporations encountered criticism in Third World nations and took the pledge to follow codes as a recovery measure. For example, Nestle was embroiled in a controversy surrounding their marketing practices of the breast milk substitutes in the Third World. Nestle responded effectively and in a socially responsible manner in 1981 by endorsing the WHO's code of marketing for Breast Milk substitutes. The experts were also engaged to monitor the company's compliance with the code.

***Personal Code of Accountability***

Ultimately, ethics are good for business and for individual reputation and goodwill. PR people likely to be bound by the internal rules of organizations, other than those designed by the professional bodies should also be aware of the rules which guide their own discretion. It is not just being a professional in all respects but also being conscientious about the larger interests of the society and organization both.

Personal code is that unwritten code the application of which demands sound judgement and some positive personality traits. Basic nature of an individual becomes the major force to drive a person on the righteous path. A faithful person is an asset and can be a brand in him/herself. She/He is always in demand, always entrusted with responsibilities, the brand ambassador of those groups she/he represents and a non-controversial leader always. The individual code is not only about the right conduct but also the professional expertise in handling the routine and complex situations.

In the corporate world, it is quite probable that the situations would arise when there is conflict between the individual sense of morality and the professional expectations. There can not be any formulae to deal with such situations, hence the importance of sound judgement. The backbone of the sound judgement would be professional integrity. The persons of integrity would in the long run earn respect of their bosses, subordinates, clients and every group they interact with.

When there is lack of will on the part of the top brass of the management or the decision makers at various levels of hierarchy to follow the fair practices in business, it leads to dilemma on part of rest of the employees, especially for the image managers.

An ideal example of such situation is Dow Corning. For years Dow was recognized by business educators as leaders in the area of corporate ethical programmes. In 1976, Dow's chairperson John S. Ludington established Business Conduct Committee and Dow also set up ethics training session for employees and audits every three years to monitor compliance with the company's ethical guidelines. Nonetheless, there were indications as early as 1977 that the breast implants manufactured by Dow were unsafe. Similar is the case of Mc Donnell Douglas. Despite their extensive ethics programme, in the late 70's and early 80's, their defence contractors were accused of severe overcharging of the government and some of these contractors were required to compensate the government for the overcharging. In 1980, Sanford McDonnell became Chairman and CEO of McDonnell Douglas and established the company's ethics programme because of his conviction that ethics must be woven into the decision process at all steps through all levels of authority. In 1983, McDonnell initiated a study to determine the best course of ethics training for MDC employees. The MDC training programme developed a conceptual model for defining ethical decision-making.

More than 75,000 employees took part in the training seminars. Subsequent to the implementation of the programme, the company discovered that the ethics became an acceptable topic for discussion. Sanford McDonnell's personal participation in the videotape sent a strong message, the case study approach highlighted ethical issues with practical benefits, an increased sense of pride developed among the employees, and MDC issued a new policy and procedures manual relative to pricing and contracting with the government. Some of the lessons learnt by MDC that could be transferable to other entities include: ethics training should be pragmatic and managerial in nature, strong leadership is needed from the top and implementation must be from the top down, managers must serve as role models, there must be a standardized training procedure and workshops should utilize a participative process. Some PR experts main point about the MDC case is that "a track record of exemplary conduct builds slowly. It requires constant tending. An honorable reputation is both precious and fragile. Opponents or competitors are rearmed by infractions." In 1988, investigations by the Justice Department, FBI and the Navy, showed evidence of bribery, fraud, and kickbacks in defense contracting. MDC was among the 75 companies named in the investigation.

All the principles and standards are rendered ineffective if their is no inner-drive and obligation to follow such practices. In other words, the professional morality can not acquire meaning if the follower's human mechanism, since child and adulthood, has not been trained in value system basic to any society.

**Summary**

The PR department is the company's conscience and the ethical heart. Various corporations in the western world have adopted general rules of corporate behavior on social, environmental and other relevant issues. The corporate world's concern over ethical issues can be traced to the rising instances of insider trading and also growing social expectations and stakeholder's demand to be responsive. It has been realized by the corporate world that ethical codes are essential not only for the corporate but also for the PR field as well and that these ethical principles result in all positive output, hence, good for overall health of an organization.

Every institution seeks to attain minimum standards of practice. Internal codes have become intrinsic part of any system as a measure of check and balance. The internal codes are meant for the employees and the staff to make them clear, aware and conscious about their rights, duties, responsibilities, constraints and liberties.

Ultimately, ethics are good for business and for individual reputation and goodwill. Personal code is that unwritten code the applications of which demands sound judgement and some positive personality traits. Basic nature of an individual becomes the major force to drive a person on the righteous path. In the corporate world, it is quite probable that the situations would arise when there is conflict between the individual sense of morality and the professional expectations. There can not be any formulae to deal with such situations, hence the importance of sound judgement.

All the principles and standards are rendered ineffective it there is no inner-drive and obligation to follow such practices.

**Self Assessment Exercise**

Q. 1. Comment on the effect of external – internal codes of PR on the overall business interest of an organization?

Q.2. How can individual codes be integrated with the professional codes of practice in PR?

**Suggested Reading**

1. Seema Sharma, "*Public- Relation*" Anmol Publications Pvt Ltd., 2005.
2. Caroline Block, "*The PR Practioner's : A Handbook*", Viva Books Pvt Ltd, 2003.
3. David, W. Wragg, *An Introduction to Public – Relations*, Blackwell Publishers, 1992.
4. Paul Burton, *Corporate PR*, Reinhold Publishing House, New York.

# 19

# Ethics in PR

## 19.1 Objectives

This chapter would allow an insight into:

- Ethics in PR
- Principles and standards of PR practice
- Professional code of conduct – code adopted by IPRA and PRSA.

## 19.2 Introduction

Every profession demands sincerity and devotion following certain written and unwritten rules of conduct. A sense of belongingness to the cause that instills a sense of morality. In the professional world – whether it is medical, engineering or law the respective graduates take the oath to abide by the professional ethics before embarking on their duties and responsibilities. PR is an area, which has earned an image of a lobbyist, publicist or propagandist – terms which bear negative connotations. Worst even, PR is considered by many as a "wine and dine" affair.

There cannot be smoke without fire and PR professional's conduct is primarily responsible for this state of affairs.

## 19.3 Image of PR

Following the growing decline in the professional standard and regular complaints from media and other quarters, the issue of ethics was brought to the fore in late 50s. Since PR is the visible face of an organization, its own image remains core concern for the public and the management. Hence, the PR practitioners world over, after series of deliberations, realized the need for certain principles of practice.

It becomes the moral responsibility of a PR professional to imbibe those qualities suggested in these guidelines and know those principles, upon which the edifice of PR rests.

## 19.4 Principles of Public Relations Practice

The modern PR concept embraces PR activity integral to the management philosophy rather than readymade formulae to sail through the troubled water. With the emergence of democracy as a sacred political ideology, the demand from the public to be informed about the public affairs had grown manifold. Public criticism also became a balancing factor for the democratic voices. To tackle this criticism the governments used PR and herefrom the PR assumed the role of a publicist and a propagandist.

PR practitioner's conduct is a reflection of the organization he/she represents; therefore his/her behaviour must go far beyond ignoring the legal ramifications. It should be fair, honest and governed by the law of the land. The public would not take long to realise whether the PR messages are flattery and non-truths or carry conviction for being logical and ethical.

Ethical rules are the governing principles of conduct and behaviour. Ethical conducts demand that the principle we act or follow should be one, which we can recommend everyone else to act upon. PR people should be aware of these rules which guide the profession and behave with discretion and extend their role to the society and catch up the idea of corporate social responsibility. PR practitioner's scrupulous dealing both with employees, clients and belongingness for the organization would go a long way in keeping the profession beyond criticism. PR's importance, misdemeanor, self- projection and publicity stunts cause unwarranted damage to the business. PR persons must realise that bridging the communication gap by increasing the flow of information and projecting the human face of his/her organization results in positive image. Hence, the responsibility to employ fair means to achieve the objectives and motivation of the organization for high-performance would finally earn the practitioners and the profession a good reputation.

The demand for a common code of conduct for the PR practitioners was realized as far back as 1965 when the international PR organizations gave the issue of ethics a serious thought .The societies of PR practitioners have prescribed code of ethics in an endeavour to build and maintain good reputation and inculcate values. The PRSI, RRSA and IPRA and others as representative bodies of the PR fraternity, have adopted the code of conduct underlining the do's and dont's of the profession.

## 19.5 International Public Relations Association[IPRA] Code of Conduct

The following code of conduct was adopted by International Public Relations Association in its general assembly in Venice. May 1961 and is in binding on all members of the association.

*Personal and Professional Integrity* :

It is understood that by personal integrity is meant the maintenance of both high moral standards and a sound reputation. By professional integrity is meant observance of the constitution, rules and, particularly, the code as adopted by IPRA.

*Conduct towards Clients and Employers:*

1. A member has a general duty of fair dealing towards his clients and employers, past and present.
2. A member shall not represent conflicting or competing interests without the express consent of those concerned.
3. A member shall safeguard the confidences of both present and former clients and employers.
4. In performing services for a client or employer a member shall not accept fees, commissions or any other valuable considerations in connection with those services from anyone other than his client or employer without the express consent of his client or employer, given after a full disclosure of facts.
5. A member shall not propose to a prospective client or employer that his fee or other compensation be contingent on the achievement of certain results; nor shall he enter into any fee agreement to the same effect.

*Conduct towards the Public and the Media:*

1. A member shall conduct his professional activities in accordance with the public interest, and full respect for the dignity of the individual.
2. A member shall not engage in any practice which tends to corrupt the integrity of channels of public communication.
3. A member shall not intentionally disseminate false or misleading information.
4. A member shall at all times seek to give a balanced and faithful representation of the organization he serves.
5. A member shall not create any organization to serve some announced cause but actually to serve an undisclosed special or private interest of a member or his client or his employer, nor shall he make use of it or any such existing organization.

*Conduct towards Colleagues:*

1. A member shall not intentionally injure the professional reputation or practice of another member. However, if a member has evidence that another member has been guilty of unethical, illegal or unfair practices violation of this code; he should present the information to the Council of IPRA.
2. A member shall not seek to supplant another member with his employer or client.
3. A member shall cooperate with fellow members in upholding and enforcing this code.

## 19.6 Public Relations Society of America [PRSA] Code of Conduct

Members of the Public Relations Society of America base their professional principles on the fundamental value and dignity of the individual, holding that the free exercise of human rights, especially freedom of speech, freedom of assembly and freedom of the press, is essential to the practice of public relations. The code of conduct adopted by the society is as follows:

1. A member shall deal fairly with clients or employers. Past and present, with fellow practitioners and the general public.
2. A member shall conduct his or her professional life in accordance with the public interest.
3. A member shall adhere to truth and accuracy and to generally accepted standards of good taste.
4. A member shall not represent conflicting or competing interests without the express consent of those involved, given after a full disclosure of the facts; nor place himself or herself in a position where the member's interest may be in conflict with a duty to a client, or others ,without a full disclosure of such interests to all involved.
5. A member shall safeguard the confidence of present and former clients as well as of those persons or entities who have disclosed confidences to a member in the context of communication relating to an anticipated professional relationship with the member and shall not accept retainers or employers.
6. A member shall not engage in any practice which tends to corrupt the integrity of channels of communications or the process of government.
7. A member shall not intentionally communicate false or misleading information and is obligated to use care to avoid communication of false or misleading information.
8. A member shall be prepared to identify publicly the name of the client or employer on whose behalf any public communication is made.
9. A member shall not make use of any individual or organization purporting to serve or represent an announced cause, or purporting to be independent or unbiased, but actually serving an undisclosed special or private interest of a member, client or employer.
10. A member shall not intentionally injure the professional reputation or practice of an other practitioner.
11. If a member has evidence that another member has been guilty of unethical illegal or unfair practices, including those in violation of this code, the member shall present the information promptly to the proper authorities of the society for action in accordance with the procedure set forth in Article XII of the bylaws.
12. A member called as a witness in proceeding for the enforcement of this code shall be bound to appear, unless excused for sufficient reason by the judicial panel.

13. A member, in performing services for a client or employer, shall not accept fees, commissions or any other valuable consideration from anyone other than the client or employer, given after a full disclosure of the facts.
14. A member shall not guarantee the achievement of specified results beyond the member's direct control.
15. A member shall, as soon as possible, serve relations with any organization or individual if such relationship requires conduct contrary to the articles of this code.

**Summary**

Every profession demands sincerity and devotion following certain written and unwritten rules of conduct. The modern PR concept embraces PR activity integral to the management philosophy rather than readymade formulae to sail through the troubled water. PR practitioner's conduct is a reflection of the organization he/she represents; therefore his/her behavior must go far beyond ignoring the legal ramifications.

The demand for a common code of conduct for the PR practitioners was realized as far back as 1965 when the international PR organizations gave the issue of ethics a serious thought.

**Self Assessment Exercise**

1. What role the PR associations play in maintaining the ethical standards in the PR field?
2. Ethics should be integral to any profession. Discuss in the light of current PR scene.

**Suggested Readings**

1. Seema Sharma, "*Public-Relation*" Anmol Publications Pvt Ltd., 2005.
2. Caroline Block, "*The PR Practioner's : A Handbook*" Viva Books Pvt Ltd, 2003.
3. David, W. Wragg, *An Introduction to Public – Relations*, Blackwell Publishers, 1992.
4. Paul Burton, *Corporate PR*, Reinhold Publishing House, New York.

# 20

# Code of All India Radio, PRSI and TV (DD)

### 20.1 Objectives

This chapter would allow an insight into:

1. Purpose of associations and professional bodies.
2. Activities undertaken by associations and professional bodies.
3. Code of All India Radio and Doordarshan.
4. Code of conduct of PRSI.

### 20.2 Introduction

The professional associations and bodies serve the interest of their members. To further these interests they enhance understanding of the professional pursuits , promote high standards of discipline , and endeavour to bridge the gap between the public and the professionals. These bodies and societies have become powerful forces to reckon with in India and abroad . India is the biggest democracy of the world and a big market too. Associations provide a platform to exercise the right to expression in a democratic nation and the market activities provide them momentum to work towards building healthy work environment.

**Purpose of Professional Bodies**

Acquiring the professional status requires lot of understanding, exposure and experience sharing. The PR associations have strived hard to establish and promote PR field as a full fledged area of management. Demands of the management have further given impetus to the PR's business and humanitarian pursuits and has bought returns in terms of frequent medical camps, health care campaigns, loan melas, etc. and conscious efforts to raise ethical standards in business etc. Professionalization in the PR field has also earned to the community recognition, individual accountability, commitment, efficiency and innovation.

With the changes in recent times, the PR has kept pace with the rising demands and aspiration of the communities they have served. Realising the growing expectation from the PR, the related associations realised the need for:

*Important Areas of Attention in PR*

1. Rigorous training in the field.
2. Saving the PR field from criticism and allegations.
3. Developing skills and techniques.
4. Inculcating sense of belongingness.
5. Acquiring understanding of management functions.
6. Promoting the talents.
7. Encouraging PR researches.
8. Building a common understanding for conduct and enforcing codes of professional practice.
9. Appreciating the latest trends in the field.
10. Facilitating exchange of ideas and experiences.
11. Bringing out publications to keep the members abreast of the organisations' activities and development in PR world.
12. Organising seminars or other activities under its banner to bring the PR fraternity at one platform.
13. Offering statistics, ranking and other information about PR industry.

Tasks of an Association

↓

Membership Communication

↓

Membership Enrichment

↓

Flow of Information

↓

Act as Pressure Groups

↓

Relations with industries and other associations

Various organisations in existence cater to most of the needs enlisted here and provide professional support to PR practitioners and PR industry both. These bodies depend on membership fee for promoting the set objectives and undertaking various enrichment programmes. The membership categories of these bodies include corporate, associate, individual, student and life members. The categories might vary according to the need and nature of the bodies. The membership status plays a crucial role with respect to reputation, recognition and market value of the respective associations. Big names would fetch better promotion and more membership and hence, improve financial status to carry out various activities. Renowned figures and wide networking would also help the bodies emerge as a big pressure builder who is listened to, taken seriously by the industry and the governments.

The associations are non - profit making bodies surviving on the membership support and contributions. The expenditures are incurred on various activities undertaken. Such associations are constantly engaged in building communication environment among its members and on the other hand building relations with the industry and the public affected. These bodies endeavour to bring professionals of common interests on one platform while organising academic programmes. One of the specific interests of most of the associations remains to seek attention of the policy makers and the concerned industries for common issues of concern. For this reason, apart from membership generation, garnering support of the influential persons remains crucial for the existence and reputation.

Though, PR is a recent craze in India, the wings of professionalism started spreading with the inception of Public Relations Society of India (PRSI) in 1958. In its Delhi convention the initiation was taken to establish PR as an independent specialised field. Recently one more professional body-Public Relations Council of India (PRCI) has been established in the year 2004. It is in the process of widening its network and membership base. In 1956, the Public Relations Society of America (PRSA) had conducted a survey to find out almost hundred colleges were offering courses in PR. Ever since the PR education and training in America and in other countries multiplied manifolds.

*A list of some of the renowned Professional Bodies*

PRSI: Public Relations Society of India
Founded in 1958
Has more than 40 chapters across the country
The respective chapters organise seminars, conventions etc. and bring out publications.

- PRCI: Public Relations Council of India Founded in 2004.
- PRSA: Public Relations Society of America.
  Headquarter - New York.
  Founded in 1948.
  Has 114 chapters and about 20,000 members.
  Activities- knowledge projects, an institute for PR research and education (1956), fellowship programmes etc.
  Publications: Public Relations Tactics; PR journal monthly; PR strategist, a quarterly; PR review.

- IPRA – International Public Relations Association.
  Headquarter -Geneva, Switzerland.
  Founded in 1955.
  Formally recognised by the United Nations.
  Publication – International Public Relations Review (quarterly)
  Members -across more than 75 countries.

- IABC – International Association of Business Association.
  Headquarter- San Francisco
  Founded in 1970.
  Members across more than 15 countries and 13,700 members
  Activities – Gold Quill and Excel awards programmes; communication world online service.
  Publication - Communication World magazine, PR Job Board
- IPR-Institute of Public Relations (UK)
  Founded in 1948.
  Have more than 12 regional groups and over 7000 members
  Activities-Sponsors the Communication Advertising and Marketing Education Foundation.
  Publication: Public Relations (8 issues per year)
- CPRS-Canadian Public Relations Society
  Headquarter-Ottawa, Ontario
  Founded in 1948.
  Has more than 8 member societies and 15,000 members
  Activity-Annual Conference.
  Publication-Communiqué- a quarterly
- PRCA- Public Relations Consultants Association
  Founded in 1969.
  Activity-works closely with IPR, promote consultancy practice, Offer counselling in PR.
  Publication-Consultancy costs, researches etc.

## 20.3 Code of AIR and Doordarshan

The All India Radio and Doordarshan have codified the norms of practice for the Broadcasters. These codes offer a word of caution to the PR practitioners with respect to the use of these media for publicity, commercial, advertising campaigns.

*Broadcast Code Governing All India Radio*

We recognize the immense power of Radio and Television for both good and evil and the solemn responsibilities this places upon all broadcasters. We believe, there, that the following cardinal principle should be enshrined in the policy and practice of all Broadcasting and Television organizations:

1. To ensure the objective presentation of news and fair and unbiased comment;
2. To promote the advancement of education and culture;
3. To raise and maintain high standards of decency and decorum in all programmes;
4. To provide programmes for the young which, by variety and content, will inculcate the principles of good citizenship;
5. To promote communal harmony, religious tolerance and international understanding;
6. To treat controversial public issues in an impartial and dispassionate manner;
7. To respect human rights and dignity.

*Broadcast on All India Radio by individuals will not permit:*

1. Criticism of friendly countries;
2. Attack on religions or communities;
3. Anything obscene or defamatory;
4. Incitement to violence or anything against maintenance of law and order;
5. Anything amounting to contempt of court;
6. Aspersions against the integrity of the president, governors and judiciary;
7. Attack on a political party by name ;
8. Hostile criticism of any state or the centre;
9. Anything showing disrespect to the Constitution or advocating change in the Constitution by violence; but advocating changes in a constitutional way should not be debarred;
10. Appeal for funds except for the Prime Minister's national relief fund, at a time of external emergency or if the country is faced with a natural calamity such as floods, earthquake or cyclone;
11. Direct publicity for or on behalf of an individual or organization which is likely to benefit only that individual or organization;
12. Trade names in broadcasts which amount to advertising directly (except in commercial services).

*A.I.R. code during elections:*

Broadcast on All India Radio will not permit:

1. Criticism of friendly countries;
2. Attack on religions or communities;
3. Anything obscene or defamatory;
4. Incitement to violence;
5. Anything amounting to contempt of court;
6. Aspersions against the integrity of the president and judiciary;

7. Anything affecting the unity and integrity of the nation;
8. Any criticism by name of any person;
9. Sponsored programme by political parties to telecast/broadcast during election period;
10. Songs sung by cine artists themselves in films who have joined politics;
11. Telecast/broadcast of programmes of the prime minister /chief minister/ ministers having a direct relation or bearing on elections. However, telecast/ broadcast of programmes on official activities of the prime minister/ chief minister will be permitted.

*Code for Commercial Advertising for Commercial Advertising over All India Radio*

*Definition:*

In this code unless the context otherwise required:

1. Government means Government of India.
2. Director General means the Director General All India Radio, or any officer duly authorized by him on his behalf.
3. Advertiser means any individual or organization including a commercial concern which has offered an advertisement for broadcast over the radio.
4. Advertising agency means any organization which is accredited to be registered with AIR as such.
5. Advertisement includes any item of publicity for goods or services inserted in the programmes broadcast by the competent authority in consideration of payment to All India Radio.
6. Spot advertisement means any direct advertisement mentioning product services, their merits and their related details.
7. The term sponsored programme means any programme material which is planned, produced and or paid for by an organization or individual, including a commercial concern to be called the sponsor for the purpose of being broadcast over the radio.

*Scope:*

2. The Director General All India Radio shall be the soul judge of the suitability or otherwise of an advertisement or a sponsored programme for broadcast and his decision in this regard shall be final.
3. Broadcast time shall be sold to the advertiser / advertising agencies at the sole discretion of the Director General, All India Radio, according to the prescribed rates.
4. The advertisement must be clearly distinguishable from the programme.
5. A sponsored programme shall constitute a substantive broadcast / programme, as distinct from material which directly advertise any specific wares or goods / products / service. The name of the sponsor shall be broadcast immediately before and after the sponsored programme.

The sponsor shall, however, undertake to indemnify All India Radio against any legal claim that may be brought against it as a result of the broadcast of a sponsored programme or any portion thereof.

6. Any such effects which might startle the listening public must not be incorporated in advertisements. For example, and without limiting the scope, the use of the following sound effects will not be permitted.
   (a) Rapid gunfire or rifle shots,
   (b) Sirens,
   (c) Bombardments,
   (d) Screams,
   (e) Raucous laughter and the like.
7. Any pretence in advertising copy must be avoided and such copy shall not be accepted by All India Radio. The 'simulation of voices of a personality in connection with advertisements for commercial products is also prohibited unless bona-fide evidence is available that such personality has given permission for the simulation and it is clearly understood that stations broadcasting such announcements are indemnified by the advertiser or advertising agency against any possible legal action.

   Note : Advertisements concerning jewellery, foreign banks, besides those Indian equity/ debenture issued for NRI will, however, be accepted as far as the external service of All India Radio are concerned.

   Note I : In all other respects, the Director General will be guided for purposes of commercial broadcasting in All India Radio by the code of ethics for advertising in India as modified from time to time.

   Note II : Notwithstanding anything contained herein, this code is subject to such modification / directions as may be made / issued by the Director General from time to time.

   Note III : AII advertising agencies shall adhere to the standards of practice as prescribed by Advertising Agencies Association of India, Bombay, as given in following :

## Annexure III

## Procedure for the Enforcement of the Code

1. Complaints or reports on contraventions of the code, received by All India Radio may in the first instance be referred by the Director General to the Advertisers Associations concerned with request for suitable action.

*A.I.R. /DD code*

Broadcast on All India Radio/DD by individual will not permit:

(1) Criticism of friendly countries;

(2) Attack on religions or communities;
(3) Anything obscene or defamatory;
(4) Incitement to violence or anything against maintenance of law and order;
(5) Anything amounting to contempt of court;
(6) Aspersions against the integrity of the President and Judiciary;
(7) Anything affecting the integrity of the Nation; and
(8) Criticism by name of any person.

## 20.4 The Code for Commercial Advertising on Doordarshan

*Definitions*

In this Code, unless the context otherwise requires:

(i) Government means, Government of India.
(ii) Director General' means, the Director General, Doordarshan or any officer duly authorized by him on his behalf and includes the Director, Doordarshan Kendra.
(iii) 'Advertiser' means any individual or organization including a commercial concern which has offered an advertisement for telecast over television.
(iv) 'Advertising Agency' means any organization which is accredited to recognized by or registered with Doordarshan as such.
(v) 'Advertisement' includes any item of publicity for goods or services inserted in the programmes telecast by Doordarshan with a view to increasing sales.
(vi) 'Spot Advertisement' means any direct advertisement mentioning product/services, their merits and other related details.
(vii) 'Advertising Association' means an Association or Society or any other body of whose constituent members are Advertising Agencies registered/recognized or accredited to Doordarshan.

*Scope*

(a) The Director General, Doordarshan, shall be the sole judge of the suitability or otherwise of an advertisement for telecast and his decision in this regard shall be final.
(b) Doordarshan time shall be sold to the advertisers/advertising agencies at the sole discretion of the Director General, Doordarshan, according to the prescribed rates.
(c) Doordarshan time shall be sold to the advertisers/advertising agencies at the sole discretion of the Director. General, Doordarshan, according to the prescribed rates.
(d) The advertisement should be clearly distinguishable from the programme by using suitable wipes/blank, in order to avoid the message of the programme getting mixed up with the content and images of the advertisement.

***Advertising***

Advertising is an important and legitimate means for the seller to awaken interest in goods and services. The success of advertising depends on public confidence. Hence no practice should be permitted which tends to impair this confidence. The standards laid down here should be taken as minimum standards of acceptability which would be liable to be reviewed from time to time in relation to the prevailing norm of viewers' susceptibilities.

The following standards of conduct are laid down in order to develop and promote healthy advertising practices in Doordarshan. Responsibility for the observance of these rules rests equally upon the Advertiser and the Advertising Agency.

All those engaged in advertising are strongly recommended to familiarize themselves with the *legislation affecting advertising* in this country, particularly the following Acts and the Rules framed under them:

(1) Drugs and Cosmetics Act, 1940.
(2) Drugs Control Act, 1950.
(3) Drugs and Magic Remedies (Objectionable Advertisement) Act, 1954.
(4) Copyright Act, 1957.
(5) Trade and Merchandise Marks Act, 1958.
(6) Prevention of Food Adulteration Act, 1954.
(7) Pharmacy Act, 1948.
(8) Prize Competition Act, 1955.
(9) Emblems and Names (Prevention of improper Use) Act, 1950.
(10) Consumer Protection Act, 1986.
(11) Indecent Representation of Women (Prohibition) Act, 1986.
(12) AIR Doordarshan Code.
(13) Code of Ethics for Advertising in India issued by the Advertising council of India.
(14) Code of Standards in relation to Advertising of Medicine and Treatments.
(15) Standards of Practice for Advertising Agencies. (The list is illustrative and not exhaustive).

*The Code*

General Rules of Conduct in Advertising:

1. Advertising should be so designed as to conform to the laws of the country and should not offend against morality, decency and religious susceptibilities of the people.
2. No advertisement should be permitted which:
   (i) Derides any race, caste, colour, creed, nationality;
   (ii) Is against any of the directive principles, or any other provision of the Constitution of India.
   (iii) Incite people to crime, cause disorder or violence, or breach of law or glorifies violence or obscenity in any way;

(iv) Presents criminality as desirable;
(v) Adversely affects friendly relations with foreign States;
(vi) Exploits the national emblem, or any part of the Constitution or the person or personality of a national leader or State Dignitary;
(vii) Related to or promotes cigarettes and tobacco products, liquor, wines and other intoxicants;
(viii) In its depiction of women, violates the constitutional guarantees to all citizens such as equality of status and opportunity and dignity of the individual. In particular, no advertisement shall be permitted which projects a derogatory image of women. Women must not be portrayed in a manner that emphasizes passive, submissive qualities and encourages them to play a subordinate, secondary role in the family and society. The portrayal of men and women should not encourage mutual disrespect between the sexes. Advertisers shall ensure that the portrayal of the female form is tasteful and aesthetic, and is within the established norms of good taste and decency.

3. No advertisement message shall in any way be presented as news.
4. No advertisement shall be permitted where the objects are wholly or mainly of a religious, or political nature; advertisements must not be directed towards any religious or political and or have any relation to any industrial dispute.
5. Advertisements for services concerned with the following shall not be accepted:
   (i) Money lenders;
   (ii) Chit funds;
   (iii) Saving schemes and lotteries other than those conducted by Central and State Government, Organizations, Nationalized or recognized banks and Public Sector Undertakings;
   (iv) Matrimonial agencies;
   (v) Unlicensed employment services;
   (vi) Fortune tellers or soothsayers etc., claims of hypnotism;
   (vii) Foreign goods and foreign banks;
   (viii) Betting tips and guide books etc., relating to horse racing, or other games of chance.
6. The items advertised shall not suffer from any deficiency as mentioned in Consumer Protection Act, 1986.
7. No advertisement shall contain references which are likely to lead the public to infer that the product advertised or any of its ingredients has some special or miraculous or supernatural property or quality, which is difficult to prove, e.g. cure for baldness, skin whitener, etc.
8. No advertisement shall contain the words 'Guarantee' or 'Guaranteed', etc., unless the full terms of the guarantee are available for inspection

by the Director General, Doordarshan, and are clearly set out in the advertisement and are made available to the purchaser in writing at the point of sale or with the goods. In all cases, terms must include details of the remedial action available to the purchaser. No advertiser shall contain a direct or implied reference to any guarantee which purports to take away or diminish the legal rights of a purchaser.

9. Scientific or statistical excerpts from technical literature etc., may be used only with a proper sense of responsibility to the ordinary viewer. Irrelevant data and scientific jargon shall not be used to make claims appear to have a scientific basis they do not possess. Statistics of limited validity should not be presented in a way as to make it appear that they are universally true.
10. Advertisers or their agents must be prepared to produce evidence to substantiate any claims or illustrations. The Director General reserves the right to ask for such proofs and get them examined to his full satisfaction. In case of goods covered by mandatory quality control orders, the advertiser shall produce a quality control certificate from the institutions recognized by the Government for this purpose.
11. Advertisements shall not contain disparaging or derogatory references to another product or service.
12. Imitation likely to mislead viewers shall be avoided.
13. Visual and verbal representation of actual and comparative prices and costs shall be accurate and shall not mislead on account of undue emphasis or distortion. Testimonials must be genuine and used in a manner not to mislead the viewers. Advertisers or Advertising Agencies must be prepared to produce evidence in support of their claims.
14. The picture and the audible matter of the advertisement shall not be excessively 'loud'. This is to ensure that between the programme and the advertisement there is a smooth changeover avoiding jerkiness or shock to the viewers.
15. No advertisement of any kind of jewellery or precious stones shall be accepted.
16. Information to consumers in matters of weight, quality or prices of products, where given shall be accurate.
17. Advertisements indicating price comparisons or reductions must comply with relevant laws.
18. No advertisement shall be accepted which violates AIR and TV Broadcast Code.
19. Any such effects which might startle the viewing public must not be incorporated in advertisements. For example, and without limiting the scope, the use of the following sound effects will not be permitted: Rapid gunfire or rifle shots; Sirens, Bombardments, Screams, Raucous laughter and the like.

20. Any pretence in advertising copy must be avoided and such copy shall not be accepted by Doordarshan Kendras. The 'simulation' of appearance or video of a personality in connection with advertisements for commercial products is also prohibited unless bonafide evidence is available that such personality has given permission for the simulation and it is clearly understood that stations telecasting such announcements are indemnified by the advertiser or
    1. Anything amounting to contempt of court.
    2. Aspersions against the integrity of the President, Governors and the Judiciary.
    3. Attack on a political party by name.
    4. Hostile criticism of any state or the centre.
    5. Anything showing disrespect to the Constitution or advocating change in the constitution.

**20.5 Advertising and Children**

1. No advertisement for a product or service shall be accepted if it suggests in any way that unless the children themselves buy or encourage other people to buy the products or services, they will be falling in their duty or lacking in loyalty to any person or organization.
2. No advertisement shall be accepted which leads children to believe that if they do not own or use the product advertised they will be inferior in some way to other children or that they are liable to be condemned or ridiculed for not owing or using it.
3. No advertisement likely to bring advertising into contempt or disrepute shall be permitted. Advertising shall not take advantage of the superstition or ignorance of the general public.
4. No advertisements of talismans, charms and character-reading from photographs or such other matter as well as those which trade on the superstition of the general public shall be permitted.
5. Advertising shall be truthful, avoid distorting facts and misleading the public by means of implications by false statements as to:
    - The character of the merchandise i.e. its utility materials, ingredients, origin, etc.
    - The price of the merchandise, its value, its suitability or terms of purchase.
    - The services accompanying purchase, including delivery, exchange, return, repair, upkeep etc.
    - Personal recommendations of the article or service.
    - The quality or the value of competing goods or the trustworthiness of statements made by others.
6. Testimonials of any kind from experts etc., other than government recognized standardization agencies shall not be permitted.

7. No advertisement shall be permitted to contain any claim so exaggerated as to lead inevitably to disappointment in the minds of the public.
8. Methods of advertising designed to create confusion in the mind of the consumer as between goods by one maker and another maker are unfair and shall not be used. Such methods may consist in:
   (a) The imitation of the trademark of the name of competition or the packaging or labelling of goods; or
   (b) The imitation of advertising devices, copy, layout or slogans.
9. Indecent, vulgar, suggestive, repulsive or offensive themes or treatment shall be avoided in all advertisements. This also applies to such advertisements which in themselves are not objectionable as defined above, but which advertise objectionable books, photographs or other matters and thereby lead to their sale and circulation.
10. No advertisement in respect of medicines and treatments shall be accepted which is in contravention of the code relating to standards for advertising of medicines and treatments.

## 20.6 Public Relations Society of India-Code of Ethics

International code of ethics for public relations as adopted by the Public Relations Society of India at the 1st All India Public Relations Conference, New Delhi, April 21, 1968.

Considering that all member countries of the United Nations Organisations have agreed to abide by its charter which reaffirms its faith in fundamental human rights, in the dignity and worth of human person and that having regard to the very nature of their profession, public relations practitioners in these countries should undertake to ascertain and observe the principles set out in this chapter.

Considering that, apart from right, human beings have not only physical or material needs but also intellectual moral and social needs and that their rights are of real benefits to them only in so far as needs are essentially met.

Considering that, in the course of their professional duties and depending on how these duties are performed, public relations practitioners can substantially help to meet these intellectual, moral and social needs.

And lastly, considering that the use of techniques enabling them to come simultaneously into contact with millions of people give public relations practitioners a power that has to be restrained by the observance of strict moral code.

Considering these grounds public relations society of India hereby declares that it accepts , as its moral charter the principle of the following code of ethics and that if, in the light of evidence submitted to the society if a member of this society should be found to have infringed this code in the course of his professional duties, he will be deemed to be guilty of serious misconduct calling for an appropriate penalty.

Accordingly, each member of the society shall endeavour:

1. To contribute to the achievement of the moral and cultural conditions enabling human beings to reach their full stature and enjoy the indefeatible rights to which they are entitled under the Universal Declaration of Human Rights.
2. To establish communication patterns and channels which, by fostering the free flow of essential information, will make each member of the group feel that he is being kept informed and also give him an awareness of his own personal environment and responsibility and of his solidarity with other members.
3. To conduct himself always and in all circumstances in such a manner as to deserve and secure the confidence of those with whom he comes into contact.
4. To bear in mind that because of the relationship between his profession and the public, his conduct even in private will have an impact on the way in which the profession as a whole is appraised.
5. Shall Undertake: to observe, in the course of his professional duties, the moral principles and rules of the Universal Declaration of Human Right.
6. To pay due regard to, an uphold, human dignity, and to recognize the right of each individual to judge for himself;
7. To establish the moral, psychological and intellectual conditions for dialogue in its true sense, and to recognize the right of the parties involved to stay at their case and express their views.
8. To act, in all circumstances in such a manner as to take account of the respective interests of the parties involved; both the interest of the organization which he serves and the interest of the publics concerned.
9. To carry out his undertakings and commitments which shall always be so worded as to avoid any misunderstanding, and to show loyalty and integrity in all circumstances so as to keep the confidence of his clients or employees, past or present and of all the publics that are affected by his actions.
10. Shall Refrain From : Subordinating the truth to other requirements.
11. Shall Refrain From : Circulating information which is not based on established and ascertainable facts.
12. Shall Refrain From : Taking part in any venture or undertaking which is unethical or dishonest or capable of impairing human dignity and integrity.
13. Shall Refrain From : Using any manipulative methods of techniques designed to create subconscious motivations which the individual cannot control of his own free will and so cannot be held accountable for the action taken on them.

**Summary**

The professional associations and bodies serve the interest of their members. Associations provide a platform to exercise the right to expression in a democratic nation. Acquiring the professional status requires lot of understanding, exposure and experience sharing. The PR associations have strived hard to establish and promote PR field as a full fledged area of management with rigorous training in the field, developing skills and techniques, encouraging PR researches etc. Some important PR bodies are PRSI, PRSA, IPRA and PRCA.

The All India Radio and Doordarshan have codified the norms of practice for the Broadcasters. These codes offer a word of caution to the PR practioners with respect to the use of these media for publicity, commercial and advertising campaigns.

The Public Relations Society of India has adopted International Code of Ethics like contributing to the achievement of moral and cultural conditions enabling human beings to reach their full stature, establishing communication patterns by fostering the free flow of essential information, which will make each member of the group feel that he is being informed and also give him an awareness of his personal environment etc. It also provides the members to establish moral, psychological and intellectual conditions for dialogue, to act in all circumstances in a manner as to take account of the respective interest of parties involved etc.

**Self Assessment Exercise**

1. Which are the major PR Associations and what are their broad objectives?
2. Do the PR Associations have a role to play in maintaining professional standards in the PR field?
3. Discuss the Codes of Conduct of PRSI.
4. What is the relevance of AIR and DD code as regards the PR industry?

**Suggested Reading**

(1) Seema Sharma, "*Public- relation*", Anmol Publications Pvt Ltd., 2005.

(2) Caroline Block, "*The PR Practioner's* : *A Handbook*, Viva Books Pvt. Ltd., 2003.

(3) David. W. Wragg, *An Introduction to Public – Relations,* Blackwell Publishers, 1992.

(4) Paul Burton, *Corporate PR*, Reinhold Publishing House, New York.

# 21

# PR Campaign

## 21.1 Objective

In this lesson we will discuss the various activities involved in PR Campaign.

## 21.2 Introduction

PR is an effort of communication link to establish a positive image of the company or organization. PR activities have to embed within the overall implementation of PR programme. It is an independent area of the of stream of communication, such as advertising and marketing. It is a link between the corporation and an organization and their target publics which are external and internal. Effective and successful PR encompass objective oriented, database and efforts evolved around a definite action plan. Today's PR is an important tool to build public opinion about the organization. These are related to both commercial and non commercial activities. PR is defined as a deliberate, planned and sustained effort to establish and maintain mutual understanding between an organization and its publics. The term campaign is used to mean systematic efforts for achieving a target. It is a unit of effort to accomplish a set of objectives. While applied to PR may be taken to mean "a unit of programmes or policies or services information distributed to accomplish a set of communication objectives. It is a series of professional and strategic plans and activities.

To achieve the PR objectives a PR campaign plan lays down the alternative strategic involving PR message and media. Campaign as it applied to PR, is a continuous extensive effort to create and maintain a mental environment conducive to the acceptance of a product\ polices\ programmes\ services, an idea or ideology, or a personality, individual or corporate.

There are four principal categories on which campaigns are conducted:-

1. Industrial and Financial,
2. Commercial,

3. Institutional,
4. Governmental.

***Industrial and Financial Campaign***

It is call for campaigns continuously for making a favorable public acceptance of a business enterprise. It includes all general public along with financial or banking community. The stock holders, the particular section of the public or trade who are the ultimate users of the product or services offered, employees and potential employees, the community or communities, and govt agencies. This campaign attempts to make a favorable news scenario in the market.

***Commercial Campaign***

Commercial campaign is related to the acceptance of a product or services. In this campaign, publicity as a tool of PR plays a significant role.

***Institutional Campaign***

It is concerned with non- profit organization for fund raising activity. It includes all non- profit social, political health, welfare and educational institutions of the country. It has voluntary nature that makes the impact of good PR and gives shape to the pattern of community life.

***Govt Campaign***

It works for tourism organizations, Transport Corporations, nationalized banks and other development corporations like State Electricity Board, LIC. These areas involve special type of campaign known as a government campaign.

***How PR Campaign Works***

PR is a way of life in an organization and must be continuous affair; it is an unfocused short term, multi- media, multi- dimensional and with specific quantifiable or measurable objectives. The following must be considered when a PR campaign is going to start:-

*Why*- Why communicating/objective of campaign?

*Who*- Who is your target group? To whom campaign want to reach?

*What*- What campaign wants to say? It means key message of the communication.

*Where*- Where do we say? By which media?

*How*- Manner of presentation of campaign\ the way campaign wants to reach our target audience\ or the strategy or action oriented programme.

*When*- Time- period or the frequency of messages.

Besides the above, two other important point via, budgeting and evaluation or feedback about the success or failure of the campaign. Its emphasis on the planned form of public- relations based on a two- way understanding. PR campaign is a process of the implementation of planned programmes. Which serve both the organization and the public interest?

So, we can say that the emphasis is on one key concept in the PR campaign, and that is planning. It is called the" action charter" while implementing a PR campaign.

Keeping in view the, the following four stage process is involved in successful PR campaign, fact finding, planning, implementation and evaluation.

## 21.3 Problem Identification or Fact Finding

The first step is defining the problem and to define the problem, there is a need to do some fact finding. Actually, problem definition begins with listening to the views of varying publics. In this reference feedback is a powerful tool. When it does not exist or is ignored then the situation engenders doubt and concern in the communicator, and frustration and sometimes hostility in the audience while defining the problem which is known as symptomatic diagnosis of the situation and will help to the organization. It will analyse the management, employees, product, competitor and its sensitive issues such as family friends, scandals, insensitive media, collective bragging, threat from pressure group, inferior product, price, vis-a vis computer etc. To find out the main problem, it is necessary to get to the depth of the issue. In fact research and fact finding is also a very integral part of structuring symptomatic" listening" into the process communication.

A PR manager must know the problem. First he\she needs to do some fact finding research. PR personnel should have thorough knowledge of the organization. This may require both formal and informal ways of researching the problem. The problem definition should ideally take the following steps:-

First: - Scan the problem thoroughly. Such as what is being said how and through which channel?

Second – Vital clues will have to be linked.

Thirdly – Analysis of the information. This means appraisal of how much of what is being said is truth and how much fallacious.

Therefore, PR practitioner uses research as a major tool. Research orientation is imperative for those plasticizing PR in the information age. It helps decision making. PR should be used in the research process and in research concept to get results. Through the research, a PR professional should be able to gather information and analyse data. But before making a research, it is important to make a problem statement which depends on:-

- What is the source concern?
- Where has the problem occurred?
- When is it a problem?
- Who is involved or effected?
- How are they involved or effected?
- Why is this of concern to the organization and their target group?

***Fact Findings***

The fact finding is a related step of problem identification. It is a formally starting point of any PR campaign. Fact finding can be carried on in three ways.

First- Organize fact findings with systematic collection of rélevant data and information.

Secondly - Maintenance of proper fact files on a subject

Thirdly- Process of Research Investigation and fact finding of the situation is the first requirement of any PR campaign. A study of what the problem is and what is involved in an effort to tackle the problem. The PR person will first study the situation and collect the readily available fact both from within his own organization and from external sources. If the situation has a different nature where the fact is not clear, research may have been necessary. Research might be necessary to discover the causes of the problem. The research might reveal for instance that some unscrupulous competitors are behind the campaign.

*Systematic Fact- Finding*

The art of fact- finding can be used for guiding the policies of an organization. The PR manager can assemble enough information to develop fairly reliable format of the campaign. Systematic fact- finding will eliminate all available uncertainties. For this there are some following essentials:-

(1) To assemble a basic fact file.

(2) To operate continuous intelligent activities constantly adding to the basic factfile.

The things that may be assembled in a basic fact file are:-

(a) Statistical figures of importance of project.
(b) List of information agencies concerned with the problem.
(c) Reference book.
(d) Pertinent legislation.
(e) Relevant clippings from mass media.
(f) List individual (may be product\ person\ organization) who may be important in the case.
(g) List of media.

*Scientific Fact- Finding or Organised Research*

Simple observation or even a study of available facts as collected in the basic fact file may not suffice to discover things that are hidden. Organized research therefore becomes necessary. So, PR campaign needs the specific research based on three following broad groups:-

- Measuring the extent of certain attitudes.
- Exploring the reasons and circumstances that favors or hinder the growth of the opinion or attitude.

- Testing the effectiveness of various plans to change the opinion or attitude. Therefore, the existence of a certain attitude offers only a starting point to the PR implement. Research can help to get a depth into the reason why certain attitudes grow or change or do not grow. Research by providing a breakdown of the attitude through such features as sex, age, economic status, geographic location and other identifications data may give significant basic clues as to the reason. Research may sometimes be obtained to decide what is the best media to reach the specific target group desired in the most exclusive way. On the other side it is also important to determine how the target audience or public view the organization. This could be tested either formally through the proper survey or informally by questioning key people.

## 21.4 Planning

The next stage through which PR campaign passes is of planning or the working out of a strategy. It is an analytical step by step programme of action, while there are a number of techniques and methods used.

Once a problem is identified and research conducted, it is found that barriers are cleared and then the next step of planning will start. It involves decision making for identified objectives alongwith strategy formulation.

Actually planning not only involves the various stages that need to be taken, the means of communication to be accepted, but an estimate of the budget, requirements of manpower and so on. The total strategy, different type of programmes, the means by which the objectives are to be attained and their budget, will have to be prepared properly or with the format document. The PR person is authorized to make and implement the plan of campaign within the framework of an overall budget. It is desirable to keep top management informed and to take their cooperation in the execution of the plan of PR campaign.

The PR man should prepare himself carefully for proper presentation of campaign strategy and plan to top management. All the facts have to be presented, the analysis on the basis of convincing case made out to show that the proposed strategy is likely to meet the objectives .In this process, there may be possibility of modified suggestion by the top management. In this situation, their suggestions should therefore, be carefully considered and if essential, modification should be introduced in the plan.

The following framework of planning should be considered for a successful PR campaign:-

- Analysis of situation
- Setting of objectives
- Identification of target group
- Selection of media and PR programme
- Determination of budget.

## 21.5 Evaluation of Result of Campaign

The above said process is mainly involved with planning and budgeting process of organization. It is a strategic thinking which decides the identification and selection of objectives. Actually will defined objectives provide a frame work of responsibility, achievement, activities along with assessment of benefit and consequences of actions?

***Aims***

Besides these, there are many ways to analyze the planning function and objectives for the PR campaign and the demerits, consequences and difficulties, of each course of action. But it should be very much clear that plan should have sufficient flexibility for mid-plan corrections and implementation. Clearly identified goals contribute to the success of plan. So, objective of the plan should be always based on the following facts:-

- To increase the public knowledge
- To enlist the support of voluntary and non governmental organizations (NGOS)
- To motivate the public to participate in the campaign
- To make a good networking on the basis of above mentioned facts the *Objectives will include* the followings:-
  (1) Defining goals and measurable objectives
  (2) Determining the nature and scope of campaign to be accomplished in key areas
  (3) Determining desired effects
  (4) Identifying resources, both manpower and financial appropriation
  (5) Fixing responsibilities
  (6) Evaluation and reconciling.

*Goals*

In PR campaign, two types of goals are identified:-

(1) Process
(2) Outcome goals

*Process goals* include all the process that must be accomplished before, during and after the campaign.

*Outcome goals* identify what needs to be gained or achieved from the total campaign outcome. Process goals are normally more than one goal.

***Objectives***

There are two following objectives being used for PR campaign

(a) Informational
(b) Motivational

Both are identified as an aspect of what has to be accomplished and are directly measurable. What information has to be disseminated through this campaign which they want to include? What are the benchmarks and from what print would the evaluation take place. For example, what percentage of the population is currently aware of the issue or problem, and what increase in percentage does the campaign want to achieve?

***Tools of Planinng***

The planning strategies process vary from organization to organization.

Generally the PR plan period exhausts for one financial year. But some time, it depends on the PR objectives, which may be long term campaign or short term. The approval of company is given by the top management. The following tools are used in the planning of PR campaign:-

(1) Idea generation
(2) Alternative pattern
(3) Score and prioritization
(4) Creative planning.

The aim of idea generation is to make a brainstorming session for collecting many ideas by the discussion. The ideas submitted are grouped together according to the concept and then constituted into a cohesive PR campaign.

Alternative pattern is a method of mixed scanning. It is firstly formulated then revised when extra information is available. The method of alternative pattern is again in another form to fit the incoming information. This is revised number of times depending upon the pattern and information possible.

Similarly, the system scores and priorities alternatives. It is know as a sequential decision making method. Through this method each alternative will be surveyed. After that, each will be then coded according to the predetermined criteria.

The coding will be use for an adding of scores and for prioritization of the alternatives. Creative plans take place when alternatives are found or when attempts are made to find solution and ideas. It is not frequently practiced all over the world along with India. Besides this it is essential to improve creative PR plans and internal part of the PR campaign. Once the PR person is clear on the plan, some of the following *PR activities* can be as follows:-

- To arrange workshop and symposium providing a platform to different NGOS for sharing their knowledge, problems and efforts in the field to help cross fertilize ideas.
- To evolve a common programme, keeping in view the local ethos.
- To earmark funds for specific activities
- To make a project for their joining as partner in govt programmes
- To reach out to identified target adopters through different channels
- To workout specific message.

To decide what action is expected from them on adoption of such programme, financial contribution, empathy towards public with specific communication.

### 21.6 The Publics: Target Publics

In the field of public relations the term 'public' has accepted with vary broad categories. Basically there are three types of public identified in the PR world :-

*Primary*: - Primary publics are those that are directly affected by the situation, issue or problem.

*Secondary*: - Secondary publics are those who are indirectly affected.

*Tertiary*: - Tertiary publics are those who could influence the situations.

In the profession of public- relations the PR personnel communicates with different type of people. It is very much essential that PR person should define their target publics clearly and should select the strategy and media to reach them perfectly.

There are some other identified public in public relation field which are considered for a major campaign:-

(1) The *employees*:- The people who work in the organization from management unit to lowest post

(2) The *potential employees*: - People who work for competitor organization.

(3) The *suppliers*: - who supply the service or materials to the company.

(4) The *traders*: - Distributor, wholesellers, retailers agents etc.

(5) The *financial contacts*: - Bankers, Shareholders, investors, brokers and insurers.

(6) The *media*: - Press, TV, Radio etc.

(7) *Opinion leaders* :- People who make influence such as social agents, bureaucrates, local leaders, public- representatives

(8) *Pressure groups*: - Trade union, labour association, employee associations etc. Besides the above mentioned list, there are some specific types of the target group with whom the organization should be ready to communicate. The target audience is never unlimited. The first step is to avoid the term general public. Broad categories should be identified whose behaviours or perception the PR person tries to influence.

The next step is to break up the broad categories of public into smaller, more definable groups. Then, one has to see as to which of the group is more "crucial "in terms of reach. In other words, the PR person must identify the primary and secondary target group. There is a need to identify the opinion – makers or leaders among the before mentioned public, those who can influence the others.

## 21.7 Message Design

For preparing an effective PR campaign the two points must be considered carefully:-

(1) The audience

(2) The message

The audience indicates the answer to question such as interest of the people, specific need of the message which fulfill the desire of audience as a whole as much as possible. The psychological appears to need will be helpful to work effectively with the target group. The requirements and interest of this segment will decide which type of content of message should be highlighted in the campaign of PR.

### *The Message*

The message designing plays an important role in the process of PR campaign. As we know communication is a stimulus which must lead to a "conditioned response. To be effective, any persuasive communication must carry its audience through a series of stages each stage being independent on success in the previous stage. In short the message must be:-

- Understandable: - It must be seen\ read\ listen to there should believe by the public.
- Rememberable: - It must be acted upon.
- Acceptable: - It must be acted upon.

A famous expert of PR Ray Eldon Hilbert suggested a *four- pronged guidelines for developing a message*

*First*: - Determine what people think of you. If you do not know that how your target public perceives you then your message will be worthless.

*Second*: - Establish what you actually are. This will be analyzed by identification of problem and research on it.

*Thirdly*: - Make desire image. There is a need to use a succinct image statement as to how would target public like to perceive the organization, such a company is either environmental conscious on consumer oriented.

*Fourth*:- Reduce image statement to key word for example while "supreme" while frequent use of key words win slowly but surely change old images and build new ones communication, in fact, involves more than semantics. Symbols and colures also communicate. We know very well that this is a comparative edge and for making the distinctiveness some companies especially focus on colors along with verbal and non– verbal means.

Therefore, the communication has to be credible in context, clear, consistent and compatible with the reliever's value system. There are following factors that should be considered for the message design:-

- Selection of words
- Length of message
- presetting of message

## 21.8 Selection of Media

After defining the publics and prioritizing them and after designing the message, the PR manager has to select the media. Media selection means using the media according to the objectives decided to project the campaign. The analysis of media effectiveness must be based on two main aspects:-

(a) Those communication channels should be selected which provide the message the best opportunity of being expressed clearly and effectively.

(b) The media selected must enable to communicate with as many of targeted audience as possible at the minimum cost.

(c) The right selection of media will be always based on money, effort and time saving.

(d) Media must be carefully selected by the PR person to maximize its reach to the target group to communicate message properly.

(e) It is also important that in any campaign not all media are used at the same stage.

Mass media like TVs, radio any newspapers\ Magazines inform and persuade a large number of people in a short time. Media relation is a key function of the PR profession. The objective of PR campaign determines the right media mix. But to educate and motivate people to take action, Interpersonal media are of utmost value. In order to make selective audience to act, the PR professionals have to go beyond the mass media. NGO's, social agent, personal contact and other specific media like direct mail or personal meeting can help to indulge action. According to Kotler and Roberto, interpersonal communication assumes a variety of roles.

## 21.9 Budget

As we know public- relations is a management discipline. It requires a proper budget for the smooth functioning of various activities and campaigns of PR. Budgeting is an important aspect of planning. It depends on the priorities.

There are generally two type of views about the way to arrive at the budget for PR campaign. One is need based budget and the other is related to sales turnover or to profits.

*Narrative budgeting system in PR*

- Benefit shadow pricing is another process in budgeting which assigns values to goods and services that may be not have a market in, for example, someone is asked how much they are willing to pay for a product (in which is not in the market) as if it is available in the market place. The assumption is that the individual estimates a price which could be aggregated to represent a fair market value.
- Cost benefit compensation is the benefit in relation to the cost involved Therefore, budget should be broadly allocated for media cost, creative charges, and other operation charges of the various promotional

activities of the campaign.

This allocation is made for particular period of time, usually a year.

Every budget should be reviewed time to time and should provide scope for effective control system on expenditure with provision for response to sudden change.

Though various methods are followed in establishing the budget, objective of task oriented method is most effective. It is realistic, appropriated and approachable.

## 21.10 Implemenation and Evaluation

Presuming that the strategy and activities suggested are approved and the necessary budget are made available; the further stage is the implementation of the plan of PR campaign. It is very much obvious that plan will not only be clear about the objectives but will also clearly have to identify target audience and the media or other means required to influence these audiences. Without identifying the audience very precisely the message is likely to get diffused and the exercise will prove too costly because there will be a considerable waste involved. If a PR man wishes every message of his\her to be carried to the teaching millions in the country, he\ she will only succeed in running his organization financially and even objectives. The more precisely therefore the audience can be pinpointed and the smaller the segment the more effective the campaign is likely to be.

The PR person will also have to decide how the program is to be implemented organizationally. For that, there should be a clear demarcation of responsibilities and a mutually agreed area of action for each. There should be careful supervision at each stage on how the plan is being implemented and if anything goes wrong corrective action should promptly be taken. In this process slight modification in the original plan in the light of experience gained may become necessary and should not be avoided merely because it marks a slight deviation from the original plan.

Once the plan has been implemented there should be a proper evaluation and through this an attempt should be made to discover how far the objectives have been achieved. Actually, effectiveness of the campaign is always a prime concern. Even before the PR campaign is released, it is necessary to evaluate its expected level of performance.

It is an integral part of the PR process. Strategic decision needs to be taken whether to take up evaluation as a "feed forward" i.e. before a PR programme is launched or only at the end of the campaign to estimate the level of its effectiveness. In this process, an evaluation can help prepare the public-relations programme. Keeping in view the perception of the public for whom the programme is being launched : How would the programme be evaluated? When and why and at what intervals? A PR person among all public via, employees, consumers, media writers, professionals etc, yet their perception also needs to be elicited before the launch can find them the campaign and after it is over to evaluate the change in perception. Perspectives from which evaluation is to be taken also need to be outlined, besides carefully deciding what to evaluate. The evaluation of effectiveness of a PR campaign may be considered with the reach, exposure and recall, credibility, understanding and readability.

Reach is and know need with a percentage of employees and external public particular relieved the campaign on a timely basis and the exposure and recall indicates how well did public recall important parts exposed in the specific campaign, credibility means did the public consider the launched campaign trustworthy. Further, understanding highlights the audiences understand the organization's position on important events and readability explains that were the external and internal public of PR able to comprehend the content of message without difficulty.

***Service Delivery and Evaluation and PR Campaign***

The evaluation can be through a questionnaire, interviews or electronic email, homilies, call center, mobile standard offices etc. These modes are known as a service delivery. The evaluation of PR programmes though taken seriously in corporate sectors abroad, is just coming into existence in India

The above framework offers the key guidelines to component parts of the PR campaign structure.

***Research for the Evaluation of PR***

*Campaign:* Research is a hallmark of the PR which is demanded by the industry or organization and govt. The main aspect of research embarked upon at the early stage of PR campaign includes exploratory, development research and concept testing. These may be undertaken using both qualitative and quantitative methodologies.

*Exploratory Research*

Research in the campaign process should be started at the very early stages of PR campaign and especially well before any substantial formation of the campaign.

Exploratory and developmental research offers guidelines for the campaign at the vary beginning and contributes to bench marking for evaluation. It also provides details as to whether a campaign is necessary to address an issue. Principally, exploratory research highlights the following:-

- Why is there a need to address the issue now?
- What is currently known about the particular issue and what previous research has been undertaken on the issue?
- Who is the community that the issue affects and what are the relevant characteristics, attitudes and behavior?

- How could the communication address the issue effectively?

*Developmental Research*

Once the above mentioned points have been cleared and vision more or less highlighted, developmental research should be started.

Once the aim, goals and objectives of the campaign have been decided, developmental research will help to invite more insight and depth into the main objective of the campaign. Apart from selected research methodologies mentioned above, the following types of evaluation research relate:-

- Benchmarking
- Tracking
- Post campaign evaluation

Benchmarking research provides a good insight into a circumstance in which the campaign is executed. Sometimes, it includes information regarding the target public's knowledge, awareness, attitudes, habits, priorities, behaviors or perception. It makes benchmark data against which the campaign could be evaluated together with any changes that may happen.

Tracking research controls and tracks the progress and changes among the external and internal publics. If the required improvement is not being completed successfully, the aim and plan of the campaign should be reanalyzed and changed. When a campaign has a nature of multi- phase, tracking will make the needs required for the next phase. Post campaign research helps to measure:-

- What has changed since the campaign started?
- How has it become different or move from one campaign to anothor?
- Why has it changed?

It may be necessary where there is some doubt or controversy with regard to the results to take recourse to the process of formal research. In other cases the outcome of the campaign and its effects may be fairly clear. Having found out the results and the extent to which the objectives originally set have been achieved, the PR person will move to the next campaign.

## 21.11 Summary

PR is a management function. Almost every company now engages in PR to some extent company managements becoming more aware of the usefulness and necessity of formal organized PR. The modern PR executive cannot expect success without complete detailed programming and campaign. Campaign is a systematic effort for finding a target. It evolves from planning to strategy. There are four principal categories on which any campaign is based they are : industrial and financial, commercial, institutional and government. PR campaign is a continuous affair. It must unfocused short term, multimedia, multi-dimensional with specific objectives. PR campaign involves four stages. These are fact finding, planning, implementation and evaluation.

Fact finding is related step of problem identification in PR campaign. The planning strategy process depends on the campaign objectives which may be long term campaign or short term. It requires a proper budget for the smooth functioning of various activities of the campaign. The PR person will also have to decide how the programme is to be implemental. There should be a clear supervision at each stage how the plan is being implemented and action should promptly be taken. Last but not least, the evaluation of the campaign is a strategic decision but it is an integral part of the PR process. The evaluation of a campaign can be through a service delivery. Today, research is a hall mark of the PR campaign demanded by industry and organizations. It includes exploratory and development research. Post campaign research may be necessary to find out the doubts or controversy. After getting the result of launched campaign, the PR person evaluates and analyzes all the activities along with profit gain and loss and then he starts to move for the next campaign.

**Self Assessment Exercise**

Q1. What do you understand by PR campaign?

Q2. Describe the type of PR campaign.

Q3. Elaborate the framework of the planning of PR campaign.

Q4. What do you understand by public in PR? Describe the types of public of PR.

Q5. Explain the message design and its guidelines.

Q6. What is the role of budget in the PR campaign?

Q7. Explain the kind and importance of research in the PR.

**Suggested Readings**

(1) Seema Sharma, "*Public-Relations*" Anmol Publications Pvt Ltd., 2005.

(2) Caroline Block, "*The PR Practioner's : A Handbook*" Viva Books Pvt. Ltd., 2003.

(3) David. W. Wragg, *An Introduction to Public – Relations,* Blackwell Publishers, 1992.

(4) Paul Burton, *Corporate PR*, Reinhold Publishing House, New York.

# 22

# Crisis Management

## 22.1 Objectives

The objectives of this lesson are :-

- To highlight the meaning of crisis and its introduction.
- To inform to types of crisis.
- To explain the concept of crisis management.
- To explain the process of preparing for crisis management.
- To analyse the various steps for crisis management.
- To elaborate the role of crisis services.
- To discuss the review of crisis management.
- To indicate the precedence for the future of crisis PR.

## 22.2 Introduction

Every organization faces a time of severe difficulty, occasionally, which is know as a crisis. Even if they have not be found crisis is always there. Crisis are often turning points in organization life. The management of crisis will help the PR person to take action even if the situation is totally paralysed. Dictionary defines "crisis" as a crucial event or turning point- an unstable period especially one of extreme trouble or danger- a course or a disease.

Besides many PR practitioners have offered other definitions :

- "Crisis is an issue in hurry"
- "Crisis is an serious incident- which has or will affect human safety, or is threatening to life and\ or health and \ or the environment The above-mentioned definitions indicate that a major issue can be at least as damaging to an organization as a following definition which attempts, to draw the close relationship between an issue and a crisis for the public relation practiones:-

"A sudden incident or a long term problem- possibly triggered by a sudden incident- which could damage an organizations its share price and impact upon the way it is able to conduct itself in future". According to the above said definition, we can say which seriously interferes with the operation of the organization and which can be regarded as unwelcome by those involved.

The above mentioned definition indicates the crisis situations which may be divided into categories- first, those that happen at fairly regular intervals and second those that occur in any organization. For example, crisis arising out of strikes, lockouts, worker unrest. There are crisis that take place rarely but draw considerably great public attention example of this type of crisis is a big accident. A suitable example of this type of crisis relates to the Bhopal gas leak.

In the case of first type of crisis the preventive measures consist of continuing efforts to establish good employees, effective management of communication within organization which not only gives for communication from the top to bottom, but will be a frequent way of communication. There must be a provision for a regular interaction with the public or employee representative group.

Crisis situations are always the concern of PR, and in many instances can be greatly alleviated by public- relations situation which has been identified as a crisis of an organization:-

(1) A disaster
(2) A strike
(3) An antitrust investigation

***A Disaster***

A disaster may be of different types, such as natural disaster which includes earthquakes, floods, droughts, civil commotion and should pay the close attention to PR process involved in a disaster situation as it does to the safety procedures designed to protect it starts, such as a fire, or explosion in a company, there is going to be a decided amount of panic. If company is totally unprepared from the PR stand point, or else its policies and process are so poor then they fail. Here, it should be very much clear that PR procedures not only prevent damage to a building, but PR practitioner can help a company to go through a disaster with lowest damage to its image.

In this situation the following steps will be helpful to avoid the abovementioned circumstances:-

(1) The moment, there is hint of disaster; the PR department must be alerted.
(2) The name of local news media must be filed by the PR office so they can call in the event of an emergency.
(3) A plan for working with press should be in existence at all times. Photograph and interviews from eyewitness, should be arranged.
(4) Police should be informed as to general type of details that would be given to the media press during the disaster.

(5) In setting up process and policies which would be implemented during disaster crisis a PR professional should keep in mind the attitude of media or press towards disaster.

*Strikes*

Strikes include mainly lockouts and acute industrial unrest. Each strike has its own characteristics and poses different problem, solutions. Some strikes are violent others merely involve picketing and across the table negotiations. It is inevitable in any strike, and emotions will run high, increasing the danger of making a PR mistake that could seriously damage the company.

On the other hand, the organization should always be quick to put forth its side on an issue. The media or press will n will feel entitled to it. In early stages of almost any strike, newsmen will want speak several times each day with a company spokesman on the progress from the organization's point of view.

*Antitrust Investigation*

This is directly related to the lawyers. The PR person associates with this field only when the trouble starts. PR people should relate to lawyer and top management educating everyone, who could move antitrust violation to possible pitfalls. The main steps of an antitrust prevention programme are to create awareness among all concerned of the difficulties in business. The first point to make in any anti- trust education programme is that enforcement is non political. From the PR viewpoint, result to a company's reputation upon conviction. It would seem that only an insane businessman would violate the antitrust laws seeing these penalties. The PR people would do well to become acquainted with lawyer of the company, either directly or through corporate channels. On so doing they will be in a better position to help the situation in the event of the company being charged with any violation. Customers antitrust pitfalls must be guarded against.

*Crisis Situation*

There are some other types of examples which have been identified as crisis f organizations:-

(1) Serious accident, involving fatalities or injurious simply affecting the ability of the organization to function.

(2) The loss of a significant market or customers.

(3) Interruption to the supply of materials or components.

(4) Industrial disuses.

(5) An unwanted takeover bid.

(6) The withdrawal of a planned takeover or the withdrawal of financial support by a major sponsor backer.

(7) The election of a government hostile to the arms of the organization.

(8) A serious product defect, requiring withdrawal.

(9) Accident, incident or sudden illness affecting the ability of a key member of the organization's management to function.

(10) The discovery of criminal or fraudulent activity related to senior member of staff or management, and putting the integrity of the organization at stake.

(11) Criminal activity against the organization, such as raids on banks or building societies.

(12) Tampering with a product.

It is significant that the effect of any such crisis on employees should be taken into account just as much as to any external audience. A crisis requires wholehearted favor from the employees. Employees can be amongst the victims of a lack of communications, it does not matter whether the crisis is self- inflicted or not, or indeed whether it is man- made or the result of natural disasters such as an earthquake. It is still necessary to display concern for those involved.

In some cases the outcome of a crisis that employees are liable to disciplinary action or prosecutions for negligence impacts their livelihood by the removal of driving or pilot's license or essential qualifications.

## 22.3 Crisis Management

Every organization makes news and the best news has some element of controversy or conflict, tension and human interest. The media spotlight is on the organization, whatever the sector and whatever the business. So the organization that finds itself in perceived misdemeanors or causes damage to society, or environment is certain to create the headline.The PR section manages the crisis at two levels:

(1) The top management should be involved directly in dealing with totality of the situation.

(2) The task is one of communicating with media and other external publics to ensure that the public is kept informed and has access to facts throughout the period of the crisis. It is in the latter area that the public-relations department is directly involved. Imporatant area which need to be taken into account and which have been referenced are :

(1) The preventive measures

(2) The contingency plans

(3) The actual operation

(1) The preventive measure are identified in the area of known or unknown crisis. The preventive measures involve constant review of safety measures and internal communication emphasizing the prime importance of safety. The contingency plan will associate the provision of a route which can be used when access to the organisation's normal office is not possible. The contingency plan would require the center away from organisation's premise through this control center measures must immediately be started to give

relief and maintain a flow of information to the media and external publics, as well as, the employees. It will require maintenance of numbers of key management functionaries so that communication between the top management and other levels of the management does not break down. The PR should maintain continuous liaison with the control center. It must also provide feedback to the control center and the media of external publics and of employees. The content of communication campaign and the forms of media to be used should emphasis on briefing the press and keeping it informed and also finding suitable channels of communication through which employees can be kept informed of management policies and on the progress of negotiations. The actual crisis is concerned with the development following the unprecedented event. This type of crisis is quite unusual as a disaster had never before taken place. There are three advance occasions that represent effective PR crisis management.

(1) Take steps to prevent a disaster before it occurs.
(2) Establish standby measures should an emergency happen.
(3) Design programme to recoup company's image.
(4) Designate an authorized company's spokesperson.
(5) Provide information on personal details of the families involved as quickly as possible as facts can be verified.
(6) Refrain from speculation on a subject.
(7) Take the initiative in informing the press if they are not already aware of the situation.
(8) The basic statement should be available in printed format and also for electronic transmission.
(9) The statement should be updated frequently as more information becomes available.
(10) Demonstrate your concern and give reassurance.
(11) Let people know where and when information will be available.
(12) Direct people to the company's website for more information.

***Crisis Management Strategy***

To deicide the strategy of crisis management, first of all there is a need to examine the nature of the crisis by following question:-

(a) Fundamental problem.
(b) Organization fault.
(c) Is there an inherent weakness that makes company vulnerable.
(d) How can we correct this?
(e) How can company prepare for a similar situation ?
(f) What is the worst case scenario?
(g) What will he target audience think?
(h) What are the timing implications?
(i) What is at stake regarding company's image.

***Communication Strategy***

Communication strategy should decide with the action plan by the following direction:-

(a) How proactive \ reactive does the company need to be?

(b) What targets does the company need to communicate with?

(c) What media need to be briefed?

(d) How do we do it?

- written\ email\ web cast\ press conference, one to one press briefing.

A p! ess conference packs containing the following:-

(a, Current statement.

(b) Backgrounders on the organization including history, aims, objectives, major documents ( e.g annual report) financial.

(c) Policy statement.

(d) Biographies of spokesperson and other board directors.

(e) Visuals if required or request for photographs\ video.

(f) Digital photography – e.g. sites- product.

(g) Video footage.

(h) Consider extra resourcing need for the crisis headquarter including staffing to cope 24 hours seven days a week.

(i) Keep employees aware of development as they occur.

(j) Staff and media should be briefed.

## 22.4 Guiding Principle for Crisis Management

Crisis management is about seizing the initiative – taking control of what has happened before it manage crisis is the key to corporate survival. Taking action in a crisis can be fraught with risk. Therefore the guiding management.

- Have a positive attitude towards crisis management.
- Bring performance all over the organization into line with public expectations. Develop credibility through such behavior.
- Obtain and act on the opportunities during crisis.

***Approach to Manage the Crisis***

The following approach may be used in the crisis:-

(1) Existing situation which have the potential to become crisis.

(2) Crises which have beset the company in the past.

(3) Planned activity.

With the above said approach, there may be a need to catalogue the area of risk. From this point it becomes sthe logical series of steps which need to be taken in the crisis management planning process.

***Planning for a Crisis***

Advance planning makes it more possible to concentrate on the actual problem when it breaks. Every organization should have an effective crisis management plan. So, planning for crisis management may be framed :

(a) cataloguing potential crisis situation.

(b) devising policies for their prevention.

(c) Formulating strategies and tactics for dealing with each potential crisis.

(d) Identifying who will be affected by them.

(e) Devising effective communication channels to those affected so as to minimize loss to the organization's image.

(f) Testing everything.

The first step is to identify the potential for a crisis which could affect the organization. PR should look at a number of matters capable of developing into a crisis.

Employees are an important factor during the crisis. They are always most sympathetic and most critical. Sympathetic simply because of knowing the business. Yet they may be critical because they know the organization better. Organization should always have a core, team of people senior members of the operational financial, leg functions, with a responsible executive director in charge. The following steps are necessary for preparing a plan for acting during the crisis :

(1) Identify issues which could escalate into a crisis.

(2) Creating a management team along with the services of specialized consultancies mainly PR used who can be investigate the problem, providing recommendations which include training for management and staff to cope with.

(3) Identify key audiences and be ready with communication targeted at these audiences during the critical early days.

(4) Will crisis be operated from head office or from a remote location? Some organizations centralize and have a limited function in branch offices.

(5) For accidents and incidents, practice emergency procedures, possibly having consultant to help.

(6) Ensure that anyone likely to face the media has the essential training. He\ she must be able to understand the what and why.

(7) The senior management of the organization should be encouraged to live within easy reach of head office.

(8) Provide guidelines on crisis management as well as corporate viewpoint on major issues along with phone numbers of those involved with this work.

(9) Additional support for press, customer and personnel department.

(10) Provide updated information as the situation develops and more information becomes available.

(11) Use the fastest means of communication available, with circulars, electronic mail, telex or facimiles and bring information internally and use a two- way communications to up- date the media. When providing information to give the priority to the leading newspapers and TV channels. To manage the crisis three separate teams are formed :
   (a) Core committee
   (b) Crisis control team.
   (c) Communication team.

*Core Committee*

This will comprise main board directors whose role is to take the high ground of the crisis. Members are grouped together. Each team member must be assigned specific, individual responsibilities for the handling of crisis core committee should have an alternate in case someone is away. The team leader must chair regular information bulletins to the entire team members. The core committee probably should be located near the head office to help the crisis control team.

*Crisis Control Team*

The second team to come into play is the crisis control team, responsible for the immediate response. The crisis team will be located at the site of the crisis to help the core committee constantly up- dated.

*Communication Team*

Communication is an aspect of the management function is generally given a high prioty in the situation essential to keep updated on the background information packs about the organization and each installation or part potentially at risk. The communication team should include colour and black white photographs , diagrams, no of the organizations, business duration, and description, names of key executives and safety records and practices.

All these informations enable the media to begin framing the story they will later write or broadcast.

***Media Centre***

To set- up a media centre is an essential part of handling the crisis. If it is not possible, those, present in company premises will be provided opportunity to tell details once or twice a day connected by media people. The press conference site should contain external telephone lines, fax machine a large diagram visual aid material, background information press packs, refreshment (not alcohol), adequate security. For the success of press conference the following useful tips may be considered :

(1) Permit those who have specific knowledge of different aspect of the incident and insure the presence in the press conference of company executive, who is a good communicator.

(2) Place a time parameter on the conference. It should not be less than 30 minutes. End the conference at the decided time.
(3) Issue a new press release at conclusion of the conference.
(4) Arrange one to one television interviews after the conference.

***Media Calls***

Incoming telephone calls from the media will far outweigh the numbers of reporters able to get the site. designate a media telephone response room equipped with sufficient handset and its own dedicated telephone number issued via the wire services on the site of emergency. There must be a constant flow of information from the crisis team with the media responders so new information may be constantly accessed and passed on the media .

***Calls from Relatives***

This is most important area in crisis communication management. It is one of the most complete communication response. Many companies family members should be identified in the crisis or accident.

***Emergency Public Information Center***

It comprises a set of rooms only in a crisis situation. In companies, the relative response team has a designated meeting room equipped in the same way as the media responders. A separate administration team should deal with logistics of getting family members to the hospital. The company will also require ensuring company rep to assist family members in hospital.

***The News Release***

It is a key communication tool in a crisis situation. News release presented by the organization's official may be used for indicating statements from senior management on how it is managing the crisis. A press detail with time and date will enable journalist to keep tabs on the chronological order of events. It also helps in attaining a consistency of message from all those involved. Press statement should always declare crisis, location of crisis, details of fatalities, details of injured or affected, details of areas affected, impact on the environment. Messages taken for public or customers, statement from senior manager expressing include regret for crisis and sympathizing and assuring for those in the emergency. It includes details about follow- up investigation and reminder about site's safety record.

***Information for Employees***

In a serious crisis it is important to keep employees well informed about the situation and they should not receive crisis information via media because employees are the ambassadors of the company.

They should have access to company press statements prior to release of the news. It can be through info letters from senior management or printed newsletters to keep them updated regularly. There should also be a policy that it is not the role of employees to talk to the media about the crisis. There is a need to convince the employee to stay out of enquiry and media should contact the press office of the organization.

### *The Role of the Crisis Services*

*The police*: - Police and security can be of enormous help in crisis of a physical nature. Ideally, the police is that accompanied by a senior company representative so that immediate assistance can be offered to the close relations. The attendance. When survivors arrive at the hospital, or relatives and media reach at the place of the accident, to maintain and organize traffic flows, establish meeting points, make secure the scene of the incident and organize appropriate measures.

### *The Fire Brigade*

The fire brigade may be requisitioned in an emergency or crises situation. It should be informed in detail as to the crisis. The key is to ensure message properly and in time.

### *Local Police*

Company site managers should keep in regular contact with local police.

## 22.5 Review of Crisis Management

The key to crisis management is crisis prevention. A comprehensive contingency planning can minimise causing great damage and a good and open communication can minimize a loss to intergrated and personal image. The companies – whatever their sphere of operation- should regulate their activites so the opportunity of crisis is well under control by offering professional counseling. It is found that while surviving a crisis the company is provided number of chances to recognize itself to ensure it never again gets itself in a similar position.

## 22.6 Precedent of Crisis Management

Crisis by their nature have a small time span available with the organization. In this time the crisis would either solve or intensify. Crisis consists of following features :

(1) As stress increases in a crisis performance worsen.

(2) Inadequate performance is directly proportionate to the complexity to the work.

(3) Behavioral patterns change during the time of intense stress and move towards simplistic and basic forms of behaviour.

(4) As stress improvers, we recommend as "displacement vision" or "tunnel vision". One tends to avoid the side effects.

(5) In the situation of crisis, communication is minimizing likely to be accept as you had planned it to be.

**Self- Assessment Question**

1. What do you mean by crisis management?
2. Discuss the various guiding principles of crisis management.
3. What is the Importance of handling media during crisis?

**Suggested Readings**

(1) Chase, W. Howard (1984) *Issue Management; Origins of the Fullers*; Sue Action Publications Inc, Hess Burg, Vir.

(2) Kinsdorf, Marion (1990) "Crisis Management" *Public-Relations Journal*, March.

(3) David, W. Wragg, (1992) *An Introduction to Public- Relations*, Oxford, U.K.

# 23

# Public-Relations in Practice

## 23.1 Objective

The objective of this chapter is to highlights the aspect of practice of public relations because the role of PR practitioner is becoming much more sophisticated and demanding. This chapter will concentrate on the day to day issues of public- relations practice and management rather then academy theory. It highlights the various aspects of public-relations i.e. marketing communication, media relations, internal communication, community relations, financial public-relations, local government and government PR, business to business communications, along with public-relation for non commercial organizations. It also emphasizes on sponsorship and environmental PR. This lesson gives you an overview of all the major functional areas of PR.

This lesson provides a good insight into the role and practice of PR within organization.

## 23.2 Introduction

The PR profession is becoming more practical oriented, sophisticated and demanding as the contribution of communication is being increasingly recognized as challenging to any organization. Because PR still has a great deal to do to escape the clichés that surround it, and to gain the respect that such a complex and powerful profession deserves but it is on the way. Presently, there are number of young people coming into the PR profession who are equipped through training and experience to take their place with fellow professionals. The skills required to act and advise as a communication professional are of the highest order, and transferable into any position within any organization.

Practice of PR covers so many specialist area .This PR profession needs both the focused specialists and there is plenty of scope for both. Marketing communication is a type of PR that most commercial organizations employ quite extensively. Internal communication is vital means to motivate and inform the staff greatly improving community relations and finding its place as a powerful weapon for those taking corporate responsibility and some time seemingly the impenetrable areas of public-affairs (government and govt PR). Besides these, the sponsorship also works well and gives real added value to PR programmes. There are some well known areas of PR. Business to business PR work often goes on quietly behind the scenes, but has a major effect on the bottom line of the company. Nowadays the non profit making sectors are also utilizing PR in powerful, cool, effective campaign that have spearheaded social change and raise crores of rupees for worthy causes. Some legislative and people ied demands have required organization to take up environmental PR. It explains why and how environmental PR can be positive asset, not just a necessity for 'forward looking companies'.

### 23.3 Media – Relations in PR

Media relations are the most important aspect of the practice of PR. It is a new concept and broadly based activity offering more than just media relations. Although, one cannot escape the fact that media relations is important in PR practice and could be fairly described as the single most important element in overall PR mix. It is found that when handled well media relations can be as precise as advertising in reaching the target audience being more persuasive and, as a result far more cost effective. Media contact of a more direct and personal nature in essential in any effective PR programme. The role of PR person is to be able to handle enquiries, providing information, and discussing the background to a particular development. The PR function knows exactly what particular journalists will find of interest.

PR person should be present at all such contacts and there are several reasons for this. Firstly, the PR person can provide guidance and support. Secondly, PR person can ensure that the rules which can or can't be quoted will be followed by the both parties Thirdly, interviews, especially with the senior person act as a briefing for the PR function, updating what is going on, and also on how the organization is prepared to be quoted on a development. Fourthly, PR ensures fair play for both parties, Finally, PR people understand the mood of the media and organization for which they are working.

#### *Establishing Relationship*

The PR function must fully understand the business, whether a commercial organization or some non – commercial activity. The PR professional must also be aware of and able to understand the philosophy of the organization and its strategy for the short, medium and longer term, it is also necessary for PR to be a part of executive or management committee taking important decisions.

It is necessary to get the essential right so that media contact and indeed contact with other interested groups or audience can be handled efficiently. PR should be always carefull that media enquiries require and immediate response or as near immediate as possible.

***Relation with Media***

Mutual trust is the key element media relationship. PR should understand that interest of the media and of the organization are not necessarily the same. Relations with media include the following events:

*(A) Press Conference*

Definitely, press conference is best effective means to establish good media- relations. But this is only suitable for a significant story. It includes major events which might include announcing details of crisis, or demonstrating a major new product launch or announcing the financial results of a major company.

*(B) Press Reception*

A reception is a very good idea if the news story is not strong enough but one can invite sufficient senior officers of the press to mark their presence for an opportunity to hold an informal discussion with leading figures in the company.

*(C) Press Launch*

Sometime press launches are useful for an interview. This is a time to meet senior officers of the management. Such launch builds contact and good relations. While in managing this programme, there are some points to be kept in mind:

- Contact them before 24 hours
- There should be record of who attended
- Brief the invitees in advance about issues of interests
- Programme, should be planned in advance. With time schedule and refreshment.
- Material for distribution during the function to the media should be arranged.

**23.4 Managing News and Features**

News and features material is the very essence of the work of a press office. The effective PR practitioner ensures that material is carefully targeted for the most suitable publication and, along with telecast on all broadcasting stations. A story which has relatively small impact nationally can often be of significance in local newspaper throughout the country. If a local aspect can be included, which that can be something as simple as attributing any quote to the local brand manager. To time the announcement of a major story in a way that it will have a better chance of being used or provide due prominence, is also important.

Weekly local morning daily, daily evening and Sunday newspapers all have different headlines. A story which surfaces in the wrong newspaper at the wrong time can be paid less attention by other newspapers. Any story which breaks in a Sunday newspaper has to be very worthwhile indeed to appear on the Monday morning.

PR must have the authority to be able to hold back or even abandon less important stories if there is a danger of flooding the media or distracting them from other more significant events within a particular organization. So quality is more important than important quantity. There are people in PR and especially in consultancy who will programme a certain number of stories per month or over a year.

The desperation for media coverage, which one sometimes finds results in all means to ensure that a particular story does receive some attention.

There is no correct length for a press release- the correct length is as short as it is possible to be while covering the necessary facts, and perhaps adding a comment which humanizes the piece, adding best information which is the best handled through a quote than in the main body of a release.

Local and regional newspapers will usually regard 500-600 words as a reasonable length, while the quality newspaper will go for 800- 1,200 words, and trade, professional and other specialized periodicals will differ in their requirements.

Most of all, managing news and features look for topical events. One should ensure that the product is brought to the attention of the media at suitable times of the year. Definitely, there are other ways of raising the relevance or topicality of a news items or a feature. There are several occasions when a PR can improve the coverage of a story.

A good photograph supplying can help one increase the amount of space obtained in the newspaper. Video clips, some background materials and an interview with a relevant expert or director, can also improve coverage.

The fastest way of reaching large numbers of newspaper, radio- TV and internal is to use a e-PR(electronic PR) services so that all receive information simultaneously on the printers in the office.

*There are few things which should keep in mind by PR offices.*

- Be aware about the news as well as good news
- Make the update contact list of media and include the best contacts.
- Angle the story for various market segments.
- Deadline and publication telecasting and broadcasting dates for Organizing press conference and press briefing occasionally.
- Be aware of seasonal opportunity for certain product or series
- Be ready to collect feedback.

- Provide visual backup with a press release.
- Provide other explanatory material such as brochures etc.
- Some products or services, such as stage production, films, recorded music, books and so on.
- Sample of product
- Provide a story with sufficient interest.
- Time- sensitive story must reach in time to media offices.
- Additional material in form of background articles or features, interviews, photographic opportunity, recorded interview with audio- video.
- Contact name on any material issued to the media.
- Avoid clashing with major announcement with competition.

### *Photography*

Photography is an important tool of PR function. Many corporate need to have a good historic photographics library. Essentially photography is essential for the following applications:-

- To promote products or services
- To announce and record, an event such as VIP visit or a factory opening.
- To maintain a record of the organization's progress
- To display and provide a visual record of the organisation work and its achievements.
- To monitor application of the corporate identities.

Therefore, PR must have control of the photography which it uses, be it for annual report or employee communications or for media use. The marketing department meets the cost of product photography for PR use but this cannot absolve the PR department of responsibility for the direction of such photography. It is not enough for the marketing department to provide extra prints to ensure good, newsworthy, photographic material. There are some essential steps involved while managing the photographs in the practice of PR:-

*Storage*:- Colour photographics should be field in special plastic hanging wallets and black and white hanging files within acid free wallets to ensure they survive.

*Indexing*: - Every item should be indexed and cross indexed by subject, location and date.

*Captioning:* - Every illustration should have a caption prints should have it pasted, using non-destructive adhesive, on the back, while transparencies or negatives should be indexed against a caption.

*Stock Control*: - Well stored collection of photography helps to enrich the PR office- even the name, address, fax and telephone\ mobile no of the photographer should be maintained on the file. Important, Photographs should be stacked separately.

*Periodic Review*: - There should be review of the stock from time to time so that the most important photography is replaced by more up- to-date illustration. On the occasion of launching a new product on the opening of new branches or new policies or equipment of any significance introduced, photography will probably be taken and copies should be added to the photo library of PR office.

*History*: - The collection and record of the photography of the past within the organization will be invaluable in the future. Generally, every organization has a historical file or section which includes photographs.

### Marketing Communication

Public- relation plays a vital role in marketing operation, particularly with the four P's- product, price, place and promotion. The discipline of marketing includes getting the right products (goods or services) in the right quantity - at the right place - at the right time and making a profit out of operation.

Role of PR in the marketing mix is very easy to communicate key message to identified target group with the marketing network to influence buying behavior and thinking. For example, IT advertising shows about the company then PR expresses what others think and say about the company. Actually, advt. and PR lies between paying for media space versus the use of editorial with implied third party endorsement to get best recognition.

PR practice is the discipline which takes care of reputation with the purpose of building establishing and influencing opinion and behavior. So, when reputation affects marketing, PR has key part to play in the marketing mix, and management functions. It enhances internal and external relationship. It makes an important contribution to a company's competitiveness and overall market position. In this process, word of month creates its own level brand, customer loyalty, retention and retention PR can assist in such cases by supporting to shape the message to be carried by word of month. Thus the PR performs the following functions:-

- Make market scenario favourable.
- Improve share of voice
- Inform and educate the consumer
- Influence the trade
- Support a sales force
- Opinion leader
- Extent promotions
- Type advertising
- Exploit sponsorship
- Manage issues
- Contain crises

All the above can be dealt by marketing communication PR.

***P R Activities for Marketing Mix***

Planning is a primary process to implement the PR activities of marketing mix. It should be in the written form with marketing data and research based information about the brand, product, and services. The marketing strategy and identified PR objectives and target group with available budget should be associated to the written document of public- relation planning in the marketing mix.

PR professional should ask the following questions in order to achieve successful understanding:-

(1) Details of organization and its mission objectives

(2) Specific marketing objectives of organization along with a copy of marketing plan

(3) Additional market research of such process of product distribution and delivery, customer profile- awareness and acceptance, potential consumer or target audience demographics or psychographics.

(4) Company\ product iterative

(5) Other marketing communication initiative in any place e.g., advertising, promotion, marchendising, derect marketing, sponsorship etc.

(6) Running image of company product

(7) Customers views about organization\ produce

(8) Characteristics\ special feature of your organization\ product

(9) Media dealing:- receive, positive, central, negative, coverage. How much coverage organization receives?

(10) Evaluation of the success of PR campaign.

(11) Comments of relevant personnel of the organization

Beyond above these other helpful information may be collected such as copies of previous media coverage, information alternative on the products or services, competition and market research two reports. Interactions with and on consumers fitting the target audience profile or media personnel within the target media may be helpful to PR marketing communication.

***Marketing Integration/(Unified Marketing)***

PR in a marketing mix can improve other marketing disciplines being used; it can be used, separately as the only marketing component. The concept of unified or integration is with other marketing disciplines such as advertising and sales promotion, or running patrolled campaigns separately which do not tally with the other advertising programmes i.e. paid for media. PR can also be used in external advertising campaign by taking a celebrity appearing in the advertisement and using him or her as product model or spokesperson in advertorial and editorial terms. Above the line advertising may be used to promote a product. This is sought to communicate product features and profits to discreet niche target group. PR can be used very effectively to potential audience sector for cost effectivity and without alienation with the larger overall audience. By using PR to target specific population, an organization may be able to provide an additional promotional boost of its product.

**Campaign/Advancement or Planning**

Independent research helps to clarify the situation before a planning approach is considered. Focus group may be used for qualitative analysis. Research may also be carried out to test the validity of the brief or a general auproach. For developing a situation analysis a careful evaluation of the SWOT – strength weakness, opportunities and threats of the product\ organization – a swot analysis should be done. It is a kind of balance sheet of the ratio from which the key messages and strategic approach may begin to be advanced. Strategy and approach should be always as simple as possible and with current status, future direction of the organization or its product.

After the determination of overall approach, the campaign will take shape by identified techniques and strategy in a practical oriented creative way along with tactical recommendations with facts, i.e. market research, forecasts, trends, logistic research etc. Marketing threats take all shapes and sizes. PR has been used to promote new products, events and new developments. Today's marketing professions realise that PR can do much more than create a flurry of editorial coverage which improves awareness and share of voice. PR in the marketing mix is becoming increasingly sophisticated. A measured approach can be used to steer public-opinion over time to re-position the image of the organization and create interest in or even build a pre-disposition to buy or motivate. Performance of PR in marketing mix continues to grow as its cost- effectivness and ability to deliver measurable impact increases.

***Product Launches***

When any product launches in the market there is a great need to create maximum noise and widespread media coverage for story or an interesting write- up. Thorough review of the market and study of competitors activity is an essential part to develop a programme. Press material, together with the sample of product should be distributed on an 'exclusive' basis to media men covering launching event and they should be provided some filler material also for the coverage.

After launching, a wide range of activities must be implemented immediately to maintain media and public's interest in the product until it goes for sale and throughout the market.

*Good News Stories*

Should be announced in a newly launched product, such as then signing of professional cricket player and hitting a sixer in a professional cricket match by a cricket star wearing the shoe.

*Media Promotion*

An offer and opportunity to win a product before they went for sale. It should be in both print and electronic media.

*One to One Coaching*

It should be held with selected media and contracted professionals players celebrities\ model\ to demonstrate product performance.

*Photo Shoot*

There should be an arrangement of photo shoot with celebrities. Seeing that celebrities can use the product- will be helpful to create a feeling that the launching product is useful to celebrities also.

*Documentary Series*

Radio, TV documentary series should be produced and may be aired in a programme about the concept and development of product, focusing on the inventor of manufacturers.

*AD Campaign*

The company can run an advertising campaign. Ad campaign can make an excellent impact. The strength of third party endorsement via media coverage persuades to accept the claims made by company's advertising campaign.

The advertising's print coverage reaches an audience of million based on circulation figures and within minutes of broadcast and telecast coverage.

***Creating Brand Equity***

The mind of a communications professional or PR professional should be full of changing trends regarding target group 'mindset'. The following points should keep in mind by the PR professional:

*Consumer Confidence*

It is related to consumer awareness as today's consumer is increasingly expecting good deals.

*Relationship*

Networking with target group and society. On the basis of above said point we can say that organizations are striving to recruit as many consumers as possible in brand and then increase that share of consumer. The following tools can be helpful to improve the equity: - (a) the company portfolio: - can be enhanced through the product which includes other personal finance and services. This type of exercise increases the share of each customers spending.

*The Positive Media Coverage*

If company is launching any new product or services, then there is a need to use an independent tracking study undertaken by CARMA computer Aided Research and Media Analysis. It determines the favorability of media coverage. It shows the cause and effect, tracking of proactive public- relations practices and initiative against resulting editorial coverage. This attempts demonstrates a remarkable improvement in the brand equity.

**Prospects of PR in Marketing Mix**

As earlier mentioned that the public relation role in the marketing mix is to communicate key message by public or third party endorsement. It defines target audience with market networking to influence buying behavior with cost effectively.

The role of PR in the marketing mix is a way in which PR is practiced. It may be changed considerably in future with the following market elements:

- Increasing complexity of the consumer and their requirements and demands
- Fast changing media technologies which are influencing and giving a shape to the marker place
- Globalization of brands and marketing

The associating media will be helpful to shape the career of marketing communication PR in the field of operation or diversification and globalization and interactive television and internet.

Nowadays the complex result of an action or event are various for public relations. Because consumers are quite aware and exposure to a knowledge-based society cannot include conflicting views or cannot be argued. There is only one way i.e. persuasion and only through logic development this may be achieved.

***Internal Communication in PR Practice***

Internal communication is best effective tool of PR practice. In other words, we say that good communication is a valuable motivator. Communication is close attention concentration that helps to make teams, strengthen pride in working for a company and motivates public (Internal) to work that bit harder to beat competition. But the communication must be in line with strategy so that public has the proper framework to work within. It is a link between an organizations' need for change and an employee's need for feeling free from fear or anxiety in a secure way. It is found that sometime staff does not know what they are doing and why, they are doing and why, they are less likely to perform well.

***Information for Public***

Communication is a two way process which involves sending and receiving or listening and telling of the messages. There are three main categories of the process of sharing the information:-

*Intergrated*: - build pride and belonging for the organization. Personnel feel proud to work for and feel good about company.

*Cascade:* - Cascade communication is especially one in a series. In this process message pour downwards rapidly and in large quality. Cascade communicates objectives.

*Personal*: - It is day to day encouragement and persuasion to achieve the desired target.

In the process of effective communication there is a need of all above mentioned three. It also motivates public to say their vision, thought about the received information. When public watch management decision or their feedback the whole communication process builds trust and credibility. In practice the communication process becomes the right tool for developing the bottom line.

***Practical Skill of Communication for PR Practices***

Special skills to communicate for the practice of PR is an essential need. Comfortable communication with the staff creates healthy environment in the organization. There are some communication techniques which may be used in the practice of PR?

*Face To Face Communication*

For the analysis and study of the attitude of public and employee, face to face communication is the most suitable technique. It is always admirable.

*Team Meetings and Large Gatherings*

Through the team meeting and large gatherings staff has the choice to listen to, and ask questions from a senior manager to facilitate focus. Group meeting provides staff the opportunity to provide feedback.

*House Journal*

House journal is the most effective medium of internal communication in practice of PR Articles and write- ups in house journal, will create positive situation among the public. Videos, audio-tapes, are easy to listen on the way to work. Actually, there is a need to be tailored to the individual of not just- the company but also the basic communication principle timeliness, openness and honesty.

As communication is a shared resource. The success or failure of communication rests with the whole organization, with the support from the person at the very top.

### *Communication and Leadership in PR Practice*

Communication is a line management responsibility and is a two-way-process between staff and management. For a long established and reputable international business the leadership communication deals with, how in general marketing business and in particular, internal communication from being soft option to a strategic imperative to helps turn the business round.

The commitment and motivation of people both work for the organization. Where knowledge and understanding of performance provide the motivation, and returns and the need to manage costs were accepted as the day-to-day way of working for everyone in the organization, right from driver to peon.

Any highly developed and decentralized organization needs to understand its local customers also.

*Preparing Description*

There are three important factors help to prepare a description or background for internal communication of company.

*First Factor: The cultural change process.*

*Second Factor: Result of Global Attitude*

A second factor support to make the ground is the result of a global attitude. When company ask its employee where they can to get information regarding their jobs and their company, definitely the answer will be "the Boss". This view is echoed in the attitude summary of most companies. Inspite of being on the internet people still want to hear what is going on from their bosses.

*Third Factors: Made Imperative*

It makes vital importance for change in the communication for company. The impact of technology also play a significant role. Today most staff of company has access to personal computer. An electronic technologies and hence to e-mail. People around the word with gossip, reunions in real time. So the PR practitioners and their communication techniques have to change. Even e-mail is a very powerful tool. This cannot be ignored and has to be managed as part of the communication process of the practice of PR.

### *Positive Attitude*

The following points must be considered to make positive attitude among the public:-

- The dialogue
- Communication
- Expertise of company

*How to Make Positive Attitude*

Good communication makes good attitude. Attitude and techniques based on the following tips should be followed by individual managers.

(1) Upward feedback and appraisal.
(2) Open thinking, i.e., openness, personal impact, empowerment and networking.
(3) Communication network
(4) Global communication network.
(5) Communication platform.
(6) Task force : identified best practices
(7) Communication with staff.

*Guideline of Positive Communication*

Communication process in PR practice varies from country to country. But who does what and where must be considered in the process of positive communication: with the followings:-

- Executive spends full 50% of working time communicating with his\her staff.
- Meet a small cross – section of staff over a lunch\ to find out what is going on their mind.
- Invite small groups of key middle managers to meet on an informal basis for discussing communication issues.
- Formal monthly meeting :- In the meetings first to appreciate the chance to be together and discuss about what was going on in their inside and immediate areas.
- Make your own cosidentral communication also.
- Consultation between management and PR professionals.
- It is a virtuous communication circle.

Therefore, to facilitate an open timely and balanced two way communication process in which messages about company and its objectives enhance company's ability to perform is the role of PR professionals. Actually the PR profession is there to help management. They have to facilitate and perform in the best way. Because communication is soft issue in any organization today, many companies are using a variety of communication tools of internal communication i.e. regular meetings – meetings during journey audio programme and awards and feed- back.

***Relation with Human Resources***

Strong relations between human resource and PR professionals are being forged because both are essentially helping staff in good management. Good PR should be always ready to listen to the staff as to what they are saying. This is the key to upward feed back and appraisal. So, the HR and PR professionals are joining forces to help coach, train and counsel managers in these vital skills. A couple of good PR communication practices are implicit to the message in the following:-

*First-* Communication best practice is to be short, simple and memorable.

*Second-* Use consistently: - Again and again to staff, city, and media – person.

*Third-* Repetition:-Use head office jargon.

To perform the above mentioned there is a need to form a team of PR professionals and live-management. They have to work closely with each other and with their colleagues to enhance the company reputation and to build image. It includes employees and financial analysis, the media and the environment lists.

Actually communication is one of the three skills management must practice, the other two are coaching and visibility. Employee communication. also is the "button" the group needs to press to continue delivering performance.

The best practice of communication is :

- Use face to face communication (with training). It is primary method of communication.
- Involve professional communicators to deliver the message in the appropriate way to various target groups and to provide feedback.
- Identify and communicate a positive change.
- Co-ordinate the timing of communication too staff.
- Avoid speculation.
- Allow maximum time for public to talk through whatever they want to talk about.
- Communicate with staff in a clear, honest, consistent and timely manner.

## Community Relations

Community relation is a series of mutually beneficial business partnership with one or more stakeholders, which enhance good corporate citizen partnership community can be either a local, regional, national or international. All community relation programmes have measurable impact on the overall perception of the company, by external and internal public.

The PR professionals should be expert and capable to demonstrate the achievable benefits of the community relations stream and can present the added value of such a programme to a company's overall business objectives.

Most of the companies now aim to maximize community programmes by adding value. Companies are now feeling the benefits of associating their staff in deciding how the community should be supported and which activities will form the key focus centre. It makes opportunities for association, personal improvement, takes pride in supporting the local community and boost up morale, as employees realize that their help is valued by both the community and the company. A community relations programme can benefit the organization in two ways. The first is by education based sponsorship. Which create awareness in local schools and or are linked to the national curriculum which helps establish a company a team of desirable employees with resultant potential and recruitment opportunity. Secondly they can provide opportunities for employees to develop their skills by working with local schools.

Community programmes can help to focus the support of the local media MPs and other key opinion leaders.

*System of community relations programme*

The systems which are usually being used in community relation programme are based on a combination of sponsorship, targeted donation, awards hospitality, employee volunteering, use of facilities, seminars, associate links with various field such as arts, sports, education, the environment, occupational health along with safety, charities, heritage, senior citizen, underprivileged group, youth, disabilities and many more categories.

Similarly, company can work with partnership with the local community also to spread awareness against crime, foeticide especially among its employees.

Community relations are consistently delivering messages to key target audiences. It can also have a direct impact on media relations, investor relations, shareholder communication strategies and many others. It is therefore both about justice to people or helping the local community.

The programme is based on the following:- (a) commercial principle of research (b) vision, (c) strategic objective (d) tactics, (e) analysis and evaluation and communication skill with key audience.

*Development of Community Relation Programme*

A regular media contact programme should be established to maximize all future publicity opportunities. This can be at a local, regional or national scale, involvement brochure, community newsletters, appropriate photographs, and exhibition can enhance the community programme.

*Evaluation*

Community programme is usually measured by the following key indicators:-

(1) Publicity achievers
(2) Employee feedback
(3) Value for many
(4) Creativity
(5) External benchmark
(6) Appreciation
(7) Preparation of opinion former

*Association of Employees in Community Programme*

The company encourages employees to become associated in the local communities. It can be through the followings ways :

- Preferential treatment.
- By the reward and recognition award presentation.
- Award presentation.
- Employee volunteering.
- Committee membership.

***Financial PR***

Getting the right messages to the right people at the right time is the essence of success. The PR strategy can succeed if the management of the company are doing their duty perfectly and recognize the significant role that communications has to play.

Financial public and corporate relation people, however successful should keep in mind at all times that they are only part of the communication process.

A good PR campaign is one that is effective, not necessarily one that gets noticed. Financial PR may require more discipline and more technical knowledge. The most aspect of communication activity, It also needs to be every bit as creative as the most sophisticates consumer PR.

A new company requires a different financial PR campaign to a company presentating results or a new stock market listing. However, there are a number of key points that need to addressed before embarking on any financial campaign:-

- Objective of the campaign with preferred time scale for achieving the objectives.
- Identified key strength along with core of the camping message.
- Identified weakness of the company and its management to develop a communication plan.
- Identified spokesperson, properly prepared and trained in media-management for presenting the case in front of media.
- Coordinated and well linked PR and marketing activity released by the company.
- Well planned format of events which matches with company's financial calander along with rules and regulation of stock exchange.
- Methods and process of evaluation of campaign.

***Importance of Financial PR***

As already mentioned in this lesson that corporative and financial PR are interlinked to the extent of often being indistinguishable. An organization's corporate image and that of its management is the basic foundation upon which financial PR is built. Financial PR can not be totally separated from the consumer and business to business PR carried out by any company. Therefore the quality and reputation of a company's services and products cannot be separated from its corporate image and the way it is seen by its financial audiences.

Political and govt. affairs activity also have to be closely coordinated with financial PR activity.

So, today's financial PR is an area where professional knowledge and skill are needed.

The communication strategy devised by management and the in- house PR director ensures an understanding of the company's business strategy and its objectives of highlighting its somewhat diverse business.

*Structure In-House- PR Department* :- The in-house PR department is set up to both manage media- and investor relations in a coordinated way to develop an understanding of the company's opinion leader whether they are journalists or investment analysis institution fund managers. The department of eight or so people divided the work into three main areas- media relations, investor relations and the rest including internal communication, events and publication.

The director PR takes on the responsibility for investor relations with one or two media- relation experts. They perform all PR functions, including handling of a press office. Their major job is as an advisor to the chief executive and finance director.

A perfect PR person knows well the nature of PR, he\ she already has a good reputation and does not disappoint shareholders.

***PR with Govt and Local Govt.***

Public – relations is a need to ensure that the organization's aim, philosophy and motives are consistent, both in terms of the way in which the organization performs with its external markers or identified target group and the way in which its internal activities reflect the organizations objectives.

Public- relation is know as public- affairs also. It is not an exact science. But there are similar methods to consider it as a public- affairs process when looking at government at central and local level for support. Actually support will not be forthcoming without knowledge and knowledge is derived from information via research and campaign planning. Such knowledge also needs to be communicated, shared, debated and agreed upon if that is an essential ingredient to aid success. In the other words, we can say that effective PR is a name of successful public affairs. It has ability to understand and influence opinion.

It is essential therefore to have a clear vision of what is trying to be achieved and what the strategic aims are? Who are the potential audiences, identifying the important messages for key people what are the effective ways of achieving and maintaining contact with public?

The range of activities expected may be planned by those involved in public affairs and communication with govt and local govt, media relations, community relations, advertising, issue management, investor relations, staff communication, corporate publications and conferences, seminars etc.

The overall objective in any campaign must be to build support for PR activity.

*Central and Local Govt.*

Today, everybody is exposed to the system followed in central and local govt. and non-elected bodies, trusts, and so on. They are responsible for running associated with education, health and water. In organizations a democracy the an every system of govt though sometimes complex, still remains in of many countries. As PR practitioners one should know their functioning and means of access.

GOVT:- It is very much difficult to identify the running of a govt department and shape and size of its cabinet since change can occur overnight. The media should be able to identify the new structure of govt or a shift in ministerial portfolios.

The role of govt remains constant i.e. to legislate and regulate, actually govt is playing a significant role in the country as a prime employer and a major customer. Nowadays extra lines of communication with govt have developed.

*Approach*: Making relations with govt has become an industry of its own. There are number of lobbying companies which will claim as part of their services to have the right contact or to effect the right introductions.

Research and making the right relations with international, national, regional and local govt will provide more productive outcome. There is a need to invest more time to key influencing figures. It cultivates a positive attitude of public towards the issue.

*PR should use influential figure for effective introduction he\she should :*

Start at or near the top of the organization to be targeted. In this process there is great need to assign a senior- in- house person to make contact and to lead the campaign. PR should develop a good rapport with those outside the organization who can help or advise.

Meetings with ministers and civil servants and dialogue with them may assist the PR efforts. It gives a point of contact while starting. The govt has its own PR officers who act as spokes person for department and are part of the govt information service and are therefore at the center of "official" govt activity.

*Local Members*: - PR should establish contact with local MLA's opinion leaders. Because contact with local leaders is less complicate than contact with the ministers. Frequent visits and correspondence with them can make long term benefit for the PR relations. It is important to remember, however, that correspondence or letters play the role of persuasion of public- affairs activity pressure negotiate and open up other channels of communication or potential support will be invaluable in the long term. Detailed knowledge of the particular process party documents, policy papers, can help to strengthen the PR relations with local and central govt. PR professionals should assist the MPs and MLA's make the key points in debate, a letter to a newspaper or in a speech.

Guidelines about gaining opportunity to approach the govt and local govt are :

- Make the right target for communication
- Make relations in a professional way.
- Do it at the first opportunity, but identify any politically important time such as in the election duration.
- Frequent relations with flow of information

Therefore, it is better to have a rapport, earn an image for credibility and demonstrate a reliable voice by ensuring your public affairs or public-relations. It should be carefully planned, managed and sustained overtime.

*Local Govt*: - Local govt is an important organ of democratic system of representation. Their constituents are present in the Parliament, so the local public has the opportunity to elect MLA's or Mayor, along with member of municipal corporation.

*Gaining Access*: - It is not essential that every organisation will be able to appoint a professional PR officer or will publish their own leaflets or newspapers. Maintaining of a comprehensive telephone directory and issue citizen's charter information centre obtained from public offices such as libraries may be the foundation of effective PR for corporate sector.

Local govt is more accessible to the public than central govt. Municipal and Panchayat offices and services are in the locality, with their committees-where the decisions are taken open to the public. So there is need to consider them as an important target for information and potential alliances in public-affairs activity. The following objective and group should be identified:-

*Objective*: - To raise public awareness through media

- To persuade the govt
- To press the govt to provide distinctly by introducing a new concept in the local and central administration system.

*The Groups*:-

- The public
- Opinion leader in local central govt
- MP's, MLA's, municipal members and its officials
- Other chief authorities of administration
- The media

*Implementation*

- Informed. Constructive, positive and supportive approach through media
- A feature article about the research
- Press conference
- Employees should be kept informed

According to the above mentioned points the scope of public- affairs is widespread in today's communication led society. The public- affairs strategy must be sufficiently robust to withstand such scrutiny and the organization's philosophy and its personnel will be tested.

***Business to Business PR***

Business to business PR is based on customer demand. In many areas of business, customer services have become a marketing tool where public relations is a valuable tool to help achieve the end. Although in the business to business environment it is going to take more than just public- relations to achieve the overall goals.

***PR Work for Business***

Business to business trade press coverage can be a fickle thing and is unlikely to give a clear vision of just what customers think.

Tracking results in the trade press are key issues which will help to give an idea of trends but PR should have to assess customer perception realty to have a clear idea of what they actuality think.

Tracking like this also helps to define the PR goals.

The trade press is worth taking a closer look at not least because of being in the specialist areas of business to business communications. PR professionals in corporate a wide variety of styles and approaches. From the small dedicated one person operations to the vast established "industry bible". PR professional should remember all communication internally should also reflect the organization's external position. So, business to business communication need to be seamless timely and have a goal that is measurable in more than just newspaper column inches or radio air time, for example: - If the company has to make difficult announcement. Something that is not going to go down too well or may be an issue of potential embarrassment then the following factors may help :

*First: Timing: Second: line of communication*

*Line of communication*

(a) Live broadcast: Radio
(b) All available commercial channels
(c) Other communication techniques: press, radio letters correspondence good news stories
(d) Press : good news stories

(e) News letters
(d) Direct marketing
(e) Mailing list
(f) Market research
(f) A pre-launch
(g) A constant feedback from clubmen's co- suppliers locally.
(e) Internal poster campaign
(f) Seminar

The above said are well tried techniques for the business to business PR. These techniques influence target groups which comprise local trading standards and local press journalists and industry representatives. Media coverage make positive and strong impact through right messages and handling. They are a part of the marketing media's annual agenda. PR can help in the traditional manner through proactive media work and the protection of the company when under attack and by improving communication link with identified audiences, and working to develop new approaches to handling a company's key clients and influence with the following directions:-

(1) Creative ideas with simplicity
(2) Message with every communicational devices
(3) Successful campaign with best ideas with effective communicational disciplines
(4) Join for us with other organizations with mutual benefits
(5) Media coverage with measurement techniques I.e. peruption views of the customers.
(6) Top priority of the company issue and development.

***PR for Non-Profit, Non-Commercial Organisation***

PR is the key ingredient of the organization. It is a highly motivated workforce. For example a charity like help the aged is knows as a non profit organisation. The variety of help for elderly people provides plenty of opportunity for proactive public- relations. This visibility provides plenty of opportunities for PR and promotions.

Non profit PR focuses attention on a neglected area of under privileged- the specific problems faced by concerned public for example. The company can provide transportation of the local level where important activities of non-profit PR take place and advice programme with other group and charities provide plenty of strong local stories and raise local awareness.

PR can distribute free information and advice leaflets to aged person and their careers. The leaflets attract media coverage because of their value and accuracy. The none profit PR activities and events every year can include award winning campaigns.

It provides the opportunity to tell story on a human scale. This proves successful in press and PR terms as well as provides a source of reassurance for needy public or community. In today's climate of increased emphasis on community care, non profit PR helps guard people's right to stay independently for as long as possible.

Non profit PR can take benefit of the growing opportunities through application of new technologies for particular group or community. Non profit PR provides specialist advice and information services which are easily accessible. Potential sponsors also offer attractive partnership with non- profit PR in delivering service to target group. Following points should be carefully considered in the non profit PR:-

- Research, statistics base clear message.
- Well planned campaign.
- Identify target audience.

  Tools of non profit PR conference, celebrity event, photo call, news release, advertisement or press conference.
- Decide the most appropriate media to carry the message-either in national, regional, radio, TVs, magazines or may be in poster or leaflets.
- Will briefed and trained staff with identified spokesperson.

*Brand Sponsorship*

Sponsorship aids in the business and brand promotion in the modern world. Famous companies invest in exciting events to increase international awareness of the product and expanding the sales. Thorough the sponsorship, the company tries to bring the product on the map of the world. It creates special attention. The origins of commercial sponsorship as we know it today are attributed to or when 1931 when Phil company sponsored the Philadelphia symphony orchestra and established a trend that others quickly followed. But the boom of sponsorship came 30 years later, when the tobacco companies found themselves increasingly restricted in the international areas of advertising and turned to sponsorship to create awareness for a growing number of different brands. Today, sponsorship has its own rightful place in the marketing mix and is seen to offer specific benefits that neither advertising or PR alone can deliver to the majority of advertising agencies which earlier tended to view sponsorship as a direct threat to their budget and profit. PR agencies have been inclined to see it as an opportunity to build business and help create a new corporate image for the client. In pursing this live, PR agencies have expressed themselves to be not only far more pragmatic, but commercially enlightened. The PR agency needs to guide to the clients to set realistic publicity objectives for the duration of the commitment and deliver the highest possible profile through the appropriate media. The television, radio, national press or even local or trade journalist should emphasize the dynamic culture of the organization to its identified target group. The PR agency should follow a well planned approach and persuade the client to quantify the value of sponsorship from the outset and creative public. Definitely, the PR inputs are crucial in communication the sponsorship and its significance. Once it is established, the sponsorship will need creative PR support to keep it in the public eye on a regular basis.

***PR with Environmental Issues***

The new millennium has seen a great improvement in public awareness over environmental issue. The media are full of coverage with environmental angle, i.e.- ozone layer, destruction of rainforests, increases in radiation levels, industrial , air, noise, and river pollution, population explosion etc.

Reflecting the increase in public awareness national govt are learning to address a wide range of environmental issues through the introduction of new legislation to cover areas as diverse as improved effluent pollution controls to the protection of endangered birds and animals. With the background of heightened public concern and ever-growing legislation, it is essential for every commercial enterprise to be clear where it stands on the environmental issues which may affect its operations.

PR can play a vital role in the management process with two counts when dealing with environmental issues.

First: It is the platform which provides management with information and monitors changing public attitude to relevant environmental issues.

Second: It can give the environmental suggestion and skill necessarily to present the environmental policy of an organization and activities related to the target group such as chemical industries are in the environmental limelight more than others. A responsible care programme was introduced a few years ago and adopted by chemical industry associations (CIA) members. They have encouraged open communication with employees and the public on environmental issues.

So, this is the right time with PR has to play an explanatory role. Effective public consultation can be achieved by undertaking research, holding public exhibition to visitors and generating positive editorial in local media.

PR has a key role to play in order to explain the benefits of development versus any negative environmental impact. They can also advise on the sensitivities of local environmental issues and on initiatives to offset negative relations by providing an environmental gain, e.g. funding a nature reserve, stocking the river with fish and so on.

The PR campaign associated with the venture generates extensive opportunities for imaginative photo- calls and editorials in national and local press.

School information packs, newsletters and promotions on a continuous basis a part of the PR campaign. These succeed in winning for the organisation a strong image as an environmentally sensitive multinational operation- as well as turning an environmental opportunity into a genuine business advantage.

Another initiative which can be successful through environmental PR is valuable publicity.

The culture of the management and staff should be in tune with environmental issues.

Constant media interest and publicity should be increased in various forms by PR. More emphasis on environment should be devoted in the companies annual reports by PR office.

**Summary**

PR is a practical oriented, sophisticated and demanding profession. Practice of PR includes so many specialized areas with plenty of scope. Media relations are the most important aspect of practice of PR. The role of PR is to know exactly what particular media will find of interest. The philosophy of the organization should be understand by PR professional. Organizing press conference, press receptions, press launch, sending news feature, writing feature, writing, photograph etc are of great help in establishing a good relationship with media. Role of PR in the marketing mix is to communicate key message to identified target group with the marketing network to influence buying behavior and internal communication in the organization. PR communication is a live management responsibility between staff and management. Strong relations between human resources and PR professionals are being forged because both are essential in helping staff and management. Community relations are a series of mutually beneficial business partnership which enhance the company's reputations as a good corporate citizen. Financial PR requires more disciplines and more technical knowledge. An organization's corporate image and that of its management is the basic foundation upon which financial PR is built.

PR is know as public- affairs which look towards govt at central and local level for support. PR practitioners should know the complexity of the central and state govt. Today's extra lines of communication with govt have come up. PR should build contact with local opinion leaders. Business to business PR is based on the customer demands. The trade press coverage can give clear vision of customer's opinion. Non profit PR is the key ingredient of any organization. It focuses attention on underprivileged or on neglected areas. It provides the opportunity to tell a good story on human scale. Sponsorship introduces the business and brand promotion in modern world. Today's, sponsorship has its own rightful place in the marketing mix.

PR has a key role to play in order to explain the benefits of development versus any negative impact of environment. It can play a vital role in the management process dealing with environmental issues.

***Self- Assessment Questions***

Q. 1. Describe the concept of the practice of PR with suitable example.

Q. 2. Explain the role of PR in various interdisciplinary fields.
Q. 3. What is role of media in public relations. Which techniques should be followed to establishing media relations?
Q. 4. What is marketing communication. How does PR is work with marketing communication?
Q. 5. What do you understand by internal communication. How can a PR make the international communication?
Q. 6. What is financial PR? How PR works as a financial PR? Describe the importance of PR.
Q. 7. Describe the PR with govt. What are the various opportunities to build approach central and state govt?
Q. 8. Describe the role of business to business PR in practice.
Q. 9. What is non profit PR? Describe the main features of non profit PR in practice.
Q. 10. Explain the importance of sponsorship in the field of public relations.
Q. 11. Explain the role of environmental PR for making and image building of an organization.

***Suggested Readings***

(1) Seema Sharma, "*Public-Relation*" Anmol Publications Pvt. Ltd., 2005.
(2) Caroline Block "*The PR practioner's : A Handbook*, Viva Books Pvt. Ltd., 2003.
(3) David. W. Wragg : *An Introduction to Public – Relations,* Blackwell Publishers, 1992.
(4) Paul Burton, *Corporate PR,* Reinhold Publishing House, New York.

# PART 3

# PR IN GOVERNMENT

# 24

# Public Relations in Government

**Aim**

PR is an essential and integrated component of public policy or service. The professional public relations activity will ensure the benefit to the citizens, for whom the policies or services are meant. This book aims in imparting such professional PR skill.

**Pre-requisite for PR**

- Knowledge about the organisations.
- Communication skill (oral and written) including language, presentation skills etc.
- Media Knowledge.

**Objective**

On completion of this book the student will:

- Be able to explain PR concept and its importance.
- Be able to explain the importance of organisational image.
- Be able to develop 'PR' programmes.
- Be able to maintain better media relations.

## 24.1 Definitions of Public Relations

"Public Relations is the deliberate, planned and sustained effort to establish and maintain mutual understanding between an organization and its publics."

**Institute of Public Relations, USA**

"Public relations is the attempt by information persuasion and adjustment to engineer public support for an activity, cause, movement or institution."

**Edward L. Bernays**

"Public Relations is a combination of philosophy, sociology, economics, language,psychology, journalism, communication and other knowledges into a system of human understanding."

**Herbert M. Baus**

"Merely human decency which flows from a good heart."

**Charles Plackard**

"Good performance, publicity appreciated because adequately communicated."

**Dale Carnegie Fortune (Magazine)**

"Public Relations is - winning friends and influencing people – writ large."

**Robert Heibroner**

"Everything involved in achieving a favourable opinion."

**George F. Meredith**

**Former President of the American Pubic Relation Association**

"The Management function which gives the same organized and careful attention to the asset of goodwill as is given to any other major asset of business."

**John W. Hill**

"Public Relations is distinctive management function which helps establish and maintain mutual lines of communication, understanding, acceptance and cooperation between an organization and its publics; involves the management of problems or issues; helps management to keep informed on and responsive to public opinion; defines and emphasizes the responsibility of management to serve the public interest; helps management keep abreast of and effectively utilize change, serving as an early warning system to help anticipate trends; and uses research and sound and ethical communication as its principal tools."

## 24.2 Origin of Public Relations

Thomas Jefferson (1807) used the phrase "Public relations" in the place of "State of thought" while writing his seventh address to the US Congress. In India, Great Indian Peninsular Railway Company Limited (GIP Railways) carried on publicity in Public Relations campaign in England to promote tourism to India through mass media and pamphlets. During the time of First World War a central publicity board was set up at Bombay (now Mumbai) for disseminating war news to the public and press. After Second World War the

Public Relations activity gained importance. Both private as well as Government started Public Relations campaigns.

## 24.3 Need for Public Relations

Investing on Public relations will help the organisation to achieve its objective effectively and smoothly. Public Relations is not creating good image for a bad team. Since false image cannot be sustained for a long time. Though the organization product or services are good it needs an effective Public Relations campaign for attracting, motivating the public to the product or service or towards the purpose of the programme. The event encourage and involvement from the public results in better image. An effective Public Relations can create and build up the image of an individual or an organisation or a nation. At the time of adverse publicity or when the organisation is under crisis an effective Public Relations can remove the "misunderstanding" and can create mutual understanding between the organisation and the public.

## 24.4 Functions of Public Relations

- Public Relations is establishing the relationship among the two groups (organisation and public).
- Art or Science of developing reciprocal understanding and goodwill.
- It analyses the public perception and attitude, identifies the organisation policy with public interest and then executes the programmes for communication with the public.

## 24.5 Elements of Public Relations

- A planned effort or management function.
- The relationship between an organisation and its publics
- Evaluation of public attitudes and opinions.
- An organisation's policies, procedures and actions as they relate to said organisation's publics.
- Steps taken to ensure that said policies, procedures and actions are in the public interest and socially responsible.
- Execution of an action and or communication programme.
- Development of rapport, goodwill, understanding and acceptance as the chief end result sought by public relations activities.

## 24.6 The Components and Tools of Public Relations

**"Public"**

A group of similar individuals; an assortment of persons having the same interests, problems, circumstances, goals; it is from such persons that

---

*Courtesy:*

1. Rex F. Harlow, Applied Public Relations p. 15, 16.
2. Rex F. Harlow, "Building a Public Relations Definition," *Public Relations Review*, 2 (winter 1976) p. 36.

opinion emanates. Public is a varied creature; it comes in many forms and sizes. Public has a multitude of wants and desires; it has its likes and dislikes, some times, strong likes and strong dislikes. Employers make for a public and employees another public; the government is a public and citizens constitute another public, and so on, each of these groups is a public of the sort, tries to attract a different audience with its own tools and techniques.

**"Relations"**

Human wants to create the need to establish relations with one another. The representative wants of the individuals will profoundly affect their relationship. To understand any relationship, therefore, one must understand the wants of those involved. Relationships are of all possible types. We have relationship by rank-superior to inferior, inferior to superior, and equal to equal. We have relationship by sentiment-benevolent, friendly, suspicious, jealous, hostile. A relationship may be active, or it may be passive it may be good or it may be bad, or it may be neutral. At any rate, the relationship is there to be accepted, ignored or altered, as desired.

**Propaganda**

Propaganda is the manipulation of symbols to transmit accepted attitudes and skills. It describes political application of publicity and advertising, also on a large scale, to the end of selling an idea or cause or success of a candidate or all three.

**Campaigns**

These consist of concerted, single-purpose publicity programme, usually on a more or less elaborate scale, employing coordinated publicity through a variety of media, aimed, at a number of targets, but focussed on specific objectives. A campaign objective may be the election of a candidate, the promotion of political cause or issue, the reaching of a sales goal, or the raising of a quota of funds.

**Lobbying**

It entails the exertion of influence, smooth and measured pressure on other, exercise of persuasion cum-pressure. In essence, it means a group putting its points of view forward in an attempt to win the other groups support.

### 24.7 Some Possibilities that Would Call for Public Relations

***Promotional Opportunity***

To inform the new service / policy which call for Public Relations to make wider publicity.

---

*Courtesy:* Raymond Simon, *Public Relations: Concepts and Practices,* 2nd ed. (Columbus, O.Grid, 1980), pp. 9, 11.

**Competition**

To overcome the resistance (pre-set mind condition).

**Controversy**

To eliminate the contradictory conditions in between the organisation and the public.

**Adverse publicity**

To inform the truth or correct issues and thereby removing the misunderstanding.

**Catastrophe**

Announcement of any unfavourable issues.

**Crisis**

Whenever threats arise.

## 24.8 Public Relations in Government

Public relations role in government:

The Government public relations contributes to:

1. Implementation of public policy.
2. Assisting the news media in coverage of government activities.
3. Reporting the citizenry on agency activities.
4. Increasing the internal cohesion of the agency.
5. Increasing the agency's sensitive to its public.
6. Mobilisation of support for the agency itself.

***National Objectives:***

The basic function of the government Public Relations department / agencies is to provide information, education/instruction to the citizens. The effort should also motivate the people directly or indirectly, to discharge these functions in a meaningful and purposeful manner, it is necessary that the Public Relations Department / wing should be clear about the broad objectives which guide their work.

The national objective should be non-political, non-controversial, and on which there should be a national consensus. The objectives should further the interests and the well being of the public as a whole and promote the many sided development of the country. The objectives should be long term and need not necessarily change with political vagaries.

## 24.7 Public Relations Objective

For developing a sound Public Relations programme, a clear well-defined Public Relations objective needs to be established. These objectives should be very specific and measurable.

Example:

Objective: To immunize two million children of the state above the age of 3 and below the age of 5 during the period of August 15 to August 30 to avert the Polio.

Evaluation: Success of the programme can be determined by the actual number immunized.

**Objective**

1. To begin to provide the public with regularly scheduled advertisements about the danger of burning plastic in open air and its associated disease like cancer, disabled child etc.
2. To personally contact once in 3 months all media representatives (press meet) in order to inform the health hazards and to seek their cooperation for highlighting the issues.

## 24.8 Public Relations Strategy

For effective implementation of the Public Relations objective a Public Relations strategy is to be evolved. The process of strategy starts with planning which consists of:

(a) Determining Key results area
(b) Define roles
(c) Selecting and setting objectives
(d) Preparing action plans relating to programming, scheduling, budgeting, fixing accountability and establishing rules and procedures.

Rice and Paisley suggest the guidelines for planning a successful campaign

(i) Assessment of the needs, goals and capabilities of target audiences.
(ii) Systematic campaign planning and production
(iii) Continuous evaluation
(iv) Complementary roles of mass media and interpersonal communication
(v) Selection of appropriate media for target audiences.

## 24. 9 Public Relations Process

The definition of Public Relations is related with the general public through publicity, those functions of a corporation, organisation, branch of military service, etc., concerned with informing the public of its activities, policies, etc., attempting to create favourable public opinions.

Public Relations is the planned effort to influence an opinion through good character and responsible performance, based upon mutually satisfactory two-way communications. It involves the following :

*(1) Research-listening:* This involves probing the opinions, attitudes and reactions of those concerned with the acts and policies of an organisation, then evaluating the inflow. This task also requires determining facts regarding the organisation: "what's our problem?"

*(2) Planning-decision making:* This involves bringing these attitudes, opinions, ideas and reactions to bear on the policies and programmes of the organisation. It will enable the organisation to chart a course in the interests of all concerned: "Here's what we can do."

*(3) Communication-action:* This involves explaining and dramatizing the chosen course to all those who may be affected and whose support is essential: "Here's what we did and why."

*(4) Evaluation:* This involves evaluating the results of the programme and the effectiveness of techniques used: "How did we do?"

**PR Process Phases**

The first phase of Public Relations process is identifying and listing out the information or message to the communicator.

The second phase of Public Relations is process to ascertain the existing image or awareness level about the issue in the target group or common public.

The third phase of Public Relations is developing of communication objectives and priorities.

The fourth phase of Public Relations is deals with developing the message and choosing the media to transit.

The fifth phase of Public Relations is the implementation of the message and media, coordination or the dissemination of message.

The sixth phase of Public Relations is communication process to check whether message reached properly and the expected action or behaviour or knowledge on image factors.

The seventh phase of Public Relations, in case the message did not reach properly is to identify the reason for the ineffectiveness and rectification of the same and disseminate the revised message.

Now, let us briefly see the above component:

**1. Listing and prioritising of information to be disseminated:**

*May wish to inform the public:*

(a) The new policy of the Government or organisation.
(b) The change in the existing policy.
(c) The new scheme promoted.
(d) The change in the existing scheme.

Public Relations activity starts with identifying the message to be disseminated and prioritised.

**2. Ascertaining the existing knowledge level or understanding the perceptions of the public**

The organisation can hold a quick survey among the target group of the public to ascertain the knowledge level of the issue for which the organisation is planning to initiate Public Relations process and in case of the image it is essential to know whether the image is positive, neutral or negative in terms of the assessment or in terms of the organisation or both.

**3. Communication objectives and priorities**

Based on the knowledge level or image factor, communication objectives is to be established which is possible to evaluate and the top management approval is required. For example, communication objective instead of using the term increasing awareness level about the scheme, it should be specific "By 2020, in the number of families where of the scheme is implemented to be at least one lakh" so that we can evaluate the impact.

**4. Message and Media**

After choosing the objective, the content of the message needs to be developed. While developing the message we should keep in mind the media which we are going to use for disseminating that message. TV/Visual media may be effective for spreading awareness. Training media may be effective where the recipient may wish to keep the gap or further reference.

**5. Implementation of message and media**

Based on the expected reaching level and target group, the budget is to be prepared and message is transmitted through the appropriate media.

**6. Impact assessment**

After release of the message, it is essential to study the impact at interval by interacting with the target group.

**7. Message redesigned**

In case, the interaction of the target group reveals the message did not reach as expected the modification in message or media needs to be done and the revised message should be disseminated.

**The research process**

Opinion, market and academic researchers have developed a pattern of research that involves nine basic steps:

(1) Statement of the problem.
(2) Selection of a manageable portion of the problem.
(3) Definition of concepts and terms.
(4) Literature search.
(5) Development of a hypothesis.
(6) Determination of a study design.
(7) Gathering of the data.
(8) Analysis of the data.

(9) Recording of the implications, generalisation, conclusions.

Research for analysis of a specific problem should include these elements:

(1) A broad overview of what has gone before that influences the present situation

(2) Changes expected in the environment in the next year or so that could affect the organisation.

(3) Social, political and economic trends foreseeable in the next five to ten years that could affect the organisation; and

(4) What the organisation can do to influence the public to accelerate favourable trends and slow down unfavourable ones.

**Public Relations Process:**

There are at least nine questions to be answered while conducting a PR campaign.

(i) What are the objectives in influencing public opinion?

(ii) What are the alternative avenues of action for attaining them?

(iii) What are the risks in taking each avenue?

(iv) What are the potential benefits in each?

(v) What are the potential consequences beyond each?

(vi) Which avenue do we choose to take?

(vii) What should be the structure of a proposal to proceed on the course chosen embodying the projects and programmes we want to carry out?

(viii) In what form do we present our proposal to best advantage for approval? To whom?

(ix) What is the minimum commitment in support and participation acceptable from administration if the plan is to go forward and succeed?

**Analytical Matrix for Public Relations Programming**

| Target group | Information Interest | Intended Effect | Message | Media | Priority | Active |
|---|---|---|---|---|---|---|
| | (Most receptive) | (Reaction or Relation effect) | (Policy and image values) | (Establish and Possible) | (Long range or Short Term or) Temporary | (Rough outline) |

**Problem statement:**

The first product of the research is a statement that summarises what was learnt about the problem situation. Written in present tense, the problem statement describes the situation in specific and measurable terms. It details most or all of the following:

*What* is the source of concern?

*Where* is this a problem?

***When*** is it a problem?
***Who*** is involved or affected?
***How*** are they involved or affected?
***Why*** is this a concern to the organisation and its publics?

# 25

# Image Building

## 25.1 Introduction

Image is the mental perceptions of the person related to an object, a product, service, an individual or an organisation. The image need not necessarily be true and image is only an indication that how a person is perceived by the other(s). The organisations do have an image in the minds of public, customer, employee, Government or for that matter in any interested group. Some organisations enjoy a favourable image, whereas some organisations do not enjoy such a favourable image. The image is beneficial for organisations for achieving their objective. Images may be friendly, speedy, honest, corruptive, efficient, etc. Though we can not say which is a right image or wrong image, we can say some images are favourable to an organisation for achieving its objective with relative easiness.

## 25.2 Image Building Exercises

The Image building exercises start with understanding the present image and to chalk out, the desired image and to channalise all the Public Relations activities towards it. Now let us see how Public Relations department can understand the present image. The Public Relations department can gather information from various sources through appropriate data collection method. Some of the data collection methods which will be helpful for understanding the image is described below:

### *(1) Primary Data through Interview*

Holding interview for primary data collection method is best-suited method. Here the organisation contacts the target groups (Public) and obtains information. This is possible by developing a structured schedule or non structured interview and encourages the respondent to come out with the information in a friendly atmosphere and as spontaneous as possible. Such information collected from various groups will form the basis for analysis.

***(2) Data from secondary sources***

Organisation can collect information / data information especially in terms of image, from published sources, informations like article or coverage by newspapers or journals, where the organisation is referred in some reports or referred at public meeting. This may provide a clue to, what the other persons views are about the organisation. This will also help the organisation in understanding and analysing the situation.

***(3) Analysis***

The data collected from primary and secondary method can form the basis for analysis and the required information is to be culled out with reference to image / public perception. This refers to the image prevailing at that time among the target group or group from which the information is obtained.

The Present image could be

Favourable

Neutral

Unfavourable/Undesirable

**Desired Image**

The organisation may prefer a certain image and they like to project that image in the minds of the public or among the target group. Normally top management and PR departments are involved in this exercise and they will identify the Mission Statement of the organisation and the preferred image that will help the organization to achieve its mission. For example: A social service organisation involved in propagating income generation programme for the poor, may like to have a image as "Friendly Organisation". Whereas, some other organisation who are also involved in the similar activity may prefer image of being "Speedy".

**Projecting the image (Image Building activity)**

'Based on the existing image and the preferred image, it is essential to note that whether the preferred image is deviated from the present image or closely associated or neutral. Based on the existing image the PR needs to be focused. In case of negative or unfavourable image, P.R. needs to focus first on either neutralizing or removing the misunderstanding about the organisation and then develop the required impressions. In case of neutral or favourable image, the Public Relations can focus on more details about the organisation for creating favourable preferred image.

Public Relations functions need to adopt the appropriate strategy, by choosing appropriate message, appropriate media for the information in the most effective manner so that the desired image can be creative and contribute to the organisation's success and growth.

**Public Opinion Research**

Public Opinion Research ascertains what people think about an organisation, its policy, service etc. and why they think so as well as their attitudes toward the organisation, etc.

**Image Study**

The image study seeks to understand how an organisation is known, its reputation and also what people think about its service, policies, etc.

**Motivation Research**

Motivation research ascertains why the public attach favour or disfavour and why they are showing positive attitude or negative attitude and also the underlying emotional factor.

## 25.3 Effectiveness Surveys

Effectiveness Surveys helps to measure the impact of Public Relations activities on public opinion. Before initiating Public Relations activities the survey is to be conducted to ascertain the attitude of the people and another survey is to be conducted after the campaign is over to see if there is any change and whether the public opinion is tilted in favour of the Public Relations objectives and thereby the result.

Public Relations plays an important vital role in enhancing the image of organisation in the eyes of the public. Public Relations is not projecting the negative as positive. Public Relations is the process of communication with the group with whom the organisation exists and functions.

# 26

# Communication and Message Development

## 26.1 Communication Programme

Communication programme consists of message, media and budget. The word communication is derived from the Latin *communis*, meaning "common." The purpose of communication is to establish a commonness. The basic elements in communication are the source or sender, the message, and the destination or receiver. Effective communication requires efficiency on the part of all three. The communicator must use a channel that will carry the message to the receiver. The message must be within the receiver's capacity to comprehend. The message must motivate the receiver's self-interest and cause him or her to respond. Communicators need to bear in mind that communication is no substitute for policy and action. A sender can encode a message and a receiver decode it only in terms of their own experience and knowledge. When there has been no common experience, then communication becomes virtually impossible. Commonness in communication is essential to link people and purpose together in any cooperative system.

The Communication programme includes:

(i) Developing the message
(ii) Selection of media
(iii) Appropriate budget for implementing the programme.

## 26.2 Message Development

For achieving the desired result, the message should be developed properly and clearly. The appropriate message will have the following three attributes:

(1) Clear
(2) Correct and
(3) Concise

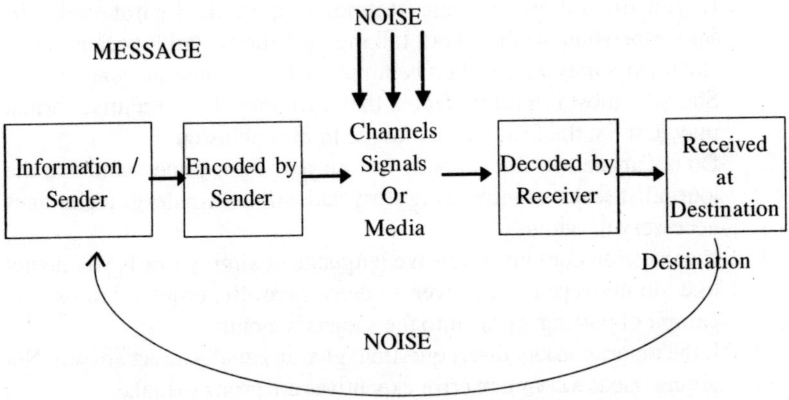


**Clear**

The message is free from ambiguity and it is necessary to ensure that slang phrases usage are avoided and also the message should be free from perceptional distortion problems. As far as possible, one should use simple language, simple style, appropriate words and right tone.

The credibility of the message is based on the credibility of the source and also the correctness of the content. It is essential to ensure that the information provided (message) is true and to unbiased and there is a source to verify it. It is essential to avoid content based on rumours, hearsay as well as source of no origin.

**Concise**

Since message dissemination involves time and effort for transmitting as well as receiving or absorbing the message should be crisp enough to and at the same time not occupy much time of the receivers valuable time. The content should revolve around the core element of the message; frills and verbose/ornamental language need to be avoided. The effectiveness of the message depends upon the above three attributes and if any component is missing or negative, the result will also be negative or not as per the expectations.

***Some Specific Guidelines***

Practitioners and executives alike can profit through a close study of these guidelines developed by an experienced counselor, Chester Burger:

1. Talk from the viewpoint of the public's interest, not the organization's. The soft drink bottler who launches a campaign to collect and recycle bottles can frankly admit that it does not want to irritate the public by having its product litter the landscape.
2. Speak in personal terms whenever possible. When many people have worked on developing a new product or adopting a new policy, it becomes difficult for the executive to say "I."

3. If you do not want some statement quoted, do not make it. Spokespersons should avoid talking "off the record," because such statements may well end up being published without the source.
4. State the most important fact at the beginning. The executive format may first list the facts that led to the final conclusion.
5. Do not argue with the reporter or lose your cool. Understand that the journalist seeks an interesting story and will use whatever techniques necessary to obtain it.
6. If a question contains offensive language or simply words you do not like, do not repeat them even to deny them. Reporters often use the gambit of putting words into the subject's mouth.
7. If the reporter asks a direct question, give an equally direct answer. Not giving one is a common error executives are prone to make.
8. If a spokesperson does not know the answer to a question, one should simply say, "I don't know, but I'll find out for you." With this, the spokesperson assumes the responsibility of following through.
9. Tell the truth, even if it hurts. In this era of skepticism and hostility, the most difficult task is often simply telling the truth.
10. Do not exaggerate the facts. Crying wolf makes it harder to be heard next time out.

These guidelines simply add up to the rule that profitable press relations require adherence to the "Five Fs" in dealing with journalists and programme producers in a manner that is : fast, factual, frank, fair and friendly.

**Essentials of Good Copy**

Essentials of good publicity copy are essentials of good news writing. A few reminders can serve as a checklist.

Will the information or news really interest the intended audience?

Does the information answer every reasonable question that readers or listeners may ask?

Is the significance of the information explained in terms of audience?

Is the copy sufficiently news worthy to survive stiff competition for public attention?

Will the information further the objectives of our institution? Is it useful?

Does the publicity accurately reflect the character and nature of the institution it represents?

Are the facts, names, and dates accurate? Are the technical terms explained?

Will the lead catch and hold the busy reader's or inattentive viewer's attention?

Will it a produce a bright, eye-catching headline? Is the lead terse or to the point?

---

*Courtesy* : Pg. No. 435, *Effective Public Relations*, 6th Edition, Scott M.Cutlip, Allen H.Center, Glen M. Brooms.

Do the facts of the story support the lead in fact and spirit?

Is it a readable copy, stripped of superlatives? Good news copy must be correct, clear,concise.

Is the copy written so as to preclude the charge that it is an effort to get "free advertising"?

Is the information presented as dramatically as possible with this set of facts? Squeeze all the news value you can into your story, but don't exaggerate.

**Print Media**

Here are some fundamental principles for print advertising:

1. Use simple Layouts
2. The illustration is usually more important than the Headline
3. Look for story appeal in the illustration
4. Photographs work better than artwork
5. Offer a benefit in the Headline
6. Don't be afraid of long copy
7. Make it easy to read
8. Every advertisement should be a complete sale
9. Break out of the mould
10. Design the advertisement for the medium.

## 26.3. MEDIA : Media Profile

| *Media* | *Target Group* | *Geographic Area* | *Usefulness* | *Remarks* |
|---|---|---|---|---|
| Cable Television | Literate and Non- Literate including children | Urban, Semi- Urban and Rural | 1. Demonstration is possible (seeing is believing).<br>2. Visuals have better impact and recall.<br>3. Cost per reach may be less.<br>4. Quick access to the mass population.<br>5. Regional Issues can be better covered.<br>Appropriate channel selection may result in better response. | 1. Appropriate.<br>2. Image of the cable television and the popularity among the target group needs to be identified. |
| Folk drama | People with no formal education | Semi-urban and Rural | 1. Possibility of concept telling through stories.<br>2. Mass (people) will identify themselves with the character.<br>3. May be effective for immediate results (emotion based). | 1. Cost factor<br>2. Space |
| Pamphlets, Brochures, Manuals and Books | Literate | Urban and semi urban and also Rural | 1. Act as Reference<br>2. Repetitive exposure is possible. | 1. Concept to action duration.<br>2. Correctness of the content is vital. |
| Spoken Word | All | Urban, Semi- Urban and Rural | **The Grapevine:**<br>The grapevine is not a formal or controlled medium, but word-of-mouth which is often the quickest | 1. Need careful attention. |
| Radio | Literate and Non- Literate | Semi-Urban and Rural | 1. Easy to reach.<br>2. Useful in disseminating voice to transit celebrities (remark or command).<br>3. Relatively inexpensive (cost per reach) | 1. Availability and use of Radio |

*(Contd.)*

*(Contd. Table )*

| *Media* | *Target Group* | *Geographic Area* | *Usefulness* | *Remarks* |
|---|---|---|---|---|
| Television | Literate and Non- Literate including children | Urban, Semi- Urban and Rural | 1. Demonstration is possible (seeing is believing).<br>2. Visuals have better impact and recall.<br>3. Cost per reach may be less.<br>4. Quick access to the mass population. | 1. Availability and use of Television.<br>2. Cost factor<br>3. Production factors |
| Motion picture (Cinema AD) | Literate and Non- Literate | Semi-urban and Rural | 1. Demonstration is possible.<br>2. Visuals have better impact.<br>3. Cost per reach may be less.<br>4. Repetition is possible. | 1. Production factor<br>2. Concept to action duration. |
| Newspaper (Regional / Regional language) | Educated | Urban and Rural | 1. Where one way communication is sufficient).<br>2. Reference is possible.<br>3. Easy to catch the attention of the reader.<br>4. Reputation of the newspaper is useful in disseminating information. | 1. The cost per reach depends on circulation figure among the target group. |
| Newspaper (English) | Educated | Urban and Semiurban | 1. The reputation of the newspaper may attach weightage to the content.<br>2. Used as a reference. | 1. The cost per reach depends on circulation figure among the target group. |

*(Contd.)*

*(Contd. Table )*

| *Media* | *Target Group* | *Geographic Area* | *Usefulness* . | *Remarks* |
|---|---|---|---|---|
| Journals / Magazines | Educated | Urban and Rural | 1. If content matches with a profile of the Journal's target group then it may be effective.<br>2. Repetitive exposure is possible. | 1. May not be possible for urgent information dissemination.<br>2. As the journals normally prepared long before the issue. |
| Hoardings | Literate and also Non- Literate | Urban and Rural, transit etc. | 1. Useful for short information.<br>2. Catching attention is possible.<br>3. Relatively inexpensive. | 1. Availability of space |
| Puppet show | People with no formal education | Semi-urban and Rural | 1. Possibility of concept telling through stories.<br>2. Cheaper than drama<br>3. People will identify themselves with the character. | 1. Concept of action duration |
| Posters | Educated | Semi-Urban and Rural | 1. Less expensive.<br>2. Easy to adopt | 1. Display near the target group is vital. |

*(Contd.)*

**A Comparative Evaluation of the Media of Advertising**

| *Sr. No.* | *Media Factors* | *Newspapers* | *Magazines* | *Direct Mail* | *Radio* | *Cinema* | *Outdoor* |
|---|---|---|---|---|---|---|---|
| 1. | Circulation | Widest Circulation | Limited circulation | Restricted to the number of mailings contacted | Good Circulation | Restricted to local population | Limited to local circulation |
| 2. | Degree of Selectivity | Generally universal in appeal. It permits Restricted Regional and linguistic Selectivity | Greater degree of selectivity | Higher degree of selectivity | Restricted regional and linguistic selectivity | Restricted local selectivity | Local Selectivity |
| 3. | Audience | Generally very large, but limited to those who can read and subscribe | Limited in scope | Limited to a live mailing list which should constantly be reviewed | Limited to those who possess radio and who tune into the programme | Limited to cinema going population | Limited to local people |
| 4. | Timeliness | Message may be varied at short notice. Current events may be capitalised | Lack of timeliness; absence of news value | Highest degree of timeliness; selection of the right time and right message possible | Restricted timeliness, depending upon programme planning | Timeliness but at a higher cost | Uneconomic timeliness |

*(Contd.)*

*(Contd. Table )*

| *Sr. No.* | *Media Factors* | *Newspapers* | *Magazines* | *Direct Mail* | *Radio* | *Cinema* | *Outdoor* |
|---|---|---|---|---|---|---|---|
| 5 | Flexibility of size design, layout and colour | High degree of flexibility | Less flexibility | Highest degree of flexibility | Restricted flexibility, depending on the availability of time | Highest degree of flexibility but at porportionately higher costs | Good degree of flexibility but uneconomical |
| 6. | Life | Very limited life | Longer life commensurate with frequency of issue and use for reference | Subsequently longer life, depending upon the usefulness of the literature | Limited Life | Very short lived unless repeated very frequently | Longer Life |
| 7. | Repetitive value | Message may be repeated every day and adopted to the day's need | Repetitive value restricted to frequency of publication | Repetitive value depends on frequency of mailing | Quick repetition possible | May be repeated in every show but not to the same audience | Seen every time prospect passes by it |
| 8. | Effectiveness | Well planned news paper advertisement is very effective in locating new customers buying in market and supporting | Very Effective in case of technical goods, has also the good will of the publication to support | Most effective because of the personal touch, undivided attention, elaborate explanations | Less effective because of shorter memory and shorter messages | Very effective because audio visual value may be made effective by use of cartoons and elaborate explanation | High memorizing value |

*(Contd.)*

*(Contd. Table)*

| *Sr. No.* | *Media Factors* | *Newspapers* | *Magazines* | *Direct Mail* | *Radio* | *Cinema* | *Outdoor* |
|---|---|---|---|---|---|---|---|
| 9. | Secrecy | No secrecy can be maintained because of universal appeal | No secrecy competitors also read it | Privacy and secrecy may easily be maintained | No secrecy | No secrecy | No secrecy |
| 10. | Economy | Moderate costs per advertisement to numbers contacted | Higher cost per advertisement but less over-all costs | Cost depend upon the size of the mailing list | Costlier | Moderate costs as a whole but higher per contract costs | Cheap on the whole but higher per contract costs |
| 11. | Suitability | Suitable for all types of goods having wide market and needing constant explorations | Suitable for specific goods according to the nature of the magazine | Very suitable for articles having a well defined limited and enlightened market | Suitable for articles of daily use in wide demand | Most suitable for local consumption goods | Very suitable to make a brand image |

*Courtesy*: Pg. No. 84-86, *Advertising: Principles and Practice*, Chunawalla.Sethia

# 27

# Press Release

## 27.1 Hints for Writing Press Release

- **Choose positive rather than passive headline**
- First paragraph should be sharp and crisp.
- Prepare small paragraphs.
- Avoid superfluous expressions.
- Avoid uncommon words.
- Avoid jargon and the use of initials.
- Check the spelling of people and place names.
- Type on one side in double spacing and leave a good margin.
- Better give, one page 25lines write up.
- Check the appearance of the information and make it attractive.
- Put the date & time and mention contact person and telephone number for clarifications if needed.

## 27.2 While Handling Press Questions

- Confidence
- Ability to think and react on questions instantly
- Tact
- Authority
- Crisis management skill

## 27.3 Ten Principles for Tv Media

1. The picture should tell the story.
   Forget every other point and remember this one, and you will be ahead of the game.
2. Too often when people look for a visual symbol.
3. Grab the viewer's attention.
4. Be single-minded.

5. Register the name of your product.
6. People are interested in people.
7. Show a payoff.
8. Reflect your brand personality.
9. Less is more.
10. Build campaigns.

**How to read a storyboard?**

The challenge is to look at a piece of paper with tiny illustrations and a few words and be able to visualise involving, dramatic piece of film. A commercial is presented in the form of a "storyboard" that pictures the main action of the commercial and describes what the viewer will see (the video) and hear (the audio). It will generally include some technical terms, only a few of which you must know. Casting and special effects are particularly hard to visualise. It helps to show clips from television shows or movies to suggest the kind of actors or actresses wanted or to demonstrate unusual production techniques. The larger issue is what to look for in a storyboard.

## 27.4 Coping With Bad Publicity
## Or
## When "Adverse Image" is projected about the Organisation

- Be prepared with factual information

(1) What are you to clarify about?
(2) Why are you writing/clarifying about particular event?
(3) What is this event?
(4) When did it happen?
(5) Where?
(6) What form (how)?
(7) Whether supporting documents are available? (Statistics/Data, Visuals (Photo/Video etc.)

***While handling press five F's are***

Fast
Factual
Frank
Fair
Friendly

# 28

# Public Relations Officer

## 28.1 Profile of Public Relations Officer

1. Help with the public relations aspects of decisions.
2. Skill in articulating principles and in enlarging understanding of the organisation.
3. Loyalty.
4. Inspiration to help all members of the department / division to do their best cheerfully.
5. Influence in restraining other members from saying or doing anything detrimental to the organisations welfare.

## 28.2 Work Assignments of Public Relations

1. *Writing*: News releases, newsletters, correspondence, reports, speeches, booklet, texts, radio and television copy, film scripts, trade paper and magazine articles, institutional advertisements, product information, and technical materials.
2. *Editing*: Special publications, employee newsletters, shareholder reports, and other communications directed to internal and external publics.
3. *Media Relations and placement*: Contacting news media, magazines, Sunday supplements, free-lance writers, and trade publications with the intent of getting them to publish or broadcast news and features about or organised by the organisation. Responding to media requests for information or spokesperson.
4. *Special events*: Arranging and managing press conferences, convention exhibits,open houses, anniversary celebrations, fund-raising events, special observances, contests, and award programmes.

---

*Courtesy:* Pg. No. 435, *Effective Public Relations,* 6th Edition, Scott M.Cutlip, Allen H.Center, Glen M. Brooms.

5. *Speaking*: Appearing before groups and arranging platforms for others before appropriate audiences by managing a speaker's bureau.
6. *Production:* Creating communications using multimedia knowledge and skills; including art, photography, and layout for brochures, booklets, reports, institutional advertisements, and periodical publications; recording and editing audio and video tapes; and preparation of audio visual presentations.
7. *Research*: Gathering intelligence – enabling the organisation to plan programmes responsive to its public and problem situations, monitoring public relations programme effectiveness during implementation, and evaluating programme impact.
8. *Programming and counseling*: Determining needs, priorities, goals, publics, objectives, and strategies. Collaborating with management or clients in a problem solving process.
9. *Training*: Working with executives and other organisational representatives to prepare them for dealing with the media, and for making presentations and other public appearances. In service staff development.
10. *Management*: Administering the operation of the public relations function – personal, budget and programmes.

## 28.3 Requirements for Success

*Skills*

- Effective writing
- Persuasive speaking

*Knowledge*

- In-depth knowledge of various media.
- Understanding of management process
- Business, financial acumen.

*Abilities*

- Problem solver
- Decision-maker.
- Deft in handling people generates confidence.
- Assumes responsibility

*Quality*

- Stability and common sense.
- Drive and enthusiasm.
- Wide-ranging interests and intellectual curiosity.
- Good listener.
- Tolerance for frustration.
- Style.

## 28.4 Cantor's Traits for Success

**1. *Response to Tension*:** Most successful public relations executives are intense people, although it may not always be evident event to themselves. Often they are at their best under fire, and rather than solving problems by abstract analysis, will reach practical solutions by direct action.

**2. *Individual Initiative*:** The successful public relations executive will usually take immediate action before a situation becomes blown out of proportion. He or she usually will not wait for instructions, but takes the initiative to solve the problem; seeks to anticipate and adjust to change; leads the public relations effort.

**3. *Curiosity and Learning*:** The public relations professionals should have an inquiring mind, should want to learn everything possible about the product, service, client or organisation, and the competition. Since Public Relations is not an exact science, frequently the public relations executive must try a number of approaches in order to solve a problem. Some of which might not work. If and when they don't work, the professional does not regard them as personal blunders but as learning opportunities. Problems are solved by persistence and intelligence. He or she never stops learning.

**4. *Energy, Drive and Ambition*:** The successful public relations person has energy, drive and ambition. He or she works rapidly and is not afraid to take a calculated risk. This is a very important element in the personality of public relations executives. Most of the top practitioners are stimulated by the problems to be solved, and are willing to work the hours it takes to reach their goals.

**5. *Objective Thinking*:** Public relations executives must be as objective and factual as possible and above all, have excellent judgment. They must know what to do and say, and when. They must have a sense of timing. They must have a capacity for intense concentration and attention to intricate detail, and keen powers of observation. This is especially critical in counseling.

**6. *Flexible Attitude*:** It is crucial that public relations executives have the ability to see things from someone else's view point, eg., executive management's a publication editor's or a hostile audience's.

**7. *Service to Others*:** Most successful public relations executives have a natural desire to help people. Pleasure in the success of others is a major motivation for the service behaviour.

**8. Friendliness**: Public relations people generally are perceived as likeable, friendly and genuinely interested in others, rarely as resentful, bitter, or hostile. They develop and maintain a wide range of personal contacts.

**9. Versatility**: The successful public relations executive is often able to perform well in a variety of areas because he or she has a venturesome spirit and a lively interest in the world at large. The best practitioners are generalists

---

*Courtesy:* Jo Proctor, "The Path to the Top", *Public Relations Journal*, Vol. 39.

with a speciality. The desire to learn and the ability to focus on varied subjects helps them adjust rapidly to new tasks and multiple client problems and needs.

**10. Lack of self-consciousness:** Successful public relations executives are much less self-conscious than other executives, perhaps because they often function as catalysts. Although some practitioners have large egos, they often are self-effacing, functioning in the background while projecting others into the limelight. This trait is indigenous to the public relations professional.

**Doyle's Communications Chart**

| *Group* | *Objective* | *Management Action* | *PR Action* | *Communication Channel* | *Type of Message* |
|---|---|---|---|---|---|
| General Public | Goodwill<br>Respect<br>Support | Conduct business in public interest support community projects | Survey plan<br>Communicate evaluate | Mass media<br>Mail replies<br>Plant tour folders | Institutional ads<br>News on basic information about company |
| Prospective customers, clients | Sales | Produce good product or service | Survey Plan<br>Communicate Evaluate | Mass Media Trade Journals Direct Mail Films | Sales ads<br>Product news<br>Institutional ads |
| Customers, employees, management ranks | Loyalty, Goodwill<br>Efficient Production<br>Good Morale | Help employees find work satisfaction, self respect, fun | Survey Plan<br>Communicate Evaluate | Company publications<br>Bulletin boards<br>Mass media<br>Direct Mail Film | News and features about company and individual employees and employee groups<br>Institutional ads |

*(Contd.)*

*(Contd. Table)*

| *Group* | *Objective* | *Management Action* | *PR Action* | *Communication Channel* | *Type of Message* |
|---|---|---|---|---|---|
| Stock holders, bankers, investment counselors | Operating capital Confidence Goodwill | Good Management | Survey Plan communicate Evaluate | Company publications Newsletter Mass Media | Progress reports Future plans Financial reports Institutional Ads |
| Government officials, civil leaders | Goodwill support Favourable dicisions | Conduct business in public interest Support community projects | Survey plan communicate Evaluate | Personal contact Speeches Mass Media Films | News about company progress and plans Editorials Institutional ads |
| Press Radio-TV | Respect confidence in statements | "Open-door" policy Truth | Survey Plan Communicate Evaluate | Personal meetings Memos Press tours General news tips | Shop talk Background on company news |
| Educators | Respect Support Goodwill | Host Plant visits Serve on PTA boards, etc | Survey Plan Communicate Evaluate | Personal Contact Speeches Direct Mail | Offers to help educators |

*Courtesy: Effective Public Relations*, 6th Edition, Scott M. Cutlip, Allen H. Center, Glen M. Brooms, Pg. No. 358.

# 29

# Terms Used in Advertising Public Relations and Mass Media

**Air Brush:** An art process widely used for retouching photographs, applied with the aid of compressed air and an air brush. Also used by many illustrators to obtain interestingtone effect.

**Air Time:** Starting time of a TV to radio programme.

**Angle:** Particular emphasis of a story or broadcast; also called "slant".

**Answer Print:** Print of a motion picture film used to check quality, before final printing.

**Art:** All types of illustration in any medium.

**Attitude:** The composition of a person's bent on any issue or question, made up from all the influences they have built up throughout the lifetime. Usually unexpressed.

**Audience:** Denotes the group or groups to whom the public relations programme, or anypart thereof, is directed.

**Backgrounder:** A document prepares to provide the facts and significance underlying a subject, as a means of "backgrounding" an editor or writer.

**Back Up:** When one side of a sheet has been printed and the reverse side is being printed, it is said to be backed up.

**Banner Head:** Headlines set in large type and usually extending all the way across the top of a page.

**Beat:**

1. An area or subject that a medium assigns to a given reporter or department, such as the criminal courts or boating.
2. An exclusive story; a "scoop".

---

*Courtesy:* Bill Cantor, *The Cantor Concern,* the New York based executive search firm specialising in public relations.

**"Blow Up":** Increase the size of any visual item by photographic reproduction.

**Booklet:** A printed piece of six or more pages, with a paper cover and prepared as abound unit, usually by stapling. (See Brochure)

**Boomerang-Effect:** In propaganda, when the affected individual reacts in the opposite from the expected way.

**Box:** A newspaper item enclosed with printed borders.

**Bridge:** Phrase or sentence connecting two stories or segments of a telecast.

**Brochure:** A printed piece containing six or more pages. More elaborate than a booklet.

**By line:** Signature of the author on a newspaper or magazine story.

**Cable Television (CATV):** Also called Community Antenna Television. A means of transmitting signals to receivers through direct cable connections rather than over the air.

**Campaign:** An organised effort to poll, formulate, or alter the opinion of any group or groups on a selected subject.

**Catalogue:** A book of reference, including a description and, if possible, an illustration of products and other pertinent data, such as instructions for their use and care.

**Centre Spread:** The two facing centre pages of a publication appearing on a continuous sheet.

**Channel:** A place on television dial where a station can be received. Also, incommunication, one of avenues for reaching an audience.

**Circular:** A mailing piece or free-distribution item, usually one sheet. An item intended for widespread, inexpensive distribution.

**Class Publication:** Periodicals designed to appeal to particular, well-defined groups, interested incertain limited subjects.

**Clip:** In broadcasting, a short segment taken from the whole or to be sliced in. In print media, a clipping.

**Community:** The adjacent geographical area influenced and affected by company policy and production.

**Conservation:** Support of the public's existing opinion and preventing it from changing.

**Consumerism:** The composite of movements and causes purporting to protect the consumer in the purchase of goods and services, product safety and other matters.

**Control Group:** Group in which the members are chosen for their characteristics or opinions.Often a group not exposed to test that is used as a comparison to test group in equating results.

**Conversion:** To sway public opinion from one side of an issue to another.

**Copy Desk:** Editor's centre at newspaper, magazine, TV or radio station where copy is edited and headlines written.

**Copy:** Written material, such as press release, the text of booklets, broadcast material, or a magazine article.

**Copy Reader:** Editor who reads and corrects copy and usually writes headlines.

**Correspondent:** Out-of-town or travelling reporter.

**Coverage:** Extent of distribution of publicity or opinion-affecting material.

**Cover Stock:** Study papers used for pamphlet and booklet covers, posters, memo cards, announcement cards and similar purposes.

**Cropping:** Changing the proportions or size of an illustration to eliminate unnecessary or undesirable background or to enable the reproduction to fit into a specific space.

**Crystallization:** Bringing into public consciousness previously vague or sub-conscious attitudes.

**Data line:** Line at start of a story giving point of origin and date.

**Deadline:** Time when story must be completed.

**Debrief:** Originally, to interrogate a serviceman after return from combat area. Now includes interviewing members of an organization or their readings of public attitudes.

**Documentary:** Informational film or television show with a unified subject or purpose.

**External Publication:** A publication issued by an organisation to people outside its own employee or membership groups, such as to customers, the local community, the financial world etc.

**Feature:**

1. A story based more on interest or background than on news.
2. The main topic of interest in a story.

**Feed:** Electronic signal sent from the source to other activities.

**File:** Send story by wire or electronic means.

**Filter:** A short bit of copy used in making up the pages of publication to fill small spaces.

**Folder:** A printed piece of four pages. Also a four-page heavy-paper container for other printed materials.

**Folio:** Page number

**Follow-Up:** A broadcast or story that follows a news report; also known as second or third day story.

**Format:** Size, shape and general make-up of a publication.

**Free-Lance:** An unaffiliated writer, photographer, cameraman, artist or other person who is available on assignment or contract basis.

**Goodwill:** The favourable attitude of other persons or groups toward any person,institution or group.

**Grapevine:** Informal word-of-mouth process of disseminating information or rumours.

**Handout:** Publicity release, especially when it is widely distributed rather than given as an exclusive.

**Head:** Headline or title of a story.

**Hold:** Restrain from publishing or broadcasting until authorization is given.

**Hold for Release:** Material not to be printed or broadcast until a designated time or under specified conditions.

**"Image":** The subconscious impression a person has of an organisation, institution or person. Based on the interaction of all exposures he has had to the subject of the image. A "corporate image" is the supposed impression toward a company held in common by a whole public.

**Input:** Information fed into a data processing system. By extension, information obtained in the process of human considerations.

**Insert:** Printed matter prepared for enclosure with letter. Also, new material insertedinto a story already written.

**Internal Communication:** Communication with personnel or membership of a company or organization.

**Interviewer:** A person who asks respondents the questions specified on a questionnaire in an opinion or market survey. Also, a person who seeks information for media use – a newspaper reporter, or a television or radio panel show moderator etc.

**Lead (pronounced "leed"):** The beginning of a newspaper story. Also, a tip on a potential story.

**Leaders (pronounced "leders"):** Dots used to direct the eye from one part of the copy to another.

**Leaflet:** A printed piece, usually of four pages.

**Live:** Performed or reported now; not recorded.

**Localize:** Make specific references to a locality in a mass-distributed story or broadcast.

**Manual:** A compilation of directions and instructions in book or booklet form.

**Mass Publications:** Periodicals having a wide variety of appeal and a large general circulation.

**Matte:** Dull finish on illustration. Needed to prevent glare from stills on television.

**Media:** Avenues through which public relations messages are transmitted. Common media (singular is "medium") include newspapers, magazines, radio, books, music, paintings, cartoons, posters, leaflets, brochures, speeches, window displays, car cards, trade or business papers, envelope stuffers, calendars, house publication, motionpictures, slide films and television.

**Monitor:**

1. TV receiver used to watch broadcasts or closed-circuit signals.
2. To review a broadcast station's content.

**Newsletter:** A publication in letter-size format, usually issued periodically.

**Network:** Linkup of two or more broadcast stations to carry the same material.

**Opinion:** A person's view on an issue or subject as he articulates it. More conscious than an attitude.

**Plug:** A free and favourable reference.

**Poll:** A survey of the attitudes, opinions, and/or desires of a specific group of people.

**Position Paper:** A document that presents an organized exposition of an organization's position on a given issue. It may be used with the media, with government bodies, or in other ways.

**Presentation:** Offering of a programme or services at a meeting. May involve written materials, graphic displays, films or other materials.

**Prestige:** The reputation and standing of a person, institution or group.

**Pretesting:** Sampling techniques in a survey to be confident they are right before setting up the complete survey pattern.

**Prime Time:** Broadcasts hours when the potential audience is largest-usually weekday evenings.

**Programme:** The planned outline of activities for a campaign.

**Promotion:** Special activities designed and intended to create and stimulate.

**Propaganda:** An effort to influence the opinion of others.

**Proposal:** Materials organized to offer plans for a programme to services. A proposal may be used at a presentation or submitted by mail or hand delivery.

**Proxy:** Written authorization given by a stockholder to someone else to vote his stock.

**Selective Attention:** Singling out particular objects from among many for concentration of the third.

**Selective Reinforcement:** Tendency to pick out of many ideas or messages those that concern an opinion or attitude already held.

**Self-Mailer:** Printed folder prepared for mailing without an envelope.

**Slant:** Emphasis given in a story or programme.

**Split run:** Publication in part of the total circulation of a newspaper or magazine.

**Squib:**A short story in a newspaper or magazine. Sometimes, a short second headingthat tells more about a long story.

**"Stunt":** A created event developed by a press agent to evoke publicity.

**Survey:** An analysis of a market or state of opinion among a specified group of persons, groups or institutions.

**Terminal:** A place in a communication system where information can either leave orenter.

**Test Groups:** A group selected for reaction to or use of a product or an idea.

**Text:** The body of any written material-the copy.

**Threshold of Consciousness:** The point at which a given subject passes out of the mass of unperceived subjects into the awareness of the individual.

**Update:** Bring the information in a story up-to-date.

**Visual Display Terminal (VDT):** Displays copy selected from computer memory and allows editing.

**Watermark:**Identification mark left in texture of paper, which can be seen when held up to the light.

# 30

# Classroom Exercise

**PR Release Exercises**

**Objective:** Writing of Press Release.

**Classroom Exercise: 1**

The student group may be asked to write a Press Release for the given topic or for the assigned PR programme.

Students may be advised to refer course material on press release,communicàtion etc.

Students may be encouraged to write on a chart paper or OHP slides or to prepare power point slides for presentation purpose.

**PR Programme**

**Objectives**

To enable the students to develop the PR programme for an organisation.This covers development of Public relations objective, communication programme content / message development, media co-ordination, impact / result monitoring etc.

**Classroom Exercise: 2**

The Facilitator may assign an organisation or, the group may be allowed to choose the organisation of their interest. We suggested that the organisation may be of government owned type or public welfare type. In case the facilitator  assigning an organisation, case should be taken that group will be able to obtain all relevant information about the organisation. In case the group chooses the organisation on their own it is essential to ensure that they have an access to information or possess inadequate information about the organisation by themselves.

***Classroom***

***Facilities Required***

In case the group prefers to go out for collecting information, vehicle facility is necessary.

The role of the facilitator: It is essential to see that the spirit is alive throughout the programme and a competitive spirit is prevailing between groups.

**Classroom Exercise: 3**

***Media Relations***

For giving the students a real life experience, a press meet session can beorganised and the participants group may be asked to play the role of Public Relations Officer or the spokesperson of the organisation. Press reporters from leading journals or newspapers may be identified and invited for an interaction with the group and they expect to play the role of reporters and media persons.Some bureaucrats or senior government officers who normally face press reporters often like Secretaries to Government, Police commissioner's etc., may be invited as an observer. At the end of the press meet session, the observer as well as the press persons may be requested to provide feedback.

***Facilities Required***

Presentation equipments and facilities to prepare charts, power point presentation, OHP slides etc. as requested by the participant group.

**Classroom Exercise: 4**

***Organisational Image***

The participants group may be encouraged to go out and interact with the target group of the organisation or the stakeholders of the organisation in a friendly atmosphere to gather information, opinion, impression and desire etc. and they may be encouraged to consolidate the information to arrive at a conclusion about the organisation image, prevailing and also appropriate / favourable to the mission of the organisation.

Facilities required:

1. Identity card
2. Vehicle facilities
3. A person to guide the geographical locations.

*Please Note : Following cases are developed for learning purpose and for classroom distribution only.*

**Classroom Exercise: 5**

***Plastic - "Dioxin"***

The Government came out with series of publicity that burning of plastic bags/ disposable etc will emit "Dioxin", the chemical which may cause cancer and birth disabled children etc. and advising the public to refrain from using of plastic carrybags, etc. and ask them to switch over to paper carry bags or cloth bags.The Plastic Manufacturers Association advertised in leading newspapers on theWorld Environment Day (June 5) that burning of the plastic materials such as polyethylene / polypropylene or polystyrene, does not release dioxin at all. When burnt they dissipate as carbon di oxide and water vapour and Plastic ManufacturerAssociation have quoted that this information was provided by the Director Generalof Central Institute of Plastics Engineering & Technology, an Institute of Repute in the field of Plastic. The Government started receiving telephone calls as well as letters seeking clarifications whether the Government advertisement stating that dioxin is released while burning? Or whether the statement issued by Plastics Manufacturers Association is true? Some other Advertisements also appeared on the newspaper with regard to Plastic.

**Note:** The above case is developed to illustrate a situation and to form a base for classroom exercise and discussion purposes only and not intended for finding fault with any organisation or their policies and procedures.

**Points for Discussion:** You are the Public Relation Officer and the Government asked you to develop a PR programmes to clarify the position to the public.

**Classroom Exercise: 6**

**University Land**

Government of "x" five days back announced that the Government is considering the allocation of land belonged to the Agricultural University, which is found to be surplus at this moment, for developing a Biotechnology Park. The plots will be allotted, on long lease, to the corporate houses with strong R & D and export potential at a concessional rate, for setting up of their biotechnology units. Two days ago, a public forum gave a petition stating that this is against the interest of the student community, as this land is meant for future expansion of the University and should not be given to industrialists and also they seek Government to revert its decision.

The opponent political party criticised the Government for allotting the land much below the market price.When announcing about the allocation of University land, Government expressed that the biotechnology units near University campus will facilitate the interaction between the students and the research units and thereby increasing the employability of the students. Further this may contribute positively to the image of University itself. A group of student were protesting and involved in dharna kind of activities, demanding the Government to revoke its decision.The police officials informed that the situation needs to be handled properly and they anticipated agitation and violence. The Government machinery is working towards handling the situation and seeks support from public.

**Note:** The above case is developed to illustrate a situation and to form a base for classroom exercise and discussion purposes only and not intended for finding fault with any organisation or their policies and procedures.

**Classroom Exercise: 7**

**Learning Objective:** Newspaper may have their own style of projecting the news.

**Purpose:** Compare different newspaper released on the same day, with respect to the news coverage, focus, words, tone, the highlight of the issue and the place in which the news is covered.

**Materials Required:** Newspaper - 5 to 6 (National / Regional language of the papers released on the same day)

These exercises may be assigned to the students and the students are asked to analyse the news coverage in detail by comparing all the newspaper. The analysis may be with respect to:

(i) News.
(ii) The highlighted point / issue.
(iii) Tone.
(iv) Whether the issue is covered in the front page / prominent place or inan eyes catchy manner or in the inner pages.
(v) Is there is any editorial comment with respect to this news.
(vi) Overall focus of the newspaper.
(vii) Types of news covered.
(viii) The language style and depth of coverage.
(ix) Any other observation.

**Presentation:** The Groups after making detailed analysis may be asked to make a presentation.

# PART 4

# MARKETING PUBLIC RELATIONS

# 31

# Marketing Public Relations (MPR)

## 31.1 Introduction

This chapter reviews the disciplines that form the foundation of this study, namely marketing, public relations and marketing public relations (MPR). It also discusses the hypothesised benefits of MPR, namely greater credibility, trust and the establishment of long-term relationships. These benefits are the factors that the study identifies for effective corporate online communication.

## 31.2 Marketing and Communication in Marketing

This section deals with definitions of marketing and provides a historical overview of developments in marketing, marketing processes and activities, communication in marketing, marketing communication and trends in marketing and marketing communication. It is necessary to highlight these areas of marketing because MPR includes thinking from the marketing concept and the societal, cause-related and relationship marketing perspectives, and also has a strong product and/or service focus.

## 31.3 Definitions of Marketing

McDaniel's (1979) argument that "marketing's responsibilities and functions have changed rapidly in the past 60 years due to changes in values, resources, technology and governments which encourage managers to change their strategies in order to meet their organisation's changing goals", underscores the variety of perceptions in this field.

There are various definitions and perceptions of marketing, which have gradually extended the four Ps of the marketing mix to include the needs and wants of an organisation's customers. The various definitions which follow illustrate the variety of perceptions of this evolving discipline.

McDaniel (1979:3) refers to the broad definition of marketing formulated by Philip Kotler, who claims that the essence of marketing is the transaction.

Kotler defines marketing as "an exchange of values between two parties" and argues that it is specifically concerned with the way in which transactions are created, stimulated, facilitated and valued (McDaniel 1979:3).

Hart (1990:1) defines marketing as the process of balancing the organisation's needs for profit against the benefits required by consumers, so as to maximise long-term earnings per share.

Another definition is that of Stanton, Etzel, Walker, Abratt, Pitt and Staude (1992:7), who define marketing as a total system of business activities designed to plan, price, promote and distribute want-satisfying goods, services and ideas to target markets in order to achieve organisational objectives.

According to the American Marketing Association (AMA), marketing is a management philosophy which includes a range of activities. This definition reads as follows (Cant, Strydom & Jooste 2004:4):

Marketing is the process of planning and executing the conception, pricing, marketing communication and distribution of ideas, products, and services to create exchanges that satisfy individual and organisational goals.

Cant et al (2004:20) define marketing as a combination of management tasks and decisions aimed at meeting opportunities and threats in a dynamic environment in such a way that its market offerings lead to the satisfaction of consumer's needs and wants in such a way that the objectives of the business, the consumer and society are achieved.

The above definition includes concepts such as management tasks, decisions, opportunities and threats, the dynamic environment, market offerings, need satisfaction and the attainment of objectives.

According to Belch and Belch (1995:6), marketing is the process of planning and executing the conception, pricing, promotion and distribution of ideas, goods and services to create exchanges that satisfy individual and organisational objectives.

This definition emphasises the facilitation of satisfying exchanges between buyers and sellers, in other words, satisfying customer needs and wants. To this end, organisations must establish what people like about their product and also what prompts people to buy and use it (Kotler 1994:7).

Boone and Kurtz's (1999:9) definition of marketing which also includes relationships with the organisation's customers, reads as follows: the process of planning and executing the conception, pricing, promotion and distribution of ideas, goods, services, organisations, and events to create and maintain relationships that will satisfy individual and organisational objectives.

Boone and Kurtz's (1999) definition of marketing is adopted for the purpose of this thesis because it accommodates many of the concepts that form the basis of today's understanding of modern marketing as well as all organisational functions and the creation and maintenance of relationships with the customer. The concepts include the marketing variables, namely product, price, place and promotion.

## 31.4 A Historical Overview of Developments in Marketing

Over the centuries, modern marketing evolved through seven stages, as indicated in table 31.1 below.

**Table 31.1: The seven stages through which the marketing discipline evolved**

| | |
|---|---|
| **First stage** | Selling (ancient times) (18th and early 19 th centuries) |
| **Second stage** | Selling, advertising (late 19th century) |
| **Third stage** | Selling, advertising, marketing research (20th century) |
| **Fourth stage** | The Marketing department developing a balanced marketing programme which coordinates all the marketing mix instruments (20th century) |
| **Fifth stage** | Market-oriented company (20th century) |
| **Sixth stage** | Cause-related and relationship marketing (20th and 21st centuries) |
| **Seventh stage** | Online marketing (21st century) |

*Sources:* Boone & Kurtz (1999); Cant et al (2004); Kotler and Mindak (1978); Strydom (1999).

The first stage of the evolution of the marketing discipline occurred in the 18th and early 19th centuries in the form of an ancient selling function. Street vendors sold goods calling out in public to attract attention. However, in the late 19th century, manufacturers started to realise that repeated advertising could enhance their sales activities. The swift growth of national markets in the 20th century increased the need for marketing information on which marketing management could base their planning. Sellers realised that they could reduce their risk by spending money to establish what customers really wanted and the way in which customers perceived the organisation and its product(s) and/or service(s). The fact that the sales, advertising and marketing research functions operated independently of one another, led to the development of the fourth stage in which they were combined into a marketing department. The fifth stage, the market-oriented company, occurred when the various departments of the organisation all began to adopt and practise a customer philosophy (Kotler & Mindak 1978:15).

Top management's realisation of the importance of actively marketing the organisation's products and/or services in order to create a competitive advantage, culminated in the sixth stage. This stage is indicative of the new attitude managers have towards the marketing function. Marketers also realise how vital it is to accommodate the needs and wants of the organisation's customers and that credibility and trust hold the key to improved productivity and long-term relationships (Strydom 1999:11).

The seventh stage includes concepts such as online marketing (or e-marketing, e-retailing and mass customisation) during which marketers realised that the Internet can be used as a valuable tool to create long-term relationships with customers because a marketing strategy for a single customer is developed (Cant et al 2004: 21).

In addition, over the years marketing evolved through a number of perspectives, namely the production-oriented, sales-oriented, marketing-oriented, societal marketing, cause- related marketing (CRM) and the relationship marketing perspectives. These perspectives will be briefly outlined in the sections below.

### *31.4.1 Production-oriented perspective*

In the production-oriented stage, the notion in production-oriented organisations was that customers would favour products that were available. Management therefore focused on improving production efficiency (Strydom 1999:11).

During this period (from the time of the Industrial Revolution until the 1920s), organisations focused on the production of a few specific products which were mass-made by machines in factories. According to Strydom (1999:11), the central notion of the production era was that products would sell themselves. Organisations therefore largely ignored the requirements of consumers because their major concern was production and not marketing. Stanton et al (1992:8) explain the underlying assumption during this stage as the fact that marketing is not required to make people buy a product when the product is well-made and cost-effective.

Consumers were relatively poor and unsophisticated and bought new products only when they could afford them. Stocks thus began piling up which made management realise the importance of stimulating demand in order to increase sales. This change in management thinking led to the sales-oriented era of marketing (Strydom 1999:11).

### *31.4.2 Sales-oriented perspective*

During the sales-oriented stage (from the early 1930s into the 1960s), sales-oriented organisations believed that consumers would not buy enough of the organisation's products unless a special promotion and selling effort was made (Strydom 1999:12). The major concern was to increase sales which were believed to be the key to profitability.

Organisations now started to take more notice of their competitors and it also became more difficult to reach the market. In sales-oriented organisations, advertisements were placed to inform consumers of the availability of products while sales representatives promoted products through direct personal contact (Strydom 1999:13).

According to Stanton et al (1992:8), it was during this period that selling acquired its bad reputation because of the "hard-selling" approach followed by dishonest used-car and door-to-door sales people.

### *31.4.3 Marketing-oriented perspective*

Cant et al (2004:12; 190) refer to the marketing-oriented stage (by the early 1950s), as the foundation of the contemporary marketing philosophy. During this stage, an organisation with marketing-orientation was customer-focused, followed a team approach and was competitor oriented. This stage is based on an understanding that a sale does not depend on an aggressive sales force but rather on a customer's decision to purchase a product. In the marketing-orientation stage, consumers had more sophisticated needs and better finances as well as access to a variety of competing products which made management realise the importance of the marketing function.

During the marketing-oriented stage the focus was on marketing rather than on selling, the top executive for this activity being called a "marketing manager" or a "director of marketing" (Stanton et al 1992:9). The marketing era emphasised the sales message, the price and quality of products, packaging, methods of distribution as well as communication to the target audience. It was further characterised by the adoption of the marketing concept as a management philosophy (Strydom 1999:13).

*The marketing concept*

According to Skinner (1994:14) and Strydom (1999:13), the marketing concept is a result of the market-orientation stage. Dalgic (1998:45) describes the marketing concept as "basically a straightforward and logical idea, which puts the customer at the centre of overall activities of the firm". The concept gained much recognition among academia in the 1960s. Skinner (1994:14) further states that in order to adhere to the principles of this management philosophy, an organisation should strive to satisfy consumer needs through a coordinated set of activities that also allows it to achieve its objectives. McDaniel (1979:4) argues that the marketing concept requires awareness of the consumer's wants and needs, but not at the expense of the organisation's goals. He also points out that members of the organisation must accept and believe the marketing concept if it is to be successfully implemented.

Strydom (1999:13) defines the marketing concept as follows:

> The marketing concept holds that achieving organisational goals depends on determining the needs and wants of the target market and delivering the desired products or services more effectively and efficiently than competitors.

Strydom (1999:13) also describes this concept as an ethical code or management philosophy according to which the enterprise's tasks are performed to satisfy customer needs and wants at a profit.

Friedman, Giladi and Lewis (1999) affirm that the marketing concept is one of the principal philosophies to influence business today. It has enabled many marketers of consumer goods to survive in today's extremely competitive and difficult economic environment. They argue that an organisation should do everything in its power to satisfy its customer's needs, thereby achieving its own goals. Focusing attention on customer's needs will not only keep an organisation viable, but also assist management to create new opportunities for new products much more readily than if the focus were on current products.

The essence of the marketing concept lies in four principles (which may vary according to the views of various authors and theorists). The four principles of the marketing concept are the target market, customer needs, coordinated marketing and profitability. It starts with a well-defined market, focuses on customer needs, coordinates all activities that affect customers and produces profits by creating customer satisfaction (Kotler 1994:19). Cantet al (2004:13-14) include profit orientation, consumer orientation, organisational integration and corporate social responsibility as the four principles of the marketing concept.

### *31.4.4. Societal marketing perspective*

Cant et al (1999:14) describe the societal marketing concept which emanates from pure marketing as a marketing management perspective which is concerned about consumer's needs and wants in the long-term. This orientation anticipates possible conflicts between consumer's short-term wants and long-term welfare. It postulates that the organisation should determine the needs, wants and interests of target markets and then deliver superior value to customers in a way that maintains or improves the consumer's and society's well-being.

The societal marketing perspective questions the adequacy of the pure marketing concept in an age of environmental problems, resource shortages, rapid population growth, worldwide economic problems and neglected social services. It also questions whether organisations that have adopted the marketing concept always have the interests of their consumers at heart. The societal marketing concept requires marketers to balance three considerations in setting their marketing policies, namely company profits, consumer wants and society's interests (human welfare) (Cant et al 1999:14).

### *31.4.5 Cause-related marketing (CRM) perspective*

Cause-related marketing is an extension of the societal marketing perspective. It links specific products or services to a specific cause and can be defined as "a commercial activity by which businesses and charities or causes form a partnership with one another to market an image, product or service for mutual benefit". Organisations increasingly develop cooperative programmes and partnerships with nonprofit and charity organisations which mutually benefit both parties. The benefits of CRM include an increase in sales, the enhancement of the organisation's reputation and brand, new customers and an increase in employee loyalty (Cant et al 2004:17).

### *31.4.6 Relationship marketing perspective*

The most recent marketing perspective constitutes relationship marketing which entails a broader view of the market. It is also an expansion of the market offering. Its main focus is the maintenance of long-term relationships between the organisation, the government, the public, suppliers, employees and current and potential customers (Cant et al 2004:18). Grossman (1998:27) refers to Evans and Laskin (1994) who state that relationship marketing will lead to greater profitability, increased consumer loyalty, opportunities for strategic advantage, reduced costs in recruiting consumers and more effective organisational planning.

According to Christopher, Payne and Ballantyne (in Cant et al 2004:18), the four Ps of the marketing mix alone are inadequate to ensure full consumer satisfaction. They conclude that two further variables, namely people and processes must be added to the four existing marketing instruments. The variable 'people' refers to the employees of an organisation who should be trained in customer service and should realise that their job satisfaction also depends on the success of the organisation. The variable 'processes' refers to integral parts of the production, administration and marketing functions (Cant et al 2004:18).

In the literature there is no agreement on a common definition of relationship marketing. All the definitions reflect differences in scope. Boone and Kurtz (1999:333), for instance, define relationship marketing as

"The development and maintenance of long-term, cost-effective relationships with individual customers, suppliers, employees and other partners for mutual benefit. The above definition explains relationship marketing as extending the organisation's relationships to integrate stakeholders, who also include distributors and retailers, into an organisation's product design and development, manufacturing as well as sales processes."

Grönroos (1996:7) formulates the following fairly comprehensive definition of relationship marketing:

Relationship marketing is to identify and establish, maintain and enhance relationships with customers and other stakeholders, at a profit, so that the objectives of all parties involved are met. This is done by a mutual exchange and fulfilment of promises.

Gummesson (1997) and Grönroos (1996) both provide an interesting European perspective on the relationship marketing theory. Gummesson (1997:7) criticises current literature on relationship marketing as "theory less" and "a stack of fragmented philosophies, observations and claims which do not converge in the direction of an emerging relationship marketing theory". He refers to his contribution to the theory of relationship marketing as the "relationship approach". Gummesson (1997:12 - 14) identifies 30 tangible relationships that exist in business and other organisations and therefore contends that relationship marketing is a paradigm shift and not an addition to traditional marketing management. These 30 relationships refer to business networks and interaction and suggest that relationship marketing is a chain of activities and part of a larger context. He suggests that the implementation of relationship marketing requires managers "to go beyond their traditionally function-bound roles". He contends that relationship marketing forces management to value the quality of the total relationship between the organisation, its customers, suppliers, referral and influence sources, as well as potential and current personnel.

Grönroos (1996:7) reiterates the above arguments that relationship marketing constitutes a paradigm shift and not a new marketing model or "another instrument in the marketing mix". He argues that major changes in the business philosophy may be required "if relationship marketing is truly to be adopted". He states that if these changes do not occur, organisations will only be paying lip service and that using direct marketing techniques and developing partnerships alone are not sufficient. Grönroos (1996:7) explains that in order to practise relationship marketing, the four Ps of the marketing mix can and should be applied, and numerous other resources and activities (related to customer care and how to approach customers) should also feature. He proposes that at least four types of resources need to be used to create good customer care, namely personnel, technology, knowledge (customers) and time which he refers to as the "resource-oriented marketing perspective". He identifies strategic issues in relationship marketing as the firm operating as a service business, managing the firm from a process management perspective and developing partnerships and networks. Tactical issues in relationship marketing include seeking direct contact with customers, building up a database and developing a customer- oriented service system.

Dalgic (1998:51) explains that effective relationship marketing will lead to a higher percentage of satisfied customers and ultimately to greater customer loyalty. But the organisation should consider both the macro environmental and micro environmental factors in order to achieve this.

## 31.5 Marketing Processes and Activities

Marketing processes and activities are rooted in the organisation's marketing strategy, which includes the four elements (four Ps) of the marketing mix (marketing instruments) to align the organisation's operations to satisfy the needs and wants of its target market. The four Ps were introduced by McCarthy in the 1960s to enable students and teachers to recall or memorise the instruments of the marketing mix (McCarthy & Perreault 1984:v). The marketing approach has been dominated by this marketing mix theory for the last four decades, but theorists increasingly add more Ps to the marketing mix, especially from the services and relationship marketing fields because they perceive the "P" approach to apply in only a few instances of marketing.

Marketing management must make decisions about the four Ps, namely the product itself, the place where it is to be sold (its distribution channel), the marketing communication methods to communicate information about the product to the consumer, and the price of the product. The four Ps combine in a market offering which the consumer may decide to buy if it meets his or her needs (Cant et al 2004:21).

Rafiq and Ahmed (1995:4) refer to Shapiro (1985), who explains that the marketing mix constitutes the idea of controllable variables or a "tool kit" that marketing managers can use by marketing managers to influence customers. They explain that, although McCarthy's four Ps framework is popular, there is still disagreement about what these controllable variables are, especially among European academics.

Rafiq and Ahmed (1995:6) indicate that over the years, numerous modifications to the four Ps framework have been proposed, but that the most severe criticism has come from people in the services marketing industry because of its unique and different approach to consumer marketing. They refer to various modifications to incorporate the unique aspects of services. Booms and Bitner's (1981) extension of the four Ps process, physical evidence and participants, has gained widespread acceptance in the services marketing literature. Quantitative exploratory research by Rafiq and Ahmed (1995:11) indicates that there is general support for Booms and Bitner's seven Ps mix, but not uniform support for the three new variables.

The most recent adaptation of the four Ps of the marketing mix refers to the *four Cs of the marketing mix* that were developed by Robert Lauterborn and proposed by Philip Kotler. The four Cs constitute a more client-oriented marketing perspective, namely customer needs and wants, cost to satisfy needs, convenience and communication. The central questions of this approach are as follows (Tenericbusiness [Sa]):

*Product becomes customer needs and wants.* What does the customer need and want?

*Price becomes cost to satisfy need.* What is the cost to the customer, both in money and time?

*Place becomes convenience.* How is the customer demanding convenience and how is the organisation responding?

*Promotion becomes communication.* What is the most effective way for the organisation to communicate with its customers?

## 31.6 Communication in Marketing

Messages and communication emanating from modern marketing have a strong customer need-satisfaction focus in order to create lasting relationships. Communication in modern marketing also links an organisation's product(s) and/or service(s) to a specific cause such as environmental projects. In this way marketing communicates the organisation's commitment to and care about society's needs (Dalgic 1998:45).

Communication in marketing is aimed at creating an awareness of the organisation and its product(s) and/or service(s) in order to increase sales and make a profit. The sender (organisation) conveys messages about the organisation's product(s) and/or service(s) to the receiver (customer) in order to persuade the customer to buy the organisation's product(s) or to make use of its service(s). In order to create a lasting relationship, messages focus on the brand, customers' needs and the organisation's commitment to society. A brand is the sum of all emotions, thoughts and recognitions that people in the target audience have about an organisation (McNamara 2001).

All elements of the marketing mix communicate specific messages to the organisation's target audience (Kitchen 1999:22). The role of communication in the "product", for instance, is to communicate the extent to which the organisation's product(s) and/or service(s) can satisfy consumer needs, compared with those of competitors. According to Burnett and Moriarty (1998:35), communication should be about how and why a product meets the needs of the organisation's target audience(s).

Communicating the second "P", namely price to the organisation's target audience is one of the most important marketing messages because it motivates consumers to purchase the organisation's product(s) and retains them as customers. This is communicated by organisations through packaging, coupons, signage, price copy advertising, price concessions and price bundling (Burnett & Moriarty 1998:54; Burnett 1993:103). service and other customers in the service environment (Rafiq & Ahmed 1995:7).

The third "P" in the marketing mix, namely the place or distribution channel, includes all the institutions, processes and relationships that facilitate the distribution of the product. The distribution channel can convey a specific message about the organisation to the consumer (Burnett 1993:95).

According to Kitchen (1999:24), the role of communication in the fourth "P", namely marketing communication (promotion), is to persuade customers to buy a product or make use of an organisation's service(s). In order to effectively communicate messages to the organisation's target audience(s), the '"what to say, how to say it, through which media/channels, to whom and how frequently" become important in all the components of promotion.

Marketing sometimes uses the tools of the marketing communication mix (promotional mix) to effectively communicate with the organisation's customers.

### 31.7 Marketing Communication

Marketing communication is the fourth P in the marketing mix, which is used to inform and persuade the target audience to buy or use an organisation's product(s) and/or service(s). Rowley (1998:384) states that marketing communication ensures that customers are aware of the organisation's available product(s) and/or service(s) and plays a key role in determining profitability and market success. Koekemoer (2004:11) defines marketing communication "as the collective activities, materials, and media used by a marketer to inform or remind prospective customers about a particular product offering and to attempt to persuade them to purchase or use it".

Although the concepts of marketing communication and promotion are regarded as having the same meaning in most of the literature on the subject, Shimp (1993:7) makes a distinction between these concepts. He describes promotion as the aspect of general marketing that promotion management explicitly deals with. Marketing communication, on the other hand, is a "more encompassing term" that includes communications via any or all of the marketing mix elements. Marketing communication represents the collection of all elements in an organisation's marketing mix that "facilitate exchanges by establishing shared meaning with the organisation's customers or clients". Rowley (1998:384) suggests that organisations should develop an appropriate marketing communication mix. Kitchen (1999) identifies the following elements (or tools) of marketing communication :

- advertising
- sales promotion
- direct marketing
- personal selling
- MPR
- sponsorship
- the Internet

Communication with customers can be either on a personal or an impersonal basis - in other words, through direct selling by the salesperson or a mass advertising campaign. Pitt, Bromfield and Nel (1994:159) refer to the mix between the personal and impersonal approach as the communication mix. When applying the tools of the marketing communication mix, Pitt et al (1994:159) argue that the organisation should consider the balance between personal and impersonal communication to its target audience. They should also accommodate the behavioural effects it requires for advertising, its advertising objectives, and how it will ensure that its advertising strategy addresses the characteristics of each customer group.

An interesting perspective is that of Kitchen (1994:21), who cautions against unwanted or incomprehensible marketing communication messages. He explains that marketing communication "does not and cannot operate in a vacuum of its own making". He also suggests that before marketing related messages can have any influence, consumers must pay attention to them. Since the volume of marketing communications is increasing rapidly, Kitchen (1994:19) points out that this form of communication represents what has been termed a *leviathan* and which has the potential to be a form of "pollution".

The elements of the marketing communication mix identified by Kitchen (1999) will now be briefly discussed.

### *31.8.1 Advertising*

Koekemoer (2004:65) defines advertising as "a means of making known what we want to sell or want to buy, a means of informing existing and potential customers about a product, its special features and benefits and a means of persuading them to buy the product. More generally the purpose of advertising is to induce potential customers to respond favourably to the offerings of a firm".

Koekemoer (2004:66) explains that the source of the information or message is known as the advertiser, which could be a manufacturer, retailer, service organisation or even the government. The message is the advertisement that is normally prepared by an advertising agency. The message is transmitted through nonpersonal mass communication such as newspapers, magazines, television, radio, outdoor advertising, direct mail, etc. When the message is transmitted, it is adopted by the target market. According to Kitchen (1999:268), advertising "takes a more remote approach" to its target audience than the other elements in the marketing communication mix and its primary role has become longer-term brand-building through building awareness, conveying information, telling a story, establishing an identity and creating a predisposition.

### *31.8.2 Sales promotion*

Koekemoer (2004:267) defines sales promotion as "a blend of marketing communication activities and materials designed to intensify the efforts of the marketer's sales force, induce intermediaries to stock and sell the marketer's product offering, and/or persuade consumers to buy the product offering within a specified, limited time period". Some of the objectives of sales promotion include encouraging sales people to increase their efforts to sell more of a specific product, to locate more prospective buyers of a product, and to build consumer goodwill.

Kitchen (1999: 292) identifies types of sales promotion as price cuts, coupons, displays and feature advertising and/or a combination of these. Communication is either personal or impersonal.

### *31.8.3 Direct marketing*

Koekemoer (2004:326) refers to the generally accepted definition of direct marketing used by the American Direct Marketing Association, namely that direct marketing "is an interactive system of marketing that uses one or more advertising media to effect a measurable response and/or transaction at any location". Koekemoer (2004:326) also refers to a more elaborate definition by Stone and Jacobs (2001:5) that "direct marketing is the interactive use of advertising media to stimulate an immediate behaviour modification in such a way that this behaviour can be tracked, recorded, analysed and stored on a database for future retrieval and use".

Kitchen (1999:311) identifies forms of direct marketing as inserts in print media, radio, television shopping, telemarketing, direct mail and database marketing. Communication with the organisation's target audience is more direct and personal.

### *31.8.4 Personal selling*

Koekemoer (2004:13) defines personal selling as "a person-to-person process by which the seller learns about the prospective buyer's wants and seeks to satisfy them by offering suitable goods or services and making a sale". Communication is extremely personal through direct contact with the purchaser.

Kitchen (1999:327) explains that personal selling constitutes personal contact with one or more purchasers in order to make a sale and is more expensive than other elements of the marketing communication mix. However, in order to be effective, marketing management needs to integrate personal selling with other marketing communication mix elements (Kitchen 1999:327). The salesperson's communication is direct and personal.

### *31.8.5 Marketing Public Relations MPR*

Kitchen (1999) regards MPR as a vital element of the marketing communication mix in that it adds value to an organisation's marketing efforts. Kitchen (1999:352) refers to the definition by Harris (1993), namely that "MPR is the process of planning, executing and evaluating programs that encourage purchase and consumer satisfaction through credible communication of information and impressions that identify companies and their products with the needs, wants, concerns, and interests of consumers".

MPR is an integrated cross-disciplinary approach with a strong product and/or service focus. Communication can be either personal or impersonal.

### *31.8.6 Sponsorship*

Koekemoer (2004:456) defines sponsorship as the "alignment of a brand with an activity in order to exploit the commercial potential created by the association, thereby positively impacting brand image and/or sales amongst the sponsor's target market, in order to attain marketing and corporate objectives". The organisation provides resources directly to a beneficiary to pursue some activity in return for rights as detailed in a sponsorship agreement. In addition to traditional advertising, it offers the opportunity of brand-building and the selling of marketer's goods and services. Communication is impersonal and concentrates on the sponsoring organisation's image.

## 31.9 The Internet

The Internet is a significant new element of the marketing communication mix. According to Kitchen (1999:387), it is not a mass marketing or selling medium but a communications medium that can establish online relationships. Various Internet resources such as the corporate website, e-mail and discussion forums are used to attain specific objectives. Communication is personal and directed at the Internet user, and there is also an opportunity for feedback.

## 31.10 Trends in Marketing and Marketing Communication

Trends in marketing and marketing communication include more emphasis on improved and long-term relationships with the organisation's customers and finding alternative media (for instance, electronic media) to communicate more effectively . Koekemoer (2004) and Kitchen (1999) both include new media in their marketing communication mixes.

Doyle (1995:23) refers to this trend as "marketing in the new millennium" and points out that those organisations that are not focused on their customers and which do not understand the needs of the market, will be "dominated by other organisations in the network with superior knowledge". He also states that marketing's impact will depend on how effective managers interact both internally and externally to adhere to the principles of the new marketing orientation.

Dalgic (1998:45) reiterates the above arguments and explains that market-led organisations make the customer the organisation's priority. This entails focusing on the customer, specialising in the customer's unique needs and communicating to the customer the "organisation's commitment and care". Grossman (1998:34) indicates that organisations use marketing communication tools to develop better and long-term relationships with customers. For instance, he refers to the frequent flyer programmes which airlines use to encourage customers to develop a sense of commitment to the airline, rapid check-in and luxurious travel lounges. Relationships with the customer are also built through perceptions of the organisation that are conveyed through marketing communication messages.

According to Rich (2000:172), a current trend in marketing is what he refers to as "one-to-one relationship marketing", which he treats as an extension of the relationship marketing theory. He emphasises that the Internet can play a crucial role in communicating more effectively with the organisation's individual customers as well as in building better long- term relationships. Schultz and Kitchen (2000:14) refer to this trend as the "interactive marketplace" and "global marketplace" which began to develop in the early 1990s with the growth and expansion of various forms of electronic communication such as the Internet, the commercialisation of the World Wide Web and the introduction of e-commerce. This resulted in marketing communication messages changing from linear to two-way communication.

Rich (2000:175) argues that because of its customer data-gathering capabilities, the Internet has the ability to apply the relationship marketing concept. He refers to the example of the *Ford Motor Company* which launched a relationship marketing programme using the Internet. This company's website links its dealers, establishes an owner e-mail network and offers ownership benefits. Ford's objective is to create an interactive medium to gather customer feedback, allowing local dealers to respond and thus to develop "added value to the Ford ownership experience".

Arguments by Cant et al (2004) reiterate the importance of being focused on the customer's needs. According to them, it is no longer enough for organisations to win new customers or to be product or technology driven. Organisations now need to provide value to their customers and to be customer-oriented and market driven in all their actions. Schultz and Kitchen (2000:30) emphasise that this can only be achieved through integrated communication or marketing communication.

# 32

# Public Relations

## Public Relations

Because MPR also includes public relations techniques, this section discusses definitions of public relations, a historical overview of public relations, theoretical and practical approaches to public relations, public relations activities, corporate social responsibility and trends in public relations.

## 32.1 Definitions of Public Relations

Since public relations is a growing and dynamic industry there are various definitions and perceptions of this field. However, there is still no final universally accepted definition. Over the years a number of definitions of public relations have been proposed, some of which are recognised by authoritative bodies in public relations. These definitions are mostly conceptual and reflect the fundamental role of public relations as an "agent" for both the organisation and the environment. A case in point is the definition of public relations that was developed in 1989 by a panel of experts in the USA (Lubbe, in Lubbe & Puth 1994:6):

> Public relations is the management process whose goal is to attain and maintain accord and positive behaviours among social groupings on which an organisation depends in order to achieve its mission. Its fundamental responsibility is to build and maintain a hospitable environment for an organisation.

Cutlip, Center and Broom (2000) debate the problems relating to a single definition of public relations and in their work refer to the many existing definitions of public relations. They address the concept of public relations in practice by referring to the definition of the public relations scholar and professional leader, the late Dr Rex Harlow, stemming from his analysis of 472 definitions of public relations. What distinguishes this definition from earlier ones is that it includes both the conceptual and operational aspects of public relations (Cutlip et al 2000:4):

> Public relations is the distinctive management function which helps establish and maintain mutual lines of communication, understanding, acceptance and cooperation between an organisation and its publics; involves the management of problems or issues; helps management to keep informed on and responsive to public opinion; defines and emphasises the responsibility of management to serve the public interest; helps management keep abreast of and effectively utilise change, serving as an early warning system to help anticipate trends; and uses research and sound and ethical communication as its principal tools.

Harris (1993:11) points out that the length and complexity of the above definition is indicative of the difficulty of defining a "multifaceted field" such as public relations.

Cutlip et al (2000:6) also provide their own definition of public relations as the management function that establishes and maintains mutually beneficial relationships between an organisation and the publics on whom its success or failure depends.

The above definition reiterates perspectives of other theorists that public relations establishes "mutually beneficial relationships" between an organisation and its various publics.

National and international public relations organisations such as the Public Relations of Society of America (PRSA) have also formulated various definitions of public relations.

PRSA's definitions refer to the role of public relations, namely (Du Plessis 2000:17):

Public relations helps an organisation and its publics adapt mutually to each other.

And Public relations is an organisation's effort to win the co-operation of groups of people.

The Institute for Public Relations and Communication Management (PRISA), which was established in 1957 as a governing body of public relations practice in South Africa, formulated two definitions of public relations. Their first and earlier definition emphasises the deliberate nature of public relations and its nature and role. This definition states that (Lubbe, in Lubbe and Puth 1994:6):

> Public relations is the deliberate, planned and sustained effort to establish and maintain mutual understanding between an organisation and its publics.

PRISA's current definition of public relations was accepted in 1998 and acknowledges public relations as the management of communication and strategic relationships with different stakeholders (Koekemoer 1998:348). It reads as follows:

> Public relations is the management, through communication, of perceptions and strategic relationships between an organisation and its internal and external stakeholders.

Some definitions of public relations include the operational aspects thereof. A case in point is the definition developed by *Public Relations News*, a leading newsletter directed at public relations practitioners in the USA which reads as follows (Lubbc, in Lubbe & Puth 1994:6):

> Public relations is the management function which evaluates public attitudes, identifies the policies and procedures of an individual or an organisation with the public interest and plans and executes a program of action to earn public understanding and acceptance.

The above definition states that the public relations management of an organisation must encourage research and communication programmes in order to gain an understanding of what the organisation's various publics expect from the organisation. It also refers to the way in which the organisation fulfils these needs and expectations in practice.

The following working definition of public relations of the British Institute of Public Relations (IPR) (Newsom, Turk & Kruckeberg 2004:2):

> Public relations is about reputation – the result of what you do, what you say and what others say about you. Public Relations Practice is the discipline which looks after reputation with the aim of earning understanding and support, and influencing opinion and behaviour.

The last definition has been adopted because it reiterates the perception of public relations in terms of earning credibility for the organisation.

## 32.2 A Historical Overview of Public Relations

This section provides a brief overview of the development of public relations.

Over the years the concept of public relations has been both misused and misunderstood "through incorrect associations with its past". In more recent literature, changes in its focus and operation have been emphasised, for instance, the scientific and professional nature of the many activities in this field (Mersham, Rensburg & Skinner 1995:5).

According to Kotler and Mindak (1978:16), the field of public relations has "its roots in ancient human activities". Public relations can be traced from primitive society where leaders controlled their people by force, intimidation and persuasion to Babylon where historians had to paint favourable images of the kings.

The public relations discipline evolved from so-called "press agentry" to creating mutual understanding between the organisation and its different publics (i.e. from one-way to two-way communication). This had a bearing on the different roles that public relations practitioners fulfil today (Mersham et al 1995:4).

Modern-day public relations originated in the USA. Mersham et al (1995:4) refer to the following significant events that impacted on the development of the discipline:

- the use of the Boston Tea Party to gain support for breaking ties with Great Britain (1773)
- Samuel Adams's use of the press to unite the colonists against the British
- The use of public relations as a political tool by the abolitionist movement to obtain support for blacks in the North through the publication of *Uncle Tom's Cabin*
- the great showman PT Barnum's use of public relations to generate publicity for attractions in newspapers (19th century).

The concept of public relations as one-way persuasive communication was still dominant when the USA entered World War I and created the Committee on Public Information, headed by George Creel. The role of this Committee was to unite public opinion during the war effort by means of a national propaganda campaign. As late as 1955 the concept of public relations as persuasive publicity was reflected in Bernays' influential book *The engineering of public consent* (1955), a view of public relations which some managers still support today (Mersham et al 1995:5).

## 32.3 Theoretical and Practical Approaches to Public Relations

The practice of public relations also evolved through several theoretical and practical approaches. Four theoretical approaches to public relations are briefly discussed, namely the asymmetrical and symmetrical, systems, process and rhetorical/persuasive approaches.

***PR Models :***

Lubbe (Lubbe & Puth 1994:8) explains that Grunig and Hunt (1984) were the first theorists to define four typical ways in which contemporary public relations is practised. This is known as the symmetrical and asymmetrical approach to public relations. These four models are important because they describe and explain how and why contemporary public relations is practiced, and comprise the two levels at which public relations practitioners operate, namely the technician and managerial levels (Lubbe, in Lubbe and Puth 1994:8):

(1) The ***press agentry model*** describes public relations as a publicity function based on the technician role of public relations.

(2) The ***public information model*** describes public relations as the dissemination of information through the mass media and controlled media, for instance, newsletters and direct mail. This model also focuses on the technician role of public relations.

(3) The ***two-way asymmetrical model*** of public relations refers to the research component of public relations practice. Information is

disseminated on the basis of research on the most suitable channels and messages to persuade publics to behave as the organisation would like. This model uses both the technician and the management roles of public relations.

(4) The ***two-way symmetrical model*** describes public relations efforts in terms of its research base and explains the use of communication to enhance understanding with strategic publics. It also requires both the technician and management role of public relations.

*Systems Approach* : Another prominent public relations theory is the systems approach to public relations. According to Angelopulo (Lubbe & Puth 1994:41), the systems approach offers a framework for the public relations process and tasks in the organisation's operations. The systems approach addresses any system, be it inorganic, social or cognitive. A system is a set of objects or entities that interrelate with one another to form a whole (Angelopulo, in Lubbe & Puth 2004:41). It emphasises the importance of maintaining the equilibrium, balance and interdependence of the various systems and subsystems in society. All systems are perceived to have five qualities, namely wholeness, hierarchy, self-regulation, openness and adaptability. The systems approach is not unique to public relations but contains principles which can be applied from the natural to the social and applied sciences (Angelopulo, in Lubbe & Puth 1994:41).

*Process Approach* : The process approach to public relations suggests that public relations should be analysed and examined as a set of routinised activities, which is an ongoing process and not limited to a specific timeframe. The process model developed by Cutlip et al (1985), describes public relations as a managed function, which is part of an organisation's problem-solving process (Du Plessis 2000:21).

*Rhetorical/Persuasive* : The rhetorical/persuasive approach to public relations is used by public relations practitioners to achieve compliance, goodwill, understanding, appreciation and action, as contacts or the production of publications (Lubbe, in Lubbe & Puth 1994:8). well as to create a corporate image for and to manage the organisation's reputation. Public relations activities or techniques are not only performed by means of communication, but also by means of persuasion (Du Plessis 2000:26).

The practice of public relations also evolved through practical approaches, which include the well-known raise formula, the four-step plan (RACE), the interactive approach and the cyclic approach to public relations.

*Raise Formula* : The raise formula for practising public relations is accepted by PRISA and comprises research, adaptation, implementation of strategy and evaluation. The focus of this approach is the needs of the target audience and it is normally used to promote an image, product or idea, or to solve a problem (Du Plessis 2000:29).

*Interactive Approach* : The interactive approach to public relations regards the needs and viewpoint of the target audience as essential to the determination of the campaign structure and message. The focus is on a "negotiated meaning", which is created by the communicator and the target audience. In order to achieve success, the communicator's aims, needs and viewpoint must be aligned with those of the audience. It involves four phases namely assessment, creation, implementation and evaluation (Rensburg & Angelopulo 1996:51 & 52).

*Cyclic Approach* : According to Wilcox, Ault and Agee (1986:11-13), the cyclic approach to public relations conceptualises public relations as a cyclic process consisting of six components, namely research, analysis, policy formation, programming, communication and feedback. After the programme assessment, the cycle is repeated to solve and modify related aspects of the problem that may require additional decision making and action. The public relations practitioner uses a variety of professional communication skills and plays a fundamental role in the organisation and between the organisation and the external environment.

*Race Approach*: The four-step plan (RACE) provides an idea of the practice of public relations and describes public relations activity as consisting of four key elements, namely research, action and planning, communication and evaluation. The primary focus of this approach is on the knowledge and technical skills of the public relations practitioner (Wilcox et al 1986:10‰).

## 32.4 Public Relations Activities

According to Mersham et al (1995:8), part of the problem of understanding what constitutes public relations has to do with the fact that it is concerned with many different activities. They refer to the International Public Relations Association (IPRA)'s list of 14 different type of activities with which public relations practitioners might be concerned:

(1) Counselling based on an understanding of human behaviour
(2) Analysing future trends and predicting their consequences
(3) Research into public opinion, attitudes and expectations and advising on necessary action
(4) Establishing and maintaining two-way communication based on truth and full information
(5) Preventing conflict and misunderstandings
(6) Promoting mutual respect and social responsibility
(7) Harmonising the private and public interest
(8) Promoting goodwill with personnel, suppliers and customers
(9) Improving industrial relations
(10) Attracting competent personnel and reducing labour turnover
(11) Promoting products and/or services
(12) Projecting a corporate identity
(13) Encouraging an interest in international affairs
(14) Promoting an understanding of democracy

The above activities which require a broad understanding of business management and the social sciences are carried out by the public relations practitioner by means of a public relations programme and/or a public relations campaign.

Public relations theorists and scholars identify various public relations tools and techniques. Not only have these tools and techniques become more sophisticated, but their numbers have also increased over the years, which is indicative of the vast area of the field of public relations. For instance, Skinner and Von Essen (1999:8) identify media relations, the researching, designing and production of publications, corporate image and identity, corporate advertising, sponsorship, promotional activities, issues management, lobbying and networking as some of the primary tools and techniques that a public relations practitioner should employ. They also refer to research, programming and counselling/planning and advising, media relations and placement, organising, writing, editing, production, speaking, training and management as important tools and techniques of public relations. Cutlip et al (2000) list the specialised parts of the public relations function as media relations, investor relations, community relations, employee relations and government relations.

To accommodate an increasing awareness of building better relationships with customers and to communicate more effectively with them, various new public relations tools and techniques have been identified. Goodman (2001:121), for instance, includes the creation of web pages, the generation of better media products, the creation and building of relationships internally and externally as well as the building of trust in all of the organisation's audiences as additional public relations tools and techniques.

## 32.5 Corporate Social Responsibility

MPR considers corporate social responsibility as an essential MPR activity to enhance the credibility of an organisation's product(s) and/or service(s).

Corporate social responsibility is also known as corporate social investment because the organisation invests in a specific cause to uplift the community, and in the process, increases its profits. Public relations practitioners manage corporate social responsibility programmes of organisations in order to create a favourable corporate image for the organisation. Public relations keeps management informed of and responsive to social needs through communication (Mersham et al 1995:78).

However, corporate social responsibility is no longer an exclusive public relations function, but is also promulgated in marketing literature.Cant et al (2004:15) regard corporate social responsibility as one of the principles of the marketing concept. They explain that corporate social responsibility is the concept "that maintains that businesses are part of the larger society in which they exist and are accountable to society for their performance."

Different perceptions and definitions of this concept exist. These all indicate that corporate social responsibility has many aspects and different levels of interpretation. Mersham et al (1995:85) refer to Carroll (1979's) definition of corporate social responsibility, which reads that "social responsibility of business encompasses the economic, legal, ethical and discretionary expectations that society has of an organisation at a given point in time". They explain that organisations are primarily socially responsible when they produce goods and services that society wants and sell them at a profit. However, an organisation is ethically socially responsible when it behaves in a specific manner because it is expected by society, even though this behaviour is not required by law. This behaviour strengthens the relationship between the organisation and society. Organisations are, for instance, financially involved in programmes that both benefit and uplift the community such as education, job creation, health services, social welfare, community development, environmental conservation, art and culture and housing.

Apart from being externally socially responsible, organisations can also be internally socially responsible when they care for their employees through the provision of appropriate housing and health programmes, etc (Cant et al 2004:15).

### 32.6 Trends in Public Relations

Goodman (2001) explains that trends in public relations especially include the acknowledgment of this discipline as a more strategic function. For instance, the results of a study by the Corporate Communication Institute *"Benchmark Study"* and the Council of Public Relations Firms "*Spending Study*" in 2000 respectively, indicate that communication has become more strategic while better relationships with the community have become a priority to many organisations (Goodman 2001:118). An earlier study by Grunig and Grunig (1998) confirms the shift in the perception that public relations has become a strategic function.

In addition, the Internet is used by public relations practitioners to build better relationships with the community and to present the organisation as socially responsible (Ihator 2001:199). Cutlip et al (2000:285) refer to the Internet as "the most ubiquitous leading edge of what is a major communication revolution". Newsom et al (2004: 57) emphasise the impact of electronic communication on public relations strategy and tactics. Because information is more readily available, public relations practitioners must practise proactive public relations tactics more often.

The Internet is increasingly regarded by public relations practitioners and scholars as a valuable medium in the practice of public relations. Advanced technology such as the Internet has changed the way communication is produced, displayed and stored. The speed of communication has changed dramatically and resulted in the Internet becoming a strategy instead of merely being used by the public relations practitioner as a tool. The Internet and Intranet in particular make better two-way communication possible which may result in better customer service (Goodman 2001:118). Ihator (2001:199) emphasises the fact that Internet technology has minimised the distance between the organisation and its publics resulting in a new relationship between organisations and their relevant publics .

Another trend in public relations includes an increasing awareness of the values of integrated communication, which is explained in more detail in Section 4.9.

# 33

# The Integration of Marketing and Public Relations

In order to understand how the marketing and public relations fields overlap and support each other, integrated communication and the debate surrounding the boundaries of the marketing and public relations disciplines will be discussed.

## 33.1 Integrated Communication

Earlier literature argues in favour of the concept of integrated communication or closer cooperation between and coordination of disciplines in organisations (Stanton et al 1992:46). More recent literature acknowledges the integration of communication to the benefit of the organisation (Ferguson 1999), or critically refers to this concept as "uncritical acceptance of integration as a panacea for communication management in the twenty-first century" (Cornelissen & Lock 2001). Cornelissen and Lock (2001:427) argue that this concept has been "polarised" amongst academics. On the one hand, academics embrace this concept as resulting in communication effectiveness (referred to as pragmatists – for instance, Schultz, 1996; Kitchen & Schultz, 1999). So-called "purists" on the other hand, see this concept as being unworthy of serious examination because academically it is not respected. They therefore support the traditional distinction between marketing and public relations in the study of communication management .

The perception of integration was already extremely prominent in the early and late 1990s. Stanton et al (1992:46), for instance, argue that public relations experts regard themselves as part of a team that includes other marketing communication mix elements, a perspective which is also promulgated by Miller and Rose (1994:15) and Erdogan and Kitchen (1998:369).

The value of integrated communication is also acknowledged in terms of better consumer satisfaction (Tourish & Irving 1995). A perspective that is indicative of what is happening in practice is that of Schultz (1996), who argues that "the consumer integrates the marketer's and advertiser's communication whether the marketing or advertising organisation does or not". According to Schultz (1996), integration is not up to the organisation, but to the consumer. Even if the organisation directs uncoordinated messages to the consumer, he or she will integrate those communication messages in some way.

Over the years, integration has been endorsed by so many academics as well as marketing and communication executives that it has become a permanent organisational practice. The concept of integration has led to different theoretical positions and different concepts such as integrated marketing communications (IMC), integrated marketing (IM) and integrated communications (IC) (Cornelissen & Lock 2001:425).

Gayeski and Woodward (1996) refer to Grates (1995) who argues that in this new era "lines between communication disciplines as well as those between communication and other related types of consulting are blurring".

Consequently, separate "islands of communication" have become more unacceptable because of fragmentation, loss of credibility in terms of communication messages and information overload (Gayeski 1993b, in Gayeski & Woodward 1996). Belch and Belch (1998:32) explain that there are various reasons why nowadays marketers adopt an IMC approach. In addition to delivering a consistent and central marketing message, organisations benefit from cost savings by eliminating duplication and coordinating human resource requirements with improved long-term results for the organisation. IMC is a relatively new approach to help manage relationship building. According to Geissler (2001:489), it is "an attempt to look at the communications effort from the consumer's perspective". It involves coordinating distinct parts of an organisation's communication efforts (for instance, advertising, public relations and sales promotion) to "generate a flow of information from indistinguishable sources". IMC's objectives are comprehensible and consistent messages as well as maximum communication impact.

Although some theorists oppose integration of marketing and public relations (for instance, Ehling, White and Grunig, in Grunig, 1992), the marketing and public relations disciples have already integrated their respective tools and techniques. Goodman (2001:18) explains that modern communication has become more strategic while better relationships with the community have also become a priority to many organisations. Based on findings of their empirical study with regard to the role and tasks of corporate communication executives, Dolphin and Fan (2000:99) reiterate that corporate communication has become recognised as one of the most valued strategic planning tools in the organisation together with other line function departments.

## 33.2 The Debate Surrounding the Integration of Marketing and Public Relations

The debate surrounding the integration of public relations with marketing and advertising is ongoing. Twenty-five years ago, Kotler and Mindak (1978:8), for instance, pointed out that marketing people tended to view public relations people as "press agents, flacks, and sponsors of pseudo-events". Public relations people, on the other hand, viewed marketers as "hucksters, number-crunchers and deodorant salesmen", both viewing the other's function in its narrowest perspective.

In the early 1990s in particular, a significant disagreement developed about the respective boundaries of both the fields of public relations and marketing. While advertising educators were in favour of the integration of public relations, marketing and advertising, public relations educators opposed this emerging trend (Miller & Rose 1994:13).

However, studies in this regard indicate that this debate is merely academic, that practitioners need a multi disciplinary and more cost-effective approach to communication, and that the integration of public relations and marketing functions has already been practised for years (Brody 1994; Kitchen & Papasolomou 1997; Miller & Rose 1994). Miller and Rose (1994:13) refer to a national study in the USA which resulted in a preliminary Task Force Report suggesting circular integration of public relations with advertising and/or marketing. The report elicited much deliberation. The study reveals that while practitioners support integration, educators are fiercely opposed to the merger. It also reveals that private practice appeals to a more interdisciplinary and cost-effective approach to communication.

Based on the above findings, Miller and Rose (1994:15) argue that perhaps the time has come for both academia and industry to cooperate in meeting this demand for a multi disciplinary approach, one that allows the advertising, marketing and public relations fields to grow together, at the same time learning from each other.

Various theorists and scholars conclude that marketing and public relations are two separate disciplines and use different arguments to substantiate their different perspectives. Other scholars argue that the two functions of marketing and public relations are frequently confused and that public relations is often "subsumed by the larger, more powerful marketing function" (Lubbe, in Lubbe & Puth 1994:10). Others again, underscore this argument by pointing out that public relations and marketing are both essential factors for a modern organisation, but that when an organisation makes public relations a marketing function, practitioners are reduced to the "technician role", which results in the "organisation losing a valuable mechanism for managing its interdependence with its strategic publics" (Ehling et al, in Grunig 1992:357).

This perspective is much criticised by Harris (1993:13). He refers to it as "hysteria expressed in some PR circles". In particular, he opposes Grunig's statement that "a marketing-oriented organisation ignores the nature of a volatile and hostile environment in which organisations, especially business enterprises, must function", arguing that marketing-oriented organisations are extremely concerned with the changing environment. Cornelissen and Lock (2001:428) classify Grunig as a "purist" in the sense that he regards the concept of integration as unworthy of further examination. Brody (1994:20) sees the debate on this changing role of marketing and public relations and other elements of the marketing communication mix as a "disservice to all these disciplines" and emphasises that "one-on-one media are growing in efficiency and effectiveness", a factor which, according to him, necessitates these changes. He criticises this resistance to integration as a perception that interests "will be better served by capturing larger shares of a shrinking market than by expanding the boundaries of their disciplines".

The confusion is also increased because marketing people are increasingly interested in incorporating publicity as a tool in the marketing mix (a function which has been controlled by public relations practitioners), while public relations practitioners have become concerned about their organisation's marketing practices because they question whether they adhere to the organisation's social responsibility (Kotler & Mindak 1978:13). Cutlip et al (2000:6) contend that there should be no confusion between the two disciplines. They argue that marketing and public relations are two different disciplines and that the transaction (exchange for something of value) distinguishes the marketing function from that of public relations.

Various authors (Boone & Kurtz 1999; Erdogan & Kitchen 1998; Kitchen 1996 & 1999; Koekemoer 2004 & Wells, Burnett & Moriarty 2003), however, realise the value of public relations for marketing purposes. They accept that public relations is part of marketing, and in particular assists marketing efforts with customer relations. They also accept that public relations not only complements but also benefits the marketing approach.

According to Kitchen and Papasolomou (1997:71), in the literature there is some confusion about the distinction between marketing and public relations. However, an increasing number of articles (for instance, those by Erdogan and Kitchen,1998; Kitchen 1996; Schultz 1996), recognise public relations and marketing communications practices as "increasingly integrated and converging concepts". A significant contribution to the debate is that these reflect a growing tendency for the public relations and marketing disciplines to be regarded as converging disciplines in both professional and academic worlds.

An interesting perspective is that of Wells et al (2003:467), who argue that public relations can add credibility to an organisation's product messages and must work hand in hand with advertising as part of the organisation's marketing plan. They also contend that integration supports marketing's product or service focus by increasing the brand and the organisation's credibility with consumers.

This debate and the respective boundaries of both marketing and public relations are perhaps best summarised in a Paper presented as early as 1989 in San Diego by Philip Kotler entitled "Public Relations and Marketing: Dividing the Conceptual Domain and Operational Turf". In his Paper, Kotler contemplates final decisions about which tools, techniques, principles and procedures belong to the public relations and which to the marketing discipline (Kitchen & Papasolomou 1997).

Kotler argues that the two disciplines of marketing and public relations are mistakenly regarded as "adversarial". He suggests that they are better viewed as "corporate allies" rather than as adversaries, a view also supported by other theorists (Kitchen 1999; Shimp 1993). Harris (1991:41) refers to five models suggested by Kotler and Mindak (1978) to illustrate MPR as an element of promotional planning. These five models explain the perceived organisational relationship between marketing and public relations. The fifth model proposes that marketing and public relations have the same function. Marketing and public relations, for instance, both consider publics and target markets, recognise the need for market segmentation, and acknowledge the importance of market attitudes, perceptions and images. In addition both formulate programmes consisting of analysis, planning, implementation and control.

Another interesting qualitative study on the debate was conducted in 1996 by Kitchen and Papasolomou (1997), of which the results indicate that this dispute has been merely academic. In the academic literature, reference has been made to the debate between marketing and public relations academics over the "respective positions and spheres of influence of the two disciplines". The research identifies an inclination among marketing and public relations practitioners to compete over power, territory and, in essence, budget control. Practitioners suggest that the debate between the two disciplines is a question of definition or merely academic - in other words, "a war of words". Some participants even state that the debate between marketing and public relations practitioners is actually about ownership of MPR and that these two disciplines are already integrated (Kitchen & Papasolomou 1997:81).

Despite all the arguments in favour of the integration of marketing and public relations, there is still resistance on the part of public relations academics especially that marketing plays a significant role in public relations. There is particular resistance among these academics to the recent move towards the concept of MPR, which has been induced by the traditional marketing view of what public relations is or should be. However, the qualitative study by Kitchen and Papasolomou (1997) indicates that MPR is not only already accepted but also used in practice (Kitchen & Papasolomou 1997:81).

## 33.3 Marketing Public Relations (MPR)

This section defines MPR, explains MPR activities and conceptualises MPR in the context of the three main benefits which, according to the literature,

MPR possesses. These benefits are greater credibility, more trust and the establishment of long-term relationships. Credibility, trust and long-term relationships are, however, universal concepts applicable to all instances of communication in the organisation. The discussion therefore focuses on how these concepts are applicable to MPR.

**33.4 Defining MPR**

Over the years, the expanded view of public relations led to MPR, a name for an integrated cross-disciplinary approach with a strong product and/or service focus. Owing to the fact that MPR is still a relatively unexplored area, there are still various perspectives on and views of what MPR is and should be (for instance, Harris 1991,1993; Kitchen 1996,1999; Kitchen & Papasolomou 1997; Koekemoer 2004; Marken 1995; Shimp 1993; Strenski 1991; Wells et al 2003).

Definitions and interpretations of MPR vary widely, also partly because of the continuous debate surrounding the integration of marketing and public relations. Public relations experts in particular cannot reach agreement about what MPR entails, but do accept that it "is not free advertising". Definitions of MPR are, however, different from definitions of general public relations because of their product and/or service focus .

At a basic level, MPR can be described in the words of Harris (1991:12) as a "new promotional discipline which comprises specialised application techniques to support marketing activities and which is referred to by some theorists and authors as product publicity".

Shimp, 1993 in (Kitchen 1999:352) defines MPR as

> The more narrow aspect of PR which involves an organisation's interactions with consumers or with other publics (such as governments) regarding marketing matters (like safety). In short it is the marketing-oriented aspect of PR.

Kotler 1991a (Kitchen 1999:352) defines MPR as

> A healthy offspring of two parents: marketing and public relations. MPR represents an opportunity for companies to regain a share of voice in a message-satiated society. MPR not only delivers a strong share of voice to win share of mind and heart; it also delivers a better, more effective voice in many cases.

According to Kitchen and Papasolomou (1997:73), MPR is

> The process of planning, executing and evaluating programmes that encourage purchase and consumer satisfaction through credible communication of information and impressions that identify companies and their products with the needs, wants, concerns, and interests of consumers.

Perhaps the foremost existing definition of MPR is that of Harris (1991:12):

> MPR is the process of planning, executing and evaluating programmes that encourage purchase and consumer satisfaction through credible communication of information and impressions that identify companies and their products with the needs, wants, concerns, and interests of consumers.

This definition includes the most frequently used definitions of public relations and marketing as well as Harris' own experience of MPR (Harris 1991:12). But while this definition links both public relations and marketing functions in a way that contributes to and complements these disciplines to achieve the organisation's marketing objectives, it still lacks a description of what benefits it has regarding the selling of the organisation's product(s) and/or service(s).

MPR constitutes an integrated and interactive way of planning, executing and evaluating communication in order to enhance credibility, trust and long-term relationships with the organisation's stakeholders and customers in the selling of its product(s) and/or service(s).

## 33.5 MPR Activities

MPR activities include both marketing and public relations techniques and tactics to enhance the selling of an organisation's product(s) and/or service(s). For instance, public relations techniques may include gaining media attention and consumer interest to generate free publicity for the organisation's product(s) and/or service(s) (Harris 1991:78).

MPR activities are directed at abundant two-way interaction between the organisation and its various stakeholders and customers, at community involvement and at making the organisation's product(s) and/or service(s) more visible.

The following are examples of some MPR activities. Although some of these activities are typical public relations techniques and tactics, they are applied in the context of selling an organisation's product(s) and/or service(s):

- advertorials
- tie-ins
- contests
- special events
- booklets and brochures
- public service tie-ins
- trade shows and exhibits
- sampling
- demonstrations
- parades
- festivals
- sports events
- entertainment

- sponsorships
- news conference
- printed and electronic publicity
- media tours
- surveys and speeches
- symposiums and seminars
- online communication
- speeches
- social responsibility

## 33.6 Main Benefits of MPR

From existing literature and research it is clear that MPR is an integrated cross-disciplinary approach with a strong product and/or services and sales focus which has been practiced for many years. Edward L Betrays, who is regarded as the founding father of modern public relations, for instance, was responsible for various MPR programmes in the early years of public relations (Harris 1991:13). Betrays applied his skills to assist Procter and Gamble to sell Ivory soap carvings among American school children. He also created one of the greatest publicity achievements of the 20th century when he staged the Golden Jubilee of Light in celebration of the 50th anniversary of the electric light bulb for his client, General Electric (Harris 1998:290).

MPR emerged in the 1980s to distinguish between the specialised application of public relations techniques which support marketing and the general practice of public relations. It has since grown rapidly and convincingly to meet the opportunities of a changing marketplace. In the process, it has adopted and incorporated techniques and tactics from traditional public relations, marketing, advertising and research (Harris 1991:13). MPR has grown dramatically which is documented by a 1993 telephone survey conducted by *The Marketing Report*. The survey revealed that more than one- third of 243 marketing executives at consumer, industrial and service organisations were spending more than 20 percent of their entire marketing budgets on public relations (Harris 1998:91). According to Kitchen and Papasolomou (1997), who conducted qualitative research on MPR, it cannot rightfully be termed a new discipline. They suggest that it is a "new label" for well-established utilisation, traditions and procedures that support marketing communications (Kitchen & Papasolomou 1997:7). However, to date no empirical research has been conducted to support their research findings.

Over the years, various theorists and scholars have not only identified uses and applications of MPR in practice, but also tactics in terms of product publicity. Therefore in some earlier literature MPR is promulgated to be essentially about product publicity (Kitchen 1996, 1999; Kitchen & Papasolomou 1997). However, this constricted focus gradually changed as MPR gained increasingly more appreciation in terms of benefits other than mere product publicity (Guth & Marsh 2000: 243; Harris 1991:12; Kitchen 1999; Kotler, 1988; Marken 1995: 48; Strenski 1991:25).

The greater part of the literature on MPR hypothesises that when organisations use it effectively to promote the selling of their products and/or services, credibility, trust and long-term relationships are enhanced. Because MPR includes techniques and tactics from both the marketing and public relations disciplines, the organisation can benefit from long- term relationships with its customers as well as greater credibility and more trust in the selling of its product(s) and/or service(s).

Table 33.1 below summarises the hypothesised main benefits of MPR.

**Table 33.1: Hypothesised main benefits of MPR**

| |
|---|
| MPR *allows for more credibility* in the selling of the organisation's product(s) and/or service(s) |
| MPR can *instil more trust* in the selling of the organisation's product(s) and/or service(s) |
| MPR plays a significant role in *establishing long-term relationships* with an organisation's stakeholders and customers in the selling of its product(s) and/or service(s) |

The above three hypothesised benefits of MPR are interrelated. An organisation's marketing activities, for instance, involve a communication process aimed at achieving desired exchange outcomes with its target markets. In order to achieve this, the organisation needs to have trust and credibility with its various target markets. Public relations is the organisational practice responsible for establishing goodwill between an organisation and its publics through continuous interaction (Kitchen & Papasolomou 1997:75). This can engender greater credibility and trust which leads to long-term relationships with an organisation's stakeholders and customers in terms of its product(s) and/or service(s).

Credibility, trust and long-term relationships are, however, universal concepts applicable to all instances of communication in the organisation. The next section therefore focuses on how these concepts are applicable to MPR.

The hypothesised benefits of MPR are now explained as follows:

### *33.6.1 MPR allows for more credibility in the selling of the organisation's product(s) and/or service(s)*

Herbig and Milewicz (1995:6) explain that "credibility is the believability of an entity's intentions at a particular moment in time". Credibility is whether an organisation can be relied on to do what it promises. It exists "when one can confidently use past actions to predict future behaviour".

For the purpose of this study, credibility refers to the trustworthiness and believability of the organisation's communication about its product(s) and/or service(s). MPR uses public relations techniques to add credibility to the organisation's product(s) or service(s) in order to increase sales and focuses on responsible action, useful information, the organisation's use of the media and social responsibility.

Marks (2002), Vice President of Public Relations, *Coca-Cola,* North America explains that public relations builds credibility through responsible action. Credibility is built when an organisation is responsive to consumer concerns and provides assistance in terms of information and service. Harris (1991:105) states that in order to achieve credibility, it is imperative for organisations to give something back to the community and to proactively participate in programmes that benefit the community. By also identifying the brand with causes that consumers care about or by sponsoring high-visibility events, MPR adds credibility to organisations and their products or services (Kitchen & Papasolomou, 1999 in Kitchen 1999:357; Wells et al 2003:461). MPR basically enhances the demand for an organisation's product(s) and/or service(s) by lending credibility (Harris 1998:293). Kitchen and Papasolomou (1997:73) reiterate that MPR "serves a distinct and unique purpose, often giving a product, service or marketer added credibility, exposure and newsworthiness".

The media are often used by organisations to establish the perception of being socially responsible. Wells and Spinks (1999:108) contend that community relations are imperative for the success of the organisation. In this regard, the public relations function "attempts to develop, influence, shape and modify public opinion". For an organisation to have a good community image, it must be featured favourably in the media. Public relations attempts to influence the content of media exposure so that the community image created by media sources will be favourable. The publics MPR targets are the organisation's customers and include intervening publics such as the news media, through which it can win an independent, third-party acceptance of a product and/or service. Media approval makes the organisation's messages about its product(s) and/or service(s) more credible (Guth & Marsh 2000:423).

According to Kitchen (1996:10), "as marketing has evolved through various orientations as a result of environmental change so public relations has also evolved towards the concept of the public-oriented company". He argues that the integration of marketing and public relations can especially be promulgated "under the societal orientation banner". According to Mersham et al (1995: 82), organisations increasingly realise that they need to be perceived as socially responsible in order to gain a competitive edge. Their social responsibility is therefore also reflected in their corporate culture .

Case studies indicate that MPR has worked well in practice and has benefited organisations in terms of credibility in the selling of their products and/or services. These case studies also illustrate how MPR can position a new product or service through various public relations techniques which are aimed at enhancing credibility.

Strenski (1991:25) refers to the case study of the *Drackett Company,* which made use of MPR when it introduced a new air freshener on the market. Even though it was the first-dry spray freshener on the market and had an advantage over its competitors, it was more expensive than other air fresheners. Its sales message also had to compete with numerous other household products that all claimed to be unique. The *Drackett Company* made use of various public relations techniques to enhance the credibility of its new product. The company, for instance, obtained the President of the British School for Butlers as the official spokesperson for the product and introduced a media tour to 12 cities. During this period, the company managed to obtain 72 media interviews in only 30 days. The Company also sent products to 500 magazine and newspaper feature editors as part of a "Do it Yourself Press Conference at Your Desk" which allowed the editors to demonstrate the product at the office and to compare it with that of a competitor. A consumer information booklet on odour control and "ways to create an ambience with air fresheners" was also offered during the media tour.

Strenski (1991:26) also refers to the Academy of General Dentistry, the second largest dental organisation in the USA with approximately 30,000 members in general dental practice in both the USA and Canada. MPR was used to obtain media attention amidst other dental organisations, which were all attempting to send messages to the media. A national media relations campaign was launched to enhance the Academy's credibility in terms of its services, which involved the following public relations techniques:

- the distribution of *Dentalnotes*, a quarterly publication of news briefs for the media
- telephonic follow-up for each issue of the *Dentalnotes* publication
- a caring attitude about AIDS prevention in the dental office

A media training seminar was also held for the Academy's officers and board members to ensure a consistent, credible message for general dentistry to the media. National coverage of the Academy's annual meeting, especially on the topic of preventing AIDS transmission in the dental office, provided publicity in media such as *Newsweek*, *USA Today*, Associated Press Reuters and *Newhouse*. The Academy's President was also invited to testify as the representative of dentistry before the Presidential Commission on AIDS (Strenski 1991:26).

In terms of the above discussion, MPR can benefit the selling of the organisation's product(s) and/or service(s) in terms of credibility because of the following actions by the organisation:

- responsible action
- media endorsement

- useful information
- social responsibility

### 33.6.2 *MPR can instil more trust in the selling of the organisation's product(s) and/or service(s)*

According to Ratnasingham (1998:162), trust enables people to take risks. She refers to Kipnis 1996 (in Ratnasingham 1998) who explains that trust consists of two components:

- "Concerns of how we feel about being trusted and to be trusted which means that you are capable of managing resources that other people value, ie you have the power over others.
- Concerns of how we feel about having to trust other people which is a bothersome activity and sometimes can bring about feelings of deterrence, anger and anxiety."

Zineldin and Jonsson (2000:248) contend that trust takes time to develop between the parties involved and that it exists when one party has confidence in a "collaborative exchange" partner's reliability and integrity.

For the purpose of this study, trust means having confidence in the organisation's product(s) and/or service(s) because they pose no risk. The concepts of credibility and trust are interrelated because credibility generates more trust.

MPR plays a significant role in building more trust between the organisation and its various stakeholders and customers, because the organisation's message about its product(s) and/or service(s) is more convincing. Through trust, the organisation minimises its customer's sense of risk. MPR uses public relations techniques to make consumers trust the organisation and its product(s) and/or service(s) more in order to increase sales and focuses on familiarity with the organisation and its brand and making the organisation more visible and accessible.

According to Harris (1991:105), public relations is the only management function that "is uniquely able to build consumer trust". Trust, however, is built up over time. In particular consumer loyalty and trust are built up through expertise and accessibility to consumers. Trust requires direct involvement with consumers, both as individuals and as members of their communities. A gradual building of impressions forms a lasting impression which leads consumers to value the organisation's product(s) and/or service(s) and to be more receptive to product publicity (Harris 1991:109).

To gain trust, organisations must be visible to consumers to build confidence and reassurance in their product's safety and value (Harris 1998: 304). According to Jarvenpaa, Tractnisky and Vitale (1999), assurances help to increase trust, especially when the parties have not interacted before and hence do not have first hand knowledge of each other. Consumers need to feel that the organisation is honest and concerned about its customers.

By becoming familiar, an organisation establishes its own familiar corporate identity. People purchase from organisations they are familiar with and with which they can associate. Kitchen and Papasolomou 1999 (Kitchen 1999:350) refer to research findings by Duncan (1995), namely that MPR builds brand awareness and confidence. They explain that Duncan (1995) conducted a survey among 286 *Advertising Age* subscribers who held marketing and advertising positions with client organisations. According to Beavers-Moss (2001), consumer involvement creates a "kind of visibility that breeds trust". The organisation's marketing strategy can reinforce leadership and generate consumer trust, while public relations can generate it by making the organisation more visible. MPR can reach the consumer directly through various nonmedia non-media tactics and personal contacts (Harris 1998:304).

In terms of the above discussion, MPR can benefit the selling of the organisation's product(s) and/or service(s) in terms of trust, because of the following actions by the organisation:

- creating familiarity with the organisation and its brand
- making the organisation more accessible
- making the organisation more visible

### 33.6.3 MPR plays a significant role in establishing long-term relationships with an organisation's stakeholders and customers in the selling of its product(s) and/or service(s)

According to Cownie 1999 (Kitchen 1999:407), credibility and trust are pivotal in building relationships with customers because these concepts are central to agreeable personal relationships.

MPR focuses on building long-term relationships with customers in order to persuade them to buy a product or to make use of a service which is based on the principles of the relationship marketing paradigm (Harris 1991:46) and to which public relations can make a considerable contribution (Cowles 1997; Miller & Rose 1994:15). According to Harris (1991:283), relationship marketing is "the ultimate public relations oriented definition of marketing, because building relationships with 'publics' is what public relations is all about".

For the purpose of this study, long-term relationships refer to loyalty towards the organisation's product(s) and/or service(s) based on two-way interaction and the fulfilment of needs. MPR uses public relations as a platform to establish long-term relationships with the organisation's customers in order to create repetitive sales of its product(s) or use of its service(s) and focuses on personal interaction, customer service and differentiated product(s) and/or service(s).

Research by Grunig and Grunig (1998) indicates that public relations facilitates the building of long-term relationships with an organisation's strategic publics. MPR provides for building of long-term relationships because it allows for more opportunities for feedback. The practice of MPR constitutes more personal contact between the organisation and its customers than the marketing and public relations disciplines allow for separately. MPR focuses more on the target audience/publics in an integrated and engaging manner. According to Harris (1998:299), MPR builds personal relationships with consumers by being helpful and by being known as a consumer's friend. Organisations create a climate of acceptance for their products, advertising and promotion. In this way MPR can bring about better, more effective relations with stakeholders and customers because of its customer and two-way communication orientation. Two-way communication assists in determining the customer's needs as well as explaining that the organisation is striving to meet those needs (Marken 1995:48). Because MPR allows for more opportunities for feedback, the organisation is able to interact more with its customers and can use the feedback to improve upon its customer service and build relationships with its customers.

Another feature of relationship marketing is that of personal interaction with the organisation's customers. This is known as personalisation. Goldsmith (1999:179) explains that when interaction with individual customers occurs, long-term relationships are established because the customer feels valued and the organisation becomes familiar and trusted. Personalisation is the result of a gradual move in marketing thought and practice from mass marketing to one-to-one marketing.

Marken (1995:47) contends that MPR has become increasingly important because of a changing business climate. Managers now realise that a product's life cycle has become too short to spend too much time, money and effort on products that will be replaced within a short period of time. They therefore ensure products of a high quality which are different from those of competitors. Managers also realise that because of uniformity in products, services and prices, advertising necessitates new "differentiations", some of which can be brought about by MPR. MPR can be used to communicate new product benefits and uses and in the process retain customers (Harris 1998:301).

In terms of the above discussion, MPR can benefit the selling of an organisation's product(s) and/or service(s) in terms of establishing long-term relationships, because of the following actions by the organisation:

- feedback
- one-to-one interaction
- customer service
- differentiated products and services

# PART 5

# TRAVEL, TOURISM AND HOSPITALITY, PR

# 34

# Travel Tourism and Hospitality PR

While Tamil Nadu may one day well become the No. 1 tourist destination in India, for domestic and foreign visitors, a lot remains to be done to make it happen. At another level, the travel and tourism industry is the largest income generator in the world and in India as well, way ahead of the IT sector that many think is the only money-spinner. India is today the world's tenth largest economy. The potential the country has for tourism is simply huge. But can we leverage on our strengths and build a national brand to emerge as one of the top tourist destinations in the world? We can, but success will have a lot to do with effective communication and PR.

Tamil Nadu is the No. 2 destination in India for foreign tourists (15 lakh tourists visited the State last year), and the No. 3 destination for domestic visitors (Five lakh are expected this year), and if we have to make the state the No. 1 destination in the country on both counts, it will only be with the help of effective PR through a Public Relation Officer. The State Tourism Department was working towards promoting various tourism initiatives: setting up a tourism police force, putting in place a team of tourist guides, extending support to those who wished to promote lesser-known places by waiving tax for the first five years, providing easy finance and clearances, promoting employment, and producing publicity material in English and Hindi. Government was keen to promote tourism in the State and make it the No. 1 tourist destination in India.

PR has undergone a sea change. It was explored all facets of providing enhanced services. The changing environment is challenging the old order, 'Indians are re-exploring their own country. The focus of this PR should be brand-building, forming strategic partnerships, networking and PR'.

India's ability to influence others through culture, religion, philanthropy and other fields is well known. It was against this background that the winds will decide the fate of life, only he survives who struggles. "*Athithi devo bhava* - a guest in like God". We can refer to how an Indian doctor had conducted a heart transplant for a Pakistani child and the wonderful bonds that resulted between people of the two countries because of it. After Independence in 1947, the country crossed another milestone in 1991 when it adopted the path of economic liberalisation and globalisation. Today, India is the tenth biggest economy in the world; Ten million Indians surf the Internet everyday. Dwelling on the resultant direct impact on tourism, booming infrastructure, and more airline services, PR practitioners should give their best. Underscoring the need for better standards in PR, " Now we need accreditation and must only encourage people with the right academic background and professional experience." This will uplift the quality of PR practice in the country.

Referring to the diverse paths in tourism and how tourism had grown by leaps and bounds, tourism was no longer about visiting temples and the usual places of interest. Adventure tourism, medical tourism, eco-tourism and wildlife tourism would constitute the rapidly growing areas.Travel and tourism, was the single largest industry in the world. Whilst the software industry earned 900 billion dollars a year, the travel and tourism industry earned 4.63 trillion dollars, equal to the earnings of the automobile, chemical and software industries put together. The travel and tourism industry employed one out of every 12 employable persons in the world. In spite of putting very little effort, travel and tourism fetched India revenue worth 6 billion dollars. "If we attain one-tenth of China's earnings, we will earn 30 billion dollars,". The tourism industry was a great wealth distributor - bellboys, darwans and children selling waste material, all made a living. If the software industry offered jobs to 120,000 software professionals every year, the travel and tourism industry had the potential to generate 5-10 million new jobs every year, the next three years. "We need to increase our share of the world tourism market. By 2020, there will be one billion travelers; one out of six people will be travelling. Seven trillion dollars will be spent every single year. India receives only five million visitors a year whereas Paris welcomes 75 million tourists," .

The kind of tourism potential India had, referred to the 3000-km long and 300-km wide Himalayan range, the 8,000-km long coastline, the desert in Rajasthan, the Deccan Plateau, Chilika, the largest freshwater lake, and Cheerapunji, which received the highest rainfall. "If we have to create one temple, we have to spend one-fourth of a billion dollars. We don't look at the return on investments. In the last 50 years we have not created even one lasting monument. At least let us maintain the ones we have." In India : "We have 14,000 monuments but the government can spare only Rs 7,000 per year for 3,000 of them. For that amount you can't even hire a watchman!" Singapore, spent 9 percent of its GDP on travel and tourism. The result was that 15 percent of its GDP came from that industry. India spent only 0.5 percent of its GDP on the sector. Making yet another comparison, It was remarked that while the total number of hotel rooms available in India was about 1,05,000, Manhattan in the USA had more than that number! With new investments being made, about 120,000 new hotel rooms would be added, "So, what has happened as a result of our apathy? Our own centres have lost the hub status, which the smaller countries (Singapore and Dubai) have taken over. Emirates Airlines takes Indians from Indian cities to Dubai and makes them change planes there for other destinations. Namaste, yoga and Ayurveda have all been usurped by others. There is no claiming what are our intellectual property rights. There is no PR or advertising. PR practitioners have a very large role to play.

"Management of chaos will be a daily occurrence in our lives. The role of government is changing, from being in business it is moving more in the direction of policy making and economic growth. Services are overtaking the world". Indeed, from 65 percent, the contribution of agriculture to GDP had reduced to 20 percent. Outlining a big role for PR, there was nobody promoting the country, there was no PR. Word-of-mouth publicity and PR was ten times more effective than advertising, . It was a plea for responsible journalism. "Bad events sell newspapers but are not good for the country. Government participation is crucial. The travel and tourism industry is the No. 1 industry and a hugely evolving industry in a hugely evolving world. Tourism trade on the Internet generates 80 billion dollars. Communication and PR are infinitely more important. The 21st Century will make the 20th Century seem like a tea party".

***'We need to be proud to be an Indian'***

The Incredible India campaign has made India one of the most popular holiday destinations in the world today. With Indians making an impact around the world in various fields, with the skies opening up and airfares becoming cheaper, there is a fresh burst of energy. Indeed, it is fashionable to be an Indian. However, there are challenges too, and one of it is taking the India brand to the world. Tourism is the largest industry in the world. The past two years have witnessed a dramatic change in tourism in India thanks to the Incredible India campaign that has made its presence felt on a London cab as well as at New York's Times Square. The campaign has turned India into a modern destination and marks a fresh beginning for Indian tourism. The country is now one of the top ten destinations for tourists world over and could well move to the top five, with better infrastructure development and PR. "People used to dread coming to India, often seen as a country of diseases and as a trouble spot. Today, it is considered a fairly safe destination and the number of foreign tourists has increased dramatically the past two years," 'India tourism rediscovered globally and by indians'.

"Indians are making an impact around the world in various fields. This has attracted other people towards India. It is almost as if the country is reborn. The skies have really opened up; airfares are cheaper, and healthcare tourism (patients want to experience more of India after treatment) has grown. People from Western countries come here for treatment, not only for Ayurveda but also because of the excellent medical facilities available." Pointing to the huge amount of interest in India, that it was fashionable to be an Indian today. With the kind of investment happening in infrastructure development, it was predicted an 8-9 per cent growth in tourism in the coming years. The international investor and traveller were sometimes awestruck by the sheer pace of development in India. In Chennai, the ECR-Puducherry Road and the IT Corridor were examples. Hotels, especially budget hotels, were mushrooming everywhere. The Taj Group itself had two or three hotels in each metro. The smaller cities were likely to take the pressure off the metros soon. "Today's destinations extend beyond the popular Agra-Jaipur, Goa and Kerala legs. Indians are rediscovering India themselves, thanks to an increased pay package, global exposure, increased awareness and wanting to travel for relaxation and adventure. The need for a break from the usual routine is helping India. A new set of airlines is allowing Indians who had never entered an aircraft before to enter one,". Young travellers are looking for a lot of fun, which they have experienced in Thailand in another perspective. "Children here are totally left out, unlike in Thailand where the hotel staff takes care of them and allow the parents to relax. Also, we shouldn't remain only a country of temples. We should showcase the more happening modern India. If Malaysia and Singapore can cooperate, why can't the four southern states get together to sell the southern peninsula and compete with the north!

As with a slew of ideas. "The Japanese are looking at new places to get married. We can market our country as an excellent marriage venue. There is nostalgia tourism, colonels and doctors who want to go on a holiday. And medical tourism hospitals here must be accredited to international chains and work in tandem with government tourism to make their facilities well known."It was bemoaned the lack of attention paid to building a good environment, such as clean toilets at airports, for instance, for convention centres having better facilities - food courts, beauty parlours and boutiques. Worried about what she called the Bollywoodisation of our culture. Indians to travel more within India and preserve the country's culture. "Our smile, our willingness to help, these are the attributes that must be packaged and sold,".

Stating that tourism in India was a small business segment before the industry 30 years ago, we have to give stress that every country that wished to develop tourism ought to market and position itself as a brand. For example, Sri Lanka spent huge sums on promoting tourism, Rs 1.7 million, compared to which India spent only Rs 0.5 million. As Orlando's example, a place that had 300 hotels and where 100 airlines operated.Speaking about India's dirty hotels, poor infrastructure, bad roads and lousy food, It has to be asked aloud whether our policies had gone wrong. "Tourism is everybody's business. We must have the aim of attracting tourists. We must know what we are selling. We can't sell beaches to Miami or wildlife to Africa. If Malaysia can sell Thai poosam, why can't we in Tamil Nadu sell our own product? If Spain is known for the Matador, why can't Tamil Nadu be known for its Jallikattu? If you want to sell India, you have to be practical,". Was public-private partnership the answer to improving tourism infrastructure? How many tourism departments used PR agencies? And was the India branding and PR adequate? It was all for a public-private partnership. "The private sector will make profits and save the tax-payer's money,". The private sector was not exactly waiting for government help, but was focused on the customer. The tourism department to work closely with dynamic airlines. The government helping private initiative, such as identifying a place for a hotel. It was against competition between the partners. There should be collaboration between the tourism department and educational institutions. "Youngsters know very little about India and its people when they go out,". As far as PR and effective communication was concerned, it played a very important role, especially in damage control. The island country Sri Lanka remained a tourist spot in spite of years of strife in its eastern parts. We don't often focus on public transport that is often used by tourists. Auto drivers can be taught to be friendly. We need to be proud to be an Indian.

# Index

**P**

**U**



**V**



**W**



**Z**